STRUGGLE FOR
THE MIDDLE SEA

STRUGGLE FOR THE MIDDLE SEA

The Great Navies at War in the Mediterranean Theater, 1940–1945

Vincent P. O'Hara

NAVAL INSTITUTE PRESS

Annapolis, Maryland

This book was brought to publication with the generous assistance of Edward S. and Joyce I. Miller and Marguerite and Gerry Lenfest.

Naval Institute Press
291 Wood Road
Annapolis, MD 21402

© 2009 by Vincent P. O'Hara

Library of Congress Cataloging-in-Publication Data
O'Hara, Vincent P., 1951-
   Struggle for the Middle Sea : the great navies at war in the Mediterranean theater, 1940-1945 / Vincent P. O'Hara.
      p. cm.
   Includes bibliographical references and index.
   ISBN 978-1-59114-648-3 (alk. paper)
   1. World War, 1939-1945—Mediterranean Sea. 2. World War, 1939-1945—Naval operations. 3. Mediterranean Sea—History, Naval—20th century. 4. Great Britain. Royal Navy—History—World War, 1939-1945. 5. France. Marine—History—World War, 1939-1945. 6. Italy. Regia Marina—History—World War, 1939-1945. 7. Germany. Kriegsmarine—History—World War, 1939-1945. 8. United States. Navy—History—World War, 1939-1945. I. Title.
   D779.M43O34 2009
   940.54'293—dc22

                          2009006310

Printed in the United States of America on acid-free paper

14 13 12 11 10   9 8 7 6 5 4 3 2

Contents

Tables and Illustrations

Tables

Maps

Acknowledgments

While the author retains complete responsibility for all opinions and errors of fact, he thanks his family, friends, and associates whose generosity has advanced this work by providing information, by reading and challenging his interpretations, or questioning facts. As always, he thanks first his father and mother, Vincent P. O'Hara Sr. and Margaret H. O'Hara. He thanks his editor, Thomas J. Cutler, for supporting and nourishing this work, and his friend Enrico Cernuschi, who reviewed the manuscript and offered many suggestions. Karl Zingham, John Jordan, Zvonimir Freivogel, Jack Greene, Carlos Rivera, David W. Dickson, Richard Worth, Stephen Dent, Dennis Dove, Barbara Tomblin, Andrew Smith, and Robert von Maier have contributed ideas, resources, or comments. The editors and staff of the Naval Institute Press have been professional and consistently helpful. Finally, he thanks his family, wife Maria O'Hara-Rhi, son Vincent T. O'Hara-Rhi, and daughter Yunuen Rhi for their interest in and patience with the long process of bringing this book to fruition.

Introduction

Anyone who wants to know about the grand strategy of the world's empires cannot do better than study closely the Mediterranean Sea.

—Joseph S. Roucek, "The Geopolitics of the Mediterranean"

Enrico Ricciardi was a young midshipman fresh from the Livorno Naval Academy serving aboard the light cruiser *Eugenio di Savoia,* flagship of Rear Admiral Luigi Sansonetti's 7th (Cruiser) Division. *Eugenio di Savoia* was about to fight in Italy's first fleet engagement against Great Britain. Ricciardi, stationed on the flag bridge, remembered his admiral's reaction when combat commenced: "When we saw the first salvo, even before the sound reached us, Admiral Sansonetti excitedly placed his hand on my shoulder and said to me these exact words. 'Take a log sheet and note this down: at 1520 on 9 July 1940 on the Ionian Sea an Italian battle fleet fired its first gunshots against the English.' He added, 'This is a historic moment, and you, young man, should be proud to be living it.'"[1]

Aboard the British warships, similar excitement reigned when the signal "Enemy battle fleet in sight" fluttered up HMS *Neptune*'s halyards. The British commander, Admiral Andrew Browne Cunningham, noted this was the first time such a signal had been seen in the Mediterranean since the time of Nelson.[2]

Italy declared war on 10 June 1940, nine months into the conflict that became World War II. The Action off Calabria, as this engagement is known in English histories, was the war's first fleet clash and Britain's first attempt to establish sea control in the central Mediterranean. Accordingly expectations ran high, but rather than leading to a crushing naval victory, like Trafalgar, Calabria proved to be just the opening round in a protracted and bitter campaign that ultimately enmeshed five of the world's six great navies and dragged on to the very end of the European war.

Initially, the Royal Navy of Great Britain and its dominions and the Republic of France's Marine Nationale faced the kingdom of Italy's Regia Marina. Within weeks, after France's defeat, a three-way conflict developed, with Britain fighting Italy on one hand and the Vichy French regime on the other. In 1941 Germany's Kriegsmarine joined Italy, while the Anglo-French conflict simmered with periodic flare-ups. In November 1942, the U.S. Navy became a major Mediterranean participant, while significant French elements reenlisted in the Allied cause. In September 1943, the Kingdom of Italy quit the Axis and joined the Allies, and from that point to the end of the war Germany battled the combined forces of Great Britain, the United States, France, Italy, and a host of minor allies.

The struggle for the Middle Sea was World War II's longest air-land-sea campaign; it was a war of attrition in which the Axis confounded London's early quest for a decisive result and then slowly ground the British down until the Americans entered the theater in force—two and a half years after the campaign began. The Axis together and then Germany with her minor allies delayed the Allies on their road to victory for another two and a half years. By May 1945 Germany had lost Berlin but still maintained a tiny, defiant naval presence on the Middle Sea.

Myths and Misconceptions

The Mediterranean was the sea of Homer, and it has retained into modern times its ability to inspire myth. The war fought there is often related in partisan terms that contain misconceptions, simplifications, or distortions.[3] These "legends" are not the subject of this work, but it is necessary to briefly identify them before moving on.

The first regards Italy's military competence. From the beginning London believed that Italy was a weak, even contemptible opponent. Britain's effective wartime propaganda promoted this notion. As one popular "official" history from 1943 related, "That the British Fleet should be pushed out of the Middle Sea by a crowd of Italian Jackals was unthinkable."[4] Shortly postwar, the prominent American naval historian S. E. Morison continued in the same vein: "There was also the Italian fleet to guard against, on paper, but the 'Dago Navy' had long been regarded by British tars as a huge joke."[5] The official British histories by I. S. O. Playfair and S. W. Roskill conveyed a similar, if more muted tone, but British writers that followed them were less subtle. "With the odds heavily in their favour, the superior Italian fleet made their usual decision—it must have been standard training in their pre-war manuals—they turned for home!"[6] Even after sixty years an American author wrote, "Mussolini's lazy sailors disdained to prepare for serious warfare. . . . the result was an utter lack of toughness and team spirit—of any degree of real professionalism—that would lead to frequent panic in battle."[7]

In fact, however, a dispassionate survey of the Mediterranean campaign supports the opposite conclusions: the Italian navy fought hard; it often fought very well; and it accomplished its major objectives. It kept Italy's African and Balkan armies supplied for three years and largely controlled the central Mediterranean.

The corollary of this legend is that the Germans did all the real fighting. The Germans themselves were not shy in advancing this claim. Hitler remarked, "So far, unfortunately, the extent of Italy's military action had been a declaration that she was in a state of war."[8] Berlin shared London's opinion about Italian competence. A German general, after visiting Libya in October 1940, reportedly told Hitler that "one British soldier is better than twelve Italians. . . . The Italians are good workers, but they are not fighters. They don't like noise."[9] A recent German history treats the campaign as if the Italians had not been there at all: "While S-boats tightened the noose around Malta from the sea, the constant bombing by II Fliegerkorps reduced the harbour . . . to rubble . . . allowing Rommel to advance at the end of January 1942."[10] German participation in Italy's aero-naval war was important—the nature of its resources and responsibilities allowed it to concentrate on offensive operations. Italian ships, however, fought the naval battles that kept the Axis armies in business. In some cases, as at Matapan and in the convoy war, questionable German advice, broken promises, and security lapses damaged Italy's war effort. Finally, when forced to conduct a naval war on its own, the Kriegsmarine's combat performance—especially in defense of traffic —proved inferior to that of its erstwhile ally.

This introduces another misconception—that the naval war ended with the Italian armistice. In fact, following the armistice Germany deployed in the Mediterranean fifty-two destroyer or torpedo boat–sized warships, several dozen submarines, and hundreds of smaller auxiliaries, minesweepers, motor torpedo boats, and amphibious craft, battling on for the remainder of the war against greatly superior Allied forces in the Aegean, Adriatic, Tyrrhenian, and Ligurian seas to defend a vital maritime traffic and conduct minor offensive operations.

The motivation and participation of the French navy is likewise subject to misunderstanding. In many histories the French are dismissed as German collaborators or traitors: "Between June 1940 and November 1942 [Admiral François Darlan's] collaboration with the Axis enemy [was] pernicious, ruinous and fatal to the true interests of France."[11] The story is that France skipped the fighting and that its only noteworthy naval deed was to sink its own fleet at Toulon. Actually, the Marine Nationale participated throughout the five-year campaign. During the first two and a half years, the navy served the French government in Vichy. That government's objective after France's sudden and complete defeat was national survival. Memories of France's rise from the ashes of defeat by Prussia in 1871 and of Germany's rapid recovery from partial Allied occupation after 1918 influenced Vichy policy. France strove under extreme conditions to preserve as much sovereignty as possible while waiting for better times and generally remaining outside the German camp. The navy proved the government's greatest asset in that difficult struggle.

It is also a myth that the Mediterranean was the last great campaign fought and won exclusively by imperial British arms. Though the Royal Navy, in particular, attained brilliant victories in the Middle Sea, on close examination, especially of the situation on the eve of American intervention, it is difficult to endorse this conclusion. In fact, Imperial arms had reached their nadir by August 1942. The Italian navy, with German assistance, was winning through the autumn of 1942 the campaign it needed to fight, despite missed opportunities, some stunning defeats, and incomplete victories. The Allied cause was at that point revitalized by infusions of American ground, air, and naval strength. A corollary to this myth—epitomized by the depiction of the Battle of El Alamein as one of the war's turning points—is that the North African campaign significantly contributed to the Allied victory. Admiral Cunningham, writing in December 1941, expressed the prevailing belief that drove British planning: "The offensive from the Mediterranean and/or from North Africa provides our chief card of re-entry into Europe where Germany must be defeated."[12] The reality was that Great Britain sacrificed vital interests, such as the home front and Singapore, and paid an exorbitant cost in shipping to maintain for three years a small army in a peripheral campaign far from the German jugular. Britain fought in the Mediterranean because from 1940 to 1943 there was no other place where it could fight without the prospect of total defeat.

Regarding the U.S. Navy, many histories hardly glance at this theater, concentrating instead on the Pacific, the struggle against German submarines, and the Normandy invasion. In fact, however, the U.S. Navy's Mediterranean involvement was profound. By the end of the war it was the greatest Mediterranean power of all.

Sea Power and Surface Warfare

Naval warfare is a complex enterprise, with many interrelated elements, like those of amphibious, air, submarine, and coastal forces, as well as technology, doctrine, and intelligence. The purpose of naval warfare is to apply sea power, which a period textbook defined in this way:"Sea power has never meant merely warships. It has always meant the sum total of those weapons, installations, and geographical circumstances which enable a nation to control transportation over the seas during wartime."[13] Nonetheless, surface warships remained the principal tools of sea power throughout World War II. *Struggle for the Middle Sea* details how five great navies applied sea power in the Mediterranean from 1940 to 1945, with a concentration on surface naval actions between major warships— in this sense, purpose-built warships, including escorts, that displaced five hundred tons or more, were armed with at least a 3.5-inch gun, and were capable of fifteen knots. The former head of the United Kingdom's Ministry of Defence Naval Historical Branch observed that surface actions are the oldest form of naval warfare and had their recorded origins in the Mediterranean. In World War II, "more warships of minesweeper size and upwards were in Mediterranean surface engagements than in any other single theatre."[14]

Major Italian warships fought thirty-four surface actions against major warships of the British, Imperial, and minor allied navies, in addition to one against the French and one against the Germans. The Germans tangled with the British on eight occasions, the Americans three times, the French once, and the Italians once. British and French forces clashed seven times.

The record of why naval surface combat occurred and of how it was conducted tells much about training, doctrine, tactics, and weapons at different points in the war. The way fleets were used and when ships were risked illuminates what nations considered critical and much about their concepts of the type of war they were fighting. The results of naval battles were often subtle, especially in the way they impacted sea control or sea denial. Battles that established or maintained sea control had much greater consequences then did those fought for the purposes of sea denial. Italy's admirals, whatever their faults, understood that to maintain sea control they needed merely to avoid defeat.

What relevance does this hold for the modern reader? Sea lanes and maritime choke points are as important today as they were in 1940—perhaps more so. Any new conflict will be fought in littoral waters. The Mediterranean is a nexus of the world's economy today as in 1939. The problems of sea control and sea denial faced by the admirals of Great Britain, Italy, France, Germany, and the United States nearly seventy years ago will be faced again. The way different navies approached the common problems of evolving weapons, technology, doctrine, and the influence of politics upon strategy holds lessons rich in relevance in the modern setting.

This book presents a complete history of the five-year naval war in the Mediterranean and Red Sea, emphasizing the fifty-five surface actions involving major warships as defined above. Other important events, like the carrier strike against Taranto, the deeds of the Italian naval special forces, the coastal forces, or the submarine war are related but not in equal depth. Every surface action described has a table associated with it. The format of these tables is consistent and contains the following elements:

Name, date, and time
Conditions (weather, visibility, sea state)
Allied participants
 Formation one (formation commander) ship type: ship name[fate]
 Formation two (formation commander) ship type: ship name[fate]
 Etc.
Axis participants
 Formation one (formation commander) ship type: ship name[fate]
 Formation two (formation commander) ship type: ship name[fate]
 Etc.

This work uses U.S. Navy abbreviations for ship types. The appendix contains a list of abbreviations, which are generally introduced in the text without explanation, but the most common are: BB for battleship; CV, aircraft carrier; CA, heavy cruiser; CL, light cruiser; DD, destroyer; TB, torpedo boat; and SS, submarine. If a ship was sunk or damaged in the action, its fate is indicated in superscript next to the ship's name, using four abbreviations: *D1* for superficial or splinter damage; *D2*, moderate damage, with combat or maneuvering ability not significantly impaired; *D3*, significant damage, with combat or maneuvering ability impaired; and *D4*, major damage, with combat or maneuvering ability eliminated. Miles are always nautical miles and measurements imperial measures, with conversions from metric being rounded (a thousand meters is stated as eleven hundred, not 1,094 yards).

The Eve of War

June 1940

We are taking up arms . . . to solve our maritime frontiers. We want to break the territorial and military chains that confine us in our sea, because a country of 45 million souls is not truly free if it has not free access to the ocean.

—Benito Mussolini, speech declaring war, 10 June 1940

In the 1930s, as Europe staggered from one political crisis to the next, it became clear to some leaders in Great Britain and France that the status quo had fractured and that another war was inevitable. A major worry of the Western democracies was the impact that war would have on their Mediterranean interests. Although it lacked a Mediterranean shoreline, Great Britain had much at stake. The Middle Sea was the straight route to the heart of that nation's imperial holdings, cutting the voyage from London to Bombay by 4,500 miles. In 1938, the last year of peace, nearly 29 million tons of shipping passed through Suez, and on any given day 185 British merchant ships were either in transit through the Mediterranean or unloading at a port.[1]

In the case of France, the Mediterranean truly united Europe, Africa, and Asia, linking metropolitan France with its North African empire, Syria, and the Far East, not to mention the prewar Eastern European coalition that French diplomacy had painstakingly constructed in the 1920s to support the status quo and form a vital second front against Germany.

Every other country in the Mediterranean littoral—Turkey, Greece, Yugoslavia, and most importantly, Italy—absolutely depended upon maritime traffic through the Middle Sea to sustain its economy. In 1938, 86 percent of Italy's imports arrived by sea, and of that total, three-quarters passed through the British-controlled chokepoints of Gibraltar or Suez.[2]

The Mediterranean's importance for London and Paris suggests these allies would have entered war with a plan to dominate the Middle Sea. However, for various reasons, the Franco-British alliance could not forge a Mediterranean policy. Instead the two nations improvised, allowing a clearly hostile and militarily inferior Italy to commence hostilities at its convenience.

Italian policy, on the other hand, was effective up to the point of war. Rome faced down Great Britain over Abyssinia in 1935 and 1936, brazenly conducted piratical submarine campaigns in support of the Spanish Nationalists in 1936 and 1937, and brutally occupied Albania in 1939. One observer likened the British Empire to "a stranded whale from which any bold hand may cut blubber with impunity."[3] Italy's aggressive initiatives were part of a sustained and largely successful bluff, one that caused London to set aside its traditional contempt of the Italian military. Because Britain believed it could not afford to see the Mediterranean become a battle zone and thereby jeopardize its imperial connections with India and the Far East, it sought to placate Mussolini, much to the surprise of Italy's military leaders, who expected Rome's bluff to be challenged. As the Danzig crisis deepened, the Regia Marina's chief of staff, Admiral Domenico Cavagnari, fretted that the Allies would strike and overwhelm Italy's battle fleet of two refurbished, pre–World War I battleships. In the navy's opinion, war was not feasible until 1942, when all four new Littorio-class battleships would be worked up. Italy's army, the Regio Esercito, wanted to wait until October 1942, while the Regia Aeronautica optimistically "thought its equipment would reach acceptable levels by the end of 1941."[4]

Why Italy Declared War

War was always an objective of Mussolini's regime; the only questions were when and with whom. Germany's rapid triumph over France's highly regarded army caught Italy's military experts by surprise. Marshal Pietro Badoglio, the high command's chief of staff, had thought it would take six months and a million men to break the Maginot Line.[5] Thus, Mussolini rushed to declare hostilities against Great Britain and France on 10 June 1940, because it seemed peace was imminent. On 26 May he had assured Badoglio that the war would be over in September, that he needed "a few thousand dead so as to be able to attend the peace conference as a belligerent."[6] In the Duce's mind, "the risks of staying out were greater than those of coming in," because the Allies would soon be defeated.[7]

Mussolini's timing has led many histories to characterize easy spoils as his chief interest. In this view, he was a jackal snapping at the heels of a stumbling Britannia, "a hyena" coming to feed on the French carcass. The German official history endorses this interpretation:"Mussolini's policy, unpredictable and arbitrary as it often seemed, generally followed the principle of seizing booty at any suitable opportunity."[8]

But characterizing Mussolini's declaration of war as just part of an unscrupulous quest for booty obscures Italy's other grievances against both France and Great Britain. Britain's power to strangle Italy's economy justified war in the context of spring 1940 more than did the prospect of snatching Tunisia or Nice. Recent history provided many examples. In August 1916, for one, London "seized on the occasion [of Italy's shortage of coal] to force Italy to make significant political and economic concessions,"including a declaration of war against Germany. In September 1918, as an ally, Great Britain extracted economic concessions by stopping American imports passing through Gibraltar bound for Italy. In 1922 the Italian naval attaché at Constantinople expressed Italy's problem when he wrote,"The essential thing at this moment is to remove the danger that the Mediterranean is transformed into an English sea, which will one day face us with the dilemma either of starving or of following England unreservedly."[9] This menace reared its head once again on 1 March 1940, when Britain ordered a naval blockade of Italian coal imports from Germany. Great Britain clearly understood the blockade's implications; in response to Italian protests London considered"a restriction of imports of a severity that might bring Italian industry almost to a standstill." Thus, while the Duce's remark to the king on 2 April that Italy was a de facto British colony was exaggerated, it contained a kernel of truth that one middle-level diplomat captured in his diary in June 1940: "It is now a fight to the death. Either we win and become in reality the principal Mediterranean power . . . or we lose, and in that sorry case the British will not pardon us . . . and will reduce us from the status of a great power to that of a secondary, more or less'protected'state."[10]

Italian Preparations and Plans

While historians debate Italy's motivations, all agree that Rome was unprepared for a long war. Italy lacked most essential resources, especially coal and petroleum. The nation's industrial base was about a fifth of the size of Germany's. It produced only 2.3 million tons of steel annually, compared to Germany's 28 million tons. Mismanagement and corruption prevented Rome from making the most of what little it did have.[11] Nonetheless, upon the outbreak of war the army's chief of staff said, "When the guns start to go off everything will automatically fall into place."[12] In fact, he was expressing an Italian military tradition. The House of Savoy had embarked upon wars on a bluff and a gamble in 1848 and again in 1859, resulting in the acquisition of Lombardy, Tuscany, and Emilia; in 1860, ending with the unification of Italy; in 1866, gaining Venice; in 1911, acquiring Libya and the Dodecanese; and in 1915, incorporating the Tyrol and Istria. June 1940 seemed, in this sense, just another step in a daredevil process that had generally yielded positive results.

Of all the armed services, the Italian Royal Navy was the best equipped and most prepared to undertake at least a limited conflict. The naval staff initially pondered a conflict with Great Britain in 1934. At that time they considered launching commando attacks against Malta, Alexandria, Aden, and Suez to secure control of the Mediterranean's central basin, followed by the dispatch of large convoys to Africa and a massive campaign to seize Suez. This scenario envisioned a friendly Soviet Union, an indifferent America, and a France mesmerized by the growing German threat. If Great Britain maintained hostilities, the Italian navy would wage cruiser warfare in the Atlantic and Indian oceans until the negotiation of a compromise peace. By 1940 conditions were different, and Italy's military leadership had little enthusiasm for what they considered a premature war. But this did not matter: "Mussolini did not consider his military leaders as important in establishing Italy's war policy."[13] The Duce intended to fight a Mediterranean and Middle Eastern war in parallel with Germany's "Nordic" war, regardless what his generals and admirals thought.

At the end of March 1940, as Vice Admiral Angelo Iachino, who served as the Regia Marina's fleet commander from December 1940 to April 1943, later remembered, "Mussolini communicated to the military chiefs . . . that our entry into war on the side of Germany was inevitable and that it only remained to fix the date. The strategic directive was succinct: defense on land and in the air on all frontiers with the exception of Ethiopia; at sea offensive down the line."[14] However, Marshal Badoglio and Admiral Cavagnari interpreted this directive to mean "defensive to the west and the east; secure control of the Sicilian Channel [and assure] supplies to the forces fighting in Libya."[15] (See map 1.1.)

Not until 29 May did the navy issue its war plans *(Direttive navali)*. They excluded opening the war with decisive action, as contemplated in 1934. While a surprise invasion of Malta seemed feasible to some planners in light of Germany's example in Norway, there was little time to improvise such an attack, and more importantly, Cavagnari feared to risk his only two battleships supporting a fixed operation where they would be easy to find and attack.

Italy's war plans specified:

> A defensive orientation in the western and eastern basins and an
> offensive or counteroffensive posture in the central Mediterranean.

Impeding the union of the enemy's eastern and western forces by
blockading the Sicilian Channel.

The conduct of insidious [surprise or special forces] attacks on enemy
bases in conjunction with air raids.

The operation of insidious and light forces against the enemy's most
important lines of communication.

The seizure and exploitation of every opportunity to fight under
conditions of superior or equal strength.

To actively seek opportunities to coordinate surface forces with air
and submarine assets.

To avoid to the utmost confrontations with decisively superior
enemy forces.

To employ, as soon as possible, the battle fleet against the enemy before
his Mediterranean force could be reinforced and while battles can be
fought closer to friendly bases than to those of the enemy.

To protect communications with the islands, Libya, and Albania.

To defend isolated territories with local resources.[16]

These directives set forth general intentions rather than specific plans, and in
some cases they appeared to contradict each other. However, they did establish that expendable units, such as light forces, submarines, and airplanes, would
assume the major risks. The navy's principal tasks were to supply the fourteen

Map 1.1 Major Convoy Routes, June 1940

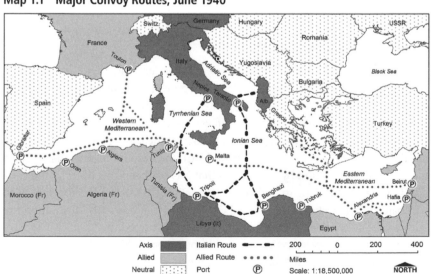

divisions in Libya, close the Sicilian Channel, dispute the British presence in the central Mediterranean, and maintain maritime communications with the Balkans and Spain. However, as Iachino summarized later, "The three armed forces never agreed upon a real operational plan, or how to complete the very difficult preparations to meet the fluid situation that existed, at that moment in France, and to accommodate the uncertain date of the critical directive from Mussolini, who dreamed of great war deeds, but lacked the means to carry them out."[17] (See table 1.1.)

Table 1.1   Italian Forces and Dispositions, 10 June 1940

Location	OBB	CA	CL	DD	TB	SS	MAS
Taranto	2	4	10	40		25	
Sicily		3			21	18	16
Libya		1*	2	4	4	10	
Tyrrhenian					24	44	25
Adriatic			2	6	16		6
Aegean				2	4	8	15
Red Sea				7	2	8	5
Total	2	8	14	59	71	113	67

*old armored cruiser used as floating battery

French Plans and Preparations

In 1939 the French Marine Nationale was a modern force with good equipment, high morale, and strong leadership. The chief of staff, Admiral François Darlan, regarded the Regia Marina as the greatest threat to French security. In 1937 he recommended action against Italy even before Germany in the event of a European war. Darlan wrote, "If we consider, at the same time, that the liberty of this sea is for Italy a question of life or death, and even more so for us, it seems that any offensive action by our armies that has not been preceded by the conquest of the Mediterranean will be useless action."[18] Admiral Darlan wanted to bombard Italy's west coast ports and cut communications with Libya upon the outbreak of a European war, whether or not Italy entered the conflict. The navy advanced this strategy in its first talks with the British in March 1939 but failed to convince its new partner. Moreover, the French army and air force were fixated on the German threat. In the end, the French government and armed forces were unable to forge a unified approach to the Italian problem and "presented themselves as internally confused and hopelessly discordant vis-à-vis Italy and the Mediterranean."[19] Not surprisingly, France adopted the British wait-and-see policy of encouraging Italian neutrality.

In April as indications of Italian belligerence grew increasingly clear, Darlan concentrated his main force in the Mediterranean and dusted off plans for a massive first strike. (See table 1.2.)

Table 1.2   French Forces and Dispositions in the Mediterranean, 10 June 1940

Location	BB	OBB	CA	CL	DL	DD	TB	DC	SS
Toulon			4		7	12		15	14
Algiers				3	6		3		
Oran	2	2		3	10			4	6
Bizerta							3	2	20
Alexandria/Beirut	1		3	1	1	2			
Total	2	3	7	7	24	14	6	21	40

British Plans

In a dispatch dated 10 May 1939 Admiral Dudley Pound, the outgoing commander of Great Britain's Mediterranean Fleet, wrote that "the strength of Italian air power and the corresponding inadequacy of British anti-air defences in the Mediterranean precluded any offensive allied action in North or East Africa." He even cautioned, "The preponderance of Italian submarines and aircraft, the vulnerability of Malta and the weakness of the French Air Force all indicated that the Royal Navy 'shall undoubtedly be subject to attrition to a much greater extent than the Italian [navy].'"[20] Pound's concerns reflected the Royal Navy's shortage of the modern ships and equipment required to meet its worldwide commitments. The Admiralty regarded Malta as necessary to maintain British power in the Middle Sea, but plans to give the island a proper air defense had been deferred due to costs and other priorities. Pound even recommended that Malta be abandoned.

Pound's pessimism did not determine British policy. The government had solved most Italian ciphers by the late 1930s, and from signal intelligence "the

British authorities possessed up to June 1940 a close knowledge of the Italian Navy and they estimated with a fair degree of accuracy the resources and dispositions of the [air force] and the Army."[21] Detailed knowledge of Rome's military situation did not diminish London's interest in placating Italy, or at least in stalling for time, but it may have instilled a sense of overconfidence at the highest levels when war in fact did arrive.

Just before the outbreak of war, Admiralty staff identified the Mediterranean Fleet's five functions as being

> To bring enemy naval forces to action wherever they can be met
> To ensure the safe passage of reinforcements to the fleet and garrisons in the Mediterranean.
> To obtain command of the sea in the Mediterranean's eastern basin, thereby denying any opportunity of seaborne Italian attack on Egypt, Palestine or Cyprus.
> Interruption of Italian sea communications with Libya
> Interruption of Italian trade with the Black Sea.[22] (See table 1.3.)

Table 1.3 British Forces and Dispositions, 10 June 1940

Location	BB	BC	BM	CV	CL	DD	DS	MS	SS
Alexandria	4			1	6	21		3	6
Gibraltar		1		1	1	9			
Malta			1			1		1	6
Port Said					2	1		1	
Red Sea/Aden					4	4	5	5	
Total	4	1	1	2	13	36	5	10	12

Several minor navies also influenced the Mediterranean balance of power. They were all potentially hostile to Italy, and all factored into the Regia Marina's calculations. In the event, Italy attacked the Greek navy even before declaring war on Greece, sinking the light cruiser *Helle* on 15 August 1940. Romania, the USSR, Turkey, and Spain never played active roles in the Mediterranean campaign, while Italy captured most of the Yugoslavian navy's assets in April 1941. Greece was the only minor navy to engage in significant combat. (See table 1.4.)

Table 1.4 Mediterranean/Black Sea Minor Navies

Nation	OBB	CA	CL	DD	TB	DC	SS	MTB
Greece		1	1	10	13		6	2
Turkey	1	2	4	2	4	6	3	
Yugoslavia			1	4	6	6	4	10
Spain		1	5	20	6	5	5	14
Bulgaria					4			4
Romania				4	3	4	1	
USSR	1	2	3	16	9		25	50

The U.S. Navy and the German Kriegsmarine were not present in the Mediterranean in June 1940, although both navies had previously fought there. The U.S. Navy had conducted America's first foreign war in 1801–5 against the Barbary Pirates along the North African coast. The German empire and America had faced off in the Middle Sea during World War I, and the Kriegsmarine had engaged in open and clandestine activity during the Spanish Civil War. These navies were to play major roles in the Mediterranean from 1943 to the end of the war.

The Naval War through June 1940

Up through June 1940 the nature of the war at sea gave the participants (and Italian observers) a taste of how action might occur in the Mediterranean. Aircraft proved effective against warships tied to specific locations, such as off the coast of Norway, but less so against ships under way at sea. Airpower also failed to prevent the evacuation of Dunkirk. Italy's own experiences in the Spanish Civil War indicated that high-level bombing would be ineffective, but naval cooperation was not the Regia Aeronautica's top priority in any case. While Italy had dive-bombers and torpedo bombers under development when war came, neither weapon was ready for action. In fact, the Italian air force staff concluded from the fate of *Courageous* and then *Glorious,* sunk by German submarines and battleships, respectively, that the emergency aircraft carrier conversion that the naval staff had been advocating since 1935 would result in a fragile asset of doubtful utility.

German and British submarines both enjoyed some spectacular successes against warships, and these encouraged Rome to trust the offensive capability of Italy's large submarine fleet. Nine months of fighting German U-boats, however,

Map 1.2   The North African Land War, June 1940–May 1943

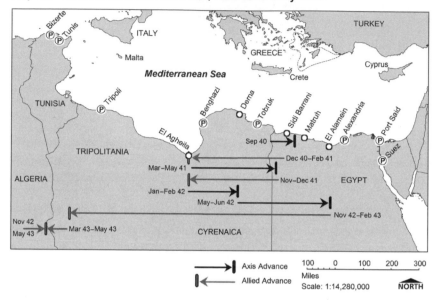

had honed British antisubmarine warfare capabilities and corrected some bad habits, while Italian training and doctrine were below German standards.

There was little foreshadowing of the type of "insidious" weapons Italy was developing, like motor torpedo boats, explosive attack craft, and manned torpedoes. Most of the major surface battles—the action against the *Graf Spee* and the two engagements off Narvik—led to conclusive results, which supported the popular belief that sea battles would be swift and deadly.

The Norwegian campaign provided a dramatic example of how the temporary application of sea power could conquer a distant objective in waters normally dominated by the enemy. This case study supported Italian planners who advocated a surprise invasion of Malta on the war's first day. On the other hand, Norway cost the Kriegsmarine dearly, and this led Cavagnari to conclude that the risks outweighed the rewards, especially if the war did prove brief.

Overall, the British certainly learned more from their direct experience of air attacks, day and night surface actions, and of submarine, antisubmarine, and mine warfare than the Italians did from their observations of them from afar. The British had ironed out many of the inevitable kinks that plague every military organization in the transition from peace to war. The French also had this experience, and both Allied fleets were eager to prove their skills on an Italian navy just coming out of the gate. The first six months of the Mediterranean war would confirm the qualitative head start enjoyed by the Royal Navy, even if the British were to fall short of the objectives they hoped to obtain. There was nothing, however, to foreshadow the seesaw nature of the African land war and the impact this would have on naval operations. (See map 1.2.)

2

The Defeat of France

No Admiral, least of all a French Admiral with his high sense of
"Honour" and dignity, would accept an ultimatum.

—Anthony Heckstall-Smith, *The Fleet That Faced Both Ways*

Mussolini announced Italy's entry into war on the balcony of Rome's Palazzo di Venezia on 10 June 1940. Franco Maugeri, captain of the light cruiser *Bande Nere,* later recalled,"I felt a strange thrill of exhilaration. . . . For one thing, the long months of doubt and uncertainty were over. For another, the hour had come for which my thirty years of training as a cadet and naval officer had served as preparation."[1] The announcement surprised no one. In fact, the British destroyer *Decoy* attacked a false submarine contact two hours before Mussolini's declaration took effect.[2] What did surprise was the way the war's first weeks failed to meet the participants' expectations.

Intentions

In the weeks leading up to Mussolini's declaration, the Marine Nationale and the Royal Navy amassed a twelve-to-two superiority in capital ships (including carriers) over the Regia Marina. The British planned a foray from Alexandria into the central basin to protect Malta. Admiral Cunningham also wanted to test the effectiveness of the enemy's air and submarine forces and attack the Italian coast.[3] The French intended to bombard targets in the Gulf of Genoa, followed by raids into the Tyrrhenian Sea and strikes against southern Italy, Sicily, and the Dodecanese. Both wanted to provoke the Italian navy into a fight.[4] However, Admiral Cavagnari had no interest in a fleet action. Instead, the submarines deployed en masse seeking targets of opportunity, the air force attacked Malta, and warships began mining the Sicilian Channel. (See map 2.1.)

Map 2.1 Defeat of France, June–July 1940

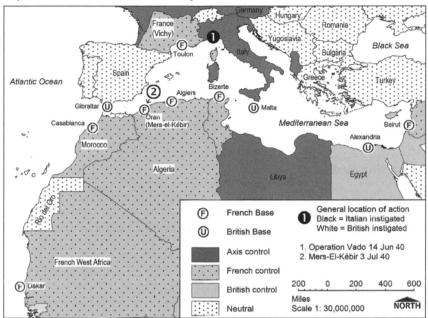

The collapse of the French army disrupted the Marine Nationale's plans. The government fled Paris on 10 June, and, against Admiral Darlan's wishes, it canceled his naval offensive; the only activity was a probe of the Aegean by four cruisers and three destroyers out of Syria from 11 through 13 June. British battleships swept the eastern basin but the Royal Navy restricted its offensive action to a cruiser bombardment of Tobruk, instead of the Italian coast.

The light cruisers *Gloucester* and *Liverpool,* escorted by four destroyers conducted this bombardment. They approached Tobruk before dawn on 12 June. Three small auxiliary minesweepers were patrolling outside the harbor, and when the cruisers engaged, they returned the enemy gunfire. In the darkness the British assumed the small-caliber shells came from shore batteries and quickly zeroed in on the source. At 0500 a 6-inch round plunged through *Giovanni Berta* (644 tons, nine knots, two 76-mm/40 guns) and forced her aground. Then *San Giorgio,* an old armored cruiser serving as a floating battery, entered the action with her 10-inch and 7.5-inch weapons. Her salvoes straddled, inflicting splinter damage, and forcing the British cruisers to withdraw.[5] The entire affair lasted eleven minutes. A concurrent air raid caused minor damage.

Italian air reconnaissance was slow in detecting the British sweep; the 3rd Cruiser Division with two destroyer squadrons sallied from Messina, and the 1st and 8th cruiser divisions with two destroyer squadrons from Taranto, but the fleets missed contact. Alexandria received a radio-direction fix on the Italian formation, but not in time for the fleet to act, causing Cunningham to complain, "I had the *Garibaldi* in the middle of a triangle of our forces but I was unaware of the fact."[6]

That same day Italian bombers attacked Bizerte. In retaliation, France's nomad government authorized a naval bombardment of enemy targets around Genoa and Savona.

Operation Vado

On the night of 13 June the Marine Nationale's 3rd Squadron departed Toulon. At 0348 on 14 June the 1st Cruiser Division, screened by six destroyers, headed for Vado, near Savona, while the 5th Cruiser Division and five destroyers targeted Sestri, west of Genoa. (See table 2.1.)

Table 2.1   Operation Vado, 14 June 1940, 0410–0425

Conditions:	Light rain, heavy onshore mist, calm seas
French ships—	3rd Squadron (Vice Admiral E. A. H. Duplat)
	1st Cruiser Division (Vice Admiral E. A. H. Duplat): CA: *Algérie*[D1] (F), *Foch*
	1st Scout Division (Captain J. G. Chardenot): DL: *Vauban* (F), *Lion, Aigle*
	5th Scout Division (Captain J. M. Chomel): DL: *Tartu, Chevalier Paul, Cassard*
	5th Cruiser Division (Rear Admiral Edmond-Louis Derrien): CA: *Dupleix* (F), *Colbert*
	7th Scout Division (Captain G. F. J. M. Reboul Hector-Berlioz): DL: *Vautour* (F), *Albatros*[D2]
	3rd Scout Division (Captain R. E. Gervais de Lafond): DL: *Guépard* (F), *Valmy, Verdun*
Italian ship—	(Lieutenant Giuseppe Brignole): TB: *Calatafimi*[D1]

The 5th Cruiser Division opened fire against the Sestri gas works and industrial zone west of Genoa at 0426 from 14,000 yards, although the weather rendered accurate spotting difficult. The eruption of gunfire surprised the old Italian torpedo boat *Calatafimi*, which was escorting the auxiliary minelayer *Gasperi* 12,000 yards to the west-northwest. The torpedo boat's commander, Lieutenant Brignole, believed the misty conditions permitted a surprise torpedo attack, so he steered a converging course. At 0431, however, the 7th Scout Division screening the cruisers to the north spotted the Italian warship and opened fire. Fragments from a near miss pierced *Calatafimi*'s hull. She returned fire and launched two torpedoes at *Vautour* from 3,300 yards as the French column passed and then another pair from her centerline tubes.

As the destroyers sparred with *Calatafimi*, the Mameli battery, west of Genoa, opened fire. A 6-inch round struck *Albatros*, penetrating the French vessel's fireroom and killing twelve men. A battery near Savona also began dropping shells around the bombarding warships. *Calatafimi* failed in an attempt to launch her last pair of torpedoes at the heavy cruisers, but under pressure from the battery's accurate shooting, the French warships ceased fire and turned south. *Calatafimi* likewise broke contact and headed for Genoa.[7]

The western bombardment force also attacked at 0426, from 16,000 yards. *Algérie* targeted oil storage tanks at Vado. The force scored hits, but afterward "the shooting was extremely difficult because of the smoke pouring from the burning tanks."[8] *Foch* shelled the Savona steelworks beginning at 0428.

The 13th MAS (motor torpedo boat) Squadron was patrolling southeast of Savona that night. *MAS535* and *MAS539* raced toward the shellfire, approaching from the northeast to within two thousand yards of *Algérie* and *Foch*. *MAS539* fired torpedoes, which missed, while *MAS535* was unable to launch, suffering light damage and three casualties in the defensive fusillade. An armored train near Savona armed with 4.7-inch guns then engaged, and its near misses peppered *Algérie* with splinters. As the French warships withdrew, *MAS534* and *MAS538* sped in from the southeast. They each uncorked two torpedoes and wheeled around to escape, but again their weapons missed.

The warships expended fifteen hundred shells. The Italian shore batteries replied with about three hundred. The French returned to base "exultantly reporting" that they had subjected their targets to a sustained and effective bombardment.[9] However, a French assessment later noted, "The results of the fire against the shore . . . were nearly null, causing damage of no importance. A more military objective would have probably been one better choice."[10] *Calatafimi*'s ineffective attack likewise provided grist for Italian propaganda mills, as her crew believed the flash of the shell hitting *Albatros* marked the detonation of one of their torpedoes. This claim, accepted at face value, lent an exaggerated aura of efficiency to the Italian coastal forces.

On 12 and 13 June the French fleet sortied to intercept a large force of German warships reported to be passing the Straits of Gibraltar to join the Italians. The sighting proved fictitious, however, and the French force's only encounter came when destroyers unsuccessfully counterattacked the Italian submarine *Dandolo,* which had fired a pair of torpedoes.

On 15 June, in retaliation for the attacks on Tobruk, the Italian 1st Destroyer Squadron from Tobruk—*Turbine, Aquilone,* and *Nembo*—bombarded Sollum through a heavy mist, expending 220 4.7-inch shells but inflicting negligible damage. They repeated the action on 26 June with better results, expending 541 rounds in the process.[11]

French cruisers and destroyers sailed on 17, 18, 19, and 21–23 June, but their only brush with the enemy came when nine Italian bombers made an ineffectual attack on *Le Malin* on the 21st. That same day *Lorraine,* accompanied by *Orion, Neptune, Sydney,* and four British destroyers bombarded Bardia with minimal results.[12]

On 23 June, the day before the Franco-Italian armistice was signed, Supermarina, Italy's central naval command, which had been activated in late May, dispatched the 7th Cruiser Division with four light cruisers, as well as the 2nd Fleet with six heavy cruisers, two light cruisers, and three destroyer squadrons, to raid French lines of communications with Africa. At 1120 a French aircraft sighted Italian warships returning toward Sardinia after a fruitless search. The French 3rd Cruiser Division sortied from Algiers, but the aircraft lost contact and no interception resulted. The next day the fighting between the Axis and France ended.

During the war's first weeks Italy's "aero-naval" offensive fell far short of expectations. Submarines deployed in force, but the British had stopped routine shipping in May, and targets were few. In fact, Italy lost ten boats through the end of June in the Mediterranean, Red Sea, and Indian Ocean, sinking in return only the light cruiser *Calypso* (on 12 June), two tankers, and a freighter. The British could, during these first weeks, read the fleet's general code, which disclosed Italian patrol areas, and facilitate the submarine slaughter.[13] However, Britain's underseas force likewise performed poorly, losing three boats in the war's first two weeks, accounting for one submarine in return.

Strategic Choices

On 28 June London activated Force H at Gibraltar, to fill the void left by the French fleet. A debate raged between the Admiralty and the joint planners as to whether the Mediterranean Fleet should withdraw to Gibraltar. The First Sea Lord, Admiral Pound, advocated withdrawal, for naval reasons, particularly to concentrate on protecting the Atlantic trade. The Admiralty was also concerned by Alexandria's limited logistical capabilities and the huge demands on shipping a Middle Eastern war would impose. Churchill vetoed a withdrawal on 23 June, however, for political reasons.[14]

Great Britain's decision to reinforce the Middle East made the Mediterranean the principal focus of the empire's war effort. In June 1940 Italy lacked the power to overthrow Britain's position in the Middle East, which the War Cabinet, using their "considerable knowledge of [Italy's] military unpreparedness for a long war," realized.[15] However, Italy did possess the world's fifth-largest fleet. To fight such a force from forward bases like Malta and Alexandria required a major commitment that could only be achieved at the expense of Great Britain's other worldwide obligations, particularly convoy protection in the North Atlantic and the defense of Singapore, which, just two years before, the chiefs of staff had designated the empire's most strategic point outside the home island.

Another factor influencing the War Cabinet's decision to concentrate on Italy was the fact that Britain could not significantly harm Germany. Only in the Mediterranean did London see an opportunity to win "early victories to encourage an embattled British nation."[16] The government "intended to take the offensive, seeing Italy as a weaker opponent that could be defeated by imperial forces unaided."[17] Even better was the possibility that a Nelsonian victory could topple Mussolini's regime and drive Italy from the war.

But before Britain could pursue such a victory, there was other business pending. London distrusted the terms of the Franco-German armistice, which specified that French ships, "except that part left free for the safeguard of French interests in the Colonial Empire, are to be collected in ports to be specified, demobilized, and disarmed under German or Italian control."[18] The Admiralty resented the way France had deserted the alliance, and it discounted assurances from Admiral Darlan that his ships would never enter the war on the Axis side.[19] The only certainty was that if the Axis seized the French fleet the Royal Navy would find itself confronted by an enemy nearly its equal—an unthinkable situation, especially given Germany's preparations to invade Britain. Churchill and the Admiralty thus determined to seize or neutralize as many French ships as possible. Admiral Pound brushed aside Admiral Darlan's protest against refusal to return French ships being held in British ports with the explanation, "We had got to win the war not only for ourselves but for them, and all trivialities and sob stuff about friendship and feelings must be swept aside."[20] The problem, however, was not the ships already in British waters but the heart of the French fleet, based in home or colonial ports.

When the nearly completed battleship *Richelieu* departed Brest on 18 June, London was relieved and issued orders for patrols to stand by to escort her into port. Unexpectedly, however, the new battleship turned south and eventually appeared at Dakar in West Africa. This caused Churchill to regard her as a major threat to British interests. "Should the dreadnought become belligerent, it alone, he reasoned, could menace all shipping lanes in the South Atlantic from the roadstead at Dakar."[21] London thus contemplated the use of force even before the French armistice commenced. When *Richelieu* suddenly departed Dakar on 25 June, the Admiralty ordered the cruiser *Dorsetshire* and the carrier *Hermes* to intercept and backed away from a confrontation only when it learned *Richelieu* was returning to the African port.

It was therefore with action against *Richelieu* no longer imminent that Force H started assembling at Gibraltar. The Admiralty instructed its commander, Vice Admiral James Somerville, to present an ultimatum to the powerful French Force de Raid at Mers-el-Kébir and, failing the desired answer, "to secure the transfer, surrender or destruction of the French warships . . . so as to ensure that they should not fall into German or Italian hands."[22] (See table 2.2.)

Admirals Dudley North (the Flag Officer North Atlantic), Cunningham (commander of the Mediterranean Fleet); and Somerville himself had strong reservations about these orders. Somerville suggested to the Admiralty that the use of force should be avoided at all costs.[23] The Admiralty and War Cabinet, especially Churchill, however, had little patience for French sensibilities or for those sympathetic with them and disregarded this advice.

Foxhound arrived off Mers-el-Kébir on 3 July at 0545 carrying Captain C. S. Holland, *Ark Royal's* skipper and former British naval attaché in Paris. He had the disagreeable task of delivering to the French the War Cabinet's terms, which contained the following options:

1. Sail with the British and continue the fight against Germany and Italy.
2. Sail to a British port with reduced crews where the ships would be safeguarded until hostilities were over.
3. Sail with reduced crews to a French West Indies port where the ships could be demilitarized, or entrusted to the safekeeping of the United States.

4. Sink all ships within six hours
5. Face the "use of whatever force may be necessary to prevent your ships from falling into German or Italian hands."[24]

Table 2.2   Mers-el-Kébir, 3 July 1940, 1656–1920

Conditions:	Light breeze north northeast, light fog onshore, visibility six miles, calm seas
French ships—	Force de Raid (Vice Admiral Marcel Bruno Gensoul)
	1st Line Division (Vice Admiral Gensoul): BB: *Strasbourg* (F), *Dunkerque*[D3]
	2nd Line Division (Rear Admiral J. F. E. Bouxin): BB: *Provence*[D3] (F), *Bretagne*[Sunk]
	2nd Light Squadron (Rear Admiral C. A. Lacroix)
	6th Scout Division (Rear Admiral C. A. Lacroix): DL: *Mogador*[D4] (F), *Volta*
	4th Scout Division (Captain M. De la Forest Divonne): DL: *Tigre* (F), *Lynx*
	Elements of 9th and 10th Scout divisions DL: *Kersaint, Le Terrible* [D1]
	Other CVS: *Commandant Teste*
	At Oran—7th Destroyer Division (Commander J. P. M. Murgue): *Tramontane* (F), *Tornade, Typhon*
	8th Destroyer Division (Commander D. F. M. de Bourgoing): *Bordelais* (F), *Trombe*
	5th Destroyer Division (Commander J. L. C. Kraft): *Brestois* (F), *Boulonnais*
	13th Destroyer Division TB: *La Bayonnaise, La Poursuivante*
	Other DS: *Rigault de Genouilly*[D3]
British ships—	Force H (Vice Admiral James Somerville): BC: *Hood*[D1] (F) BB: *Resolution, Valiant;* CV: *Ark Royal;* CL: *Arethusa, Enterprise*
	8th Destroyer Flotilla (Captain A. F. de Salis): *Faulknor* (F), *Foxhound, Fearless, Forester, Foresight, Escort*
	13th Destroyer Flotilla (Lieutenant Commander E. G. Heywood Lonsdale): *Keppel* (F), *Active, Wrestler, Vidette, Vortigern*

Admiral Gensoul refused permission for *Foxhound* to enter the port, as this could have been construed as a violation of the armistice, so the destroyer anchored thirteen hundred yards outside the harbor entrance. He also refused to receive Holland and instead sent his flag lieutenant to see what the British wanted. Meanwhile the French ships began to raise steam, furl awnings, and hoist boats—tasks delayed because many sailors were ashore and the ships had already begun the process of demobilizing. At 0847 the French ordered *Foxhound* to depart immediately; Holland embarked in the destroyer's motorboat and continued to await Gensoul's reply.

At 0910 Force H appeared on the horizon. A signalman aboard *Hood* was to remember, "It was a shimmering hot morning. . . . Looking towards the dun-coloured hills cloaking Oran, the scene was tranquil enough. Three miles to the west of Oran harbour I could see a forest of masts. This then was the French fleet moored at Mers-el-Kébir."[25] (See map 2.2.)

Map 2.2 Mers-el-Kébir, 3 July 1940

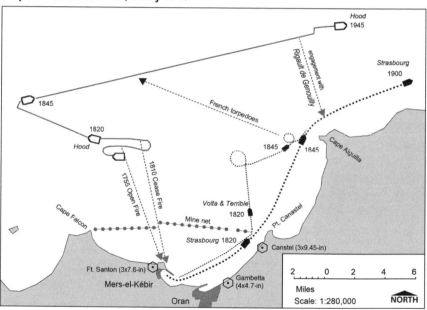

At 1000 Gensoul's flag lieutenant delivered the French admiral's curt reply; it repeated assurances given to Admiral North one week before that his ships would never fall into Axis hands and made clear that force would be met with force.

Neither Gensoul nor Somerville wanted a fight, for which reason negotiations continued. However, given the political consequences of surrendering to British demands, not to mention Gensoul's obligation to follow his government's orders, there was no way out, at least in the time allotted. At 1307, when it seemed the negotiations would fail, Somerville ordered *Ark Royal*'s aircraft to mine the harbor entrance. Though angered, Gensoul ignored this provocation and, in the face of Somerville's continued threats to open fire, agreed to meet Holland at 1440. *Foxhound* was now seven miles offshore, and Holland did not reach *Dunkerque* until 1615. After a discussion lasting more than an hour, Gensoul offered to disarm his ships in place. Holland felt this solution might work; Somerville, however, had already demonstrated too much flexibility for London's taste. At 1646 an impatient Admiralty prodded, "Settle matters quickly or you will have reinforcements to deal with."[26] Somerville immediately signaled Gensoul that he would open fire at 1730 unless one of his original options was accepted. Holland left *Dunkerque* at 1725. Somerville ordered an air strike to take off and the battleships to assume their bombardment stations.[27]

At 1730 Gensoul ordered his destroyers to cast off. The seven destroyers and four submarines in Oran harbor also began to stir, causing Somerville to drop two mines there and to send *Wrestler* to take over the inshore patrol from *Vortigern*.

The British battle line proceeded east-northeast at twenty knots. The French capital ships, moored along the mole with their bows facing the shore, formed a compact target. *Hood* was still behind Cape Kébir when Somerville hoisted the signal to open fire. The time was 1754 and the range 17,500 yards. The response was immediate: "The guns of the *Resolution* and *Valiant* roared in murderous hair-trigger reaction. Then came the ting-ting of our firing bell. . . . It was an awesome sight as shells continued to plunge into the harbour area."[28]

Gensoul was standing on *Dunkerque*'s flag bridge when lookouts reported gun flashes. He dropped his binoculars and gave the order to open fire.[29] French sailors sprang into action, stunned, like their admiral, that their allies of a fortnight past were actually shooting at them. Gensoul intended to form a battle line, led by the destroyers followed by *Strasbourg, Dunkerque, Provence*, and finally *Bretagne*. The destroyers were already under way, but as *Strasbourg* cast off, massive geysers spouted a hundred yards beyond the mole. The first British salvo was short but good on deflection. As *Strasbourg* pulled into the fairway a huge geyser erupted in water swirled by the wash from her propellers; the concussion shook everyone aboard, and splinters sliced through the flagship's flagstaff, dropping the pole in her wake. *Dunkerque* got a reprieve as shells slammed into the high mole just short of target and filled the air with clouds of pulverized cement.

Provence's 13.4-inch battery retaliated at 1758. Her gunnery officer, winner of the prior year's fleet shooting competition, sent the salvo over *Dunkerque*'s superstructure, disregarding the blast damage his big guns could cause to the flagship."A number of 13.4-inch shells . . . fell close to, and in some cases straddled, the British ships"[30] Splinters fell aboard *Hood*, wounding two men and slicing through radio antennas.[31] The French shore batteries—Fort Santon, with three 7.6-inch/50-caliber guns; Battery Canastel, with three 9.45-inch/50s; and Gambetta, with four 4.7-inch/40s—engaged, and their opening rounds followed those of *Provence* by a few seconds.

Dunkerque got under way at 1759, just as the third British salvo arrived. A 15-inch shell ricocheted off B turret's roof to starboard, disabling the nearest pair of guns and spraying the area with a deadly shower of metal fragments. One splinter struck *Provence*'s rangefinder, effectively silencing her guns. A second shell penetrated the airplane hangar and exited the port side without exploding. Rounds from this salvo also detonated aft on *Bretagne*, sparking a devastating explosion. *Strasbourg*'s captain saw "*Bretagne*'s whole stern shake while human bodies and hunks of metal debris of all kinds flew up into the air. A thick black cloud rose to the bridge. The rear funnel vomited a mixture of russet-red smoke, vapors, sparks and then flames."[32]

Mogador, followed by *Volta, Lynx, Le Terrible,* and *Tigre,* steamed down the channel, building speed. *Kersaint* had engine problems and lagged behind. At 1758 *Mogador* was only 2,200 yards short of the gap in the antisubmarine net. She targeted *Wrestler* patrolling offshore but then needed to dodge a tug crossing her path. Meanwhile, British salvos dropped into the fairway, and at 1759 a 15-inch shell struck *Mogador* aft, detonating the destroyer's depth charges and blowing away her stern. *Mogador* had fired twenty-two rounds up to that point. She anchored in shallow water with forty-two men dead. The other destroyers steered around her, making for the open sea. An officer aboard *Volta* recorded, "We are surrounded by splashes and shell bursts. Everything hurtles by, shell splinters and stones torn from the jetty, giving the effect on the water of one of those heavy rain storms so frequent in these parts. Already at full power we pass the stationary *Mogador.* . . . The spectacle is horrifying."[33]

Dunkerque finally engaged, with her forward turret trained 140 degrees to starboard. *Hood* was just coming into view from behind Cape Kébir, but the French battleship's stereoscopic rangefinders were confused by smoke and drifting dust and her initial salvo dropped short. The Santon battery also targeted *Hood* and nearly hit the screening destroyers."In one destroyer which was straddled, an unexpected hazard was the dye used by the French to distinguish splashes of their fall of shot, causing white uniforms to turn green."[34]

At 1801 two 15-inch shells penetrated *Dunkerque*'s main armor belt amidships. One struck the starboard side just above the waterline. It entered the shell-handling room of the no. 3 secondary turret but fortunately did not explode. The other detonated in no. 2 boiler room, disrupting electrical power and sending smoke surging through the ventilation ducts into the other boiler rooms. *Dunkerque*'s big guns fell silent. She fired only forty rounds in seven minutes and never obtained a good target solution.

At 1803 *Volta*, followed by *Le Terrible*, burst from the harbor at forty knots. Confident in the aerial mines dropped five hours earlier, the British destroyers on guard were surprised to see an enemy division break through the smoke with guns blazing. A French witness enthusiastically recorded, "A first target, hit, vanishes in the cloud. A second also, then a third . . . received a salvo from us on her stern, at over 15,000 metres: smoke, flames, and she disappears behind the cloud."[35] In fact, the French shells all missed their targets, but they were enough to put the British pickets to flight.

At 1803 several shells struck *Provence* while she waited for *Dunkerque* to clear. Large fires erupted, and the ship rapidly flooded. At 1809 *Bretagne* capsized in shallow water with the tragic loss of 977 men. *Dunkerque* was under way but proved too damaged to continue. At 1813 she beached with 210 crewmen dead.

Meanwhile, with shells from Fort Santon falling uncomfortably close, *Hood* ceased fire at 1812 and turned west making smoke.[36] Battery Canastel's heavy guns, on the other hand, were ineffective, because they could aim only at masts poking up through the mist. The two batteries fired thirty and thirty-six rounds, respectively. The British battleships discharged thirty-six salvos, with *Hood* accounting for ninety-four 15-inch rounds of this total.

Somerville's new course took him beyond range of the shore batteries but left the harbor exit uncovered. The admiral reported that "my appreciation of the situation at this time was that resistance from the French ships had ceased and that by ceasing fire I should give them an opportunity to abandon their ships. . . . Since the French knew that the entrances to the harbour had been mined, I felt quite positive that no attempt would be made by them to put to sea."[37] In fact *Strasbourg* had been steaming down channel, working up to fifteen knots, just ahead of every salvo. At 1809 the battleship turned northeast, broke through the mined gap in the antisubmarine net, and came to twenty-eight knots as she headed up the coast.

At 1820 Somerville discounted a report that some ships were escaping. He took a second report, made ten minutes later, more seriously. At 1834 the British admiral ordered the cruisers and destroyers to the van and, leaving the two older battleships behind without a screen, set off with *Hood* in pursuit. Somerville also diverted six Swordfish armed with 250-pound bombs to attack *Strasbourg*, even though such light bombs had little chance of slowing the battleship.

Strasbourg was now nearly eighteen miles ahead of *Hood*. At 1840 *Volta* and *Le Terrible*, guarding the French formation's rear, fired torpedoes back toward the British set to run 22,000 yards at twenty-nine knots; twenty minutes later *Tigre* and *Lynx* did the same. In total they launched twenty-two torpedoes, knowing they were unlikely to score a hit but hoping to slow the pursuit. During the chase *Strasbourg* fired twelve 13-inch rounds at *Wrestler* and *Vortigern* and 152 rounds of 5.1-inch during the two subsequent aircraft attacks. *Volta, Le Terrible, Tigre,* and *Lynx* fired 88, 99, 43, and 62 rounds of 5.45-inch, respectively.

At 1900 *Ark Royal*'s spotters signaled that the seven destroyers stationed at Oran had joined *Strasbourg*. An hour later the two torpedo boats based there fell in with the battleship's growing escort. The colonial sloop *Rigault de Genouilly* also sortied but could not catch up. The bomb-armed Swordfish attacked at 1925 and erroneously claimed one hit.

At 1933, as *Rigault de Genouilly* was returning to Oran, she encountered Force H. Aboard *Hood*, a crewman later remembered, "Where there had been six destroyers in our screen on the starboard wing, there was unaccountably a seventh, and this interloper was heading straight for the *Hood* at full speed."[38] *Arethusa* and *Enterprise* engaged from twelve and eighteen thousand yards, respectively, and *Hood* tossed in a few 15-inch salvos for good measure. The British believed the sloop was a destroyer making a torpedo run; witnesses even reported a trail of bubbles missing astern. In fact, however, *Rigault de Genouilly* carried no torpedoes. She fired nineteen 5.45-inch rounds in self-defense but got much the worse of this brief action, which ended at 1945 after *Enterprise* damaged the French warship. The next day the British submarine *Pandora* sank *Rigault de Genouilly* off Algiers, mistaking her for a cruiser. In an example of the topsy-turvy distinctions being made at this time, the Admiralty expressed deep regret to the French embassy for the mistake.[39]

At 2025 Somerville broke off the chase, concerned that *Strasbourg* would shortly join with the cruisers streaming from Algiers and quite rightly declining to risk a night engagement against so superior a foe. At 2155 the British delivered their last air strike. This time the Swordfish had torpedoes, but they were unable to hit. Five seaplanes of the Aéronautique Navale launched unsuccessful individual attacks against Force H.

Two days after the action Somerville wrote to his wife, "I shouldn't be surprised if I was relieved forthwith. I don't mind because it was an absolutely bloody business to shoot up these Frenchmen who showed the greatest gallantry. The truth is my heart wasn't in it and you're not allowed a heart in war."[40]

Mopping Up an Old Alliance

The Mers-el-Kébir action was one of several simultaneous British operations against its former ally. Many French warships had fled to Great Britain upon their nation's collapse. On 25 June their government began requesting their return. Instead, on the morning of 3 July armed parties captured every ship in English ports. This included the two old battleships *Paris* and *Courbet,* two large and two fleet destroyers, six torpedo boats, seven submarines, sixteen sloops, four subchasers, a corvette, a minelayer, seven patrol vessels, seven MTBs, and three auxiliaries. The French crews, caught completely by surprise, managed only to scuttle partially one destroyer. While the British congratulated themselves on a small loss of life, the subsequent treatment of the interned French personnel incited Gallic resentment. "Presently guards with fixed bayonets marched the crews to the railroad station, locked them in the coaches, and transported them to the camps in the vicinity of Liverpool just as though they had been prisoners of war."[41]

The happiest result came at Alexandria, where Vice Admiral Réne Godfroy commanded the battleship *Lorraine;* the cruisers *Duquesne, Tourville, Suffren,* and *Duguay-Trouin;* the destroyers *Basque, Forbin,* and *Fortune;* and a submarine. On 3 July Godfroy disregarded an order from Darlan to "fight his way to sea forthwith," an act that would have made the loss of life incurred at Mers-el-Kébir seem trivial, and finally came to an accord with Cunningham—who himself disregarded the War Cabinet's order to settle the affair on 3 July—whereby the French ships discharged their fuel oil, reduced their crews, and deposited the breechblocks of their guns in the French consulate.[42] In return the British agreed to respect Godfroy's control over his ships.

Despite these results, the Admiralty continued to worry about the modern French battleships. On 6 July a strike from *Ark Royal* against *Dunkerque* inflicted additional damage: a torpedo sank the patrol vessel *Terre Neuve,* and then a second torpedo hit the wreck and detonated the forty-two depth charges carried aboard. The massive explosion that followed sent a tower of debris-strewn water into the air, severely damaged *Dunkerque,* and killed or wounded another 154 men.[43]

At Dakar the French had *Richelieu,* destroyers *Milan, Epervier,* and *Fleuret,* a colonial sloop, two submarines, and seven AMCs. The British conducted a daring but unsuccessful raid in which a motorboat forced the harbor boom and dropped depth charges under the battleship's stern. Then *Hermes* launched on 8 July an air strike that torpedoed *Richelieu* aft, preventing her from sailing until repairs were completed ten months later.

The Tally Board

The attacks of 3 and 6 July killed 1,297 French personnel and wounded 351 more. If the British objective had been to incapacitate the French fleet, it failed; the Forces Maritimes Françaises (FMF), the naval service of the post-armistice French state, remained a powerful navy, and the squadron at Toulon, now named the Force de Haute Mer, or High Seas Force, remained an effective fleet in being that both the British and the Italians had to always consider. But sinking French ships was only part of the program; Churchill also wished to send a message to the British public and the world at large that "the British War Cabinet feared nothing and would stop at nothing."[44] The *New York Times* acknowledged the message when it wrote, "[Great Britain] would never have cut the last tie with the French except as grim prelude to a battle to the death."[45] Rome also took note. On 4 July Italy's foreign minister, Count Galeazzo Ciano, wrote, "For the moment it proves that the fighting spirit of His British Majesty's fleet is quite alive, and still has the aggressive ruthlessness of the captains and pirates of the seventeenth century."[46]

The British, however, paid a price for advertising their resolve in this fashion. They confirmed the Anglophobic Admiral Darlan as their bitter enemy, and with him the entire French navy. They destroyed whatever immediate allure de Gaulle's Free French movement may have had, and they assumed another military commitment. As the Admiralty noted on 12 July, "Further maintenance of present state of tension between the French Navy and ourselves is very undesirable and might even lead to war with that country."[47]

This was likewise the feeling in the Axis capitals. Mussolini, still seeking to annex Corsica, Nice, and Tunisia, worried that France was "trying to slip gradually into the anti-British camp."[48] On 11 July Hitler and *Grossadmiral* Raeder discussed France's role in the war against Britain and agreed that, with Italian permission, Vichy could actively participate in the Mediterranean.[49] Hitler also offered to send German troops to Dakar and other African ports to help protect them from the British.

Ironically, the attack benefited France in several ways. On 3 July the Germans, angered that the French naval units in English harbors had not been returned, threatened to reconsider the entire armistice.[50] After Mers-el-Kébir both the German and Italian armistice commissions were more relaxed about the

Table 2.3 Organization of the Forces Maritimes Françaises, 1 October 1940 Toulon

High Seas Force

Battleship	*Strasbourg*
1st Cruiser Division	*Algérie, Foch, Dupleix*
3rd Cruiser Division	*Marseillaise, La Galissonniére*
3rd Light Squadron	*Volta*
5th Scout Division	*Tartu, Vauquelin, Chevalier Paul*
7th Scout Division	*Vautour, Albatros*
8th Scout Division	*L'Indomptable, Cassard*
1st Destroyer Division	*Bordelais, La Palme, Le Mars*

Metropolitan Police Division

1st Destroyer Squadron	
10th Destroyer Division	*Epée, Mameluk*
13th Destroyer Division	*Baliste, La Bayonnaise, La Poursuivante*
3rd Escort Division	*Commandant Bory, Élan, La Batailleuse, La Curiesuse, Chamois, L'Impétueuse*
1st Patrol Squadron	

Submarines	Eight (on seven-day standby)
Under repair	*Le Terrible*
In reserve	One battleship, two cruisers, one seaplane transport, ten large destroyers, six destroyers, twenty-two submarines

Bizerte

2nd Destroyer Division	*Tramontane, Tornade, Typhon*
12th Destroyer Division	*La Pomone, L'Iphigenie, Bombarde*
In reserve	Three torpedo boats, three sloops, nine submarines

Oran

5th Patrol Squadron	*L'Ajaccienne, La Toulonnaise, La Sétoise*
In reserve	Four submarines
Under repair	*Dunkerque*

Table 2.3 continued

Algiers		
	4th Patrol Squadron	*Engageante, Tapageuse, Estafette*
Dakar		
	Battleship	*Richelieu*
	4th Cruiser Division	*Georges Leygues, Montcalm*
	10th Scout Division	*Le Fantasque, Le Malin*
	Destroyers	*Le Hardi*
	Sloops	*D'Entrecasteaux, D'Iberville, Calais, Commandant Riviére, La Surprise, Gazelle*
	Submarines	*Persée, Ajax, Bévéziers*
	Under repair	*L'Audacieux*
Casablanca		
	Under repair	*Jean Bart*
Beirut		
	3rd Scout Division	*Guépard, Valmy*
	Sloops	*La Grandière, Annamite*
	10th Submarine Division	*Phoque, Dauphin, Espadon*
Diego-Suarez, Madagascar		
	Submarines	*Le Héros, Souffleur*
Indochina		
	Light cruiser	*Lamotte-Piquet*
	Sloops	*Amiral Charner, Marne, Tahure*
North America		
	Aircraft carrier	*Bearn* (Martinique)
	Light cruisers	*Jeanne d'Arc* (Guadeloupe), *Emile Bertin* (Martinique)
	Sloops	*Ville d'ys* (St. Pierre et Miquelon)

deployment and armament status of French units. The reinvigorated FMF had in fact been granted a new mission: to defend France against the Royal Navy and, faced by a British blockade, to protect French commerce and the homeland's ties to its empire—the single greatest asset remaining to France and the ultimate guarantee of its hope of becoming, once again, a great power. More importantly, however, whatever the emotions or provocations; whatever the thoughts of certain French ministers who may have favored entering the war on the side of Germany; and regardless of the short-term benefits of cobelligerency with the Axis—Vichy France did not go to war with Great Britain.

Negotiations regarding the FMF's status finalized after the British attack on Dakar in September, which is covered in a subsequent chapter. The fleet's organization on 1 October 1940 was as shown in table 2.3.

3

Italy's Parallel War

June and July 1940

We had all expected, and such was the general conviction, that soon as the war broke out, the British would hover in the middle of the Mediterranean with all their air and sea forces to sever all maritime links between Italy and Libya. This they did not do, nor even attempted to do.

—Captain Aldo Cocchia, *The Hunters and the Hunted*

Italy entered World War II with the notion that it was fighting a parallel war alongside Germany in its own sphere of influence—the Mediterranean and the Middle East. After its Libyan army captured the Suez Canal, Italy intended to dominate the Balkans and Middle East and establish direct communications with Italian East Africa, the Black Sea, and Spain. Two major factors in this war were intelligence and logistics.

Intelligence

Prewar British intelligence enjoyed success reading Italian army, navy, air force, and diplomatic codes. However, on 10 June the army and air force changed their ciphers, as did the navy's submarines on 5 July and the surface warships on 17 July. This came as "a great shock to [British] intelligence authorities long accustomed to receiving a steady supply of Italian Sigint [signals intelligence]."[1] The Italian armed services also tightened their radio security, forcing the British to rely mainly on an inadequate number of reconnaissance aircraft for operational intelligence and on the reading of Italian air force codes used to send sighting reports. Moreover, "Italy's main naval book cyphers . . . used by her fleet for most of its important communications, were never read again after July 1940 except for brief intervals as a result of captures after the middle of 1941."[2]

The Royal Navy, in contrast to the Royal Air Force and British army, did not use a cipher machine but instead relied upon a manual subtractor system that proved vulnerable to Italian cryptologists. The Regia Marina was able to operationally exploit signal intelligence in this period, although Italy started the war with only seven men, supported by thirty clerks, handling all deciphering tasks. (The number of personnel engaged in these activities would rise to over two hundred by 1942.)[3] Thus, with respect to signal intelligence Italy enjoyed the initial advantage, although not enough resources were put into this vital area.

Both sides deplored the quality of the operational intelligence provided by their aircraft. In 1923 most of the Regia Marina's considerable aviation assets were transferred to the newly established air force, the Regia Aeronautica, and the navy went to war with nearly no control over its aviation except for shipborne reconnaissance planes. Cooperation with the air force was never good; the latter grudgingly assigned aerial assets to meet the navy's needs. For example, in August 1940 the air force's chief of staff managed to have many routine reconnaissance flights canceled after he complained to Mussolini that the boring missions were wearing out planes and crew. The British appreciated the importance of aerial reconnaissance, and once they committed more resources to the Mediterranean the quality of their operational intelligence improved greatly. However, Italy never solved this basic problem. "Poorly conceived and executed aerial reconnaissance influenced almost all missions of the Italian battle fleet . . . and formed the Regia Marina's true Achilles' heel."[4]

Logistics and the African Land War

All the supplies and personnel required to wage war in North Africa and the Middle East had to be shipped there, because, with the exception of oil (for the British) and some food, the theater produced nothing. In the case of Italy, men and materiel arrived at a few small ports: Tripoli, Benghazi, and Tobruk. Secondary anchorages included Derna and Bardia. Prewar Tripoli had a daily capacity of two thousand tons, Benghazi a thousand, and Tobruk less than a thousand. Then, once men and materiel arrived in port, they had to be either trucked or transshipped in coastal craft to wherever they were needed. In August 1939, based on the premises that Anglo-French naval superiority made offensive operations from Libya impossible, Marshal Badoglio set the army's objectives as being to safeguard the colony against armed uprisings. Beyond that, forces in Libya were to be self-sustaining for at least twelve months. North Africa's prewar infrastructure reflected this defensive orientation. It was not until 10 May 1940 that Mussolini directed the chiefs of staff to build up an offensive force in Libya and assigned to the navy, by default, the task of maintaining this force across the Middle Sea.[5]

Britain's supplies traveled up the Red Sea from around Africa or across the Indian Ocean. The immense distances involved in bringing materiel from the factory to the front tied up huge amounts of shipping and limited Britain's ability to respond quickly to opportunities or crises. (See map 3.1.)

Map 3.1   Italy's Parallel War, June and July 1940

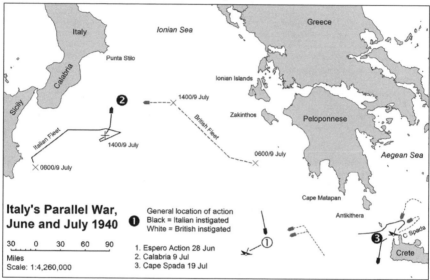

Italy began running regular convoys to Tripoli the day after France surrendered. Because Tobruk lay within range of enemy air, warships initially transported vital supplies to that port. On 27 June the 2nd Destroyer Squadron departed Taranto loaded with ten 20-mm/65-caliber AA guns, 162 men, and 120 tons of ammunition—450,000 rounds of 20-mm, about 7 percent of Italy's entire inventory. Two torpedo boats sailed from Taranto on a similar mission several hours later.

Attack on *Espero*

On the morning of 28 June a Sunderland flying boat from Malta reported Italian destroyers fifty miles west of Zakinthos, the southernmost of the Ionian Islands. The Mediterranean Fleet, at sea in force for the first time since 11 June to cover convoys sailing to Egypt from the Dardanelles, Greece, and Malta, was southwest of Crete when it received the sighting report.

Ramillies, Royal Sovereign, Eagle, and eight destroyers remained behind while Vice Admiral John Tovey led the 7th Cruiser Squadron north to intercept. At 1640 another signal pinpointed Italian warships thirty-five miles west of his position. Tovey formed his ships into two divisions on an extended line of bearing and turned southwest. (See table 3.1.)

Table 3.1 Attack on *Espero*, 28 June 1940, 1833–2200

Conditions: Fair, fresh wind, slight chop	
British ships—	7th Cruiser Squadron (Vice Admiral Tovey)
	Division 1: CL: *Orion* (F), *Neptune, Sydney* (AU)
	Division 2: CL: *Liverpool*[D1] *Gloucester*
Italian ships—	2nd Destroyer Squadron (Captain Enrico Baroni) *Espero*[Sunk] (F), *Ostro, Zeffiro*

At 1833, when seventy-five miles west-southwest of Cape Matapan, *Liverpool* sighted Baroni's ships silhouetted against the afternoon sun. Three minutes later the cruiser lofted a salvo from twenty-two thousand yards. When geysers erupted nearby, *Espero* immediately turned west-southwest. The old and laden destroyers increased speed, but a machinery defect in *Espero* prevented her third boiler from steaming and limited her to twenty-five knots. *Orion*'s division received *Liverpool*'s report and sighted the enemy at 1855. At 1859 *Orion* opened fire from eighteen thousand yards.

With cruisers pursuing on each quarter and aware of his ship's limited speed and the need to "chase" salvos so as to confuse the opponent's aim, Baroni concluded that the enemy would run him down before dark. Thus, he ordered *Ostro* and *Zeffiro* to escape while he returned fire and made smoke. *Espero* also launched three torpedoes toward *Orion*, chasing on her starboard quarter. At 1905 *Neptune* spotted wakes, and Tovey altered course for three minutes to "comb the spread," paralleling the courses of the torpedoes so as not to be hit by them. The British admiral then tried to work around the smoke to get at *Ostro* and *Zeffiro*, while *Liverpool*'s division, firing rapidly to force a decision before dark, focused on *Espero*. The solitary destroyer fought back; however, the British described *Espero*'s return fire as "being good for range but bad for line."[6] By 1920 *Liverpool* had closed to fourteen thousand yards, but her quarry proved elusive. In fact, *Espero* hit first, a 4.7-inch shell striking *Liverpool*'s hull three feet above the waterline. Splinters penetrated the warheads of two torpedoes, which did not explode. *Liverpool* turned away, and *Gloucester* followed. Observing this, Tovey ordered *Orion, Neptune,* and *Sydney* to the attack, and they deluged the destroyer with 6-inch salvos. By 2000 *Espero* had been hit in her engine spaces and brought to a halt. Tovey then resumed his chase of *Ostro* and *Zeffiro,* but with darkness falling and his supply of ammunition dwindling, he broke off after only ten minutes, setting course for Malta and leaving *Sydney* to dispatch the cripple.

Sydney approached the drifting destroyer and was greeted by several rounds. The cruiser retaliated with four broadsides from six thousand yards, and shortly thereafter *Espero* capsized. Over the next two hours the *Sydney* rescued forty-seven of the 225 men aboard. The Italian submarine *Topazio* saved another six after they had drifted fourteen days on a raft. *Ostro* and *Zeffiro* safely made Benghazi on the morning of 29 June.

"Morning showed the muzzles of [*Sydney's*] guns stripped of paint, which hung in long reddish-grey streamers almost to the deck."[7] Tovey's command had expended nearly five thousand 6-inch rounds to sink one destroyer. Only eight hundred remained in the entire theater; Cunningham postponed two Malta convoys scheduled for 29 June because the action had "denuded" the cruisers of ammunition.[8] For Supermarina this engagement seemed to confirm the danger of running supplies to Africa, even on warships, but at least two of the old destroyers had survived their encounter with a faster and far more powerful foe. The Admiralty staff, on the other hand, considered that the Italians should have shadowed the cruisers and launched nocturnal torpedo attacks, concluding, "This action afforded an early example of the Italian's lack of experience in sea-warfare."[9]

The Battle of Calabria

On the evening of 6 July an important Italian convoy consisting of a passenger liner and five freighters loaded with 2,200 men, 72 tanks, 237 vehicles, and more than 16,000 tons of fuel and supplies, departed Naples and Catania bound for Benghazi. The 2nd Cruiser Division (*Bande Nere* and *Colleoni*), the 10th Destroyer Squadron, and six torpedo boats constituted the convoy's escort. Comando Supremo, Italy's supreme military command, considered this convoy's arrival critical to the pending invasion of Egypt and the favorable development of the naval war.

Two days before the convoy sailed Italian naval intelligence had deciphered British orders for an upcoming Malta operation. In response, the Regia Marina's two battle fleets readied for action. On 7 July Supermarina received further intelligence that enemy cruisers (actually two destroyers) had arrived at Malta. That

day the 2nd Fleet, with six heavy cruisers, four light cruisers, and sixteen destroyers, commanded by Vice Admiral Ricardo Paladini aboard *Pola*, sailed from
Augusta, Messina, and Palermo. At 1410 on 7 July Vice Admiral Inigo Campioni
led his 1st Fleet's two battleships, six light cruisers, and twenty destroyers from
Taranto to support Paladini.

The ships spotted at Malta formed a small part of the British operation. On
7 July Cunningham departed Alexandria with three battleships, an aircraft carrier, five light cruisers, and sixteen destroyers to meet two Malta convoys (the
ones delayed by the *Espero* engagement). On 8 July Somerville, who had just
refueled after attacking *Dunkerque*, sailed from Gibraltar in a diversionary sortie
with one battle cruiser, two battleships, one aircraft carrier, three light cruisers,
and eleven destroyers. Cunningham suggested to Somerville that he undertake
a bombardment of "Naples, Trapani, Palermo or Messina in that order of pref-
erence."[10] Somerville elected the more realistic option of an air strike against
Cagliari, Sardinia. On 8 July an Italian flyover of Alexandria confirmed that the
Mediterranean Fleet had sailed. Likewise, agents around Gibraltar passed word
when Force H raised anchor.

Commencing at 1000 on 8 July, Italian aircraft flying out of the Dodecanese
and Libya subjected the Mediterranean Fleet to a series of high-level bombing
attacks. Cunningham reported that "for this type of attack their accuracy was
very good. We were fortunate to escape being hit."[11] Actually, one bomb did find
its mark, striking *Gloucester*'s bridge, killing the captain and seventeen other
men. Near misses lightly damaged *Warspite* and *Malaya*.

As intelligence of Italy's fleet movements arrived, Cunningham formed the
impression that "the Italians might be covering the movement of an important convoy—probably one to Benghazi."[12] He decided to interpose the
Mediterranean Fleet between the enemy and Taranto—a decision consistent
with his intentions stated a month before. "I am convinced that to knock Italy
out of this war the practical application of it must be brought forcibly home to
them. Furthermore, attack on enemy coasts seems the possible way to draw
their Fleet to sea."[13]

The Italian convoy reached Benghazi on the evening of 8 July. Campioni, at
sea off the Libyan coast, knew of the enemy's approach and correctly concluding Force H was a decoy. He ordered Paladini's fleet to turn north-northwest
at 1430. At 1521 the 1st Fleet followed, and both Italian units steered toward
Cunningham's position as reported by a shadowing floatplane.

As the fleets steamed toward a confrontation, Supermarina intercepted
British signals suggesting that Cunningham intended to be off Calabria at
noon on 9 July and from them concluded that the British planned to bombard

Augusta. Mussolini himself ordered Campioni to postpone battle so the Regia Aeronautica could attack the British the next day. By 1840 both Italian fleets had turned away to the north-northwest.

On 9 July at 0732 Sunderlands from Malta found the 1st Fleet and shadowed it for nearly four hours. Italian planes, meanwhile, unaware of Cunningham's northerly change of course, fruitlessly crisscrossed the seas south of the British track. The British admiral ordered *Eagle* to launch an air strike, but not until 1315 did a group of nine Swordfish find Paladini's heavy cruisers forty-five miles east-southeast of Cape Spartivento. For eleven minutes the biplanes braved heavy antiaircraft fire, which damaged three of their number, launching two torpedoes at *Trento*, two at *Bolzano*, and one at *Zara*. All missed.

The sight of carrier planes told Campioni that British warships were nearby. His cruisers launched six more floatplanes, and one of these finally located the enemy only eighty miles northeast. Although the Regia Aeronautica had not delivered its promised attacks, Campioni reversed course to seek battle. For his part, Cunningham headed northwest until 1415, when, satisfied he was between Campioni and Taranto, he turned west to close. His ships steamed in three groups, each ten miles apart. Vice Admiral Tovey's light cruisers of the 7th Squadron, along with *Stuart*, led the fleet. Next came Cunningham's flagship, *Warspite*, screened by *Nubian, Mohawk, Hero, Hereward,* and *Decoy.* Rear Admiral H. D. Pridham-Wippell aboard *Royal Sovereign*, three knots slower than *Warspite*, brought up the rear. He also had *Malaya, Eagle,* and the other ten destroyers. The cruisers carried scarcely 50 percent of their ammunition load; given the experience with *Espero* just nine days before, Cunningham apparently hoped to fight a quick, decisive, close-range action.[14] It is not clear why he entered action with his fleet strung out in three nonsupporting formations.

On the afternoon of 9 July conditions favored battle, with clear skies, perfect visibility, a fresh north-by-west breeze, and a slight sea. Campioni steered north-northeast at fifteen knots, his ships in four columns spaced five miles apart. From west to east these consisted of the 7th Division, the 3rd and 1st divisions, the 5th Division, and the 8th and 4th divisions. Sixteen destroyers screened the various units. Supermarina's orders were specific: "Your action today is inspired by the following concepts: do not go beyond the range of our aero-naval bases so as to permit simultaneous preemptive aerial actions against the enemy. Contact is allowed against main armored groups while they remain separate. Delay gun action to permit disabling of enemy forces by aerial bombardment. At sunset return with larger units to base. If conditions are favorable, make nocturnal contact with torpedo boats."[15] Campioni's actions were, in fact, aggressive in light of these orders. (See table 3.2.)

Table 3.2   The Battle of Calabria, 9 July 1940, 1520–1645

Conditions: Clear, slight breeze, slight swells, extreme visibility

British ships— Mediterranean Fleet (Admiral Andrew B. Cunningham): BB: *Warspite* (F)

1st Battle Division (Rear Admiral H. D. Pridham-Wippell): BB: *Royal Sovereign* (F), *Malaya*

7th Cruiser Squadron (Vice Admiral John Tovey): CL: *Orion* (F), *Neptune*[D1], *Sydney* (AU), *Liverpool*

10th Destroyer Flotilla (Commander Hector Waller): *Stuart* (AU) (F), *Dainty*, *Defender*, *Decoy*[D1]

14th Destroyer Flotilla: *Nubian*[D1] (F), *Mohawk*, *Juno*, *Janus*[D1]

2nd Destroyer Flotilla (Captain H. Nicolson): *Hero* (F), *Hereward*[D1], *Hyperion*, *Hostile*, *Hasty*, *Ilex*

Italian ships— 1st Fleet (Admiral Inigo Campioni)

5th Division (Rear Admiral Bruto Brivonesi): BB: *Cavour* (F), *Cesare*[D2]

4th Division (Rear Admiral Alberto Marenco di Moriondo): CL: *Da Barbiano* (F), *Di Giussano*

8th Division (Rear Admiral Antonio Legnani): CL: *Abruzzi* (F), *Garibaldi*

7th Destroyer Squadron (Commander Amleto Baldo): *Freccia* (F), *Saetta*

14th Destroyer Squadron (Captain Giovanni Galati): *Vivaldi* (F), *Pancaldo*

2nd Fleet (Vice Admiral Riccardo Paladini)

3rd Division (Rear Admiral Carlo Cattaneo): CA: *Pola* (F), *Bolzano*[D2], *Trento*

1st Division (Rear Admiral Pellegrino Matteucci): CA: *Zara* (F), *Fiume*, *Gorizia*

7th Division (Rear Admiral Luigi Sansonetti): CL: *Eugenio di Savoia* (F), *Duca d'Aosta*, *Attendolo*, *Montecuccoli*

9th Destroyer Squadron (Captain Lorenzo Daretti): *Alfieri*[D1] (F), *Oriani*, *Carducci*, *Gioberti*

11th Destroyer Squadron (Captain Carlo Margottini): *Artigliere* (F) *Camicia Nera*, *Aviere*, *Geniere*

12th Destroyer Squadron (Captain Carmine D'Arienzo): *Lanciere* (F), *Carabiniere*, *Corazziere*, *Ascari*

At 1447 *Orion* and *Sydney* spotted smoke on the western horizon, and Tovey detached the damaged *Gloucester* to join *Eagle,* which also hauled out of line, escorted by the old destroyers *Voyager* and *Vampire.* At 1452 *Neptune* reported two ships southwest by west, twenty-eight thousand yards distant. This was Rear Admiral Legnani's 8th Division. Meanwhile, lookouts aboard the 4th Division's *Barbiano* spotted the enemy at 1505. The 8th and 4th divisions steered north-northeast, screened by the 9th Squadron's destroyers and two ships of the 14th Squadron, which had arrived from Taranto that morning.

The range closed rapidly, and at 1508, as more masts poked above the horizon, *Neptune* reported two enemy battleships fifteen miles to the west-southwest. Tovey immediately swung north and then northeast. Racing at thirty knots, *Abruzzi* and *Garibaldi* gave chase. At 1512 however, Cunningham ordered Tovey to engage. The British cruisers turned back, and the action commenced at 1520 when the Italians sent salvos arcing toward the enemy from 23,600 yards. *Neptune* and *Liverpool* replied two minutes later from twenty-two thousand yards, followed by *Sydney* against the 4th Division from twenty-three thousand yards. Italian gunnery was good. *Neptune's* captain, R. C. O'Connor, later reported, "*Neptune* was straddled almost at once. . . . Frequent small alterations of course were made to throw off the enemy's cruiser's straddles." As the pugnacious *Alfieri* closed to seventeen thousand yards, he further noted, "the gunfire of modern 4.7" gun destroyers can be most threatening to cruisers, when the enemy remains unfired at."[16]

At 1519 *Alfieri* spotted large warships in the distance behind the cruiser's smoke. Four minutes later Campioni swung his battleships and heavy cruisers to the east-northeast to support the light cruisers. At the same time Sansonetti's 7th Division approached the action from the southeast. (See map 3.2.)

At 1524 a shell fired from *Garibaldi* peppered *Neptune's* catapult and seaplane with metal shards. British salvos fell tightly bunched, and—as with *Espero*—kept missing. *Warspite* advanced at seventeen knots, and at 1525 great gouts of smoke erupted from her guns as she sent shells streaking toward Legnani's ships.

At 1526 the 4th Division came into range, but when giant geysers erupted around its ships they turned away, spewing smoke. *Warspite* discharged ten salvos at the fleeing cruisers in four and a half minutes, alternating guns to maintain a steady stream of fire. Then Cunningham's flagship turned away, making a 360-degree circle, flinging another six salvos at the enemy cruisers between 1534 and 1536. At 1531 Tovey's cruisers likewise turned away. *Neptune* expended 136 6-inch shells during this opening phase.[17]

Admiral Cunningham was known for his impatience. "He would pace one side of the Admiral's bridge, always on the side nearest the enemy; the speed

Map 3.2 Battle of Calabria, Tactical Action, 1520–1630

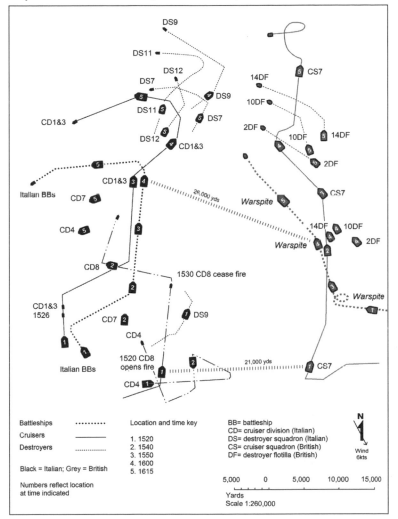

of advance of the battleship was never fast enough for him. . . . This mood was known colloquially among the staff as the 'caged tiger act.'" However, even Cunningham did not intend to fight enemy battleships if he was outnumbered. His signal to Tovey revealed his thinking: "Do not get too far ahead of me. I am dropping back on [battle force]. Air striking force will not be ready till 1530."[18] Three minutes later Legnani spotted Campioni's battleships approaching and turned west, followed by the 4th Division, clearing the line of fire by cutting between the two Italian dreadnoughts. Campioni later praised his conduct:"He duplicated exactly what we had executed during our frequent peace time tactical exercises, did not expose himself to 381-mm gunfire after he was certain our large ships were heading toward the enemy, and succeeded in withdrawing his ships quickly and brilliantly from the line of fire."[19]

The shooting faded away from 1536 to 1548, as the Italians advanced and the British regrouped. Cunningham radioed Tovey, "Sorry for the delay, but we must call upon reinforcements."[20] At 1540 Campioni's battleships turned north-northeast, steaming at twenty-five knots, their top gunnery speed. Paladini's six heavy cruisers had reached a point seventy-five hundred yards ahead of *Cesare*. Paladini's flagship, *Pola*, trailed, because the column had executed a simultaneous turn to reach its vanguard position more quickly. Sansonetti fell in behind *Cavour*. As for *Warspite*, by 1550, when her lookouts fixed the enemy battleships, she was again heading north-northwest at fifteen knots, while Tovey's light cruisers steered west-northwest, thirteen thousand yards ahead. *Malaya* had closed to within three thousand yards of the flagship, but *Royal Sovereign* lagged five miles astern. The British destroyers concentrated by flotillas off *Warspite*'s starboard bow.

At 1552 *Cesare*'s 12.6-inch guns erupted with yellow smoke and flame, propelling 1,157-pound shells toward *Warspite* on a trajectory of nearly twenty-nine thousand yards. *Cavour* fired next, targeting *Malaya* by Campioni's order (which obliged her to switch her main directors at the last minute), on the principle that every opponent should be engaged. Concentrating the twenty big guns of both ships against *Warspite* might have complicated spotting, but it still would have represented Campioni's best opportunity to exploit Cunningham's failure to concentrate his battle line. As it was, *Warspite* replied at 1553, firing 1,938-pound shells at an estimated range of twenty-six thousand yards. *Malaya* could not yet engage, while *Royal Sovereign*, straining her engines, was far out of range.

The Italian gunners fired deliberately, observing the fall of each salvo and correcting as required. Some Italian"overs"landed amid the British destroyers; splinters sliced into *Hereward* and *Decoy*, while heavy rounds straddled *Nubian* twice. Her report noted,"The second time two shells fell within 10 yards over. One shell grazed the starboard strut of the foremast abreast the steaming light."[21]

While the heavyweights slugged it out, Paladini steered to close. At 1555 *Trento* lofted three salvos at *Warspite* from her maximum range of twenty-eight thousand yards. At 1558 the others, following Paladini's orders, engaged the British light cruisers from ranges of around twenty-two thousand yards. Tovey's ships, now steering west by northwest, returned Paladini's fire. *Warspite*'s gunners, meanwhile, shot as quickly as they could load. The Italians noted that "the enemy salvos had small dispersion and were progressively centered."[22]

Both sides shot well. *Warspite*'s Captain D. B. Fisher noted that from 1556 enemy salvos straddled *Warspite* and that at 1600 a broadside bracketed the British flagship.[23] Concerned that *Cesare* had found the range, *Warspite* altered twenty degrees to port and increased speed to seventeen knots. Her guns temporarily fell silent as the ship swung to her new heading.

Lookouts on *Freccia, Cesare,* and aboard *Barbiano*'s Ro.43 floatplane circling overhead observed the course change and what appeared to be a small fire and concluded *Warspite* had been hit. Then a 15-inch shell from the British flagship's last salvo completed its thirty-three-second flight and, in one of the longest-range gunnery hits in the history of naval combat, plowed into *Cesare*'s aft funnel. The shell detonated prematurely on the funnel's thin inner plating and blasted a twenty-foot hole. The round's nose pierced a 37-mm magazine and a petty officers' mess before an armored bulkhead stopped it. Fires erupted, and ventilators pushed asphyxiating smoke into the boiler rooms. Boilers 4, 5, 6, and 7 fell off-line, and within three minutes *Cesare*'s speed dropped to eighteen knots. Campioni assumed the worse, and declining to face three more powerful enemy units with only one effective battleship, he ordered his battle line to turn away.

This order came at an opportune moment for the British. Paladini's heavy cruisers were pulling ahead of Tovey as his captains fretted about their dwindling supply of ammunition.[24] *Malaya* and *Royal Sovereign* remained widely separated and out of range.

Cavour followed *Cesare* around. Both ships fired their aft turrets at a more rapid rate until 1608, when their targets vanished in the smoke. During fifteen minutes of action *Cesare* had expended seventy-four rounds, while *Cavour* contributed forty-one. *Warspite*'s big guns shot their last round at 1603 and thirty seconds. In eleven minutes she had fired seventeen salvos. *Malaya* tried a ranging salvo at 1603 and then three more at 1608. All fell well short, though the blast from the last damaged an aircraft on her catapult.[25]

At 1606 Campioni ordered Paladini to retreat and the destroyers to cover the withdrawal. Nonetheless, the heavy cruisers shot as long as they had targets. *Zara* engaged *Warspite* through a gap in the smoke from 1612 to 1617, and at 1617 *Malaya* observed an 8-inch salvo straddle *Warspite*.[26] The others sparred with Tovey's light cruisers. *Neptune* later reported, "[We] straddled the target and 'rapid groups' was ordered. Eleven broadsides were fired in rapid in 2½ minutes. Only one small line correction was needed."[27] At 1605 one of *Neptune*'s shells punched through *Bolzano*'s hull aft and exploded. The wing, or outermost, rudders jammed to port, swinging the ship into a 180-degree turn while three hundred tons of water flooded in. Then a round detonated in the torpedo room, killing two men and discharging six torpedoes. Another exploded three feet from the end of B turret's starboard gun, spraying one barrel with metal shards. Nonetheless, *Bolzano* continued to fire. She freed her rudders within ninety seconds and came back around, steaming at thirty-six knots.

As *Bolzano* regained station at the column's head, Cunningham's ace in the hole appeared overhead. At 1610 nine Swordfish launched by *Eagle* twenty-five minutes before attacked *Bolzano* and *Trento* in three groups. *Bolzano* maneuvered wildly, dodging streaking torpedo wakes. *Eagle*'s flyers counted one hit, while Italian gunners claimed they downed several attackers, but both reports were incorrect. As the smoke thickened and targets disappeared, Paladini's heavy cruisers stopped firing, beginning with *Fiume* at 1605 and ending with *Bolzano* at 1620.

By the time Campioni ordered his destroyers to attack, their screening duties had scattered them throughout the battle zone. Daretti's 9th Squadron, sailing a mile north-northeast of *Bolzano*, charged the British line at 1607 and launched five torpedoes from ranges of up to 13,500 yards. (Italian torpedo doctrine called for reserving at least a third of available weapons in the expectation that multiple attack opportunities would arise during an action. This doctrine contrasted sharply with the tested Royal Navy practice of expending all torpedoes against the enemy whenever opportunity arose.) Daretti then ordered his ships to produce white chemical smoke. As he swung away, a shell grazed *Alfieri*'s bow.

Next the 7th Squadron's *Freccia* and *Saetta* emerged from behind the battle line's unengaged side. They sallied northeast trailing smoke and closed to within eighty-five hundred yards of Tovey's cruisers. At 1618 this pair turned, fired ten torpedoes, and ducked into the thick haze deposited by Daretti's ships. *Saetta*'s captain spotted a tall column of water spouting up beside *Sydney* and incorrectly claimed a hit.

As the Italian destroyers charged, the British flotillas formed columns off *Warspite*'s starboard side in order of, from northeast to southwest, the 14th, 2nd, and 10th. Cunningham ordered them to counterattack, and the 10th Flotilla turned due west at 1616. *Stuart* engaged the 9th Squadron two minutes later from 12,600 yards with her forward mounts. Within five minutes, however, the 10th Flotilla had turned north-northwest to maintain distance.

The 11th Squadron executed the third Italian destroyer attack. At 1606 its ships left their position along the 1st Division's port side and turned to starboard, cutting between *Gorizia* and *Fiume*. A forest of shell splashes surrounded the leader, *Artigliere,* as the squadron advanced northeast, trailing dark smoke.

She launched at 13,800 yards, and her squadron mates followed at 1620 at ranges down to eleven thousand yards. Collectively they put ten torpedoes in the water before retiring unharmed.

The 12th Squadron followed the 11th. Smothered in smoke, it had difficulty spotting targets as it charged from under the rear of the heavy cruiser column. At 1622 *Corazziere* fired three torpedoes at *Malaya,* and *Ascari* aimed one toward a cruiser. Then the squadron broke into the clear, attracting concentrated fire from every enemy warship in view. As the 12th fled back into the sheltering smoke, *Nubian* avoided two torpedoes. However, the squadron continued to observe and radio British movements to Campioni over the next half hour.

British accounts of enemy torpedoes indicated the Italian attacks were not as futile as generally depicted. For example, *Decoy*'s captain reported, "At 1700 two torpedo tracks were observed, one passing under the ship and one astern, and one torpedo surfaced on the starboard side about 50 yards away."[28] Another torpedo "narrowly missed" *Mohawk.*[29]

The old and large Navigatori-class ships of the 14th Squadron also attempted to attack but could not obtain a suitable firing position.

Between 1620 and 1645 the British destroyer flotillas headed west by northwest, keeping their distance from the blowing curtains of smoke and engaging when enemy ships emerged into view. Commander Waller's report summarized, "By 1630 enemy destroyers were dodging in and out of the smoke, and were being spasmodically engaged by our flotillas for a few salvos at a time until about 1640, when the enemy was enveloped in the smoke screen, and fire was finally ceased."[30] *Stuart* expended only fifty-five shells throughout the entire action. *Hasty* recorded, "Enemy destroyers observed making smoke and disappearing behind smoke screen making spotting most difficult."[31] She fired a few hopeful broadsides at ranges greater than ten thousand yards. *Nubian* took sporadic, long-range potshots. British destroyers all kept their distance, and none launched torpedoes.

At 1645, just as the first Italian air force bombers that Campioni had requested several hours before appeared, the 12th Squadron delivered the day's final attack. It zigzagged southeast between the battle lines, seeking an opening. When *Warspite*'s 6-inch guns began rumbling at *Lanciere,* she emptied three tubes and cleared the area. The 12th Squadron expended four hundred rounds between 1620 and 1645. By this time dense, multilayered curtains of smoke separated the fleets.

British aircraft reported *Cesare* and *Cavour* heading southeast at 1700, but during the melee Tovey continued steaming north. His ship's guns had fallen silent by 1633 after relatively moderate expenditures of ammunition. *Sydney* had fired

411 rounds and *Neptune* 512, for example. Moreover, the 7th Cruiser Squadron was an early target of the Italian air attacks, and dodging bombs absorbed its attention. Cunningham, naturally, did not plunge through the enemy smoke with his battleships, instead ordering the 14th Flotilla ahead to scout. The destroyers worked north of the screen by 1700 and beheld an empty sea.

After reorganizing, the British battleships pushed on briefly, looking for the cruiser that *Eagle*'s airmen claimed they had torpedoed. At 1735, when this proved a wild-goose chase, Cunningham turned back toward Malta. Over the next several hours seventy-six Italian bombers rained ordnance on the British, while fifty bombed their own ships in error. "No ships were hit during any of the attacks though a few splinters from near misses fell on board one or two ships without causing damage."[32] *Eagle* attracted the most attention, and many near misses loosened the pipes that carried aviation fuel and caused machinery problems that, patched up but not thoroughly repaired, would ultimately force her to miss the Taranto operation in November 1940.

The Myth of Moral Ascendancy

The Italians had a good plan. Pushed by Cunningham's aggressiveness (aware that his prime minister had already accused him of being pussyfooted), the Mediterranean Fleet sailed into a trap.[33] However, when the trap's jaws failed to spring, Admiral Campioni did not hesitate to engage. Indeed, considering the balance of forces against him—the three more heavily armored British battleships could hurl 93,000 pounds of metal a minute, compared to the Italian total of 46,000 pounds—and Cavagnari's policy of minimizing risk, Campioni had little business fighting Cunningham in the first place. Nonetheless, the Italian admiral judged the opportunity worth a gamble, and he proceeded to outmaneuver his opponent. Then, when an extreme-range hit tipped the already unfavorable odds too far against him, Campioni withdrew, adeptly keeping the enemy's superior battle line at bay. If all the British reports of torpedoes narrowly missing, or even passing under, their warships are correct, the Royal Navy was fortunate not to suffer losses during this portion of the battle.

Overall, the battle's results heartened the Italian navy, even if the subsequent bombardment by friendly aircraft proved frustrating. A midshipman from *Eugenio* expressed the mood when he wrote his mother the day after the battle, "After a happy baptism of fire, I am proud."[34] Admiral Paladini wrote, "I think that one result that occurred in the battle, and not the least important, was the fact that all personnel, even the most humble, felt the deeply rooted conviction of the necessity and beauty of battle, and our ability to confront and beat the enemy."[35]

Nonetheless, in his report to the Admiralty written in January 1941 Admiral Cunningham stated that the action had "established, I think, a certain degree of moral ascendancy."[36] These exact words appear in most English accounts of the action.[37] In fact, the politically astute Cunningham was basking in the afterglow of his unquestioned victory at Taranto when he made this claim. His comments shortly after the battle better reflect its impact. He noted that *Warspite's* hit "might perhaps be described as a lucky one" and that "the action has shown . . . how difficult it is to hit with the gun at long range, and therefore the necessity of closing in, when this can be done, in order to get decisive results."[38] On 16 July he requested a fast, modern battleship ("whose guns can cross enemy line at 26,000 yards"), two heavy cruisers, an antiaircraft cruiser, and a modern aircraft carrier. He worried to Pound about the dangers of taking his old battleships so deep in enemy waters—"My heart was in my mouth lest *Royal Sovereign* should be hit"—and felt it necessary to add the qualification, "Don't think I am discouraged. I am not a bit."[39]

Tip and Run

The naval campaign Italy fought against Austria-Hungary in World War I had been one of raids, shore bombardments, and small-unit actions. From it the Regia Marina developed a concept of hit-and-run naval warfare based upon large numbers of fast, heavily armed, expendable warships. Its first post–World War I class of cruisers, the *Colleoni*s, were constructed with this concept in mind, meant to serve as fast raiders in a sea-denial campaign against the French. Carrying little armor, they achieved forty-two knots during their trials, winning fame as the world's fastest warships. This was a false reputation, however, because they achieved these speeds with light loads in perfect conditions and by forcing their machinery.

Naval staff desired to employ these vessels for their designed purpose. When Supermarina received intelligence that a group of small British tankers, leaving Romania after that nation's change of alliance, were passing through the Bosporus into Greek waters, it decided to dispatch Rear Admiral Ferdinando Casardi's 2nd Division to Leros in the Italian Dodecanese to attack them. Casardi departed Tripoli on 17 July, and British aircraft spotted his ships the next day. Supermarina promised aerial support, but this never developed, and the Italian admiral chose not to catapult his own floatplanes because of rough seas. Thus, he had no knowledge that British warships were operating along his route sweeping for submarines in advance of a convoy from Port Said to Greece. The result was the Battle of Cape Spada.

At 0617 on 19 July the Italian ships entered the Aegean Sea via the Antikithera Strait, northwest of Crete. They had orders to ready boarding parties in expectation of encountering the tanker convoy, but instead they spotted the 2nd Flotilla headed in their direction inshore, ten miles away. The Australian light cruiser *Sydney* and the British destroyer *Havock* cruised independently forty miles to the north-northeast in the Gulf of Athens. (See table 3.3.)

Table 3.3   Battle of Cape Spada, 19 July 1940, 0617–0930

Conditions: Strong wind, mixed visibility, rough seas	
British ships—	Support Force (Captain John Collins): CL: *Sydney*[D1] (AU) (F); DD: *Havock*
	2nd Destroyer Flotilla (Captain H. Nicolson): *Ilex*, (F), *Hero, Hasty, Hyperion*
Italian ships—	2nd Division (Rear Admiral Ferdinando Casardi): CL: *Bande Nere*[D1] (F), *Colleoni*[Sunk]

Upon sighting enemy cruisers, the flotilla immediately hauled round to the northeast. Casardi pursued at thirty knots on a slightly diverging course, suspecting that the destroyers were the van of a larger force. He opened fire at 0627 from nineteen thousand yards. The destroyers replied at 0632, but their salvos fell well short.

Collins received Nicolson's enemy report at 0633 and immediately turned toward the contact, maintaining radio silence. Nicolson, unaware of Collins' exact position, fled under a deliberate, long-range bombardment (the Italian 6-inch guns had a theoretical range of thirty-one thousand yards, while the British 4.7-inch destroyer guns could reach seventeen thousand). Aboard one of the destroyers a crewman observed they could do nothing but dodge and "watch the fall of the Italian shot—an unpleasant pastime since the Italians frequently had the range, but were unaccountably out of line."[40]

Rolling swells limited the cruisers to thirty-two knots, while mist and the morning sun made long-range spotting difficult. The destroyers emitted smoke trails that further confused Italian range finders. Casardi suspended fire at 0648 and turned east at 0650 to close. The range dropped steadily from its maximum of twenty-one thousand yards as Nicolson steered northeast, hoping to draw the Italians toward *Sydney*, but even so Casardi noted in his report, "The enemy destroyers had disappeared in smoke and my attempts to re-engage them with gun fire proved useless. Practically speaking from 0648 to 0730, though continuing to chase the enemy at a speed of 32 knots, our fire was suspended."[41]

At 0730 an orange glare lit a fog bank north of the Italian cruisers, and medium-caliber shells splashed around them. *Sydney* and *Havock* had arrived at a point twenty thousand yards to the north-northeast. The Italians came ninety degrees to starboard at 0732 and responded with their aft turrets. Casadi reported, "We could make out only the flash of the fire, nothing more could we distinguish, not the silhouette of the ship nor their number."[42] Nonetheless, Collins reported several straddles. *Sydney*, shooting rapidly, hit *Bande Nere* at 0735; a round passed through the Italian's forward funnel and exploded on deck, killing four men and wounding four more. At 0738 Nicolson brought his destroyers around to make a torpedo attack.

At 0746 Casardi turned southwest and made smoke. He believed he faced two cruisers (of the *Sydney* and *Gloucester* types) and, concerned about being trapped against the Cretan coast if he continued toward his original destination, he decided to retreat and run past the island to gain sea room.[43] Collins followed, and the two forces settled into a stern chase, trading fire from roughly eighteen thousand yards. Casardi was to complain that "the rolling caused by the heavy north-westerly wind rendered gunlaying very difficult," but on *Sydney* the Italian gunfire seemed accurate, if very slow,[44]

During the chase Nicolson's destroyers caught up to *Sydney*, and the Allied ships advanced in line abreast, with *Sydney* periodically swerving to fire broadsides. The Italian cruisers replied, and at 0821 a 6-inch shell blasted a large hole in *Sydney*'s forward funnel and wounded one man. Then the Italians passed Cape Spada. At 0825, as the sea room Casardi wanted opened before him, a 6-inch round hit *Colleoni*, jamming her rudder in the centerline position. Then two more shells struck, one in the armored conning tower and another amidships, disabling boilers 5 and 6, destroying the cruiser's main steam line and damaging the 6-inch ammunition hoists. Fires erupted, and with the boilers starved for water, the cruiser lost way.

As the British closed range *Colleoni* vainly tried to stand them off with her 3.9-inch secondary guns, firing under local control. At 0840 *Hyperion* launched three torpedoes from seventy-five hundred yards and missed. *Ilex* discharged a salvo next, and one of her torpedoes struck forward of the cruiser's A turret, blowing off the tip of her bow. An Italian sailor was to recall, "As I was going down these bulkheads there was some chaps coming out from the engine room all scalded with the steam, they were in a horrible way. . . . I thought I'll go to the next bulkhead . . . so I opened it, look out and there is no ship! There is the sea. I thought, 'Good Lord, we've had it now!'"[45] Shortly thereafter *Hyperion* fired her last torpedo and scored a hit amidships.

Bande Nere circled, but Casari decided he could not help. At 0850 the surviving cruiser turned west at her best speed, with *Sydney, Hero,* and *Hasty* in pursuit. At 0859 *Colleoni* capsized and sank six miles off Cape Spada.

In the pursuit *Sydney* hit *Bande Nere* again; the shell penetrated the cruiser's quarterdeck, killing four men and wounding twelve but not slowing her down. Finally at 0937, with the range slowly opening and down to ten rounds for her forward turrets, *Sydney* broke off. *Bande Nere* made port at Benghazi. *Ilex, Hyperion,* and *Havock* pulled 545 of *Colleoni*'s crew from the water, but 121 men died, including her severely wounded captain.

The Italian cruisers had fired five hundred shells, scoring no hits on the destroyers and only one on *Sydney* over the course of three hours. *Sydney,* fighting her third surface engagement in a month, had expended thirteen hundred shells and obtained five long-range hits in two hours. In this instance, the British practice of freely spending ammunition returned the better result. Supermarina considered the battle further proof of the inadequacy of their aerial reconnaissance and concluded that lightly armored "expendable" warships operating in enemy-dominated waters could not expect to survive long. So much for tip and run.

4

No Quick Peace
August–December 1940

There can be no departure from the principle that it is the prime responsibility of the Mediterranean Fleet to sever all communication between Italy and Africa.

—Winston Churchill, letter to
Admiral Cunningham, 24 April 1941

The war's first two months disappointed British and Italian hopes for a quick decision: Supermarina's policy of minimizing risk frustrated London's quest for a Mediterranean Trafalgar, while Italian bombers and submarines proved ineffective, although just how ineffective Supermarina did not realize, due to overly optimistic action reports.

On 2 August, Force H raided Cagliari and sent a dozen Hurricanes and a pair of Skuas to Malta. On 17 August *Warspite, Malaya, Ramillies,* and *Kent* shelled Bardia. Italian cruisers and destroyers sowed seven minefields in the Sicilian Channel and around Malta in August and September. These fields sank the British destroyer *Hostile* on 23 August 1940 and seriously damaged the destroyers *Imperial* and *Gallant* on 10 October and 10 January 1941, respectively. The Regia Marina possessed mostly surplus contact mines, and because its fields were vulnerable to sweeping, it needed to refresh them constantly.

In August the modern battleships *Littorio* and *Vittorio Veneto* entered service, although they required workup and "problems with their main armament were not sorted out until October."[1] The first attempt to practice insidious warfare with the secret weapons of the Tenth Light Flotilla (*Decima Flottiglia MAS*, or, more commonly X MAS), Italy's naval commando force, failed on 22 August, when Swordfish happened upon and torpedoed their transport submarine off Alexandria. A similar attempt on 30 September resulted in the loss of another submarine, and a third operation against Gibraltar was aborted. Great Britain's tensions with France continued, and Force H in particular suffered from divided duties. As Admiral Somerville wrote his wife on 12 September, "I simply loathe this French stuff as you don't know where you are and a wrong step might bring about all sorts of reactions."[2]

On 22 August Admiral Cunningham opined to the Admiralty that Malta could, if built up with 400,000 tons of supplies, act as an offensive base for warships and submarines by April 1941. The Admiralty agreed, and reinforcing the island became a major duty for both Force H and the Mediterranean Fleet.[3] (See map 4.1.)

Map 4.1 No Quick Peace, August–December 1940

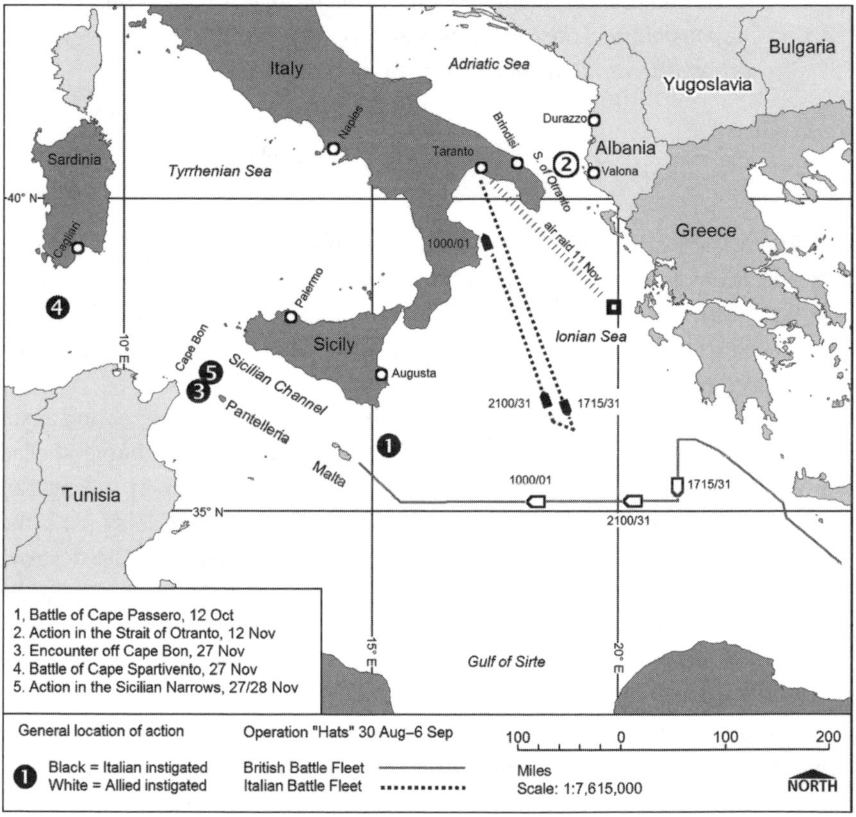
Italy
Adriatic Sea
Bulgaria
Yugoslavia
Durazzo
Brindisi
Naples
Taranto
Albania
Valona
S. of Otranto
Sardinia
Tyrrhenian Sea
40° N
Cagliari
Greece
air raid 11 Nov
1000/01
Palermo
Ionian Sea
Sicily
Cape Bon
10° E
Sicilian Channel
Augusta
Pantelleria
2100/31
1715/31
Malta
1000/01
1715/31
Tunisia
35° N
2100/31
1, Battle of Cape Passero, 12 Oct
2. Action in the Strait of Otranto, 12 Nov
3. Encounter off Cape Bon, 27 Nov
4. Battle of Cape Spartivento, 27 Nov
5. Action in the Sicilian Narrows, 27/28 Nov
15° E
Gulf of Sirte
20° E
General location of action
Black = Italian instigated
White = Allied instigated
Operation "Hats" 30 Aug–6 Sep
British Battle Fleet
Italian Battle Fleet
100 0 100 200
Miles
Scale: 1:7,615,000
NORTH

Operation Hats

On 30 August the Mediterranean Fleet sailed with two battleships, one carrier, five cruisers, and twelve destroyers for Operation Hats, to cover Malta Convoy MF2, consisting of two cargo ships and an oiler, and to meet the aircraft carrier *Illustrious,* the modernized battleship *Valiant,* and two antiaircraft cruisers arriving from Gibraltar. To Churchill's regret Admiral Pound vetoed as too risky a plan to pass two transports loaded with tanks directly through the Mediterranean.[4]

Radio intelligence tipped Supermarina to the British sortie, but the objective remained unclear, because the Royal Navy feinted a raid into the Aegean and was using a new code that remained unbroken for several weeks. During the day a debate ensued between both Admiral Giuseppe Fioravanzo and Raffaele De Courten over whether the fleet should sail immediately or wait until British intentions were clear. Fioravanzo tried to enlist Mussolini's support, but the Duce, ensconced with his mistress, was unavailable.

Supermarina finally pinpointed the Mediterranean Fleet's location on 31 August and determined that a convoy operation was under way. Led by Vice Admiral Campioni, four battleships, thirteen cruisers, and thirty-nine destroyers, "in magnificent condition as to effectiveness, readiness for action, and fighting spirit," set sail early on 31 August from Taranto, Brindisi, and Messina. Vice Admiral Angelo Iachino, Paladini's replacement as commander of the 2nd Fleet, ranged ahead to establish contact. Campioni anticipated an engagement late that afternoon. However, Supermarina supplemented his orders with the proviso that if contact did not occur before dusk (1900) he was to withdraw toward Taranto.[5]

Air attacks against the convoy began at noon and severely damaged the refrigerated cargo ship *Cornwall,* which nonetheless continued on, steering with her engines. At 1600 the British fleet, which was northwest of the convoy, altered course to due south to give the impression that it was returning to Alexandria. At 1815 Admiral Cunningham received a report of two enemy battleships, seven cruisers, and eight destroyers 140 miles to the northwest heading straight for him. Rather than turn toward the enemy, the British admiral continued south to close the convoy, still fifty miles to his southeast.[6]

At 2120, after joining the convoy Cunningham turned to a westerly course to forestall a night attack. However, Campioni had already come about, according to his orders. During the night a storm blew up, and the fleets lost contact. Ten Italian submarines in ambush positions accomplished nothing, and the convoy reached Malta without further incident.

On the other end of the Mediterranean, Force H detached reinforcements for the Mediterranean Fleet and then raided the airfield at Cagliari, on the way back to Gibraltar.

English historians have condemned the Italian fleet as "pusillanimous" for failing to engage, but it was Cunningham who streamed away from the Italian battleships for nearly three hours after they were sighted.[7] In fact, a sense of missed opportunity that "provoked disillusion in the public opinion and aboard the ships" pervaded the Italian fleet. Admiral Iachino submitted a memorandum to the high command advocating "a more dynamic conduct of the naval war."[8]

The August arrival of S.79s rigged to carry torpedoes improved the Regia Aeronautica's effectiveness against shipping. They torpedoed the cruisers *Kent* on 19 September, *Liverpool* on 14 October, and *Glasgow* on 3 December. These aircraft were, however, so few that they nicknamed themselves *I soliti quattro gatti*, the "four same old cats," and used four cats on a torpedo as their squadron insignia.

On 7 September Campioni sortied, at Mussolini's direct orders, upon learning that Force H had weighed anchor, but this proved a wild-goose chase as Somerville headed into the Atlantic. The navy was still operating under the assumption that the war would last less than a year and was expending its oil reserves freely. Throughout the month the Regia Marina worked up its new battleships and ran sixteen small convoys to North Africa and fifty-eight more to Albania. Italy's 10th Army finally entered Egypt on 13 September. After a three-day, thirty-mile advance, the invaders halted at Sidi Barrani and dug in while they improved the rear infrastructure and prepared for a further advance to Marsa Matruh.

In mid-September British gunboats and destroyers bombarded Italian positions in Libya and Egypt. The Mediterranean Fleet planned a major operation on 25 September but delayed it to ensure that French forces quarantined in Alexandria remained quiet during the attack on Dakar.

In a major assessment published on 16 September, Comando Supremo evaluated the war's progress, noting that "we have guaranteed one hundred percent our communications with Libya and Albania, permitting traffic to continue undisturbed." However, placing more credit in combat reports than was warranted by results, it also claimed that "we have contested with light ships, submarines, and aviation in effective actions enemy convoys producing enemy losses." It concluded that the navy should "follow the path taken so far." A prime factor in Italian calculations was the expectation that the army would reach Marsa Matruh. From there Alexandria would be within fighter range and vulnerable to a much greater scale of air attack. Supermarina expected this would drive the Mediterranean Fleet's major units to the western Mediterranean, giving submarines, torpedo boats, and airplanes an excellent opportunity to exact a heavy toll during the enemy's passage of the Sicilian narrows.[9]

The Franco-British Cold War

After teetering on the brink of open warfare in July, tensions between France and Great Britain cooled to a simmer. France retained 1.65 million tons of shipping and maintained a vital maritime commerce that fed the country, and during August the Royal Navy allowed French merchant ships to sail largely unimpeded. Admiral Darlan, meanwhile, continued to bargain with the Axis armistice commissions, trying to improve his navy's situation.

London cultivated a French resistance movement, led by the leader who was to show the most spirit for the job, Brigadier General Charles de Gaulle. De Gaulle swallowed the indignity of Mers-el-Kébir: "In spite of the pain and anger . . . I considered that the saving of France ranked above everything."[10] However, most Frenchmen stranded in British territories did not see things that way and elected repatriation rather than service under the Union Jack or de Gaulle's Cross of Lorraine. By mid-August Free French forces amounted to just a weak brigade. However, a big boost came on 26 August, when the governor of Chad, in French Equatorial Africa, declared for the Free French and Gaullist agents seized the Middle Congo's capital.

Vichy reacted swiftly to these events. On 1 September Darlan secured permission from the armistice commissions for a naval expedition to reassert French authority in Equatorial Africa. On 9 September the light cruisers *Georges Leygues, Montcalm, Gloire*, and the large destroyers *Le Fantasque, L'Audacieux*, and *Le Malin*, commanded by Rear Admiral C. J. L. Bourragué, left Toulon bound for Dakar, the capital of French West Africa. The British Admiralty's rules of engagement issued on 12 July specified, "For the present French warships under control of French Government should be treated as neutral war vessels if approaching a defended port."[11] Thus, British forces did not interfere when Bourragué's ships passed Gibraltar on 11 September; Admiral North even signaled, "Bon Voyage." Unfortunately for North and his career the Admiralty had not informed him that it was mounting an expedition to attack Dakar. Churchill and Pound were dismayed when they learned a powerful French flotilla was loose in the Atlantic. They dispatched Force H to intercept Bourragué, but it was too late, and after a stopover in Casablanca, the French made Dakar on 14 September.

Dakar was strategically positioned on Africa's bulge. Its excellent port dominated the mid-Atlantic and the vital shipping route from South Africa. De Gaulle's representations that he could occupy the city with little or no bloodshed resonated with Churchill. The Germans too appreciated Dakar's value. On 9 July Raeder advised Hitler that France must keep a firm grip on northwestern Africa, because British or American possession of Dakar would severely threaten Germany's ability to conduct war in the Atlantic.[12]

The British operation, codenamed Menace, called for the Free French brigade to occupy Dakar while the British contingent, which included elements of the Home Fleet, Force H, and the West African station, as well as 4,270 troops, remained in the background to guarantee success.

Darlan had no intelligence of the British operation, and on 18 September *Georges Leygues, Montcalm,* and *Gloire,* each carrying eighty troops, slipped south to rendezvous with the light cruiser *Primauguet* and the tanker *Tarn* at Libreville. However, the cruisers *Cornwall* and *Delhi* had accosted *Primauguet* and *Tarn* the day before. After a long standoff, Bourragué ordered *Primauguet* to accept an escort to Casablanca. The heavy cruiser *Australia,* later joined by *Cumberland,* had, meanwhile, encountered Bourragué's force and begun to follow. With his mission clearly compromised, Bourragué reversed course and increased speed. *Georges Leygues* and *Montcalm* eluded their shadowers in a rainstorm and returned to Dakar, but *Gloire* suffered an engine breakdown and had to accept an escort to Casablanca. "These various contacts on the high seas . . . were characterized by a running exchange, not of shells, but of polite messages that reflected the mutual anxiety to avoid the use of force."[13] (See table 4.1.)

Table 4.1   Battle of Dakar, 23–25 September 1940

Conditions: Fog first two days, clear third day, calm seas

Allied ships—	Force M (Vice Admiral John Cunningham): BB: *Barham*[D1] (F), *Resolution*[D4], CV: *Ark Royal;* CA: *Australia*[D2], *Cumberland*[D3], *Devonshire;* CL: *Delhi*[D1], *Dragon*[D1]; DD: *Eclipse, Echo, Escapade, Fortune, Foresight*[D1], *Fury, Faulknor, Forester, Greyhound, Inglefield*[D1]; DS: *Milford, Bridgewater, Savorgnan de Brazza* (FF), *Commandant Duboc* (FF), *Commandant Dominé* (FF)
French forces—	(Vice Admiral Emile Lacroix) BB: *Richelieu*[D2]
	4th Cruiser Division CL: *Georges Leygues, Montcalm*
	10th Scout Division DL: *Le Fantasque, L'Audacieux*[D4], *Le Malin*
	Others DD: *Le Hardi;* DC: *D'Entrecasteaux D'Iberville, Calais, Commandant Riviére, La Surprise, Gazelle;* SS: *Persée, Ajax,* and *Bévéziers;* and five shore batteries

The British units united off Dakar on the morning of 23 September. De Gaulle called upon the Vichy authorities to join him, but he had grossly overestimated sentiment for his cause, and his naïve attempts to subvert the colony's loyalty failed absolutely.

Vice Admiral Cunningham still anticipated an easy victory by intimidating the French with a show of force, but an unseasonal fog bank forced the British warships inshore to undertake their bombardment; when their shapes emerged from the mist, French batteries opened fire. By 1115 they had hit *Dragon*, *Foresight*, and *Inglefield*. Then a 9.45-inch shell severely damaged *Cumberland* and forced her withdrawal. The battleships expended more than a hundred 15-inch rounds, but all they hit was a merchant ship, although destroyers sank the submarine *Persée* at 1137 when she tried to sortie.

Cunningham ordered the Free French troops to land, but the transports got lost in the fog and did not gather at the proper point until 1630. Meanwhile, at 1620 *L'Audacieux* attempted to leave the harbor. *Australia*, *Fury*, and *Greyhound* were standing about four thousand yards off *L'Audacieux*'s sally point. At 1634 the cruiser engaged and with her third salvo dismasted the French destroyer; the next hit her bridge and ignited a large fire. *L'Audacieux* lost power and, burning fiercely, drifted ashore with the loss of eighty-one men. However, the defenders easily repulsed a halfhearted landing attempt by De Gaulle's troops that followed.

The British opened the second day's action by sinking the French submarine *Ajax*. Then, at 0935, the battleships renewed their bombardment, from fifteen thousand yards. The French cruisers chased salvos in the inner harbor, although several 15-inch projectiles landed close enough to drench them with tremendous splashes and splinters dusted *Richelieu*. The French battleship's guns malfunctioned, but the shore batteries kept the British at a distance, and little harm was done on either side until the afternoon, when four shells struck *Resolution*. *Richelieu* took a light hit, but the city suffered the most, with eighty-four residents killed and 197 wounded.

Surprised by the tenacity of French resistance, Cunningham decided to land the British brigade on the third day. That morning *Beveziers*, the last surviving French submarine, was lurking in the path of the British battleships as they streamed to begin their bombardment run. Lookouts reported torpedoes tracks in time for *Barham* to dodge the spread, but one weapon struck *Resolution*, blowing open a hole "big enough to take a double-decker bus" and putting her main batteries out of action due to a heavy list.[14] The British commenced action nonetheless and scored a 15-inch hit on *Richelieu*, but at 0916 two 6-inch cruiser rounds staggered *Australia*. Then a 6-inch and a 9.45-inch shell struck *Barham*, and a 15-incher burst short, underwater, forcing the bulge structure inboard and causing slow flooding.[15] Admiral Cunningham concluded that the accuracy of the French fire made more damage inevitable and terminated the bombardment.

The British withdrew shortly thereafter. *Resolution* came close to foundering and required a tow to Freetown.

This unexpected victory restored a portion of the pride and honor the French navy felt it had lost at Mers-el-Kébir. It also enabled Darlan to argue that he needed a large naval force ready for immediate action to oppose new British attacks.[16] The Axis armistice commissions agreed and authorized the French High Seas Force on 25 September.

On 24 September, sixty French aircraft dropped forty-five tons of bombs on Gibraltar. The next night eighty-one planes dropped sixty tons. Four destroyers sortied from Casablanca on 24 September to sweep up the Moroccan coast. (See table 4.2.)

Table 4.2   Action off Gibraltar, 25 September 1940

Conditions: Night, poor visibility
French ships— 2nd Destroyer Division: *Fougueux, Frondeur, Epée, Fleuret*
British ship—   DD: *Hotspur*

The French flotilla encountered *Hotspur* patrolling off Gibraltar early the next morning. *Epée* opened fire but only shot fourteen rounds before all her 5.1-inch guns developed defects. *Fleuret* did not engage, because her fire-control equipment could not follow the target, and the last two French destroyers fired six rounds total. Following this brief encounter the French squadron continued through the strait, making port in Oran. In her report *Hotspur* stated that she likewise engaged, but the French did not notice return fire.

Tensions remained high. On 27 September Force H remained at sea upon receipt of a "charming message [that] the whole of the Toulon fleet was coming out to have a scrap with us."[17] However, Vichy did not take the final step and declare war. Instead the British and French navies reached a *modus operandi* whereby the British respected superior French forces and French ships in port, but everything else remained fair game."Though British commanders had precise instructions regarding the interception of French shipping, discretion might prove the better part of valour if Vichy escorts were liable to inflict serious loss."[18] France could operate within these limits, and from the fall of 1940, when it ran the first convoy through the Straits of Gibraltar, through the end of the year, few incidents troubled relations.

Fortress Malta

Because of the French situation, September marked a relatively quiet period in the Italo-British war. However, at the end of the month the British transferred troops to Malta in a pair of cruisers escorted by a portion of the Mediterranean Fleet. Five Italian battleships sortied on 29 September. Misreading British intentions and poorly served by air reconnaissance, Campioni failed to make contact, but he scared Cunningham, who wrote, "The sudden discovery on 30 September of a numerically superior battlefleet within 100 miles of our Fleet, in spite of the shorebased reconnaissance from Malta, was disquieting."[19]

On 8 October four Malta-bound steamers departed Alexandria escorted by four battleships, two aircraft carriers, a heavy cruiser, five light cruisers, and sixteen destroyers. Cunningham felt that such a strong escort was necessary because four Italian battleships had been sighted during the previous operation.[20] Assisted by heavy weather, the convoy reached Malta undetected on 11 October. That same day, however, an Italian airliner flying to Libya reported enemy warships a hundred miles southeast of the island. Supermarina dispatched several light squadrons in accordance with its system for guarding the straits—*the Dispositivo del Canale di Sicilia*, which employed torpedo and MAS boats combined with minefields and submarines to attrite enemy forces transiting the narrows at night.

Three MAS boats loitered outside Valletta while the 11th Destroyer Squadron and the 1st Torpedo Boat Squadron sailed from Augusta to patrol east of Malta. The 7th Destroyer Squadron and another MAS unit guarded the Sicilian Channel and cruiser divisions at Palermo and Messina raised steam, just in case.

The empty transports departed Malta at 2230 on 11 October. The Mediterranean Fleet's main body waited south of the island, while the 7th Cruiser Squadron formed an extended scouting line northeast of the fleet. The wing ship, the light cruiser *Ajax,* zigzagged at seventeen knots a hundred miles east of Malta. (See table 4.3.)

Table 4.3   Action off Cape Passero, 12 October 1940, 0135–0300

Conditions: Clearing from earlier storms; bright, nearly full moon	
British ship—	(Captain E. D. B. McCarthy): CL: *Ajax*[D2]
Italian ships—	11th Destroyer Squadron (Captain Carlo Margottini): *Artigliere*[D4] (F), *Geniere, Camicia Nera, Aviere*[D2]
	1st Torpedo Boat Squadron (Commander Alberto Banfi): *Airone*[Sunk] (F), *Alcione, Ariel*[Sunk]

Alcione, Airone, and *Ariel* sailed west at seventeen knots in a line of bearing—what the Italians called a "rake" formation—with eight thousand yards between ships, to maximize the chance of spotting the enemy at night. On the same course and speed eight miles south of *Ariel,* Margottini's squadron formed the rake's southern prongs, with *Geniere* the most northerly unit and *Aviere, Artigliere,* and *Camicia Nera* in that order to the south. The two squadrons could theoretically sweep a swath of sea thirty-two miles wide. (See map 4.2.)

Map 4.2   Action off Cape Passero, 12 October 1940

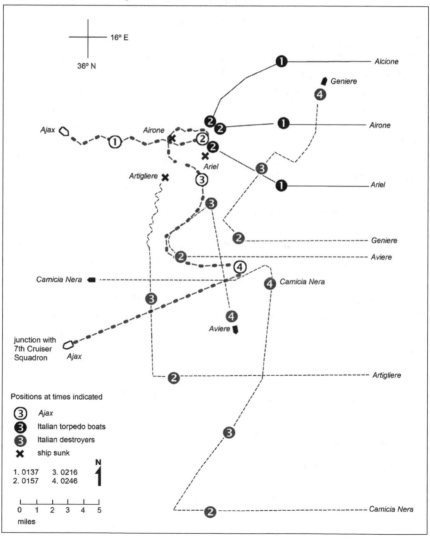

At 0135 *Alcione* detected *Ajax* in the bright moonlight twelve miles off her port bow. *Alcione* requested assistance and altered southwest toward the enemy. At 0142 *Airone,* and shortly thereafter *Ariel,* spotted the cruiser. All *Airone* needed to do was maintain her heading while *Ariel* steered northwest. At 0148 Banfi ordered a simultaneous torpedo attack. At this point the 11th Squadron's destroyers had not responded to the contact and were still sweeping due west.

At 0155 *Ajax*'s lookouts reported two unidentified ships off her bow— in fact *Airone* to port and *Ariel* to starboard. As the cruiser challenged, *Alcione* approached undetected broad on the cruiser's port beam and fired two torpe- does at 0157 from slightly under two thousand yards, target bearing 60 degrees. The Italian ship then turned northwest to bring her other tubes to bear. At the same minute *Airone* launched two torpedoes off the cruiser's port bow, range twenty-two hundred yards, bearing 50 degrees, and *Ariel* one more off the star- board bow. Five torpedoes were thus speeding toward the British warship from three different angles.

Having received an inappropriate response to *Ajax*'s challenge, her com- manding officer, Captain E. D. B. McCarthy had already ordered full speed and altered course. This maneuver, as well as Italian errors in calculating the British cruiser's speed and heading, resulted in all five torpedoes missing.[21] *Airone* closed rapidly and veered to port to bring her starboard torpedoes to bear, launching at 0158 from only a thousand yards. As her second salvo hit the water, the torpedo boat's 3.9-inch guns snapped off four quick broadsides. Two shells exploded on *Ajax*'s bridge, and another penetrated her hull six feet above the waterline, ignit- ing a blaze that burned for three and a half hours. The torpedoes missed astern. *Ariel* and *Alcione* engaged within seconds of the flagship. *Alcione* discharged fif- teen salvos, but her aim was off. She could not obtain a firing solution for her last two torpedoes, so she conducted a separation maneuver intending to line up for another attempt.

In response to the sudden attack *Ajax*'s main guns erupted to starboard at *Ariel,* range four thousand yards, and her 4-inch weapons to port at *Airone,* range two thousand yards. The cruiser's first salvos crumpled *Ariel*'s bridge and cracked her hull. The unarmored torpedo boat sank within minutes, the captain and senior officers going down with their ship.[22]

As *Airone* bore down, *Ajax* turned to port to open firing arcs (that is, to allow guns to fire that otherwise would be masked by the ship's own superstructure or fittings). Commander Banfi ordered smoke, thinking to disengage, but with the range so close and *Ajax* swinging to a parallel heading astern of *Airone* the torpedo boat had little chance. A broadside of 112-pound shells smashed her aft 3.9-inch mounts and ignited a large fire amidships. More shells plowed into

Airone's rudder and engine room. Then *Ajax* closed to point-blank range, and her machine guns raked the drifting ship. The cruiser swept past, maneuvering to confuse enemy gunfire, and flung two torpedoes back at *Airone*. Both missed, but that hardly mattered, because the Italian flagship was already down by the stern and burning fiercely.

At 0155 the 11th Destroyer Squadron's *Geniere* turned northwest, and a minute later *Aviere* swung north. *Aviere* sighted *Ajax* first at 0210 and closed from eight thousand yards, firing a salvo and seeking to launch torpedoes. The moon hung low in the sky behind the Italian destroyer and facilitated the cruiser's accurate marksmanship. One 6-inch shell disabled *Aviere*'s aft 4.7-inch mount, and another punched through the hull, causing major flooding forward. *Aviere* staggered to starboard at 0216 and lost contact two minutes later.

Geniere saw *Ajax* at 0218 as the cruiser headed south. She loosed "a few salvos" that fell astern of her target and then withdrew.[23] Meanwhile *Alcione*, returning from her extended separation maneuver, found the enemy gone, *Ariel* sunk, and *Airone* sinking. *Alcione* briefly probed south and then returned and rescued 125 of *Ariel*'s and *Airone*'s crew. *Airone* finally sank at 0334.

Artigliere turned north at 0200. She had covered nearly eight miles when, at 0229, geysers began erupting around her as *Ajax*, lurking unseen "up-moon" just a few thousand yards northeast, opened fire. *Artigliere* launched one torpedo before a 6-inch salvo devastated her bridge and killed the squadron commander. Another round detonated the forward 4.7-inch ready ammunition and sparked a large fire. However, as *Ajax* steamed past the destroyer retaliated with four shells that damaged the cruiser's compass bridge and disabled a 4-inch mount and her radar (which, despite Italian postwar claims, had played no part in the action). Then three rounds rattled into *Artigliere*'s forward engine room, and a fourth holed her central boiler. Leaving *Artigliere* adrift and burning like a torch, *Ajax* turned port at 0247 and continued east.[24]

Camicia Nera, the southernmost destroyer, sighted *Ajax* at 0246, five thousand yards to the northwest. The moon hung near the western horizon, and *Camicia Nera* enjoyed the advantage of light. She and the British cruiser swapped a few ineffective salvos. *Ajax* lacked flashless gunpowder, and repeated broadsides had ruined her crew's night vision. From her perspective, her enemy looked like a cruiser, and when this adversary disappeared in what seemed a smoke screen, *Ajax* took the opportunity to reverse course southwest to seek the rest of the 7th Cruiser Squadron, which Cunningham had "ordered to retire on the battlefleet, in the belief that the enemy's whole fleet might be in the vicinity."[25] Steaming to catch up, the Italian ship turned west-southwest at 0250 and then west a few minutes later. *Camicia Nera* crossed *Ajax*'s wake, on a diverging course, and did not reestablish contact.

Ajax suffered thirteen killed and twenty-two wounded in this action. She expended 490 6-inch shells and four torpedoes. She would patch her damage at Alexandria and return to action by 5 November. Strenuous damage control finally doused *Artigliere*'s fires and got one boiler functioning, but a lack of boiler feed water stopped her again an hour later. At 0500 *Camicia Nere* took the crippled destroyer in tow, but a British flying boat reported them at 0710. At 0840 the masts of the heavy cruiser *York* and the light cruisers *Gloucester* and *Liverpool* poked into view from the south, forcing *Camicia Nere* to abandon her tow and flee. *York* torpedoed the helpless *Artigliere* at 0905, after repeatedly missing her drifting target with deliberate 8-inch gunfire.[26]

Supermarina dispatched the 3rd Division's *Trieste, Trento,* and *Bolzano* and three destroyers of the 14th Squadron from Messina at 0800, far too late to help *Artigliere.*

In their action the Italian torpedo boats achieved surprise and attacked at point-blank range, but all their torpedoes missed. This led Supermarina to conclude "that [they] were technically inferior to the British, at least as far as carrying out night encounters at sea was concerned."[27] Vice Admiral H. D. Pridham-Wippell meanwhile congratulated Captain McCarthy for repelling the attacks of "four destroyers and two cruisers" and handling his ship with "promptitude, ability and great determination."[28] In fact, Italian weapons and tactics contributed to McCarthy's success. Commander Banfi conducted a brilliant approach, but his ships could only put five (of a maximum potential of six) torpedoes into the water. This feeble barrage was half the broadside of one modern Allied destroyer. The 11th Destroyer Squadron, which possessed greater torpedo capability, never attempted to concentrate; instead its four ships presented themselves, silhouetted in moonlight, to *Ajax*'s gunners one by one at close range. Confronting a light cruiser in this fashion proved deadly—the damage a thirty-pound 3.9-inch or fifty-one pound 4.7-inch shell could inflict on a lightly armored vessel was far less, all things being equal, than a 112-pound 6-inch shell could inflict on an unarmored vessel.

Taranto Night

In mid-October, despite the desert stalemate and his recent demobilization of 600,000 troops, Mussolini made perhaps the biggest miscalculation of his career and ordered the invasion of Greece, which commenced on 28 October. The navy disliked this campaign. "[It] complicated our maritime problems, since the

English, occupying Crete and having the free use of Greek ports, could exercise a total control of the Archipelago, isolate the Dodecanese, and intensify the aerial bombardment of the peninsula."[29] The navy was supposed to land an infantry division and the San Marco Marine Regiment on Corfu, but weather forced a delay, and then the unfavorable situation on the main front absorbed the amphibious contingent.

On 29 October the submarine *Sciré* penetrated Algeciras Bay near Gibraltar and dropped off three X MAS commando teams. Due to mechanical defects with their manned torpedoes, this attack failed, although one detonated near enough to *Barham* to cause a scare and alert the British to the existence of some kind of insidious threat, although not its exact nature.

The Royal Navy launched Operation MB.8 on 4 November. This consisted of ten separate movements spanning the entire Mediterranean, designed to bring supplies and reinforcements to Malta from both the east and west, to provision Crete and Greece, recover empty freighters from Malta and Greece, reinforce the Mediterranean Fleet, raid Italian sea lanes, and, finally, launch an air raid against Taranto. Part of the design behind these overlapping operations was to confuse the enemy by overloading their reconnaissance capacity. Although they detected some of these movements, the Italians missed the approach of *Illustrious* and her eight escorts to their attack point, thanks to the carrier's radar-directed Fulmars that swept the Regia Aeronautica's slow reconnaissance floatplanes and flying boats from the sky.

Table 4.4   Action in the Strait of Otranto, 12 November 1940, 0125–0155

Conditions: Light breeze, bright three-quarter moon, and calm seas	
British ships—	Force X (Vice Admiral H. D. Pridham-Wippell): CL: *Orion* (F), *Sydney* (AU), *Ajax*; DD: *Nubian, Mohawk*
Italian ships—	(Commander Francesco De Angelini): AMC: *Ramb III* (F); TB: *Fabrizi*[D3]
	Convoy: *Antonio Locatelli*[Sunk] (5,691 GRT), *Premuda*[Sunk] (4,427 GRT), *Capo Vado*[Sunk] (4,391 GRT), *Catalani*[Sunk] (2,429 GRT)

On 11 November twenty-one Swordfish flying in two waves from *Illustrious* swooped down and attacked Taranto. They torpedoed *Littorio* and knocked her out of the war for four months, *Duilio* for six, and *Cavour* for the duration. The raid occurred just hours before a planned sortie to cover a bombardment of Suda Bay

by the 1st (Cruiser) Division, which Mussolini insisted upon as a reply to Greece's unexpectedly stiff resistance, and of which the British had no inkling. As the raid was under way, and while the rest of the Mediterranean Fleet retired, a cruiser-destroyer group, Force X, under Pridham-Wippell penetrated the lower Adriatic to attack traffic between Italy and Albania as a means of "enheartening [sic] the Greeks and dealing the enemy a blow in his own waters."[30] (See table 4.4.)

That night four steamers were returning in ballast to Brindisi from Valona escorted by an old torpedo boat and an auxiliary cruiser. The whole force chugged west at eight knots with no reason to expect anything other than a routine "milk run."

Force X swept up the strait and, reaching the apex of its patrol at 0100, turned to rejoin the fleet, thinking its foray had failed. On account of the bright moonlight, Pridham-Wippell kept his cruisers concentrated in column, with *Orion* in the lead and *Sydney* at the rear. *Nubian* screened twenty-seven hundred yards to the west and *Mohawk* an equal distance east.

At 0115 *Mohawk* sighted the darkened convoy to the southeast eight miles away. The British closed, hoping to achieve surprise, but Italian lookouts had likewise spotted the British. *Fabrizi* steered toward the enemy, while the steamers starting coming about.

Mohawk's guns broke the silence at 0125, engaging *Fabrizi* from four thousand yards. The cruisers charged the convoy's west flank and lofted star shells from their secondary batteries. *Orion* peppered *Fabrizi* with 4-inch shells, while her main battery concentrated on *Capo Vado*, the third freighter, at a range of sixty-four hundred yards. *Fabrizi*'s skipper, Lieutenant Giovanni Barbini, tried to launch a torpedo attack, but *Orion*'s gunfire disrupted communications, and his torpedo officer did not receive the order to fire. At 0128, *Fabrizi* swung to starboard forty-five hundred yards east-southeast of *Orion*, opened fire with her 4-inch guns, and made smoke, trying to give the convoy time to scatter. It was already too late. *Ajax* targeted *Ramb III*, while *Sydney* pumped shells at *Antonio Locatelli* from seven thousand yards off her starboard bow and was rewarded by the sight of flames. At 0132 *Sydney* shifted fire to *Premuda*, while *Ajax* targeted one of the leading steamers. A minute later *Orion* dispatched a pair of torpedoes at *Capo Vado* and claimed a hit.

Meanwhile, on the convoy's far side, *Ramb III* turned northeast, aimed seventeen rounds in the direction of the enemy gun flashes, and "continued on a withdrawal course in order to avoid the sacrifice of the ship, which her captain judged would be useless."[31] *Fabrizi* was made of sterner stuff. She reversed course, keeping between the enemy cruisers and the merchant ships. At 0135 a shell knocked out her main generator. A minute later another landed amidships near the no. 3 mount. At 0139 a third round struck her bow. Nevertheless, *Fabrizi's* midships and stern guns continued in action.

After expending thirty-one 6-inch salvos, as well as torpedoes, *Orion* considered her target destroyed and shifted to *Catalani,* the rear ship, from fifty-three hundred yards. Flames quickly flared up, and *Orion* finished the job with torpedoes. *Ajax* missed with a torpedo at one of the two lead steamers but judged that she scored hits with two salvos that left her target burning. *Sydney's* description of the period from 0136 to 0140 captures the action's rapid tempo.

> Target was shifted to escorting destroyer [*Fabrizi*] which steaming from left to right making smoke. Five salvos fired at this target which drawing ahead. At 0138 fire shifted to original targets, now close together [*Locatelli* and *Premuda*]. Several salvos fired and more hits seen. These targets disappeared and target shifted again one ship right to ship apparently stopped [*Capo Vado*]. Other ships also firing at this target and many hits seen.[32]

The destroyers formed their own column, bombarding each merchantman in turn as they passed down the convoy's port beam. *Catalani,* "hit by a salvo aft[,] was laying stopped emitting clouds of steam."[33] But at 0150, just as *Mohawk* was about to turn and launch torpedoes, Pridham-Wippell ordered a course of south-southeast at twenty-eight knots to rejoin *Illustrious.*

As they departed, the British admiral calculated that Force X had sunk one ship, left two burning and likely lost, and observed one fleeing in flames. In fact, he had sunk all four (*Antonio Locatelli* went down with all hands). *Ramb III* returned to Bari undamaged, where her commander was relieved and faced a court-martial for desertion. *Fabrizi* suffered eleven killed and seventeen wounded. The torpedo boats *Curtatone* and *Solferino* sortied from Valona and rescued 140 survivors.

This action marked the first night surface attack against an Italian convoy, and it foreshadowed how deadly British surface strike forces would be. This was also the only time Allied surface warships successfully attacked Italy's Balkan supply route, which at the time engaged about a quarter of the nation's merchant shipping. As a consequence, the Italian navy increased the escort to three torpedo boats and one auxiliary cruiser for every four merchantmen. Further sweeps of Otranto Strait by British cruisers and destroyers on 19 December 1940 and by Greek destroyers on eight occasions between 14 November 1940 and 6 January 1941 proved fruitless.

The Strategic Balance of Power

About the air raid at Taranto Churchill exulted, "By this single stroke the balance of naval power in the Mediterranean was decisively altered."[34] Cunningham wrote, "The Taranto show has freed our hands considerably & I hope now to shake these damned Itiys up a bit. I don't think their remaining three battleships will face us and if they do I'm quite prepared to take them on with only two."[35] However, the distance the strategic balance had really shifted was demonstrated six days later. On 17 November Force H sallied from Gibraltar to fly a dozen Hurricanes to Malta. Italian agents in Gibraltar promptly alerted Supermarina, and Vice Admiral Campioni sortied with *Vittorio Veneto, Cesare*, six cruisers, and fourteen destroyers. When Malta reported a battleship at sea south of Naples, Somerville reasoned that the Italians "might well consider the possibility of engaging Force H with superior forces in the hope of balancing to some degree their losses at Taranto." Therefore, he "decided to fly off the Hurricanes from a position as far to the westward as weather conditions would admit."[36] This left the aircraft facing a flight of four hundred miles; eight of the twelve ran out of gas and crashed at sea. Campioni ventured as far as Bône before, unable to fix Force H's location and with his destroyers reaching the limit of their range, he returned to base.

The British Admiralty next planned Operation MB.9, Malta convoys from Alexandria and Gibraltar, considering this a critically important operation because of the ongoing Italo-Grecian war. Caught in the pinch of worldwide obligations, the Admiralty signaled Cunningham on 22 November that "urgent considerations," including the appearance of the German armored ship *Admiral Scheer* and five surface raiders, "demanded some redistribution of the fleet."[37] In response Cunningham agreed to surrender the old battleship, *Ramillies*, and two cruisers suffering from mechanical problems, *Berwick* and *Newcastle*, and to coordinate their return with the convoy operation.

Operation MB.9 commenced on 23 November. One benefit accrued from Taranto was the fact that the Mediterranean Fleet could operate in two units, each built around a pair of battleships and a carrier. Pridham-Whipple departed Alexandria with two battleships, a carrier, four cruisers, and eight destroyers. The Malta convoy, MW4—four merchant ships escorted by two antiaircraft cruisers and four destroyers—left Egypt latter the same day. Finally, at 0330 on 25 November, Cunningham raised anchor with two battleships, a carrier, three cruisers, and nine destroyers. On the other end of the Middle Sea, Force H cleared Gibraltar at 0800 on 25 November to shepherd three transports to Malta, one continuing all the way to Alexandria along with four Flower-class corvettes.

Supermarina learned that the British had major forces at sea, and Campioni sortied from Naples at 1150 on 26 November with *Vittorio Veneto* and *Cesare*, the 1st Cruiser Division, and the 7th, 9th, and 13th destroyer squadrons. The 3rd Cruiser Division and the 12th Destroyer Squadron under the command of Rear Admiral Sansonetti sailed from Messina at 1230 that same day. Campioni and Sansonetti rendezvoused north of Sicily and then headed west to challenge Force H. Four torpedo boats and two MAS squadrons departed Trapani at 1700 to patrol the Sicilian Channel.

Force H included *Renown*, *Ark Royal*, the light cruisers *Despatch* and *Sheffield*, and the destroyers *Faulknor*, *Firedrake*, *Forester*, *Fury*, *Encounter*, *Duncan*, *Wishart*, *Kelvin*, and *Jaguar*. The convoy consisted of the transports *Clan Fraser*, *Clan Forbes*, and *New Zealand Star*, escorted by the light cruisers *Manchester* and *Southampton* (ferrying nearly seven hundred air force personnel each), *Hotspur*, and the four corvettes. Somerville planned to rendezvous with *Ramillies* at noon on 27 November southeast of Sardinia, proceed toward the Sicilian narrows, and then return to Gibraltar, while the convoy continued to Malta under the cover of darkness.

The Alexandria convoy arrived in Malta at 0800 on 26 November. At noon Force D, *Ramillies*, the cruisers *Newcastle*, *Coventry*, *Berwick*, and the destroyers *Defender*, *Gallant*, *Griffin*, *Diamond*, and *Hereward* departed the island for their meeting with Force H the next day.

At 0033 on 27 November *Sirio*, while on patrol, spotted seven "unidentified" warships off Cape Bon. She approached cautiously, according to new instructions issued after the Cape Passero debacle, and sent a pair of torpedoes churning toward the enemy at extreme range. Lookouts aboard at least one of the British ships noted the torpedo boat's presence, but the force swept on, holding fire to avoid broadcasting its position.

At dawn Campioni's fleet loitered off the southwestern tip of Sardinia in three formations awaiting news of the enemy. The 1st Division and 9th Destroyer Squadron under Rear Admiral Iachino were nineteen miles east of Cape Spartivento sailing west-southwest at sixteen knots, while Sansonetti's 3rd Division with the 12th Destroyer Squadron cruised on the same heading five miles farther south. The battleships and two more destroyer squadrons followed fourteen miles behind the 1st Division. Campioni's orders, which required him to stay under Sardinia's air cover, represented a masterpiece of contradiction:

> Avoid action with the enemy if he enjoys an evident superiority; favor any opportunity for naval guerrilla actions; try to fight near base; be animated by a highly aggressive spirit at all times and remember that the

material difficulty of replacing our warship losses during the war dictates that we must coolly examine of the convenience of any action. However, the possibility of losses is not justification to refuse an encounter or to interrupt the fighting after beginning an action.[38]

When Campioni received *Sirio*'s report of enemy ships transiting the Sicilian Channel, he correctly assumed they sought to join Force H, and, hoping for an opportunity to fight within the constraints of his orders, he launched two spotters to augment three Cant Z506s that had left Sardinia at 0755. (See map 4.3.)

Map 4.3 Battle of Cape Spartivento (Teulada), 27 November 1940

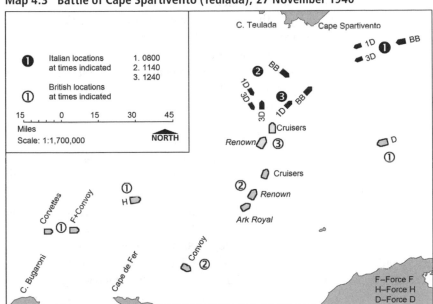

As the Italians awaited news, Somerville's ships proceeded east in three groups. At 0800, a half hour before dawn, ninety-five miles southwest of Cape Spartivento, *Ark Royal*, accompanied by *Renown*, *Sheffield*, and four destroyers, launched seven Swordfish to scout ahead of the fleet. Vice Admiral Lancelot Holland, with the cruisers *Southampton*, *Manchester*, *Despatch*, five destroyers, and the convoy, followed twenty-five miles to the west-southwest; the corvettes, their top speed only fourteen knots, had fallen ten miles behind.

Throughout the morning delayed, ambiguous, and inaccurate reconnaissance reports frustrated both admirals. A Swordfish reported five enemy cruisers and five destroyers sixty-five miles to the northeast at 0852, but this message did not reach Somerville until an hour later. By 1015 other British aircraft had radioed the presence of enemy battleships. After dispatching two destroyers to guard *Ark Royal* and two more to screen the convoy, *Renown* altered course to the east-northeast to join *Ramillies* and increased speed to twenty-eight knots.[39]

A Cant Z506 spotted the British at 0930, but not until 1015 did Campioni receive his first, somewhat perplexing intelligence from *Bolzano*'s aircraft, which reported that at 0945 a battleship, two light cruisers, and four destroyers were heading east at sixteen knots 135 miles southwest of Cape Spartivento. As Campioni later reported, "The number of ships [signaled by the *Bolzano*'s aircraft] coincided with the number reported at night off Cape Bon by the torpedo boat; the position however, was noticeably more to the west than that which was possible on the basis of the Cape Bon sighting, even if the English naval force had inverted its course only some minutes before the sighting."[40]

Nonetheless, Campioni swung southeast at 1045 and increased speed to eighteen knots, hoping to intercept this group before it could join other enemy forces he suspected were in the area. He did not know that Force D had slipped by to the south and that his opportunity to fight under the best possible odds was already gone.

Force H and Force D rendezvoused at 1130. *Coventry* sped away to join the convoy already guarded by *Despatch* and the destroyers *Wishart, Duncan,* and *Hotspur* (damaged on 20 October in ramming the Italian submarine *Lafolé*). The convoy headed southeast. *Jaguar* and *Kelvin* escorted *Ark Royal,* which ranged a strike force on deck. Somerville then turned north with two capital ships, five cruisers, and ten destroyers to confront the Italian fleet. (See table 4.5.)

At 1152 an Italian cruiser plane reported a battleship and four destroyers south of Campioni's position, steaming east. Three minutes later, he received a forty-five-minute-old signal from a land-based aircraft that it had sighted a convoy escorted by a battleship, three light cruisers, six destroyers, and an aircraft carrier. This information was the Italian admiral's first intimation of an enemy convoy. As he later reported, "A state of affairs was thus created which on the best hypothesis was unfavorable to us numerically and qualitatively. . . . It was a situation not only at variance with the directive given to me by [Supermarina], but with that imposed by military necessity."[41] At 1207 Campioni ordered Iachino and Sansonetti to increase speed and concentrate on his flagship.

Several mishaps prevented units from following this order. First, *Lanciere* experienced an engine failure and dropped back, disrupting her entire squadron. Next, *Trento* misread a signal, causing the 3rd Division to circle to starboard and leaving flagship *Trieste* in the formation's center rather than at its head. Then, at 1215 *Alfieri* reported enemy cruisers and one battleship due south.

At 1215 Holland's cruisers were pushing north on a ragged line of bearing—in order (west to east) *Sheffield, Southampton, Newcastle, Manchester,* and *Berwick*—when they observed "puffs of smoke" on the horizon bearing 006 degrees.[42] Mechanical difficulties were likewise afflicting the British. A balky turbine limited *Berwick* to twenty-seven knots. She had been dropping back toward *Renown* when Holland, wanting the support of her bigger guns, ordered her to rejoin the cruiser line. Meanwhile, boiler problems prevented *Newcastle* from gaining station. Finally, *Renown* had developed a hot bearing on one propeller shaft, which reduced her top speed to 27.5 knots.

Table 4.5   Battle of Cape Spartivento (Teulada), 27 November 1940, 0128–0155

Conditions: Wind force 3 to 4 from the southeast, excellent visibility, slight swells	
British ships—	Battle line (Vice Admiral J. Somerville): BC: *Renown* (F) BB: *Ramillies*
	Cruisers (Vice Admiral L. E. Holland): CA: *Berwick*[D2]; CL: *Manchester*[D1] (F), *Southampton, Sheffield, Newcastle*
	8th Destroyer Flotilla (Captain A. F. De Salis): *Faulknor* (F), *Firedrake, Forester, Fury, Encounter*
	Force D Destroyers (Commander W. R. Marshall A'Deane): *Greyhound, Defender, Gallant, Hereward, Diamond*
Italian ships—	1st Fleet (Vice Admiral I. Campioni): BB: *Vittorio Veneto* (F), *Giulio Cesare*
	7th Destroyer Squadron (Commander Amleto Baldo): *Freccia, Saetta, Dardo*
	13th Destroyer Squadron (Captain Vittorio de Pace): *Granatiere, Fuciliere, Bersagliere, Alpino*
	2nd Fleet (Vice Admiral A. Iachino)
	1st Cruiser Divison (Rear Admiral Pellegrino Matteucci): CA: *Pola* (F), *Fiume, Gorizia*
	9th Destroyer Squadron (Captain Lorenzo Daretti): *Alfieri, Carducci, Gioberti, Oriani*
	3rd Cruiser Division (Rear Admiral L. Sansonetti): CA: *Trieste*[D1], *Trento, Bolzano*
	12th Destroyer Squadron (Captain Carmine D'Arienzo): *Lanciere*[D4], *Ascari, Carabiniere*

Somerville remained uncertain about the Italian fleet's composition because a report by a Sunderland out of Malta suggested there were an additional six cruisers to the west. Nevertheless, he ordered the destroyers to take position ten thousand yards northeast of *Renown*"in order to be placed favourably to counterattack any destroyers attempting a torpedo attack on the [battleships]"[43]

On the Italian side, 1215 found Matteucci's 1st Division heading east at twenty-eight knots in line ahead. Sansonetti's 3rd Division followed 8,750 yards behind Matteucci. The battleships deployed thirteen miles east-northeast of the 1st Division, closing at twenty-five knots. Admiral Matteucci ordered his division to open fire, despite Campioni's strongly worded signal,"Do not, repeat, do not engage in battle."[44] He judged that the situation, not apparent from the flagship, warranted his action. At 1220 *Fiume* lofted a ranging salvo at *Berwick* from twenty-four thousand yards. Then *Pola* targeted *Berwick,* while *Gorizia* squared off against *Southampton.* By 1222 the 3rd Division had also opened fire from 23,500 yards. The Italian ships also altered course to port, away from the British, to maintain long range, which Italian doctrine favored, and the 3rd Division began making smoke.[45]

Holland noted,"The enemy's first salvo fell close to *Manchester* being exact for range but a hundred yards out for line." However, the Italians corrected quickly. At 1222 an 8-inch shell exploded on *Berwick's* Y turret barbette. From a nearby destroyer a witness recalled,"We saw on *Berwick* suddenly a red flash that was not gunfire. Simultaneously splashes hid her after part. As she drew clear she trailed a thin brown smoke behind her that was not gun smoke."[46] The blow killed seven men, wounded nine others, and ignited a fire that took an hour to subdue.

Manchester, Sheffield, and *Newcastle* returned fire against *Trieste* while *Berwick* targeted *Trento,* Sansonetti's rear vessel. *Southampton* engaged *Fiume.* At 1224 *Renown* hurled six salvos toward *Trieste* from a distance of 26,500 yards before losing sight of her in the smoke. *Ramillies* discharged two ranging salvos that splashed far short. Straining to achieve 20.7 knots, the old battleship could only watch the action slowly recede to the northeast.

Sansonetti's 3rd Division altered course to the north, even north by northwest, and thus drew away from Matteucci's 1st Division, which continued sailing northeast. At 1227 Campioni reversed course to starboard to close the 1st Division.

A brisk gunnery action ensued between 1220 and 1242 as the cruisers fought in a northeasterly direction. The British ships employed their forward turrets and the Italians their aft guns at ranges between sixteen and twenty-three thousand yards. "Many straddles were obtained, but smoke rendered spotting and observation exceedingly difficult."[47] In fact, neither side was impressed with the other's shooting. Admiral Iachino commented, "The English, as usual, fired rapid salvoes with a limited spread, making frequent turns to disturb our fire and so as to bring all their guns to bear. The general result was ineffective and not well directed."[48] British reports commented that "the enemy's fire was accurate during the early stages, but when fully engaged it deteriorated rapidly, and the spread became ragged."[49] Nonetheless, at 1235 another 8-inch shell struck *Berwick*, destroying the after breaker (electrical switchboard) room and cutting power to the ship's aft section.

Renown, after losing sight of the 3rd Division, altered course to starboard chasing a distant glimpse of the 1st Division, which Somerville believed might be the enemy battleships. Then *Bolzano* flitted briefly into view, which earned her two salvos. Swinging to starboard to bring her Y turret to bear, *Renown* launched eight salvos at *Trento* from an estimated range of 30,700 yards before, at 1245, the Italian cruiser vanished in the haze. *Manchester* and *Sheffield* continued pumping shells at *Trieste* until 1236 and 1240, respectively, but after eighteen salvos *Newcastle* shifted to *Trento*. Meanwhile, *Southampton* discharged five broadsides at *Fiume* and then targeted *Lanciere*, which was lagging due to her engine problems. At 1240 a 6-inch shell tore through the destroyer's engine room. She had restored speed to twenty three knots, but then at 1245 a dud penetrated her hull and a second hit alongside. It too failed to explode, but the shock severely shook the ship.

At 1240 eleven Swordfish attacked *Vittorio Veneto*. Campioni's flagship dodged ten torpedoes, even though they hit the water from as near as seven to eight hundred yards (the flight leader overshot his target and attacked *Cesare*). The aircraft likewise escaped damage.

Holland tried to separate the two enemy cruiser divisions. *Manchester* shifted fire to *Fiume*, the 1st Division's left-hand ship, twenty-one thousand yards off her starboard bow, and the rest of the cruisers began to target the same division, including *Berwick*, which remained in action with two turrets. However, at 1245 Holland came to starboard, worried that the enemy might work around and cross his T should he continue pounding north. This maneuver opened the range, as Matteucci continued northeast and Sansonetti north-northeast.

Renown nearly blasted a pair of French liners that inadvertently stumbled into her gun sights but then, at 1250, detected two battleships. Somerville, not liking these odds, turned south to concentrate on *Ramillies*, "as [the enemy ships] appeared to be on a closing course."[50] Then, when he saw they were withdrawing, Somerville came back to the northeast to pursue. Holland likewise returned to a northerly heading at 1258.

By 1300 *Lanciere* had lost all feed water in her boilers and was drifting without power.

After *Vittorio Veneto* emerged unscathed from the air attack, she launched a spotter and at 1300, still sailing northeast, engaged Holland's cruisers. Campioni later wrote:"When the range had diminished to 32,000 yards I opened fire with the after turret, and kept a steady course in order to maintain the approach of the First Division. If the range had continued to diminish to 28,000 yards (the maximum range for *Cesare*'s guns) I should have altered course to starboard in order to bring all guns to bear."However,"no sooner had the first of the *Veneto*'s salvos straddled the leading English cruiser [*Manchester*] than the English formation turned sharply to starboard, and in about three minutes the range had opened to over 40,000 yards compelling us to suspend our fire."[51] In fact, as giant waterspouts erupted around *Berwick* and *Manchester* Holland ordered smoke, and his ships fled southeast to close *Renown*.

Vittorio Veneto ceased fire at 1310, and the guns of the 1st Division were silent by 1315. Campioni continued northeast, and as the British ships dropped out of sight, he reduced speed to twenty knots. He had requested air support when he received the first sighting report and again after the gun action commenced, but to his disgust he had seen only British torpedo bombers.

As the Italian ships withdrew, Sansonetti asked for permission to return and tow *Lanciere* to safety. Iachino, the senior officer in signaling range, approved, on the condition he abandon *Lanciere* if threatened by a superior enemy.

As the Italians disappeared over the horizon, Somerville reviewed his situation. He was rapidly approaching the Sardinian coast, his air attack had apparently failed, and an important convoy under his protection was fading far astern. At 1312 he turned to close the convoy before dark. At 1335 he received word of a disabled enemy cruiser (*Lanciere*) to the north, but he resisted the temptation to dispatch a pair of cruisers to investigate.

During the remaining hours of daylight both sides delivered ineffective air attacks. At 1530 Swordfish dropped nine torpedoes against the 1st Division, while Skuas dive-bombed the 3rd Division at 1535. Ten Italian S.79s attacked Force H at 1420, narrowly missing a screening destroyer. At 1645 fifteen S.79s gave *Ark Royal* a scare: Somerville reported,"*Ark Royal* was completely obscured by bomb splashes two at least of which fell within ten yards of the ship."Bomb fragments damaged *Firedrake* and *Defender*.[52]

The adversaries fought this hour-long battle at extreme ranges. *Pola* expended 118 8-inch rounds, *Gorizia* 123, *Fiume* 210, *Trieste* 96, *Trento* 92, and *Bolzano* (masked by *Trento* for most of the battle) only 27. *Vittorio Veneto* fired nineteen 15-inch salvos. On the British side, *Renown* discharged sixteen salvos.

The light cruisers expended their typically prodigious quantities of 6-inch shells, while *Berwick* fired forty-seven 8-inch salvos between 1238 and 1308.

After the battle Churchill demanded Somerville's scalp, having questioned the admiral's offensive spirit ever since his objections to attacking the French at Mers-el-Kébir. However, a board of inquiry exonerated Somerville, who enjoyed the strong support of several fellow admirals. As for Campioni, although he had a mandate to be conservative, he had presided over the loss of Italy's best opportunity to deal the British a sharp setback in a fleet action. As Iachino remarked, "The use of these ships, which constituted at that moment nearly all of our fleet's effective units after the blow at Taranto, was decided by Supermarina mainly for reasons of morale, and to demonstrate that our combative spirit remained intact.[53] Cavagnari and Mussolini both endorsed his actions, but Campioni's days of command at sea were numbered.

Encounter in the Sicilian Narrows

During the night of November 27/28, the British convoy, which now consisted of three cruisers, the 13th Destroyer Flotilla, four corvettes, and three merchant ships, continued through the narrows. (See table 4.6.)

The 10th Torpedo Boat Squadron departed Trapani, at 1705 and a dozen MAS boats sallied from various bases. The torpedo boats assumed a rake formation, with five miles between ships in order (from northeast to southwest) *Sagittario, Sirio, Vega,* and *Calliope.* They cruised west at twelve knots to the longitude of Cape Bon, where at 2250 they reversed course. At 2334 *Sagittario* reported eleven enemy units crossing astern at eighteen knots. She came to twenty knots to attack one of the cruisers, but according to her report, three destroyers leading the enemy formation turned to follow her, holding fire but driving her northeast until she lost contact.

Table 4.6 Encounter in the Sicilian Narrows, 27–28 November 1940, 2334–0127

Conditions: Night, mixed visibility	
British ships—	Force F (Vice Admiral L. E. Holland): CL: *Manchester* (F), *Southampton, Coventry*
	13th Destroyer Flotilla (Captain A. D. B. James): *Duncan* (F), *Hotspur, Defender, Gallant, Hereward*
	DC: *Peony, Salvia, Gloxinia, Hyacinth*
Italian ships—	10th Torpedo Boat Squadron (Commander Giuseppe Fontana): *Vega* (F), *Sagittario, Sirio, Calliope*

Six minutes later *Sirio* sighted a silhouette three thousand yards to port. She approached, but once again destroyers intervened. *Sirio* withdrew, reporting that torpedoes had been fired against her. At 0028 on 28 November *Vega* made contact. Her tubes were trained and ready to launch when the convoy changed course and destroyers appeared, but in the process of avoiding them she also lost contact.

Finally, *Calliope* came upon the convoy at 0055. She made a silent approach on a parallel course, for once unseen by the vigilant British escort. At 0127 she fired two torpedoes at twenty-two hundred yards at what she believed was an aircraft carrier but was in fact one of the three merchant ships. Both missed.

Italian tactics in this action attempted to incorporate the lessons of Cape Passero. The torpedo boats approached individually and cautiously, following revised instructions. They only put two torpedoes into the water as a result. Even this feeble effort had an impact, however, because two months later a British convoy attempted a daytime passage of the Sicilian Channel and suffered grave consequences as a result.

On 9 December the Army of the Nile attacked the Italian positions in Egypt and in a series of stunning victories routed the enemy and propelled it into a retreat that ended only on the border of Tripolitania. The Royal Navy supported the army's advance with two bombardment forces, an air support squadron, and an inshore flotilla to move supplies.

On 10 December the Regia Marina began a major reorganization that saw the two fleets consolidated into one. Admiral Cavagnari lost his job as chief of staff to Admiral Arturo Ricardi. Admiral Campioni was kicked upstairs and became deputy chief of staff, while Admiral Iachino took over the fleet command. Ricardi's first orders were for a cruiser bombardment of the Ionian Islands, supported by the battleships, to draw off enemy naval units operating against the African army's hard-pressed flank. These instructions included the condition that "upon sighting enemy naval forces [the fleet] will engage only under definitely favorable conditions." In a demonstration of the frustrations within the Italian high command, Iachino fired back a memorandum asking whether it was up to Supermarina or the commander at sea to determine what constituted "definitely favorable conditions." Ricardi acknowledged that this was Iachino's prerogative.[54]

The successful course of the ground war and its battleship superiority, gained as a result of the raid against Taranto, allowed the Mediterranean Fleet to commence operations MC.2 and 3, which included an air attack against Rhodes and Stampalia, a battleship bombardment of Valona, a sweep of the Adriatic, a fast and a slow convoy to Malta from Alexandria, the return of accumulated shipping from Malta to Egypt, two Aegean convoys, and the dispatch of *Malaya*, five destroyers, and two empty merchantmen through the Sicilian Channel to Gibraltar. All these activities were accomplished with the loss of only the destroyer *Hyperion* to the submarine *Serpente*. The Italian fleet had relocated to Sardinia from 15 December to 20 December, while Naples' defenses were improved after an air attack there the day before had severely damaged *Pola*. Reconnaissance completely missed the British operation until 21 December. For example, the first notice of the attack against Valona was shells dropping into the harbor.

No Quick Peace

By the end of 1940 British and Italian warships had fought eight surface actions in the Mediterranean and three in the Red Sea: five at night and six during the day. Allied surface forces had sunk a cruiser, three destroyers, and two torpedo boats and had damaged eight others. In turn, Italian surface forces had damaged five British cruisers and five destroyers, most of them superficially. The British had demonstrated clear superiority at night. The four attempts by Italian light units to intercept British forces in the Sicilian Channel and Red Sea had resulted in four unsuccessful torpedo attacks and moderate damage to one British cruiser, at the cost of one destroyer and two torpedo boats sunk and two destroyers damaged. The one British night convoy attack, made with overwhelming force, destroyed its target. The two daytime battleship actions had been a draw, and the Regia Marina's surface forces had been defeated during the day only in the Battle of Cape Spada. Considering Britain's greater war experience and its tested doctrine, the Regia Marina's performance was credible. The U.S. Navy, when it first measured its doctrine and peacetime training against a more practiced foe in the first eight months of the Pacific War, lost four heavy cruisers, three destroyers, and a gunboat in ten surface actions and sank only a patrol boat in return.

Many histories imply that German intervention rescued Italy from military defeat. The Germans themselves believed this most of all. As early as 14 November Raedar was ranting to Hitler, "The Italian leadership is wretched," and further, "The Italian armed forces have neither the leadership nor the military efficiency to carry the required operations in the Mediterranean area to a successful conclusion." He identified a "close connection between victorious German warfare and the Mediterranean-African problem."[55] Indeed, important aspects of the war were going poorly for Italy, especially on the ground in North Africa and Albania. The expectation of a short war had led to the elevation of politics over military needs and to the pursuit of short-term goals—exemplified by the September 1940 dispatch of nearly two hundred aircraft to assist Germany in its air campaign over Great Britain and the demobilization of 600,000 soldiers just before the invasion of Greece. But in some other respects, the war was going better than Italy had a right to expect.

In terms of mission fulfillment, Italy had kept North Africa, Albania, and the Dodecanese Islands supplied. Up through January 1941 the Regia Marina convoyed to Africa 331 freighters carrying 41,544 men with losses of 0.6 percent, and 346,559 tons of supplies with losses of 2.2 percent.[56] The British battleships stationed at both ends of the Mediterranean sortied sixteen times up through the end of 1940 and successfully brought seven convoys, with a total of twenty-seven merchant ships, to Malta, three convoys to Greece, and one to Egypt. Another six convoys returned in ballast from Malta to Egypt or Gibraltar. Italian efforts to interdict this traffic, as well as shipping in the Aegean (thirteen convoys totaling fifty-nine merchant vessels, not counting coastal traffic) and the Red Sea, proved largely unsuccessful. However, only one merchant ship made the transit from Gibraltar to Alexandria. After six months of war, the Axis sea lanes to Libya were open, while Britain's direct route from Gibraltar to Alexandria was closed. Every other aspect of the sea war paled before this dynamic. London's decision to create an army in Egypt despite this closure affected Britain's imports, which collapsed from 4.18 million tons in May 1940 to 2.97 millions in September 1940.[57] The blockade of the Sicilian Channel and the need to base fleets at both ends of the Mediterranean facilitated Germany's submarine offensive, which sank an average of 28,000 tons of merchant shipping a month from January to May 1940 and 174,000 tons a month from June to December 1940.[58]

Italy, meanwhile, imported by rail 13.55 million tons of coal from the Reich, the greatest availability of energy in its history; more than 1.5 millions tons of iron, wood, and other items arrived from Spain nearly uncontested. For the Italian leadership these hopeful trends helped offset the gloom of military failures in North Africa and Greece. Even the king of Italy, Victor Emmanuel III, well known for his anti-German sentiments, stated to Ciano on 6 January 1941 that "the war will end in a German victory, because Hitler has unified the European continent against England."[59]

5

Enter the Germans
Winter 1941

The essence of night fighting is surprise followed by prompt action. . . . Results at night will depend on the action taken in the first minute or so, and if the most effective action is not taken immediately it is unlikely that there will be time to recover.

—Admiralty, *The Fighting Instructions 1939*

The winter of 1940/41 started well for the Allied cause. By February the Army of the Nile had conquered Cyrenaica and destroyed the Italian 10th Army. Imperial forces invaded Italian East Africa on 19 January. Greek armies pushed deeper into Albania. Winston Churchill rejoiced, "We had not failed, . . . [W]ith a gasp of astonishment and relief the smaller neutrals and the subjugated states saw that the stars still shone in the sky."[1] However, while these victories menaced Germany's southern flank, they were not the reason Berlin intervened in the Mediterranean.

As early as July 1940 the Reich had plans to move south.[2] On 26 September 1940 Grand Admiral Raeder met with Hitler and advised him that the British considered the Mediterranean the pivot of their world empire and that the "Mediterranean question needed to be resolved during the Winter of 1941."[3] Hitler agreed. In October he explored constructing a pan-European, anti-British coalition meeting with the heads of state of France and Spain, Marshal Henri Philippe Pétain and Generalissimo Francisco Franco. Hitler proposed to Franco a German attack on Gibraltar; the generalissimo, grateful for the German and Italian help that had brought him to power and foreseeing further benefits by hitching himself to Germany's cause, conditionally agreed to join the conflict. However, because its brutal civil war had devastated Spain, Franco wanted specific territorial guarantees and massive economic assistance before sending up the balloon. Berlin, however, did not wish to alienate Vichy France, or cause the defection of North Africa to the Allies, by promising Morocco and western Algeria to Spain, or to provide aid until Madrid committed to a firm date. On 8 December, during a German attempt to pin him down, the Spanish *caudillo* declared, "Spain could not enter the war so long as the British navy remained so strong, the Canaries so exposed, and Spain's own economic and military problems so great." Upon hearing this Hitler concluded that Spain's demands were too high and abandoned plans to attack Gibraltar before the Soviet Union.[4]

On 15 December Luftwaffe units began staging southward and by 9 January 156 aircraft of Fliegerkorps X had arrived in Sicily.

As these events unfolded Great Britain launched a major naval operation, codenamed Excess, to force the Italian blockade. Excess involved five freighters sailing east from Gibraltar to Malta, with four continuing on to Piraeus, Greece.[5] Two ships from Alexandria would replenish Malta, and eight vessels would return from Malta to Egypt. To cover these movements the Mediterranean Fleet and Force H collectively deployed a battle cruiser, three battleships, three aircraft

Map 5.1   Enter the Germans, January–March 1941

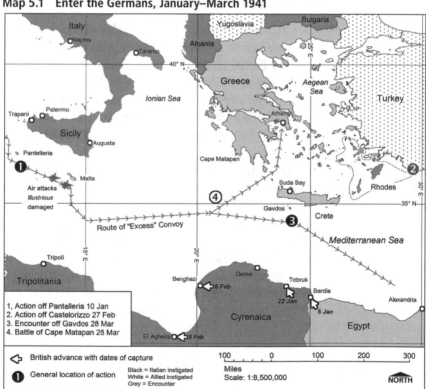

carriers, eight cruisers, twenty-eight destroyers, four sloops, and three submarines. (See map 5.1.)

The convoys weighed anchor on 6 January. By 9 January Supermarina knew that a major operation was under way, but the battle fleet remained inactive, because on 8 January British aircraft bombed Naples and lightly damaged *Cesare*. She withdrew to La Spezia for repairs, accompanied by *Vittorio Veneto*, the Regia Marina's last fully operational battleship. This left only light units to patrol the Sicilian Channel. The Alexandria convoys likewise proceeded unmolested, because Taranto's defenses were still being improved and no major warships were there to dispute their passage.

Heavy weather in the Sicilian Channel on the night of 9 January kept Italy's MAS boats in port. Torpedo boats *Circe* and *Vega* remained on patrol, however, and at dawn on 10 January, six miles south of Pantelleria, they discovered the Gibraltar convoy and its powerful escort, Force F (the new antiaircraft cruiser *Bonaventure* and four destroyers) and Force B (two cruisers and a destroyer), which had been sent ahead by the Mediterranean Fleet the day before in case Italian warships intervened. The Mediterranean Fleet itself hovered just over the horizon. The transit of the most dangerous part of the narrows was timed to occur in daylight, because of the late-November experience with repeated night attacks. (See table 5.1.)

Table 5.1   Action off Pantelleria, 10 January 1941, 0741–0820

Conditions: Poor visibility, heavy chop	
British ships—	Force B (Rear Admiral E. de F. Renouf): CL: *Gloucester*, *Southampton*; DD: *Ilex*
	Force F (Captain H. J. Egerton) CL: *Bonaventure*[D1] (F); DD: *Jaguar*, *Hereward, Hasty, Hero*
Italian ships—	(Commander Giuseppe Fontana): TB: *Vega*[Sunk] (F), *Circe*[D1]

Bonaventure, which was sailing astern of the convoy's two columns, and *Jaguar*, on the port side, sighted the Italian torpedo boats at 0720 off *Bonaventure*'s port beam. Both ships queried Rear Admiral Renouf, the convoy commander, thinking the contacts might be elements of the Mediterranean Fleet. Meanwhile *Circe* and *Vega* charged straight for the enemy, despite the long odds and choppy sea, which reduced their effective speed by several knots. *Bonaventure* challenged and then steered toward the strangers. She fired star shell and then aimed a salvo at *Circe*. The convoy turned away, and the port-side escorts, *Southampton*, *Jaguar*, and *Hereward*, hauled out of line to engage.

At 0741, at a range of four thousand yards, the Italian ships launched seven torpedoes and turned away. *Bonaventure*, however, which had been pumping rapid salvos at *Vega*, combed their tracks. The cruiser's evasive maneuvers cleared the range for the destroyers; these veteran ships targeted *Vega* and quickly silenced her guns and disabled her engines. *Jaguar* closed to three hundred yards and raked the helpless torpedo boat, igniting fires along her entire length. Then shells splashed close alongside *Jaguar*, which sheered away, assuming that Pantelleria's shore batteries, about twelve miles to the northwest, had her in their sights. In fact, these were *Circe*'s parting shots.

Vega remained afloat, so at 0820 *Hereward* torpedoed the drifting wreck. *Vega* exploded and sank with only two survivors. *Circe* escaped with splinter damage. Splinters also damaged *Bonaventure*, killing one man and wounding four.

Another Italian torpedo attack had failed and again at a heavy cost. However, from the Italian perspective, not all had been in vain. The destroyer *Gallant* struck a mine south of Pantelleria at 0830, shortly after the convoy resumed course, because the action had pushed the British ships south of their intended route. *Mohawk* towed *Gallant* to Malta, where she sat out the war as a hulk.

Jaguar had fired eighty-eight rounds of 4.7-inch SAP and six rounds of 4-inch HE, but *Bonaventure* had expended six hundred 5.25-inch rounds during the brief action and was to prove of limited help in the heavy air attacks by Fliegerkorps X that followed on 10 and 11 January.

The appearance of German aircraft surprised the British.[6] German and Italian dive- and torpedo bombers sank *Southampton*, severely damaged *Illustrious*, and lightly damaged *Warspite* and *Gloucester*. The merchant ships arrived without loss, but a British assessment noted, "Had some of the dive-bombers attacked the convoy instead of the supporting men-of-war . . . all four transports must inevitably have been sunk."[7] German aircraft repeatedly struck Malta to finish off *Illustrious*, but on 23 January the patched-up carrier escaped to Alexandria and thence to the United States for permanent repairs.

In the Aegean on 31 January the torpedo boat *Lupo*, under the command of Lieutenant Commander Francesco Mimbelli, encountered the tanker *Desmoulea* (8,120 GRT) in passage from Alexandria to Suda Bay off the north coast of Crete, just west of Kaso Strait. At 1800 the Italian warship torpedoed and severely damaged the tanker. The crew abandoned ship, but two hours later the destroyer *Dainty* arrived and towed her to Suda.[8] The large tanker was to be towed to Port Said three months later, shortly before the Germans captured Crete, but the British repair capacity in Egypt was so limited that this valuable ship never returned to service.

The Bombardment of Genoa

Following Operation Excess, London continued to seek ways in which the navy could pressure Italy. The temporary loss of *Illustrious* made it dangerous for the Mediterranean Fleet to operate in the central Mediterranean, so Force H tried to take up the slack. Meanwhile, Supermarina needed to reinforce Libya through the only port remaining in Axis hands, Tripoli, which could accommodate only several freighters a day under optimal conditions. Given that one German armored division required sixty freighter loads, this presented a serious bottleneck. Starting in February, however, the Italians increased capacity, thanks to the arrival of German barges and pontoons, while later in the year they obtained floating cranes and barges from the French.[9]

On 5 February an important convoy of three small German freighters loaded with the first German troops, escorted by an old destroyer and three torpedo boats, left Naples bound for Tripoli. The next day Force H sailed to bombard Genoa after bad weather had caused Somerville to abort an earlier attempt. On 8 February Supermarina received word of a British carrier south of the Balearic Islands and assumed a Malta operation was under way. However, Somerville's force surreptitiously turned north, and at 0714 on 9 February two-ton shells began dropping on Genoa. At that moment Vice Admiral Iachino was waiting to intercept Somerville southwest of Sardinia with *Vittorio Veneto*, *Doria*, *Cesare*, three heavy cruisers, and ten destroyers.

In a half hour *Renown*, *Malaya*, and *Sheffield* fired 273 15-inch and 782 6-inch rounds through a heavy mist into Genoa and its crowded harbor from ranges of between eighteen and twenty-one thousand yards. Aircraft spotted for the ships, but the poor visibility forced the shore batteries, which included two 15-inch, two 7.5-inch, and eight 6-inch guns, to aim at the flashes of the British weapons; they replied with only fifty ineffective rounds. The bombardment sank four freighters and a training vessel; splinters damaged another eighteen ships. Many shells fell in the city, killing 144 civilians.[10]

Iachino's fleet was well positioned to intercept Force H, but hazy weather hampered the Italian aircraft scouring the Gulf of Genoa for the enemy and kept Iachino mostly in the dark. Then Supermarina sent him chasing in the wrong direction, mistaking a French convoy for his quarry. By the time the Italians sorted out Force H's course, Somerville had escaped. The British admiral noted that his "guardian angel, to whom he had become accustomed to paying respectful homage, was evidently in a good mood."[11]

The first Italo-German troop convoy arrived in Africa on 11 February, evading an attack by the British submarine *Unique*.

Castelorizzo

The Genoa raid delighted Churchill. He continued to champion other possible operations, like an attack on Pantelleria ("if successful, would be electrifying") or Rhodes ("most urgent").[12] Cunningham feared such adventures would strain his resources and instead agreed to seize Castelorizzo, the most exposed of the Italian Dodecanese, located off the Turkish coast sixty-five miles east of Rhodes and 145 miles west of Cyprus, as a forward motor-torpedo-boat base.

On 23 February *Hereward* and *Decoy* embarked two hundred men of Commando 50 at Suda Bay and set sail escorted by *Gloucester, Bonaventure,* and the gunboat *Ladybird.* They arrived at Castelorizzo before dawn on 25 February. After a confused landing and a sharp fight, in which the thirty-five-man garrison suffered thirteen casualties, the commandos secured the island.[13] The cruisers withdrew as *Ladybird* entered Megisti, the only harbor, to provide support and a communications link until the permanent garrison arrived the next day.

The naval commander in Rhodes, Rear Admiral Luigi Biancheri, reacted swiftly to the British attack. Between 0800 and 0930 aircraft bombed the invaders and damaged *Ladybird.* The gunboat's captain decided to return to Cyprus, recommending that the boarding vessel *Rosaura,* which was bringing a regular infantry company from the Sherwood Foresters regiment, land its troops at night. Accordingly, Rear Admiral Renouf, the reinforcement convoy's commander, arranged to arrive at 0300 on 26 February.

That night *Hereward,* sailing ahead of the convoy, picked up a report from the commandos' short-range radio: two ships were attacking north of the harbor, possibly landing troops. Renouf, nervous about becoming enmeshed in a surface action, decided to retreat to Alexandria and transfer the Sherwood Foresters to destroyers. He ordered *Hereward* to engage the enemy, but she failed to find *Lupo* or *Lince,* the Italian torpedo boats involved. They had landed a reconnaissance party that shot up the town and then reembarked and withdrew. On the morning of 27 February a small flotilla, under the personal command of Admiral Biancheri and consisting of *Lupo* and *Lince,* along with *MAS546* and *MAS561,* returned with more troops, who this time landed to stay. Later that day destroyers *Crispi* and *Sella* arrived with reinforcements. All told, the warships delivered 258 soldiers and eighty sailors. The Italian counterattack pinned the lightly armed commandos at Nifti Point while *Lupo,* ranging offshore, peppered them with 3.9-inch rounds.

That same morning *Decoy* and *Hero* reembarked the Foresters and departed Alexandria escorted by *Perth, Bonaventure, Hasty,* and *Jaguar.* The flotilla arrived at 2300 on 27 February, and the destroyers gathered off Nifti Point while the cruisers patrolled offshore. The troops, who began landing shortly after midnight, found the commandos in a desperate situation; after conferring, both army commanders recommended evacuation. (See table 5.2.)

Table 5.2 Castelorizzo Harbor, 27 February 1941, 0200–0215

Conditions: Windy with rising swell	
British ship—	DD: *Jaguar*
Italian ship—	DD: *Francesco Crispi*

Many warships had concentrated in a small area. *Crispi, Lince,* and *Lupo* patrolled south of the island, *Sella* to the west; the MAS boats guarded Megisti. During the withdrawal, *Jaguar* poked her nose into the port and emptied her tubes at one of the MAS boats inside. The British crew reported four explosions, but apparently these resulted from torpedoes hitting shore. *Crispi*, meanwhile, after tossing twenty shells into the British positions, was slowly cruising east while awaiting orders when the lookout reported two large shapes, evaluating one as a "*Coventry* type" cruiser. The captain snapped off two torpedoes, but both malfunctioned and ran deep. As *Crispi* maneuvered to disengage, *Jaguar* came about and illuminated. *Crispi* opened fire with her main batteries, but "another serious technical problem" with the fire control resulted in first-salvos misses, despite the close range and the advantage of surprise. *Jaguar* quickly replied and would report hitting *Crispi* twice, but in fact her salvos likewise missed. The machine guns on both ships rattled into action. *Crispi*'s gunnery officer felt a burst pass just over his head and dropped to the deck. A 40-mm round snuffed out *Jaguar*'s searchlight, and in the darkness *Crispi* broke contact. By the time *Jaguar* fired star shell, the Italian destroyer had vanished, suffering just one man wounded by a small-caliber round.[14]

The British completed their evacuation by 0300 and retreated to Suda Bay. An embarrassed and frustrated Churchill wrote, "I am thoroughly mystified about this operation."[15] Cunningham agreed that it had been a "rotten business" and blamed Rear Admiral Renouf, who he believed had "cracked in the middle of it."[16] In fact, this small episode demonstrated that the Italians exerted sea control around even their outlying bases, and it would not be the last time the British suffered embarrassment in an operation where success depended upon a lack of Italian initiative.

Operation Lustre

In February 1941 the Mediterranean naval war took a new turn when Greece, nervously watching the German buildup in Bulgaria, consented to receive British troops on the mainland. Shortly thereafter the Royal Navy commenced Operation Lustre to transport divisions lately victorious in Africa, along with newly arrived formations, into Piraeus. The Mediterranean Fleet's War Diary commented, "The move to Greece so completely absorbed all resources . . . that any question of considered offensive action against the enemy had to be ruled aside."[17] Moreover, it came at a time when Axis air-dropped mines were shutting down the Suez Canal. At the end of March, 110 ships were logjammed at Suez waiting to head north.[18]

The Axis powers meanwhile poured Italian and German troops into Tripoli, with convoys departing on 8, 12, and 24 February and on 1, 3, 8, 9 (two convoys), and 12 March. From this traffic Allied submarines sank just two merchant ships and the light cruiser *Diaz*.[19]

Between 12 and 14 February the Italian and German naval high commanders, Italy's new chief of staff Admiral Riccardi and *Grossadmiral* Raeder, held a face-to-face meeting. As one historian observes, "Relations between the partners were far from pure. Teutons were always telling Latins what to do and what they had missed doing; Latins were recoiling in resentment against Teuton condescension and criticism. The dominant note was mistrust."[20] In fact, Raeder wanted to "persuade the Italians to adopt [the German] idea of offensive operations." Riccardi wanted German oil and parried Raeder, stating that air reconnaissance needed to improve and that the battleships damaged at Taranto had to return to action before he could consider offensive operations. Nonetheless, Raeder left the meeting feeling he had made his point.[21]

Admiral Iachino likewise wanted the fleet to be more aggressive and advanced an old plan for a sweep into the waters around Crete, if both air support and surprise could be guaranteed. Riccardi considered such a foray impractical, because of the distances involved, the lack of fuel, and the likelihood that any targets would be alerted before surface forces could bring them to action. Nonetheless, as the date of Germany's invasion of Yugoslavia approached, British convoys to Greece became a pressing concern. Finally, acceding to German pressure, Comando Supremo ordered action.[22] Prospects seemed to brighten on 16 March when the Luftwaffe reported that it had damaged two enemy battleships. Germany also promised long-range fighter coverage and aerial reconnaissance to support the Italian strike, even assigning liaison officers to work directly with Iachino.

Operation Gaudo

On the evening of 26 March the Regia Marina commenced Operation Gaudo, a battleship-cruiser sweep into the Aegean Sea and eastern Mediterranean. Iachino departed Naples at 2030 aboard *Vittorio Veneto*. Obsessed with secrecy, the fleet commander had not conferred even with the four admirals who would be sailing under him. *Vittorio Veneto's* escort consisted of the 10th Destroyer Squadron, later replaced by the 13th Squadron. The 1st Division, under Vice Admiral Carlo Cattaneo, sailed from Taranto at 2300. He commanded heavy cruisers *Zara, Pola,* and *Fiume* and the 9th Destroyer Squadron. The 3rd Division, under Vice Admiral Luigi Sansonetti—heavy cruisers *Trieste, Trento,* and *Bolzano* and the 12th Destroyer Squadron—sailed from Messina at 0530 on 27 March. Rear Admiral Antonio Legnani's 7th Division—light cruisers *Abruzzi* and *Garibaldi* and the 16th Destroyer Squadron—sailed from Brindisi. *Vittorio Veneto* joined the 3rd Division at 1100 on 27 March east of Augusta.

After *Lupo* had torpedoed a valuable tanker in January the British avoided Kaso Strait, and Allied convoys sailed south of Crete and entered the Aegean via the Antikithera Strait west of the island. The plan called for the 1st and 7th divisions to probe into the Aegean north of Crete while *Vittorio Veneto* and the 3rd Division swept east to the vicinity of Gavdos Island off Crete's southwestern coast, the effective limit of their destroyers' range. If the two prongs failed to encounter a target, they would turn for home at 0700 on 28 March.

Intelligence frustrated this plan from the start. The British received hints from decrypts of German air force Enigma code and the rarely used Italian navy Enigma that an operation into the eastern Mediterranean was pending, but they remained uncertain as to its objective. The Admiralty forecast a raid into the Aegean or eastern Mediterranean, or a landing operation on the Libyan coast, while Cunningham believed a convoy to the Dodecanese was a possibility.[23] Even as the Italian fleet cleared harbor he canceled one southbound Aegean convoy and ordered another to turn back after dark.

On the evening of 27 March, Force A—three battleships, the newly arrived aircraft carrier *Formidable* (which carried an air group of thirteen Fulmars, ten Albacores, and four Swordfish), and four destroyers of the 14th Flotilla—departed Alexandria. Vice Admiral Pridham-Wippell's Force B, the 15th Cruiser Squadron and the 2nd Destroyer Flotilla, had been escorting troop convoys and was already in the Aegean. Cunningham ordered Pridham-Wippell to join Force A south of Crete on the forenoon of 28 March. Finally, Force C, consisting of five more destroyers from the 10th Flotilla, left Alexandria after Force A. Just as Iachino was worrying about British spies in Naples, Cunningham felt the need to put on a show for Axis agents in Cairo, going so far as to visit his golf club with an overnight bag on the afternoon of 27 March for the benefit of the Japanese consul general, himself an avid golfer.[24]

At 1220 on 27 March, just eighty minutes after Iachino's force had united, *Vittorio Veneto's* cryptoanalysis group decoded a British sighting report; then *Trieste* spotted a shadowing aircraft. Iachino had lost the crucial element of surprise. However, he made the controversial decision to press on, in part because Supermarina did not specifically cancel the operation and also because at 1400 aerial reconnaissance reported the British fleet still in port. Moreover, the British aircraft missed *Vittorio Veneto* in the hazy conditions, and from interceptions of Cunningham's repeated queries as to whether a battleship had been sighted, it seemed to Iachino that the enemy lacked the whole picture. These factors led him to conclude that *Vittorio Veneto* might still obtain tactical surprise over the cruisers that Supermarina knew were at sea.[25] At 2200, however, Supermarina radioed a change in plans: the 1st and 7th divisions would abort their sweep north of Crete and join Iachino south of the island.

Table 5.3   Encounter off Gavdos, 28 March 1941, 0741–1118

Conditions: Fair visibility, overcast with moderate northeast breeze and slight swell	
Allied ships—	15th Cruiser Squadron (Vice Admiral H. D. Pridham-Wippell): CL: *Orion*[D1] (F), *Ajax, Perth, Gloucester*[D1]
	2nd Destroyer Flotilla (Captain H. St. L. Nicolson): *Ilex* (F), *Hasty, Vendetta, Hereward*
Italian ships—	(Rear Admiral Iachino): BB: *Vittorio Veneto* (F)
	13th Destroyer Squadron (Captain Vittorio De Pace): *Granatiere* (F), *Alpino, Bersagliere, Fucilere*
	3rd Division (Vice Admiral Luigi Sansonetti): CA: *Trieste* (F), *Trento, Bolzano*
	12th Destroyer Squadron (Captain Carmine D'Arienzo): *Corazziere* (F), *Carabiniere, Ascari*

Dawn on 28 March found the Italians approaching Gavdos, with the 3rd Division preceding *Vittorio Veneto* by ten miles and the 1st and 7th divisions fifteen miles northwest of the flagship. There was a light northeasterly breeze and limited visibility. Pridham-Wippell's Force B was twenty miles south of Gavdos steaming southeast toward the Mediterranean Fleet, which at the time was 150 miles south of Crete's eastern extremity. *Formidable* was launching reconnaissance patrols toward the enemy's anticipated position. (See table 5.3.)

At 0600 *Vittorio Veneto* and *Bolzano* catapulted Ro43 float planes. Iachino planned to push east for an hour and then turn for home if no targets appeared. However, at 0635 the flagship's aircraft reported enemy cruisers heading south forty miles southwest of Sansonetti's division.

Aboard *Vittorio Veneto* "the Ro43's sighting report electrified our sailors, beginning with Iachino."[26] It seemed the fleet's luck might be on the change. At 0657 Iachino ordered 3rd Division to seek contact. *Vittorio Veneto* came to twenty-eight knots so she could support Sansonetti. Cattaneo's divisions likewise increased speed, although they never caught up to the action that developed. Iachino, hoping to lure the British into range of *Vittorio Veneto,* instructed Sansonetti to concentrate on the flagship as soon as he contacted the enemy. (See map 5.2.)

Map 5.2   Encounter off Gavdos/Battle of Cape Matapan

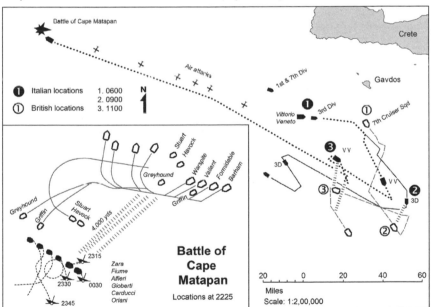

Meanwhile, *Formidable's* aircraft reported Sansonetti's cruisers, but hearing the contact was the same size, on the same course, and in nearly the same position as his own ships, Pridham-Wippell was, he later noted, "in some doubt whether it was not, in fact, my own force that was being reported."[27] Shortly before 0800 hours these doubts were resolved when *Orion*'s lookouts reported enemy ships bearing down from the north.

At the sight of Italian cruisers Pridham-Wippell immediately rang up thirty knots and turned sixty degrees, straight toward the Mediterranean Fleet, ninety miles southeast. He believed he was "out-ranged and out-gunned" and wanted to draw the Italians toward friendly battleships. At the sight of British cruisers running Sansonetti disregarded Iachino's orders; *Trieste*, followed by *Trento* and *Bolzano*, gave chase.[28]

Sansonetti opened fire at 0812. He believed the enemy bore twenty-two to twenty-four thousand yards from his flagship, but hazy conditions confused the outdated coincidence range finders equipping his old heavy cruisers. Pridham-Wippell gauged that the enemy's initial salvos came from 25,500 yards. In fact, the range probably exceeded twenty-six thousand, and the Italian shells splashed well short. Running at thirty-one knots, the maximum he could safely coax from his old cruisers, Sansonetti maintained a slow but regular fire. At 0822 Iachino asked Sansonetti if he was closing range, and at 0830 he radioed to instruct that if he was not closing to break off and withdraw toward the flagship. At 0829 *Gloucester* fired three test salvos from 23,500 yards, which fell short. However, Sansonetti cautiously adjusted course twenty-five degrees to port to stay out of 6-inch range.

Although the 3rd Division bombarded the British cruisers for twenty-five more minutes, none of its subsequent salvos reached. By 0855 Sansonetti had followed Pridham-Wippell halfway to Africa, and Iachino, worried that the 3rd Division was running into a trap, insisted that his subordinate break off. Aboard the British cruisers, in fact, "careful plots were being kept of all the movements and it was calculated that if the rate of closing was maintained, the enemy would be sighted from the *Warspite* about 10.0 o'clock."[29] Before that could happen, however, Sansonetti turned away.

In forty-two minutes of action *Trieste*, *Trento*, and *Bolzano* fired 132, 214, and 189 8-inch rounds, respectively. Iachino's report described this bombardment as "deliberately slow, but with a regular rhythm."[30] Pridham-Wippell commented that the Italian fire was "accurate to begin with[;] . . . [*Gloucester*] snaked the line to avoid hits."[31] But for the last twenty minutes of the action it was consistently short. The long range and outdated fire control equipment hampered Italian gunnery, but Sansonetti also enjoyed one advantage—at least there was little return fire and so he could follow a steady course.

When Pridham-Wippell saw he was no longer being chased he came about, maintaining contact from beyond the range of the 3rd Division's guns. To Cunningham the situation remained murky. He received Pridham-Wippell's

0812 sighting report at 0827 and immediately increased speed to twenty-two knots. A jumble of ambiguous information followed, including one notice of an enemy battleship. At 0939, still questioning the enemy's size and intentions, he ordered *Formidable* to launch a strike against Sansonetti's cruisers. By 1000 six Albacores and one Swordfish observer, escorted by two Fulmars, were winging their way northwest.

Iachino too was dissatisfied with his aerial reconnaissance. At 0913 Rhodes reported one carrier, two battleships, nine cruisers, and fourteen destroyers heading southeast, currently in a position he had occupied ninety minutes before. Discounting the report of a carrier, he assumed that these were his own ships. The flagship's cryptoanalysis team provided the Italian admiral with better information, quickly decoding messages being sent by Pridham-Wippell from which Iachino concluded the British still did not know his battleship was nearby. In the gloom of another failed mission Iachino sensed renewed opportunity. At 1017 Iachino signaled Sansonetti, "I am reversing course to try to cut off the enemy's withdrawal. Continue your present course until ordered, but maintain readiness to resume combat." At 1035 *Vittorio Veneto* came about, with, Iachino wrote, "the intention of putting myself, unseen, east of the enemy unit and to head south thereafter so as to arrive behind."[32] It was a good plan, but it did not work, because the British cruisers were north of where the Italian admiral expected them to be. He encountered them at 1050 just beyond the jaws of his trap.

An officer eating a sandwich on *Orion's* bridge remarked to a companion, "What's that battleship over there? I thought ours were miles away."[33] The Italians eavesdropped on *Orion's* signal that she had sighted an unknown unit and was going to investigate; at 1055 *Orion* duly challenged. *Vittorio Veneto* replied thirty seconds later from twenty-five thousand yards with six 1,951-pound shells. As Pridham-Wippell expressed it, "No time was lost in altering to the southward, increasing to full speed and making smoke."[34]

Vittorio Veneto's initial salvos flew overhead, but "with remarkable accuracy the Italians quickly found the range."[35] Massive columns of water two hundred feet tall sprang up on either side of the British flagship, and splinters pelted her hull. *Orion* endured ten uncomfortably close salvos, but then the battleship suspended fire for three minutes due to misfires, principally in A turret. Meanwhile, the British light cruisers steered southwest. However, the 3rd Division had also reversed course, and when Sansonetti's division advanced into view Pridham-Wippell, finding himself squeezed between the enemy columns, circled south and then southeast in line abreast. By 1115 he was flying directly toward the Mediterranean Fleet.

This loop left *Gloucester* outside to windward of the spreading screen of smoke being expelled by the British ships.[36] Iachino wrote,"It was the moment in which I hoped to obtain a positive result."[37] *Gloucester* dodged salvos with radical course alterations of up to thirty degrees. A British pilot who observed this portion of the battle later wrote,"The battleship was doing some good shooting at our cruisers and appeared to be straddling them frequently. I suspect that the only reason that they did not score any direct hits was that the spread of their individual salvoes was too large."[38] However, the visibility, poor to begin with, was rapidly deteriorating, especially after *Hasty*, spewing black funnel smoke, managed to claw to windward, giving *Gloucester* some protection.

Meanwhile, the air strike, which located the battleship at 1058, spent twenty minutes passing up *Vittorio Veneto*'s port beam. One of the flyers remembered, "She was steaming at 30 knots, the wind at our height was 30 knots against us, so that since our air speed was only 90 knots we were catching up at a relative speed of only 30 knots."[39] At 1115 the Albacores swung around to attack from ahead. After expending ninety-two 15-inch shells in twenty-nine salvos (with eleven misfires), *Vittorio Veneto* could no longer accurately spot the fall of her shot. When Iachino observed the aircraft beginning their run he ceased fire and ordered the helm hard to starboard. The planes attacked through an intense antiaircraft barrage, and all torpedoes missed astern.

As the enemy aircraft vanished southeast, *Vittorio Veneto* set course for home. When Pridham-Wippell emerged from the smoke at 1148 the horizon was clear, so he joined Cunningham. At this time *Valiant* was forty-five miles from the enemy. The British could not catch the Italian fleet unless they reduced *Vittorio Veneto*'s speed.

Iachino did not realize the Mediterranean Fleet was so near. Throughout the morning he had received contradictory and incomplete reports from Italian and German aircraft and from radio-direction fixes. These indicated there were enemy forces, certainly one carrier and probably a battleship, maybe eighty, or 170, miles east of his position. However, bitter experience made him doubt the accuracy of such reports, and on the principle that "positions fixed by the intersection of radio D/F bearings were, as a general rule, likely to be much more accurate," he concluded that the carrier and battleship were 170 miles away.[40] This was a strangely optimistic assessment, considering he had watched carrier aircraft disappear out to sea, but between 1215 and 1615 he heard nothing to shake this assumption.

As Iachino sailed for home, British aircraft attacked eight times.

At 1205 three Swordfish from Maleme vainly dropped torpedoes against the 3rd Division.

At 1420 three Blenheims from Greece attacked *Vittorio Veneto* from high level and missed.

At 1450 another six Blenheims bombed *Vittorio Veneto* from high level, without result.

At 1510 *Formidable*'s second strike, three Albacores and two Swordfish, escorted by a pair of Fulmars, attacked *Vittorio Veneto* and obtained one torpedo hit that damaged the battleship's port screws. *Vittorio Veneto* came to a standstill for several minutes and four thousand tons of water flooded through the hole, but she worked back up to fifteen, then nineteen knots using her starboard screws. Based upon enthusiastic pilot reports, Cunningham believed multiple bomb and torpedo hits had crippled the Italian battleship; the news "produced a thrill of elation throughout the fleet."[41]

At 1520 four Blenheims bombed 3rd Division and missed.

Between 1515 and 1645 eleven Blenheims bombed 1st Division, without result.

At 1700 six Blenheims bombed 3rd Division and missed.

Between 1930 to 1950, at last light, six Albacores and two Swordfish from *Formidable* and two Swordfish from Maleme struck the combined Italian fleet. Iachino deployed his ships in three columns and used smoke, searchlights, and a heavy barrage to protect *Vittorio Veneto*. This tactic succeeded, but one torpedo hit *Pola*, which had nearly stopped in order to avoid running into *Fiume* and could not take avoiding action. This blow knocked out five boilers and the main steam line. *Pola* lost electric power and drifted to a stop.

Battle of Cape Matapan

At 1644 Admiral Cunningham concluded he would not catch *Vittorio Veneto* before dark, so he dispatched Pridham-Wippell to hunt down the crippled battleship. His last air attack "reported probable hits, but no definite information of damage."[42] Cunningham also sent the 14th and 2nd flotillas out to hunt the Italians, retaining only four destroyers to screen his capital ships.

Cunningham based his action on his appreciation of the situation. At 1745 *Warspite* catapulted her spotter plane, and from 1831 it made a series of reports that led him to believe *Vittorio Veneto* was steering west by northwest at fifteen knots about forty-five miles from his position; based on other, less accurate reports, he also believed that another enemy force, two battleships with cruisers and destroyers, lay to the north-westward, and these figured in his dispositions.

Dark descended at 1940, and with the Italian and British forces both splintering into three formations, the situation rapidly grew complex. Pridham-

Wippell, who had been only twenty-four thousand yards behind the Italian fleet at 1945, slowed to twenty knots to reduce bow waves (which are visible in moonlight). Iachino learned of *Pola*'s distress at 2010, and eight minutes later he ordered Cattaneo's 1st Division to return and assist her. Cattaneo, worried that his destroyers were running low on fuel, had communicated with *Pola*'s captain. He wanted to send two destroyers to rescue the crew and scuttle the ship if her engines could not be restarted, but Iachino rejected this suggestion. Iachino's faulty appreciation of the situation determined his decision. At 1745 Supermarina had advised him of an enemy formation about seventy-five miles east of *Vittorio Veneto*. Iachino assumed this referred to Pridham-Wippell's cruisers and felt the 1st Division could handle them. He later wrote, "I had not the slightest idea that we were being pursued so closely by the British Fleet. [Otherwise] I should have abandoned the *Pola* to her fate."[43]

At 2015, as *Pola* wallowed in the slight swell without power, *Orion*'s radar pinged the stricken ship. Pridham-Wippell plotted the contact for eighteen minutes. He determined that it was a large vessel, probably a battleship, stopped or moving very slowly, although he never confirmed visually.[44] Pridham-Wippell reported his discovery at 2040 and stood off to the northwest to scout for the other Italian ships, supposing the 14th Flotilla's Captain Mack, would attack. The destroyer commander, however, was speeding off to circle ahead north of where he expected the Italian fleet to be and never received Pridham-Wippell's report. Cunningham, however, did, and at 2110 he altered course to investigate, just four minutes after the 1st Division itself had started back to succor its damaged mate. (See table 5.4.)

At 2048 *Vittorio Veneto* increased speed to nineteen knots and altered course to north by northwest. This put her north of where the British expected to find her and may have saved her from a surface action.

Cattaneo, meanwhile, sent his last message to Iachino at 2150; it read, "The range remaining to the *Alfieri* Squadron is very limited and does not permit an emergency engagement, which we think is almost certain." He foresaw a clash with British forces, but he saw it happening the next day, with *Pola* under tow. At 2100 three of his destroyers had only 145 tons of oil and *Carducci* only 125 tons. This was 28 percent of capacity and good for less than two hundred miles of steaming at battle speeds. Iachino did not answer this message.[45]

At 2155 *Ajax*'s radar detected three vessels five miles to the south. Pridham-Wippell was passing Cattaneo, but the British admiral thought the contacts represented Mack's ships, and so he stood farther north to avoid a tangle with friendly forces. Mack received this sighting report and likewise assumed it referred to his destroyers. Ensign Vito Sansonetti, the son of the admiral, was aboard *Alfieri*. He

Table 5.4   Battle of Cape Matapan, 28–29 March 1941, 2228–0403

Conditions: Overcast with light southwesterly wind, no moon, and a slight swell	
Allied ships—	1st Battle Squadron (Admiral Cunningham): BB: *Warspite* (F), *Barham, Valiant,* CV: *Formidable*
	10th Destroyer Flotilla (Captain H. M. L. Waller): *Stuart* (AU) (F), *Greyhound, Griffin, Havock*
	14th Destroyer Flotilla (Captain P. J. Mack): *Jervis* (F), *Janus, Mohawk, Nubian*
	2nd Destroyer Flotilla (Captain H. St. L. Nicolson): *Ilex* (F), *Hasty, Hereward*
Italian ships—	1st Division (Vice Admiral Carlo Cattaneo): CA: *Zara*[Sunk] (F), *Fiume*[Sunk], *Pola*[Sunk]
	9th Destroyer Squadron (Captain Salvatore Toscano): *Alfieri*[Sunk] (F), *Gioberti, Oriani*[D?], *Carducci*[Sunk]

later wrote, "I had always thought that when the captain told me to verify that our ships were in the correct formation [line ahead] and I observed instead they were in a wide rake formation that it was very strange indeed. Some years later having read the British proceedings I had no doubt the ships I had seen in the night were not Italian, but British."[46]

At 2210 *Valiant*'s radar pinpointed *Pola* about six miles to the southwest. At this same time Cattaneo approached from the south, with *Fiume*'s crew getting ready to pass a tow. The night was moonless and cloudy, and visibility hovered below five thousand yards. *Pola* sighted shapes to the north and, believing they were friendly, fired a red flare to advertise her location. *Zara*, south of *Pola*, saw the flare forty degrees off her port bow and turned in that direction. The British, meanwhile, closed with *Warspite, Valiant, Formidable,* and *Barham* in a line of bearing. All lookouts focused to port, where they expected the enemy ship to appear. One officer on the admiral's bridge, however, was sweeping the seas to starboard and at 2225 noticed large warships off the bow. Cattaneo was unwittingly crossing the British T (see map 5.2, inset).

Cunningham reacted rapidly. Over the short-range radio he ordered the giant ships to turn simultaneously forty degrees starboard to course 280 and assume a line-ahead formation to unmask their aft turrets. Then the admiral and his staff climbed one level and crowded onto the captain's bridge, where there was a "clear all-round view." *Formidable* hauled out to starboard. Aboard *Barham* the helmsman swung the wheel as Captain C. G. Cooke wondered why the admiral had ordered a turn away from the enemy and whether he should open fire anyway.[47] The battle line now approached the Italian column (*Zara, Fiume, Alfieri, Gioberti, Carducci,* and *Oriani*) on a slightly converging heading.[48]

Aboard *Zara* Captain Corsi was concerned because the flare he had seen was not a proper recognition signal. Then at 2228 *Greyhound,* the closest British ship, snapped on her searchlight and pinpointed the *Zara* as a "silvery-blue shape in the darkness."[49] A survivor later reported that Corsi exclaimed, "Why is he using his searchlight? Is he mad?"[50] Then 15-inch guns erupted at the point-blank range of three to four thousand yards. From *Stuart,* to the north of the battle line, it seemed as if "all of a sudden . . . the sky opened up. . . . [T]he leading cruiser burst into a mass of flames right from one end of the ship to the other. Then the second cruiser burst into flames as a salvo from either the *Barham* or *Valiant* caught her. By this time, a matter of seconds after the first gun, the air was full of noise, searchlights, tracers and spray."[51]

Aboard *Warspite* observers reported that five 1,938-pound shells from the flagship's first six-round salvo had smashed into *Fiume,* just thirty-eight hundred yards away, blowing her no. 4 turret completely overboard. The British flagship fired fourteen 15-inch rounds in two salvos and sixteen 6-inchers in four salvos before targeting *Zara* with four more 15-inch broadsides. *Valiant* sent her first six-gun salvo into *Fiume* as well (as well as about seventy 4.5-inch rounds) before aiming thirty-five rounds in five salvos at *Zara. Barham* initially had her guns trained on *Pola;* when *Greyhound* illuminated *Zara,* she "fired a broadside into her from 3,100 yards. Brilliant orange flashes were seen, and hits were obtained along the whole length of the ship."[52] The action caught many of the *Barham*'s crewmen by surprise. The ship's surgeon wrote,

> When we heard the sound of gunfire the Pay [paymaster] and I made for the boat deck, hoping to see what was happening. I was leading, and just as I pushed open the bulkhead door leading to the boat deck, our port after 15-inch guns opened fire. I was blasted back into the Pay's arms. . . . The padre was actually on the boat deck near the guns; he was blown off his feet and almost went over the side. It was his first exposure to gunfire let alone gunfire at night, so you can imagine what a shock he got.[53]

The shock *Barham*'s padre received was nothing compared to the one suffered by Corsi. The sudden transition from silence to dazzling searchlights, starshells, explosions, and death overwhelmed Italian reactions. The captain initially rang up full speed and ordered his ship to sheer to starboard, but loss of electrical power and damage to boilers four and five rendered this action impossible. The 8-inch guns were manned, but the massive damage and nearly immediate loss of power aboard the cruisers kept these and their 3.9-inch guns silent as well. Only a few machine guns fired in meager defiance.

Aboard the Italian destroyers the surprise was just as absolute. *Alfieri* was the target of medium batteries, probably *Barham*'s. Ensign Sansonetti related, "I opened the door of the bridge . . . when, through the glass, I suddenly saw an enormous flame a few hundred yards in front of the bows, which grew larger on the starboard side. . . . [S]uddenly I heard the sound of explosions. I ran out and saw large pieces flying through the air from the cruiser which had been hit."[54] He would recall that Captain Toscano of *Alfieri* ordered full ahead and a starboard turn, but at 2232 shells exploded aboard, disabled the engines, and jammed the rudder to starboard. Turning in a broad circle, the destroyer began to lose headway.

Gioberti and *Oriani*, the second and fourth destroyers, immediately turned starboard and maneuvered away undamaged. *Carducci* veered starboard and then returned to her old course, laying a thick smoke screen. This left her as the only ship in plain view, and 6 to 4.7-inch shells piled aboard, massacring the crew and quickly immobilizing her.

At 2231 Cunningham imagined that he saw three enemy destroyers on his port bow and that had one fired torpedoes. He ordered the battleships to execute a simultaneous ninety-degree turn to starboard to avoid this threat. However, the 10th Flotilla, which was swinging ahead and to port of the British battleships, was probably the source of this perceived danger—it certainly was not the Italian destroyers. In fact, *Warspite*'s last 6-inch salvo barely missed *Havock*.

At 2233 the battle line steadied on course 010 degrees, and by 2235 their guns had fallen silent. At 2238 Cunningham ordered his destroyers to finish off the cruisers; all units not actually engaged were to withdraw northeast. The admiral intended to prevent friendly attacks on his capital ships, but the wording of his instructions confused his subordinates. Picking up the signal, Pridham-Wippell and Mack believed it applied to them as well, and both turned northeast. Then Mack sought clarification, and Cunningham signaled him to attack first. Pridham-Wippell, however, lost any hope of finding Iachino, who at the time was thirty miles away.

The Italian destroyers were already out of sight when the three British vessels and *Stuart*, their Australian leader, set off southwest in pursuit. The destroyer action was, as the Australian history put it, "spent, mostly at high speed on constantly changing courses, in blackness lit only by the phosphorescent gleam of wash and wake; under the pallid light of star shells; among briefly seen silhouettes of ships firing streams of coloured traces . . . [amid] the crash and flash of gun fire."[55]

Fires raged uncontrolled on *Zara* and *Fiume*. *Alfieri* drifted as her crew struggled to restore power. She fired four ineffectual salvos with her bow mount at the shadows of large and small enemy ships.[56] *Carducci* was likewise immobilized; her flames attracted *Stuart* and *Havock*, which had reversed course at 2240 and headed southeast along the port side of the Italian column. *Greyhound* and *Griffin* chased southwest after *Oriani* and *Gioberti*. *Oriani*'s captain had intended to come up on the enemy's other side and attack with torpedoes. He returned fire briefly but at 2240 reported, "Hit by medium shell, probably 114-mm at the waterline, which penetrated fuel compartment 18, exploded inside and threw splinters into the forward engine room causing a rupture in the main auxiliary steam pipes on the starboard side." Following this blow *Oriani* retired south emitting black funnel smoke.[57]

Gioberti, the only Italian ship to escape undamaged, headed west at 2236 in a separation maneuver so that she could come back around to make a torpedo attack. However, *Griffin* and *Greyhound* frustrated this intention, and by 2320 *Gioberti* had fled southwest behind a smoke screen. Her captain explained, "The principal reason I did not employ guns during the night tactical action is because so many enemy units used searchlights, which, when they stayed focused directly on the destroyers, constantly concealed their shapes and canceled the flashes of their salvos past the distance which would have allowed a useful salvo."[58]

Stuart and *Havock* closed the biggest fire, preparing a torpedo attack, and then spotted what they believed was a second cruiser circling the burning ship; they launched torpedoes at this target. *Stuart* pegged this attack at 2300, and from the evidence of an explosion, she concluded that one of her eight torpedoes had struck its mark. *Alfieri* saw *Stuart* rush pass, and Ensign Sansonetti took action. "The enemy destroyer [*Stuart*] passed not more than 200 yards away. . . . I helped to aim the tubes and to fire the torpedoes . . . in such conditions and at such short range that I could not hope for hits. I did this because I felt that the *Alfieri* would soon sink. More or less in the same circumstances I fired the third torpedo at an enemy ship farther away."[59]

The Australian aimed a few rounds at *Fiume* and then, thinking *Zara* might be moving off, she switched fire toward her. Suddenly at 2308 a shape emerged from the dark. *Stuart* swerved as the two ships passed 150 yards apart, exchanging ineffectual gunfire. British accounts identify this ship as *Carducci*, but as she was dead in the water it must have been *Havock*. *Stuart* then disappeared to attack a burning cruiser. *Havock*, meanwhile, found *Alfieri* and launched four torpedoes from very close range, claiming one hit at 2315. The British destroyer then blazed away, circling so close that Italian survivors later said they could see her captain on the bridge giving orders and smoking a cigarette as their ship replied with its machine guns.[60] At 2330 *Alfieri* sank. The boats and rafts were full of holes, and 211 of her men died. *Carducci* went under at 2345. She lost 169 men. *Fiume* capsized and sank at 2315 with the loss of 812 men.

Pola helplessly witnessed the slaughter. Expecting at any moment to become a target, her captain ordered sea cocks opened; some of the crew began to abandon ship, but as she settled slowly and the water was cold, many returned aboard. At 0010 *Havock* sighted the cruiser's silhouette. She fired a few rounds and then withdrew to the northeast to radio that she had made contact "with a ship of the *Littorio* class . . . undamaged and stopped."[61] Mack's destroyers had sailed nearly sixty miles to the west-northwest. When he received *Havock's* report at 0030 Mack immediately came about. However, he missed *Havock's* 0110 correction that it was an 8-inch cruiser, not a battleship, until twenty-four minutes later. By that time there was no hope of engaging *Vittorio Veneto* before daylight.

Mack's seven destroyers arrived in the battle zone and steered through a sea filled with "boats, rafts, and swimming men" toward a fire glowing on the horizon—and thus found *Zara*. *Jervis* fired three torpedoes at the drifting wreck. There was a giant explosion, and the cruiser vanished at 0240, with the loss of 783 men.[62]

Meanwhile, from 0140, *Havock, Griffin,* and *Greyhound* had been flocking around *Pola* (*Stuart* had disappeared, apparently chasing "ghost" sightings). Only two miles from *Zara's* sinking point, "she appeared to be undamaged and lay wallowing in a slight swell."[63] However, these destroyers had expended their torpedoes. *Jervis* came alongside at 0325 and rescued 257 crewmen. Then she stood off and fired one torpedo; *Nubian* launched another. At 0403 *Pola* blew up and sank. She had lost 328 men.

Vittorio Veneto was forty miles away when the pyrotechnics erupted astern. Iachino queried the 1st Division but got no response. He reached Taranto on 29 March. If Cunningham had pursued aggressively, he could have instigated a surface action that day, but the British admiral declined to venture so deep into enemy airspace.

Italian historians have bitterly noted that Iachino's force received barely any of the air support it was promised; they list the series of unlikely circumstances and coincidences that led to the 1st Division's destruction.[64] However, every operation has risk, and none go as planned. The real question is: What impact did the Battle of Cape Matapan have?

Matapan was Italy's greatest defeat at sea, subtracting from its order of battle a cruiser division, but the battle was hardly decisive. The British lost two cruisers in the same period: *York* fell victim to explosive motor boats that penetrated

Suda Bay on 26 March in X MAS's first success, while the submarine *Ambra* torpedoed *Bonaventure* on 31 March. Italian convoys departed for Africa on 1, 2, 8, 9, and 10 April, losing only one merchantman. Force H sailed to within four hundred miles of Malta twice in April to fly off Hurricanes. Italian cruisers sortied on several occasions to thicken the mine barrages off Cape Bon. In other words, the war continued much as before, and by July Italy had three battleships back in action, more than offsetting the loss of three cruisers.

The fact that the Italians had sortied so far to the east established a threat potential that forced the British to keep their battleships ready to face another such sortie during the operations off Greece and Crete, in spite of postwar assessments that Matapan "certainly eliminated the possibility of surface ship interference with the current troop movements to Greece."[65]

Iachino wrote that the battle had "the consequence of limiting for some time our operational activities, not for the serious moral effect of the losses, as the British believed, but because the operation revealed our inferiority in effective aero-naval cooperation and the backwardness of our night battle technology." In fact, it shocked the Regia Marina's leadership that even its most modern battleship seemingly could not conduct an offensive operation with reasonable hope for success. This seemed to vindicate the fleet-in-being strategy and provided a cautionary lesson in the value of German cooperation, but also in the danger of adopting German ideas of offensive naval warfare. "According to the government's orders, I and our naval forces were not to venture outside land fighter aircraft range, and were to avoid night clashes until we were also equipped with radar."[66] The Duce had already ordered the oft-delayed conversion of the liner *Roma* into an aircraft carrier. The navy also began a serious effort to equip its ships with radar. One of the three prototypes went into testing in April. The war was ten months old. The Italian government was finally realizing it might continue for a long time.

6

The Red Sea

1940–41

Long months of torture in the blazing heat and incredible humidity of Massawa had left us apathetic and drained of hope of escape.

—Edward Ellsberg, *No Banners No Bugles*

Italy's East African possessions, particularly its Red Sea base at Massawa, were situated strategically astride the sea route to Suez. With the Sicilian Channel closed to normal transit, Italy theoretically possessed the ability to block maritime access to Egypt.

Between 1935 and 1940 Italy's planners envisioned the construction of an oceanic fleet that, in its most realistic version, would have consisted of two cruisers, eight destroyers, and twelve submarines, all fitted for tropical service and supported by a network of bases along Italian Somaliland's Indian Ocean coast.[1] However, this *Flotta d'evasione* proved more than Rome could afford. Thus, Rear Admiral Carlo Balsamo, who commanded Italy's East African naval squadron, deployed eight modern submarines, seven middle-aged destroyers, two old torpedo boats, five World War I–era MAS boats, and a large colonial sloop, all concentrated at Massawa. In Supermarina's view, the squadron's limited stocks of fuel and ammunition restricted its role to one of survival and sea denial, relying mainly upon the submarines, for the duration of a six-month war. (See map 6.1.)

Great Britain intercepted Italy's 19 May orders for the "immediate and secret mobilization of the army and air force in east Africa," whereupon the Royal Navy reinforced its Rea Sea Squadron, which consisted of the Dominion light cruisers *Leander* and *Hobart*, the old antiaircraft cruiser *Carlisle*, three sloops, and four ships of the 28th Destroyer Flotilla.[2] This force was tasked with preventing

Italian reinforcements, engaging the Massawa squadron, blockading the coast of
Italian Somaliland, and protecting the shipping lanes to Suez and Aden.[3]

On 10 June Italy's Red Sea submarines occupied, or were on their way to,
their patrol stations, but their forewarned enemy had already halted all mercantile
shipping to the Red Sea on 24 May. They enjoyed only one success, when *Galilei*
sank the Norwegian tanker *James Stove* (8,215 GRT) on 16 June.[4] In exchange the
Italians lost four boats. Crew poisoning caused by the release of methyl chloride,
used as a cheap substitute for freon in the air-conditioning system (a defect that
inadequate testing and training under realistic battle conditions failed to reveal),

Map 6.1   The Red Sea, 1940–1941

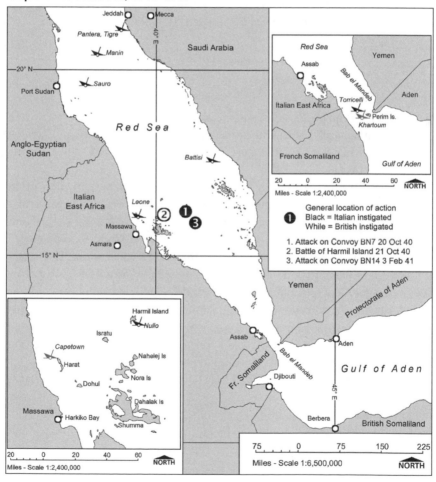

led to the stranding and wrecking of *Macallé* on 15 June. *Galilei* attempted to fight it out on the surface with the 650-ton trawler *Moonstone* on 19 June, but two well-aimed shells from the auxiliary's 4-inch gun killed *Galilei*'s captain and all the officers except a midshipman. A British boarding party captured the submarine and a set of operational orders. These enabled the sloop *Falmouth* to track down and sink *Galvani* in the Persian Gulf on 24 June. The same intelligence led to the interception of *Torricelli*, the fourth Red Sea submarine lost in the war's first fortnight.

On 14 June *Torricelli* sailed to relieve *Ferraris* after she too suffered methyl chloride poisoning off Djibouti. On 21 June British warships attacked and damaged *Torricelli*, forcing her to abort her mission and begin the long trip back to Massawa. The destroyers *Kandahar*, *Kingston*, and *Khartoum*, along with sloops *Shoreham* and *Indus*, intercepted *Torricelli* north of Perim Island, at the entrance to the Red Sea, at 0418 on 23 June. The Italian submarine, initially seeing only one sloop, and considering her damage and the clear waters that made a submerged boat easy to track, elected to run on the surface for the Italian shore batteries at Assab. In the ensuring fight, *Torricelli*, firing her deck gun, almost hit *Shoreham*, which reported "two shells falling close ahead."[5] Then the three destroyers appeared and closed rapidly.

Kingston opened fire with her forward guns at 0536. *Torricelli*, trailing a wide ribbon of oil, launched four torpedoes back at the destroyer, but their wakes were clearly visible in the calm sea and *Kingston* easily evaded. At first the British tried to clear the submarine's decks, to permit a boarding attempt. However, *Kingston*'s 40-mm shells struck one of her own antennas and wounded eight crewmen. After that the destroyers shot to sink, but they had to expend nearly seven hundred 4.7-inch rounds before a shell finally wrecked *Torricelli*'s forward bow planes at 0605 and flooded the torpedo room. The submarine sank at 0624.

After rescue operations *Khartoum*, with prisoners embarked, set course for Perim while the other ships headed for Aden to refuel. At 1150 a torpedo in *Khartoum*'s aft quintuple mount suddenly exploded, igniting a huge fire in the after lobby. The crew could not control the conflagration, and *Khartoum* ran for Perim Harbor, seven miles distant. There her men (and the prisoners) abandoned ship, swimming for their lives. At 1245, no. 3 magazine blew up, rendering the destroyer a total loss.[6]

Red Sea Convoys

The first of the Red Sea convoys, collectively the BN/BS series, consisting of nine ships including six tankers, gathered in the Gulf of Aden on 2 July. Thereafter these convoys sailed up and down the Red Sea on a regular schedule. Admiral Balsamo attempted to attack this traffic, but the war's opening months held little but frustration for his destroyers. On six occasions in July, August, and September, they sortied at night in response to aerial reports of Allied vessels but in every case failed to make contact. Aircraft and the surviving submarines did little better. *Guglielomotti* torpedoed the Greek tanker *Atlas* (4,008 GRT) from Convoy BN4 on 6 September 1940, while high-level bombing attacks damaged the steamship *Bhima* (5,280 GRT) from BN5, which four Italian destroyers had failed to locate, on 20 September.

As Italian warships burned their oil reserves on unsuccessful sorties, the Allied Red Sea Squadron grew stronger, deploying by the end of August four light cruisers, three destroyers, and eight sloops. Other warships passed through on their way to and from the Mediterranean. In September, as traffic volume swelled, the Mediterranean Fleet lent the newly arrived antiaircraft cruiser *Coventry*, which alternated with *Carlisle* along the Aden–Suez route to provide extra protection against air attacks.

By October the Italian ships faced mechanical breakdowns, the increasing exhaustion of crews by the extreme climate, and a growing shortage of fuel. Nonetheless, they continued to sail. On the evening of 20 October, four destroyers weighed anchor to search for BN7, which aerial reconnaissance had spotted sailing north. The plan called for the slower and more heavily armed *Pantera* and *Leone* to distract the escort while *Sauro* and *Nullo* slipped in to send a spread of torpedoes toward the merchant ships.

Table 6.1   Attack on Convoy BN7 and Battle of Harmil Island, 20–21 October 1940, 2320–0640

Conditions: Bright moon, calm sea	
Allied ships—	BN7 Escort (Captain H. E. Horan): CL: *Leander* (NZ) (F); DD: *Kimberley*[D2]; DS: *Auckland* (NZ), *Indus* (IN), *Yarra* (AU); MS: *Derby, Huntley*
	BN7: thirty-two merchant ships and tankers
Italian ships—	
	Section I (Commander Moretti degli Adimari): DD: *Sauro* (F), *Nullo*[Sunk]
	Section II (Commander Paolo Aloisi): DD: *Pantera* (F), *Leone*

The convoy timed its progress to pass Massawa around midnight. The moon was bright, but haze reduced visibility toward the African coast. At 2115 the Italian sections separated, and at 2321 *Pantera* detected smoke off her starboard bow. She reported the contact to *Sauro* and began maneuvering at twenty-two knots to position the low-hanging moon behind the contact. (See table 6.1.)

BN7 was thirty-five miles north-northwest of Jabal-al-Tair Island (itself 110 miles east-northeast of Massawa) when *Yarra*, zigzagging in company with *Auckland*, sighted Captain Aloisi's ships ahead. *Yarra* challenged and *Pantera* replied with a pair of torpedoes at 2331 and then another pair at 2334, at ranges fifty-five and sixty-five hundred yards, respectively. Shooting over *Yarra*, she "lobbed a few shells" into the convoy. According to a wartime British account, "a lifeboat in the commodore's ship was damaged by splinters, but otherwise no harm was done." *Leone*, which trailed *Pantera* by 875 yards, never fixed a target and thus did not fire torpedoes.[7]

Yarra saw the torpedo flashes from broad on her port bow and turned toward the enemy. Both sloops opened fire as torpedoes boiled past, narrowly missing. The Italian ships altered away, shooting with their aft mounts. Aloisi reported explosions and claimed two torpedo hits, but in fact, his weapons missed. *Kimberley* was trailing the convoy. She rang up thirty knots and steered northwest to close the action. *Leander*, sailing on the convoy's port beam, headed southwest, while the sloops and minesweepers stayed with the merchantmen. *Pantera* and *Leone*, considering their mission successfully accomplished, continued west-southwest and broke contact. They eventually returned to Massawa via the south channel.

After the gunfire died away, Captain Horan steered *Leander* northwest to cover Harmil Channel believing the enemy ships had retired in that direction.

Upon receiving *Pantera*'s report, *Sauro* and *Nullo* had turned to clear the area while the first group attacked and to put themselves in a favorable position relative to the moon. This involved a ninety-degree port turn at 0016 on 21 October and another at 0050. The section then headed southeast, but for nearly an hour it encountered nothing. Finally, at 0148, *Leander* and another ship hove into view. *Sauro* snapped off a single torpedo at the cruiser (another misfired). In response *Leander* lofted star shell, and then ten broadsides flashed from her main batteries in two minutes before she lost sight of the target. Italian accounts say this engagement occurred at sixteen hundred yards, while *Leander*'s report stated the enemy was more than eight thousand yards away.[8]

Sauro turned south by southwest and at 0207 attempted another torpedo attack against the convoy. One weapon misfired, and although *Sauro* claimed a hit with the other, it missed. At the same time *Nullo* detected flashes that she believed came from an enemy torpedo launch, and within minutes a lookout shouted that wakes were streaking toward the Italian destroyer's bow. At 0212 *Sauro* turned north and disengaged, eventually circling behind the British and taking the south channel to Massawa. *Nullo*'s captain, however, put his helm over even harder, "because it was [his] intention to attack, being still in an opportune position to launch against the convoy, before taking station in formation."[9] However, the rudder jammed for several minutes, causing *Nullo* to circle and lose contact with *Sauro*.

At 0220 *Leander*'s spotlights fastened onto "a vessel painted light grey proceeding from left to right"—in fact, *Nullo* steaming north. The cruiser engaged from forty-six hundred yards off the Italian's starboard bow. *Nullo* returned fire, first against "destroyers" spotted astern (probably *Auckland*) and then at *Leander*. The ships dueled for about ten minutes. The Italian enjoyed one advantage: she employed flashless powder (the British noted only two enemy salvos), whereas British muzzles flared brightly with each discharge. *Leander* fired eight blind salvos ("little could be seen of their effect"), but several rounds nonetheless hit home, damaging *Nullo*'s gyrocompass and gunnery director. With this the Italian destroyer abandoned her attack attempt and turned west-northwest running for Harmil Channel at thirty knots. In the two actions *Leander* fired 129 6-inch rounds.[10]

Guessing *Nullo*'s intention, the cruiser pursued in the correct direction. At 0300 *Kimberley* joined, and at 0305 *Leander* turned back, "appreciating that the enemy was drawing away from her at the rate of seven knots and that the convoy might be attacked."[11] *Kimberley* continued, hoping to intercept.

The British destroyer arrived off Harmil Island before dawn. At 0540 her lookouts reported a shape to the south-southeast, and she closed to investigate. *Nullo*'s lookouts likewise reported a contact. The sharp angle of approach made it impossible to be certain, but the Italian captain assumed it was *Sauro*, especially when it seemed to signal the Harmil Island station. He was more "worried about the shallows scattered around the mouth of the northeast passage and above all of the 3.7 meter sandbank immediately north of his estimated 0500 position."[12]

At 0553 the British destroyer opened fire from 12,400 yards. Surprised, *Nullo* took four minutes to reply and at 0605 swung sharply from a northwest heading to a south-by-southwest course. By 0611 the range was down to 10,300 yards. Due to her prior damage, *Nullo*'s gunners fired over open sights, while human chains passed shells up from the magazine. Harmil Island's battery of four 4.7-inch guns joined the action at 0615 from eighteen thousand yards. At the same time, with the range now eighty-five hundred yards, *Kimberley* turned south, emitting black funnel smoke, causing *Nullo*'s gunners to think they had scored a hit.[13]

At 0620 *Nullo* scraped a reef, opening her hull to flooding and damaging a screw. Then, while the ship was setting course to round Harmil Island, a shell exploded in the forward engine room and a second slammed into the aft engine room. *Nullo* skewed sharply to the left and lost all power; splinters swept the upper works. The captain ordered his men to prepare to abandon ship while he angled the ship toward Harmil in an attempt to run it aground. The aft mount continued in action until the heel became excessive.

Having expended 115 salvoes, *Kimberley* launched a torpedo to dispatch her adversary; it missed, so she closed range and uncorked another. The second torpedo slammed into *Nullo* at 0635 and blasted her in two. Meanwhile, the Harmil battery finally found the range, and a shell struck *Kimberley*'s engine room, wounding three men. Splinters cut the steam pipes; the British destroyer lost power and came to a halt.

Kimberley's men frantically patched the damage while the drifting ship's guns remained in action, shooting forty-five rounds of HE from no. 3 mount, and achieving some hits that wounded four of the shore battery's crew. After a few long minutes, the destroyer restored partial power and pulled away at fifteen knots. The shore battery fired its final shots at 0645, when the range had opened to nineteen thousand yards. During the battle Kimberley expended 596 SAP and 97 HE rounds.

After she was clear the destroyer lost steam pressure again. Finally *Leander* arrived and towed *Kimberley* to Port Sudan. *Nullo* remained above water; her guns ended up equipping a shore battery. On 21 October three Blenheims reported destroying a wreck east of Harmil Island. This led the British to conclude two enemy ships had been involved in the action.

The Aden command faulted the escort (except for *Kimberley*) for demonstrating a lack of aggressiveness, although deserting the convoy to chase unknown numbers of enemy destroyers through a murky night does not in retrospect seem the best course of action either. The Italian ships, although outnumbered, delivered two hit-and-run torpedo attacks, according to their plan. However, while using widely separated divisions increased the probability of finding the enemy, a natural consideration given the history of failed interception attempts, it also guaranteed that the Italian forces would lack the punch to take on the escort and deliver a meaningful attack. In fact, the first Italian attack seemed more formulaic than a serious attempt to cause damage.

The Italian East African squadron conducted another (fruitless) sortie on 3 December 1940. It aborted a mission planned for early January after British aircraft damaged *Manin,* one of the participants, and on 24 January it sortied again, without results. On the night of 2 February 1941, however, three destroyers departed Massawa and deployed in a rake formation to search for a large convoy known to be at sea. (See table 6.2.)

Table 6.2   Attack on Convoy BN14, 3 February 1941

Conditions: n/a	
Allied ships—	Convoy Escort: CL: *Caledon;* DD: *Kingston;* DS: *Indus* (IN), *Shoreham*
	Convoy BN14: thirty-nine freighters
Italian ships—	DD: *Pantera, Tigre, Sauro*

Sauro spotted the enemy, made a sighting report, and immediately maneuvered to attack. She launched three torpedoes at a group of steamships and then, a minute later, at another dimly seen target marked by a large cloud of smoke. She then turned away at speed. Her two sisters did not receive the report, but ten minutes later *Pantera* stumbled across the enemy and also fired torpedoes. The Italians heard explosions and later claimed "probable" hits on two freighters. *Tigre* never made contact.

On her way to Massawa's south channel, *Sauro* encountered *Kingston.* Out of torpedoes, the Italian retreated at full speed. Concerned that the British were attempting another ambush, the squadron concentrated on *Sauro* and radioed for air support at dawn. In the event, the three destroyers safely made port. The Italian East African press reported two freighters as probably hit, but despite this claim, all torpedoes missed.

By April 1941 Imperial spearheads were probing Massawa's defensive perimeter. With Supermarina's approval, Rear Admiral Mario Bonetti, Balsamo's replacement from December 1940, ordered a last grand gesture—an attack by the three largest destroyers (*Leone, Pantera,* and *Tigre*) against Port Suez, five hundred miles north, and a concurrent raid by the smaller destroyers *Battisti, Manin,* and *Sauro* against Port Sudan. The British Middle Eastern command had considered such an attack possible and had reinforced Port Suez with two J-class destroyers and sent *Eagle's* experienced air group south to Port Sudan, while the carrier waited for mines to be swept from the Suez Canal so she could proceed south.

The Italian venture ran into problems early when *Leone* struck an uncharted rock forty-five miles out of Massawa. Flooding and fires in her engine room forced her crew to abandon ship. Her two companions returned to port, as the rescue operation left insufficient time for them to continue the mission.

On the afternoon of 2 April the remaining Italian destroyers sailed once again, this time against Port Sudan, 265 miles north. British aircraft attacked them about two hours out of port but caused no damage. Then *Battisti* suffered engine problems and scuttled herself on the Arabian coast. The other four continued at top speed through the night and by dawn were thirty miles short of their objective. However, *Eagle*'s Swordfish squadrons intervened, sinking *Sauro* at 0715. The other ships headed for the opposite shore, under attack as they went. Bombs crippled *Manin* at 0845. She eventually capsized and sank about a hundred miles northeast of Port Sudan. *Pantera* and *Tigre* made it to the Arabian coast and were scuttled there.

Caught off guard by the Italian sortie, British warships rushed north. At 1700 *Kingston* found *Pantera*'s and *Tigre*'s wrecks. The two ships had already been worked over by Wellesley bombers, but *Kingston* shelled *Pantera*'s hulk and then torpedoed it, just to be sure.

The biggest Italian naval success in the Red Sea was a Parthian shot that occurred on 8 April, with Massawa's defenses breached and ships scuttling themselves on all sides. *MAS213*, a World War I relic no longer capable of even fifteen knots, ambushed the old light cruiser *Capetown*, which was escorting minesweepers north of the port, and scored a torpedo hit from just over three hundred yards. After spending a year in repair, the cruiser sat out the rest of the war as an accommodation ship.

This was the Italian navy's final blow in East Africa. The capture of Massawa relieved Great Britain of the need to convoy the entire length of the Red Sea and released valuable escorts for other duties. On 10 June an Indian battalion captured Assab, Italy's last Red Sea outpost, eliminating a pair of improvised torpedo boats. After that President Franklin D. Roosevelt declared the narrow sea a nonwar zone, permitting the entry of American shipping.

However, German aircraft continued to exert a distant influence over the Red Sea, by mining the Suez Canal and attacking shipping that accumulated to the south of the canal. As late at 18 September Admiral Cunningham complained to Admiral Pound that "the Red Sea position is unsatisfactory . . . about 5 of 6 ships attacked, one sunk [*Steel Seafarer* (6,000 GRT)] and two damaged. . . . The imminent arrival at Suez of the monster liners is giving me much anxiety. They are crammed with men and we can't afford to have them hit up."[14] In October 1941 the Suez Escort Force still tied up four light cruisers, two fleet destroyers, two Hunt-class destroyers, and two sloops. The British maintained a blockade off French Somaliland until December 1942.

7

A Close-Run Thing

Spring 1941

This great battle for Egypt is what the Duke of Wellington called "A close-run Thing."

—Winston Churchill, letter to Admiral Cunningham
dated 1 May 1941

At the start of April 1941, flush from their victory at Matapan, the British surveyed their position in North Africa, the Middle East, and the Balkans with satisfaction. Imperial forces were completing the conquest of Italian East Africa, a royal coup in Yugoslavia had installed an anti-German government, and the Greeks seemed firmly ensconced in Albania. German airpower had proved troublesome to the Mediterranean Fleet, but not decisively so. Admiral Cunningham considered that the major area of concern "overshadowing everything else" was the position in Cyrenaica.[1]

On 24 March 1941 Axis forces burst forth from El Agheila and swiftly erased Britain's stunning conquests, taking Benghazi on 4 April and steamrolling to the Egyptian frontier two weeks later. A stream of men and equipment pouring into Tripoli enabled this turnabout. From October 1940 to January 1941 the Regia Marina landed a monthly average of 49,435 tons of materiel and 6,981 men; only 0.9 percent of the men and 3.9 percent of the materiel failed to arrive. From February through June 1941 the monthly averages rose to 89,563 tons and 17,912 men, respectively, with 5.1 percent of the men and 6.6 percent of the materiel lost en route.[2] From this traffic the British sank four merchantmen in January, three in February, and another four in March. (See map 7.1.)

With Imperial troops in retreat, choking the Libyan supply line became critically important; under pressure from London, Cunningham reluctantly ordered four destroyers under the command of the 14th Destroyer Flotilla's skilled

Captain Mack to Malta to supplement the submarines and aircraft already operating there.[3] These ships arrived on 11 April, the same day Axis troops encircled Tobruk and one day before Belgrade surrendered to the German army. Coincidentally, April was also the date by which Cunningham had proposed back in August 1940 to have Malta functioning as an offensive base for warships, although only about two-thirds of the tonnage he had estimated necessary had been delivered.

Map 7.1   Convoy Routes, April–May 1941

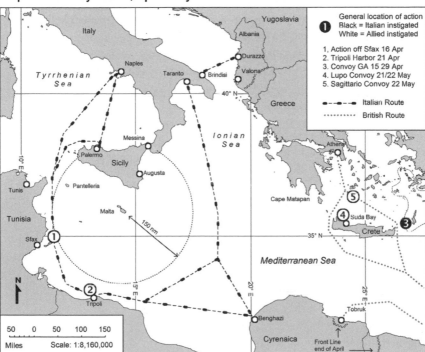

Mack's first sorties, on the nights of 11 and 12 April, were unproductive. On 13 April a convoy of three troopships and two munitions ships departed Naples for Tripoli, escorted by the 8th Destroyer Squadron, following the customary route west of Sicily, past Cape Bon, and along the Kerkenah Banks. A Malta-based Maryland sighted the convoy on the morning of 15 April, and Mack's destroyers weighed anchor that evening.

The convoy had experienced a rough passage. Heavy winds scattered the ships, and it had fallen four hours behind schedule by the time it regrouped off

Cape Bon at 2200 on 15 April. Captain Pietro De Cristofaro, the escort commander, knew aircraft were shadowing his force through cloudy skies, although
he had no idea the British had based a surface force at Malta. (See table 7.1.)

Table 7.1   Action off Sfax, 16 April 1941, 0220–0400

Conditions: Fresh NW breeze; low clouds and rain; low, short swells	
British ships—	14th Destroyer Flotilla (Captain P. J. Mack): *Jervis*[D1] (F), *Janus*[D1], *Nubian*[D1], *Mohawk*[Sunk]
Italian ships—	8th Destroyer Squadron (Captain Pietro De Cristofaro): *Tarigo*[Sunk] (F), *Baleno*[Sunk], *Lampo*[D4]
	Convoy: *Adana*[Sunk] (GE 4,205 GRT), *Arta*[Sunk] (GE 2,452 GRT), *Aegina*[Sunk] (GE 2,447 GRT), *Iserlohn*[Sunk] (GE 3,704 GRT), *Sabaudia*[Sunk] (1,590 GRT)

After arriving at a point they estimated was well ahead of their target, the
British swept northwest but saw nothing. In fact the convoy was farther inshore
than expected and the destroyers passed it to port at 0145. At 0155, acting on a
hunch, Mack turned south-southwest, and just three minutes later a sharp-eyed
lookout aboard the flagship sighted shadows six miles ahead. The wind was
gusting at forty miles per hour, and the air was heavy with dust blowing off the
continent. As Mack maneuvered for twenty minutes to position the newly risen
quarter moon behind the Axis ships, Italian and German lookouts saw nothing of the danger approaching them from astern. When he gave the order to
open fire at 0220, *Jervis*, now heading southeast, was a mere twenty-four hundred yards off the destroyer *Baleno*'s starboard quarter.

The action that followed was typically confused.[4] *Jervis*'s initial salvo missed
Baleno, but *Janus* was on target and her 50-pound shells sliced through the
Italian destroyer's bridge, slaughtering her officers and the captain, who had
just ordered his ship to make smoke. Then *Jervis* found the range, and within
five minutes *Baleno*, hit repeatedly in the engine rooms, was adrift, burning
from stem to stern. There was confusion about the source of this attack, but De
Cristofaro saw the flat trajectory of tracers and brought *Tarigo* around from her
position at the convoy's head.

The rear British destroyers, *Nubian* and *Mohawk*, targeted *Sabaudia*, the convoy's tail-end ship. *Nubian*'s captain wrote: "This vessel was hit about third salvo,
there was an explosion and a large fire broke out aft."[5] As the two Tribal-class
destroyers pushed up the convoy's starboard side, *Nubian* engaged *Iserlohn* and

Aegina, claiming hits on both, while *Mohawk* checked fire, as all targets seemed heavily engaged. Meanwhile the two Js mixed with the merchantmen at ranges from fifty to two thousand yards; in fact, *Jervis* barely avoided being rammed. They fired so rapidly that empty shell casings piled up around the mounts and interfered with the working of the guns.[6] *Iserlohn* blazed up, and *Janus* launched three torpedoes toward *Sabaudia, Iserlohn,* and *Aegina,* which had clustered together.

At 0235 *Nubian* spotted *Tarigo* speeding north. De Cristofaro likewise saw the outline of a warship emerge from the smoke. When it opened fire he hesitated, thinking it might be *Baleno.* Then a lookout shouted that it was an English cruiser. *Nubian* and *Tarigo* traded salvos from a thousand yards. Metal shards cut through both vessels. One severed De Cristofaro's leg, and he bled to death at his post.

Tarigo's passage attracted the fire of the other British destroyers. *Jervis* hit the Italian's bridge, sparking a blaze amidships. *Janus* could not train her mounts fast enough to track the rapidly moving target; she rushed two torpedoes into the water, but they missed astern. *Tarigo* likewise shot in haste, and her "tracer could be seen going high and wide."[7] Then at 0240 *Jervis* blasted *Tarigo* with a torpedo. *Nubian* and *Mohawk* passed, and *Mohawk's* captain, Commander J. W. Eaton, considered the Italian flagship neutralized.

At 0245 *Nubian* crossed *Arta's* bow at the convoy's head. As *Mohawk* followed *Arta* attempted to ram, forcing *Mohawk* to veer hard to starboard. Suddenly a torpedo walloped *Mohawk* on the starboard side abreast the Y (farthest aft) mount, blowing away the ship's aft section but leaving her propellers and rudder intact. Eaton, uncertain where the blow had originated, engaged *Arta* with his forward mounts. In fact, an enterprising ensign aboard *Tarigo* had manually aimed and fired the torpedo just a minute before.

Mack heard about *Mohawk's* plight at 0252, and he turned toward the stricken ship, ordering her to burn recognition lights. Meanwhile *Janus,* cutting through the convoy at high speed, torpedoed *Sabaudia* and touched off the unfortunate ship's cargo of munitions. *Jervis,* fifteen hundred yards away, "was showered with pieces of ammunition, etc. . . . [T]he sea around appeared as a boiling cauldron."[8] At 0253 the same ensign aimed another torpedo at *Mohawk;* it hit and exploded, and the large British destroyer began to settle.

Lampo, located on the convoy's far side, was slow to enter action. First encountering *Nubian, Lampo* fired her guns and launched three torpedoes. *Nubian's* counterblast staggered the Italian, heavily damaging her stern mount and steering mechanism. With many dead and wounded, *Lampo* retreated. She eventually grounded on Kerkenah Bank to keep from foundering.[9] After dispatching *Lampo, Nubian* chased down *Adana,* which was fleeing southeast, and set her ablaze. *Adana* and *Arta* eventually joined *Lampo* on the banks. *Baleno* finally capsized on the morning of 17 April.

Janus found *Tarigo* and pumped rapid salvos into the helpless ship for ten minutes before moving on. However, the Italian refused to sink and at 0311 launched a torpedo at *Jervis*, which passed under the British ship's bridge. *Jervis* pummeled *Tarigo* until her guns no longer bore and then ordered *Janus* to return and sink her, which she did.

The three surviving British destroyers "suffered no casualties and slight damage from splinters."[10] They lingered for an hour, rescuing all but forty-one of *Mohawk*'s men. Supermarina learned of the disaster the next day and mounted a large rescue effort, but the Axis still lost 1,700 men, 300 vehicles, and 3,500 tons of supplies.

Convoys continued despite this debacle, however. Two arrived in Tripoli without loss four days later, and Supermarina was able to regard the destruction of the *Tarigo* convoy as an anomaly based upon lucky air reconnaissance.

Tripoli Harbor

The fact that it had taken the Royal Navy ten months to intercept successfully an African convoy with surface warships demonstrated the difficulty of the task. Churchill calculated that the flow of supplies could be more easily cut if there was no place to unload them; via the First Sea Lord, he ordered the Mediterranean Fleet to use *Barham* and an old C-class cruiser to conduct a close-range bombardment of Tripoli and then scuttle themselves to block the port. This plan horrified Admiral Cunningham, who protested, "I am of the opinion that if these men [aboard *Barham* and *Caledon*] are sent into this operation which must involve certain capture and heavy casualties without knowing what they are in for, the whole confidence of the personnel of the fleet in the higher command . . . will be seriously jeopardized if not entirely lost."[11] Finally London backed down, and as a compromise, Cunningham reluctantly agreed to bombard the port instead.

Elements of the Mediterranean Fleet departed Alexandria on 18 April, combining the bombardment with a supply operation to Malta. Mack's flotilla left Malta on 20 April to shepherd four empty freighters partway back to Alexandria. After completing these movements the fleet turned south. Against expectations, Italian aircraft failed to spot the British during their approach. *Formidable*, with *Orion*, *Perth*, *Ajax*, and four destroyers, stood by while the battleships moved in. The port, which occupied an area roughly one mile square, was crowded that morning with a dozen freighters and more than a hundred small vessels like minesweepers, barges, tugs, and water tankers. Six warships were also present. (See table 7.2.)

Table 7.2 Tripoli Harbor, 21 April 1941, 0502–0545

Conditions: Calm sea, poor visibility	
British ships—	1st Battle Squadron (Admiral A. B. C. Cunningham): BB: *Warspite, Barham, Valiant*[D1]; CL: *Gloucester*
	14th Destroyer Flotilla (Captain P. J. Mack): *Jervis* (F), *Janus*[D1], *Juno, Jaguar, Hotspur, Havock, Hero, Hasty, Hereward*
Italian ships—	11th Destroyer Squadron (Captain Luciano Bigi): *Aviere*[D1], *Camicia Nera, Geniere*[D2]
	TB: *Partenope*[D1], *Calliope, Orione*

The submarine *Truant* acted as a marker for the battleships so they would know their exact position. However, she was several thousand yards east of her intended location, causing the bombardment to be conducted at a closer range than planned. At 0440 the British warships "circled the *Truant* in line ahead just like rounding a buoy." Cunningham remembered, "The silence was only broken by the rippling sound of our bow waves, the wheeze of air pumps, and the muffled twitter of a boatswain's pipe on the *Warspite*'s messdeck."[12] *Hotspur, Havock, Hero,* and *Hasty* led by two thousand yards, sweeping for mines; then came *Warspite, Valiant, Barham,* and *Gloucester,* while *Juno* and *Jaguar* screened the heavy ships to starboard and *Jervis, Janus,* and *Hereward* screened to port. At 0502 *Warspite* opened fire from 12,400 yards.

The fleet steamed east, shooting steadily, until 0524. The first impacts raised "a vast cloud of dust and smoke [which] thickened by shell bursts, made it difficult for the spotting aircraft and practically impossible for the ships to observe the fall of shot."[13] The British were off target, and the Italian shore batteries, two army-manned positions with eight formerly Austro-Hungarian 7.5-inch/39 guns, held fire so as not to provide a point of aim. However, when the column simultaneously came about to the west, putting *Gloucester* in the lead, accuracy improved, and the batteries and destroyers in the harbor engaged the British gun flashes. The battleships were beyond range, but shells straddled *Hereward,* and splinters lightly damaged *Janus.*

At 0545 after expending 478 15-inch, 1,500 6-inch, and 4.7-inch rounds, the British battle line ceased fire and continued west at maximum speed. These 530 tons of ordinance sank the freighters *Assiria* (2,704 GRT) and *Marocchino* (1,524

GRT), as well as the customs boat *Cicconetti* (of sixty tons). Splinters damaged the steamship *Sabbia* (5,788 GRT). One of *Gloucester*'s shells hit *Geniere*'s funnel, and pieces from this blast damaged *Aviere*. Fragments from a different round sprayed *Partenope* and killed her captain. Many of the heavy shells fell in the city, demolishing a dirigible hangar at the airport. The docks were moderately damaged, but the convoy of four steamers that had arrived the day before nonetheless finished unloading that afternoon. An air attack delivered an hour before the bombardment was ineffective.

This blow caught Italy in the process of expanding the minefields protecting Tripoli; in fact, two existing fields had been cleared in mid-April because they interfered with the process of sowing the new barrage. *Valiant* did touch a mine during the operation and was slightly damaged.[14] The new fields, after completion, sank on 18 August 1941 the British submarine *P32*, the wreck of which supplied Regia Marina code breakers with useful material. Then, in December 1941, Force K ran onto the field, losing one cruiser and one destroyer sunk and two cruisers damaged.[15]

British surface forces from Malta continued to probe for Axis convoys but without much success. On the night of 23 April Mack's flotilla sailed after air reconnaissance reported five transports. At 0024 on 24 April *Juno* found the armed motor ship *Egeo* (3,311 tons, two 4.7-inch/45 guns, and fifteen knots) sailing independently and, after a prolonged engagement, finally torpedoed and sank the outgunned auxiliary. The convoy saw the flash of gunfire on the southern horizon and turned away. Mack searched for but failed to find the greater prize.

On 28 April the 5th Destroyer Flotilla, under Captain Lord Louis Mountbatten, replaced Mack's 14th Flotilla. *Gloucester* stayed in Malta to provide support, because the Italians had begun to supplement their escorts with pairs of light cruisers. Then, on 2 May while entering Valletta's Grand Harbor, *Jersey* detonated a German air-dropped magnetic mine and sank, blocking the narrow entrance channel. This closed the port for a week while the wreck was blasted away. Stranded outside, *Gloucester, Kipling,* and *Kashmir* proceeded to Gibraltar instead of Alexandria, unwittingly avoiding an encounter with the Italian cruiser *Abruzzi* and a destroyer, which had been hurriedly detached from a convoy to intercept them after an Italian cryptologist read a signal regarding their situation.

Retreat from Greece

If at the beginning of April the British Empire's situation had seemed good, by the end of the month it was terrible. Axis armies had driven to the borders of

Egypt and ejected Imperial troops from Greece, the last Allied toehold on the European mainland. Operation Lustre, the buildup in Greece, lasted from 4 March to 24 April 1941. So "confused and constantly changing" was the military situation that Operation Demon, the evacuation of Greece, commenced the day Lustre ended.[16] Demon ran six days—the time it took the German army to close the Aegean coast. (See map 7.2.)

Map 7.2   Greece and Crete

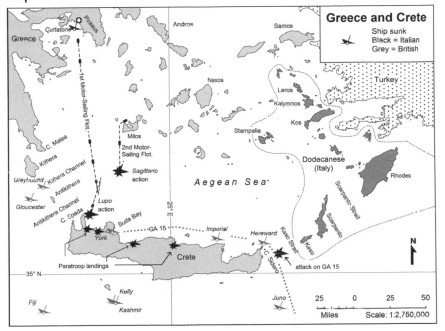

Crete served as a way station for the evacuation convoys, and on 29 April transports crowded Suda Bay. Vice Admiral Pridham-Wippell, commanding Operation Demon, formed Convoy GA 15 to evacuate to Egypt 6,232 troops and 4,699 others, including Italian prisoners of war, nurses, and consular staff.

GA 15 sailed at 1100 and proceeded east at ten knots toward Kaso Strait, joined at 1400 by Force B. Pridham-Wippell chose the eastern passage around Crete; although the route was closer to Italian bases in the Dodecanese, he considered it, after the Gavdos experience, safer from surface attacks, except from destroyers and MAS boats at night. (See table 7.3.)

Table 7.3   Attack on Convoy GA 15, 29–30 April 1941, 2315–0300

Conditions: New moon, set 2248	
Allied ships—	Convoy Escort CLA: *Carlisle;* DD: *Kandahar, Kingston, Decoy, Defender;* DS: *Auckland* (NZ); DC: *Hyacinth*
	Force B: (Vice Admiral Pridham-Wippell): CL: *Orion* (F) *Ajax, Perth* (AU), *Phoebe;* DD: *Hasty, Hereward, Nubian*
	Convoy GA 15: *Delane* (6,045 GRT), *Thurland Castle* (6,372 GRT), *Comliebank* (5,149 GRT), *Corinthia* (3,701 GRT), *Itria* (6,845 GRT), *Ionia* (1,936 GRT), *Brambleleaf* (5,917 GRT)
Italian ships—	DD: *Crispi;* TB: *Lince, Libra*

The convoy rounded Cape Sidero, on Crete's northeastern extremity, and entered Kaso Strait after dark. Beginning at 2315, *Crispi, Lince,* and *Libra,* sailing out of Leros, made several unsuccessful torpedo attacks as the convoy transited the restricted passage. *Lince* reported hitting a large destroyer with two torpedoes, while *Libra* claimed a probable hit. *Hasty, Hereward,* and *Nubian* stood them off with heavy gunfire until the Italian flotilla disengaged at 0300. *Decoy* encountered on the other flank a torpedo boat, which, in the dark, she misidentified as a much smaller MAS boat, and opened fire: "We heard the E-boat's engines start with a roar and by the time we could see again after the gun flash there was only a white streak of a wake and a noise like an aeroplane fading into the blackness."[17]

Pridham-Wippell's report noted, "Some torpedoes were fired but no damage was caused to the convoy. Own destroyers chased the enemy off several times."[18] Rear Admiral H. B. Rawlings, with *Barham, Valiant, Formidable,* and six destroyers, joined the convoy at 0600 on 30 April about eighty miles south of Kaso Strait, and GA 15 arrived safely in Alexandria the next day.

Tiger

While Imperial troops could be rescued from Greece, they had to leave their heavy equipment behind. In addition, the retreat from Libya had cost the British 2nd Armored Division most of its tanks. In this crisis the British War Cabinet decided to send equipment to Egypt directly via the Mediterranean rather than around Africa. Code named Operation Tiger, the plan called for Force H and the Mediterranean Fleet to combine efforts to get a fast convoy of five merchant ships loaded with 295 tanks and fifty-three Hurricanes, along with the battleship

Queen Elizabeth and the cruisers *Naiad* and *Fiji,* from Gibraltar to Alexandria. Simultaneously, convoys from Alexandria would reinforce Malta.

Clouds, fog, occasional rain, and "the luck of the gods" favored Force H and reduced the level of Axis air attacks.[19] An Italian bomber heavily damaged the destroyer *Fortune* on 19 May, and *Queen Elizabeth* barely avoided a torpedo attack during the night of 8 May. *Renown* and *Ark Royal* likewise dodged Italian bombs and torpedoes. Somerville wrote, "We were combing one [torpedo] successfully [when] the damn thing suddenly altered 90° to Port and came straight for our bow. Now we're for it I thought but, would you believe it, the damn thing had finished its run & I watched it sinking about 10 yards from the ship."[20] Supermarina dispatched the light cruisers *Abruzzi, Garibaldi, Bande Nere,* and *Cadorna* and five destroyers from Palermo on 8 May to set an ambush, believing the British intended to bombard that port, but rough weather prevented contact—probably fortunately, given their opposition's strength. "The information received in those days from the air reconnaissance service was so confused that Supermarina did not have the least idea that a British battleship, the *Queen Elizabeth,* had made the passage eastward with the convoy."[21] The convoy's only loss was the steamer *Empire Song* (9,228 GRT), which hit a mine off Malta on 9 May.

The British also conducted a number of ancillary actions, including a bombardment of Benghazi on the way in by *Ajax* and destroyers *Havock, Hotspur,* and *Imperial* and on the way back by 5th Destroyer Flotilla. The *Ajax* force also swept the waters south of Benghazi and sank the Italian steamers *Tenace* (1,142 GRT) and *Capitano Cecchi* (2,321 GRT) on 8 May. Churchill "was delighted to learn that this vital convoy, on which [his] hopes were set, had come safely through the Narrows."[22] But, even before it reached port his thoughts had turned to Crete.

The Battle for Crete

On 9 April the Middle Eastern command decided to hold Crete, because "from the naval point of view it was vital."[23] After being swept from the continent, Imperial and Greek troops organized, in an atmosphere of haste and defeat, to defend the island. Luftwaffe Enigma gave the British two weeks' notice of Germany's intention to assault Crete with paratroopers, and the Mediterranean Fleet, which had been built up to four battleships, one carrier, ten light cruisers, and twenty-nine destroyers, girded for action.[24] Cunningham was "quite sure that if the soldiers were given two or three days to deal with the airborne troops without interference by sea-borne powers, Crete could be held."[25] On 15 May cruiser/destroyer squadrons began to patrol the island's approaches.

Reconnaissance had sighted three battleships at Taranto, so the heavy units loitered southwest of the island ready to pounce if the Italians sortied. Cunningham did not know that the Luftwaffe had asked the Regia Marina to stay away, ostensibly because the aerial forces committed to the invasion were not trained to tell the difference between friend and foe.

On 20 May German paratroopers descended on Crete. Imperial troops, principally New Zealanders and Australians, and about ten thousand Greek levies resisted stoutly, and after the first day it appeared the German attack would fail. Conventional wisdom, in fact, held that paratroopers could not defeat emplaced regular troops; thus even before the first planes took off, a largely Greek manned collection of twenty-one small steamers, caiques, and fishing craft, dubbed the 1st Motor-Sailing Flotilla, departed Piraeus crammed with 2,331 German mountain troops to reinforce the precarious aerial toeholds.

On the night of 19 May torpedo boat *Sirio,* the convoy's sole escort, damaged her propeller near Milos, eighty miles north of Crete. The Aegean command immediately dispatched *Curtatone* to replace her, but she struck a Greek mine off Piraeus and sank. The job of escort then rotated to *Lupo.* This latter ship, commanded by Lieutenant Commander Mimbelli, located the scattered formation at dawn on 21 May fifty miles south of Milos. There were only thirty miles left to travel—an easy journey in daylight even at an average speed of three knots—but at 0715 the sector commander, the German "Admiral Southeast," Admiral Karl Schuster, ordered the convoy to wait in place. Then, based on incorrect Luftwaffe reports of British ships between Crete and Milos, he ordered it to reverse course. By the time Schuster had sorted out the intelligence situation and radioed orders to proceed, the time was 1100, and the convoy was eight miles farther north than it had been four hours before. A daytime passage under the Luftwaffe's protective umbrella was no longer possible.

Lupo led the ragged flotilla south once again, but during the afternoon head-winds kicked up a heavy sea through which the caiques wallowed at barely two knots. Evening brought low clouds and visibility between two and four thousand yards. By 2230 the convoy was five miles north-northeast of Cape Spada after a plodding journey of nearly three days.

As the 1st Motor-Sailing Flotilla labored south, British air reconnaissance had "reported groups of small craft, escorted by destroyers, steering towards Crete from Milo."[26] On the morning of 21 May Cunningham received signal intelligence that Canea would be attacked from the sea during the day and accordingly deployed four surface action forces.[27] With darkness, three groups penetrated the Aegean. The Antikithera Strait, north of Cape Spada, was the responsibility of Force D, commanded by Rear Admiral Irvine G. Glennie. He probed north with four destroyers in a line of bearing and his three cruisers following in line ahead. (See table 7.4.)

Table 7.4 *Lupo* Convoy Action, 21–22 May 1941, 2230–0030

Conditions: Low clouds, strong southerly winds, heavy chop; moon 12 percent, rise 0339

British ships—	Force D (Rear Admiral Glennie) CL: *Dido, Orion*[D2], *Ajax*[D1]; DD: *Janus, Kimberley, Hasty, Hereward*
Italian ship—	(Lieutenant Commander Francesco Mimbelli): TB: *Lupo*[D3]

At 2229 *Janus*, which had lost contact with the other destroyers, sighted a shape ahead and rapidly closed range, believing it was *Kimberley*.[28] In fact, she had stumbled upon *Lupo* leading the convoy. At 2233, according to Mimbelli's report, an Italian lookout signaled, "1,000–1,200 meters distance, an enemy cruiser to starboard bearing approximately 20 degrees off the bow."[29] The Italian ship attempted to launch a pair of torpedoes from her stern tubes (*Lupo* was configured with single tubes mounted fore and aft on each beam) but *Janus* made a slight alteration in course that unintentionally ruined the torpedo boat's set-up. Mimbelli ordered a smoke screen and held fire as his ship passed through the line of British destroyers.

At 2235, the Italian ship spotted *Dido* looming out of the dark beyond *Janus*. The cruiser had already detected *Lupo*, and at nearly the same moment British gunfire erupted. *Lupo* launched her forward torpedoes from seven hundred yards and then returned fire. In response, *Dido* turned sharply to starboard. *Lupo* held steady and crossed the cruiser's bow to starboard. Then *Orion* suddenly appeared dead ahead, in the process of turning to conform with the flagship's maneuver. Mimbelli pressed on. He later reported, "I passed just meters, repeat meters, beneath [*Orion's*] stern." During this three-minute span, the torpedo boat's three 3.9-inch guns and 20-mm/65 shot continuously to starboard, claiming hits, although the British reported that only 20-mm gunfire from *Dido* struck *Orion*, killing two and wounding nine men. After passing *Orion*, Mimbelli observed a vivid flash illuminating *Dido*, and he claimed a hit. In fact, a torpedo had passed astern of *Dido* and exploded in *Orion's* wake, slightly warping the second crusier's hull. The shock also shook her masts and reduced her speed to twenty-five knots.[30]

With his ship lucky to still be afloat and noting that "some enemy ships, instead of concentrating on [*Lupo*] were exchanging cannon-fire between themselves," Mimbelli used the confusion to escape at high speed. The British believed they sunk her. One participant aboard *Ajax*, the third ship in the British cruiser line, related, "[*Ajax*] suddenly came across a small Italian destroyer in the mist and smoke of the melee. She was no more than a few hundred yards away and *Ajax* blew her to bits with one six inch salvo."[31] In fact, the cruisers struck *Lupo* eighteen times (but only three shells exploded), killing two and wounding twenty-six men. Somehow, all this ordnance missed the thin-skinned torpedo boat's engines.[32]

With the escort brushed aside, only darkness, thick weather, and confusion protected the caiques. For their part, *S8*'s experience was typical. She carried 125 soldiers and sailed at the formation's rear, following the stern lights of the vessels ahead. Her commander's biggest worry was his ship's delicate engine. Then he spotted a vast shape looming from the darkness, and his worries multiplied. Searchlights played over the water, and bright muzzle flashes temporarily blinded him. Two salvos passed overhead. He saw an explosion, and flares arced into the sky. The cruiser rushed by so close that her machine guns could barely rake the crowded boat.

For two hours the British crisscrossed the area, sweeping the dark sea with searchlights. Warships passed *S8* twice, perforating her deck and hull with automatic weapons. To the south her men could see "five torching hulks light a large semicircle; some burn out, and new torches to the northwest light up—all told seven."[33] The ship had her mast shot in half, but the men stayed aboard. At 0300 the British withdrew, and after calm returned *S8* headed north. In addition to the damage suffered by *Dido, Ajax* bent her bow by ramming a caique.

Overall, the 1st German Motor-Sailing Flotilla lost eight of fourteen units in this clash. Force D had put eight hundred men into the water, of whom 324 drowned.[34]

Sagittario Convoy Action

Early on 22 May the 2nd German Motor-Sailing Flotilla, thirty small steamers and caiques loaded with four thousand German troops, departed Milos escorted by the torpedo boat *Sagittario*. At 0830, when the convoy had reached a point thirty miles south of Milos, Admiral Schuster ordered a retreat due to reports of British ships in the area, this time correctly—Force C, under Rear Admiral E. L. S. King, was indeed hunting the convoy. King was not to have much to show for his risky excursion north. At 0830 *Perth* bagged a straggler from the 1st Motor-Sailing Flotilla, and Mack's destroyers sank a small steamer not involved in the invasion. Then King ran into the convoy's tail end. (See table 7.5.)

Table 7.5 *Sagittario* **Convoy Action, 22 May 1941, 0840–0930**

Conditions: Clear weather, good visibility	
Allied ships—	Force C (Rear Admiral E. L. S. King): CL: *Naiad, Perth* (AU); CLA: *Calcutta, Carlisle;* DD: *Kandahar, Kingston*[D1], *Nubian*
Italian ship—	(Lieutenant Giuseppe Cigala Fulgosi): TB: *Sagittario*

The withdrawal order found the flotilla somewhat scattered. *Sagittario* was collecting stragglers when, at 0847, she spotted the unwelcome sight of smoke and then masts on the southeastern horizon. Lieutenant Fulgosi ordered the transports to disperse while he laid smoke in their wakes. Then, to buy more time, *Sagittario* charged the British formation, opening fire at 0904 from thirteen thousand yards. *Kingston,* sailing in the British van, traded salvos with *Sagittario,* and the torpedo boat tagged the large British destroyer twice on the bridge with 3.9-inch shells.[35] Even when *Perth* and *Naiad* engaged the Italian pressed on, closing to eight thousand yards and then launching four torpedoes at the cruisers.

At 0914 Italian observers reported brown smoke rising from the second cruiser in the enemy line (*Naiad*), and this caused Fulgosi to claim that one of his torpedoes had scored a hit.[36]

At 0928, with the enemy hidden by smoke, Admiral King decided to withdraw west—he did not realized how many small transports were nearby, *Carlisle* had unrepaired damage that limited his squadron's speed to twenty knots, and antiair ammunition was running low. Every mile north brought him a mile closer to German airfields. Cunningham later condemned this decision, writing that King's "failure to polish off the caique convoy" was the principal mistake made during the entire operation off Greece. Churchill sniffed: "The Rear-Admiral's retirement did not save his squadron from the air attack. He probably suffered as much loss in his withdrawal as he would have done in destroying the convoy."[37] In retrospect, these harsh judgments seem unfair and to have been inspired by the losses subsequently suffered throughout the campaign without a naval victory to balance them.

In the end Crete succumbed to the paratroopers in a contest of wills. By 26 May the German situation had become so desperate that Wehrmacht staff requested Italian assistance, which Mussolini gleefully provided. That same day the Imperial commander, General Bernard Freyberg, advised Cairo that his troops had reached the limit of their endurance and received permission to withdraw.[38] The only significant body of Axis troops to arrive by sea was a force of three thousand Italians that landed near Cape Sidero on 28 May, occupying the eastern part of the island against slight opposition.

Withdrawal from Crete

Supporting the Imperial troops on Crete and then withdrawing seventeen thousand of them cost the Mediterranean Fleet dearly. On 21 May Italian aircraft sank *Juno* and damaged *Ajax*. On the morning of 22 May German planes damaged light cruisers *Carlisle* and *Naiad* (assuming the torpedo hit on *Naiad* was aerial, not surface launched) from Admiral King's squadron. That afternoon German aircraft hit *Warspite* and sank the long-suffering *Gloucester*, with the loss of 693 men, and destroyer *Greyhound*. That evening German aircraft crippled *Fiji* and she was subsequently scuttled, while *Carlisle, Naiad,* and *Valiant* sustained lighter damage. One brief account can represent hundreds. A lieutenant aboard the destroyer *Decoy* was to recall,

> We were so placed on the screen that we were about abeam of the leading battleship, Warspite, and I happened to be watching her when suddenly two Messerschmitts appeared from high out of the blue diving on to her from right ahead. At the same moment they were spotted from Warspite and the barrage crashed out, but we saw a stick of bombs leave each plane as it dived through the pom-pom bursts. I remember shouting to the Captain "They've got her, sir!" and his shouting back, "I think they'll miss." But one at least did not, and there was a cloud of smoke, followed by masses of white steam which almost hid the ship.[39]

The 5th Destroyer Flotilla shelled the German position at Maleme on the night of 22 May, but German aircraft jumped the flotilla as it sped south after the attack, sinking *Kashmir* and *Kelly*. That same day German fighter-bombers destroyed five MTBs in Suda Bay.

In a highly questionable operation ordered by Cunningham, *Formidable* raided the German air base at Scarpanto on 26 May with six Albacores escorted by two Fulmars, inflicting light damage. While they were withdrawing, a German counterattack smashed the carrier, driving her to the United States for repairs. An Italian bomber crippled *Nubian* the same day, and *Barham* received moderate damage the next. The day after that the British command decided to withdraw, so the navy suspended its attempts to reinforce the island and concentrated on evacuating the survivors.

On 28 May Italian bombers hit *Ajax* and the destroyer *Imperial. Imperial* was scuttled, being too damaged to escape.

On 29 May German aircraft badly damaged the cruisers *Dido* and *Orion* (causing 540 casualties among the thousand soldiers crowded aboard *Orion*) and crippled *Hereward,* which was likewise loaded with troops. She was later scuttled in the face of an attack by Italian MAS boats.

On 30 May German aircraft hit *Perth* and the destroyer *Kelvin.*

On 31 May German aircraft damaged the destroyer *Napier.*

The final blow in this torturous campaign fell on 1 June, when German bombers sank the antiaircraft cruiser *Calcutta.* Altogether 2,011 Royal Navy personnel died in the battle for Crete.

One solace the British took from this miserable sequence of events was that the Italian battle fleet never intervened. This lack of activity they ascribed to the impact of the Battle of Matapan. In fact, on 1 May the German naval attaché in Rome had advised Comando Supremo that the Germans would conduct a"blitz" operation against Crete but had not divulged the date or plan. The Germans asked only for the support of the two torpedo boat squadrons assigned to the German zone.[40] Because the British were privy to the Luftwaffe signals and the Italians were not, London knew German plans and intentions better than did Rome. On 14 May Comando Supremo considered a fleet sortie, but Supermarina, which did not appreciate the Royal Navy's dire situation, judged it had enough destroyers to escort either convoys or the battle fleet but not both. Admiral Riccardi did not wish to risk the few large ships that remained operational, considering that it was their presence as a fleet in being that kept the sea lanes to Africa open. However, as Iachino concluded postwar,"Now knowing how things were, we can say that the best solution for us would have been to use the fleet to jab toward Crete to alarm the enemy and make him suspend operation 'Demon,' and then retire before coming into contact with the English heavy ships."[41]

The Routine of the War at Sea

Elsewhere in the Mediterranean, Force H, using the aircraft carriers *Ark Royal* and either *Furious* or *Victorious,* concentrated on delivering fighters to Malta. On 19–22 May, in Operation Splice, Somerville's squadron flew forty-eight Hurricanes to Malta without loss. On 5–7 June, Operation Rocket sent thirty-five Hurricanes to Malta without loss. On 13–15 June, in Operation Tracer, forty-seven Hurricanes took off for Malta, of which forty-three arrived. Operation Railway, which ran from 26 June to 1 July, delivered fifty-seven Hurricanes.

The Axis reconquest of Cyrenaica in April 1941 was only partially successful, as Imperial troops retained Tobruk. However, the besieged garrison needed to be maintained, requiring the dedication of the 10th Destroyer Flotilla and various auxiliaries to that task. These ships began making almost nightly runs from Alexandria to Tobruk (except during the height of the battle for Crete) on

5 May. They unloaded and left as quickly as possible, to minimize the exposure to air attacks on the return voyage. One participant recalled, "Having berthed, all hands turned-to and pitched our cargo into waiting lighters. Boxes and sacks of provisions stowed on the upper deck to a height of four or five feet were simply flung over the side while ammunition and land mines . . . were slid down chutes. . . . Everyone worked like demons, for the sooner we got away the further from enemy air bases and the nearer to our own fighter protection we should be at dawn. We never stayed longer than an hour."[42] Nonetheless, Axis aircraft sank the sloop *Auckland* on 24 June, destroyer *Waterhen* on 29 June, and destroyer *Defender* on 11 July.

The Regia Marina focused on supplying Libya and on laying minefields. The navy's fuel situation had become critical, with only 342,000 tons in reserve.[43] The two operational battleships, *Doria* and *Cesare*, kept to their base at Naples, and the cruisers saw only limited use providing distant cover for African convoys. Nonetheless, during May and June 1941 the following convoys reached Libya with the loss of only one ship among them:

1 May of five ships, unsuccessfully attacked by air and submarines
1 May of four ships, unsuccessfully attacked by aircraft
5 May of seven ships, unsuccessfully attacked by aircraft
13 May of six ships, arrived without incident
14 May of six ships, arrived without incident
21 May of seven ships, unsuccessfully attacked by submarine
25 May of four passenger liners, liner *Conte Rosso* (17,879 tons) sunk
    by a submarine
5 June of four ships, arrived without incident
9 June of three transports, arrived without incident
12 June of six ships, arrived without incident
24 June of five ships, unsuccessfully attacked by aircraft
29 June of four transports, unsuccessfully attacked by aircraft.

While it was business as usual at sea, on 15 June the British launched Operation Battleaxe, an ambitious offensive intended to drive past Tobruk and compensate for the loss of Crete by regaining the air bases between Sollum and Derna. However, Battleaxe failed to reach even its initial objectives, as Axis anti-tank guns chewed up most of the tanks delivered by the Tiger convoy. Even as this operation began, however, the British were undertaking other offensives in Iraq and Syria.

8

France Defends the Empire

*The French fought like mad all along the line. We had got their
psychology all wrong. They may not have been politically very
pro-Vichy, but they had orders from their generals to fight.*

—Lieutenant Commander Hugh Hodgkinson

U p through the spring of 1941 relations between Vichy France and the
British Empire remained frigid. London profoundly distrusted Marshal
Pétain's regime and suspected it of deeper collaboration with the Axis
than was the case. British naval policy, which Admiral Somerville called "sheer
lunacy," was to harass French shipping and blockade French ports, even in the
unoccupied zone, on the theory that whatever arrived in a French port would
ultimately benefit the Axis.[1] France, meanwhile, was experiencing one of the
most difficult periods in its long history. Most of the metropolitan territory was
enemy occupied and subject to onerous conditions imposed by the German
and Italian armistice commissions. However, Vichy still controlled most of the
world's second-largest empire, and the fleet remained largely intact. Berlin did
not wish to bully France past a certain point, lest the fleet and the colonies rejoin
the Allies. The consequences of that event, as the Grossadmiral Raeder explained
to Hitler in a March 1941 memorandum, would be dire: "Every bridgehead in
Africa would be lost. . . . All anti-Axis forces in the world would be given fresh
encouragement both politically and propagandistically. France would be missing
when it comes to rebuilding Europe."[2]

Given the amount of French traffic, incidents at sea between the erstwhile
allies were remarkably rare. The Royal Navy intercepted three French ships in
September 1940, three in October, two in November, and none in December.
However, on 25 December the Admiralty ordered Force H to capture French

merchantmen, "to prevent the French making a hole in our blockade."[3] On 1 January 1941 the 13th Destroyer Flotilla—*Duncan, Jaguar, Foxhound, Firedrake,* and *Hero*—intercepted four ships two days out of Casablanca en route for Oran, escorted by the trawler *La Toulonnaise.* When *Jaguar's* armed boarding party met resistance, she fired on the liner *Chantilly* (9,986 GRT), killing two passengers, including a young girl. The destroyers forced the entire convoy to Gibraltar, provoking Somerville to complain to his wife, "It seems to me that we are just as much a dictator country as either Germany or Italy and one day the Great British public will wake up to ask what we are fighting for."[4] During the balance of January, the British stopped five more French merchant vessels. In February three ships ran afoul of the British and in March four more.

On 30 March 1941 six French merchantmen escorted by the destroyer *Simoun* left Casablanca for Marseilles. *Sheffield* and four destroyers sallied from Gibraltar to seize *Bangkok,* one of the steamers, in the mistaken belief that her cargo included three thousand tons of rubber. The British intercepted the convoy in French territorial waters. *Fearless* attempted to board, but *Bangkok* fled to the protection of a 6-inch battery at Nemours in Algeria that drove the destroyer off. Shortly thereafter a French plane dive-bombed *Sheffield,* landing a 250-kg bomb within fifteen yards of the cruiser and causing damage that required five days to patch up.

By May the British had seized or sunk 143 French vessels grossing 792,000 tons, although the bulk of the seizures occurred shortly after the armistice.[5]

Germany monitored Anglo-French tensions with interest and hope. When an anti-British government seized power in Iraq in April 1941 and began hostilities against British forces on 2 May, Berlin quickly answered its appeals for assistance and sought French permission to stage aircraft flying to Iraq through Syria. France agreed, in return for concessions in armistice and occupation conditions. On 9 May German planes refueled in Syria on their way to Mosul in northern Iraq. On 11 May Admiral Darlan met with Hitler and was told that "Britain was beaten and that France, if she wished to hold a place in the New Europe and keep her overseas possessions, had no alternative to collaboration."[6] While the French admiral basically accepted this position, the mere fact of the meeting brought London's suspicions to a boil.

Despite the Balkan crisis, the impending offensive in the Western Desert, the ongoing East African fighting, and the new campaign in Iraq, Britain massed Australian, Indian, and Free French units in Palestine and Transjordan. On 15 May and again on 18 May the Royal Air Force bombed Syrian airfields. In Iraq, an Indian division advancing from Basra and a brigade from Transjordan overthrew the pro-Axis government by 30 May. By 3 June signals intelligence indicated that

Germany was terminating its Middle Eastern adventure. Nonetheless, London remained anxious, still staggered by the speed and power of Berlin's attack on Crete and fearful of a similar descent on Syria with little advance notice.[7] Thus on 8 June 1941 the 7th Australian Division, elements of the 1st Cavalry Division, the 5th Indian Brigade, and a Free French brigade invaded Syria. (See map 8.1.)

Map 8.1 Action off Sidon/Naval War off Syria

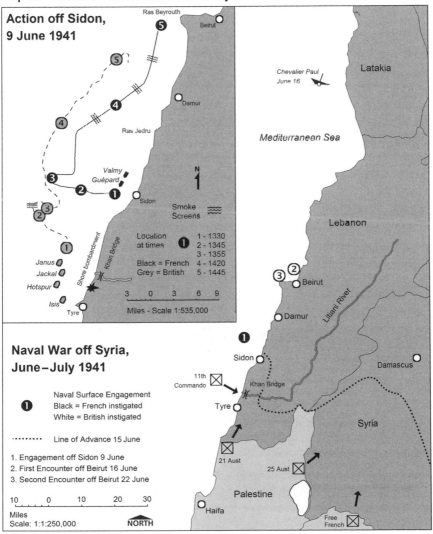

French naval assets in the area consisted of the large destroyers *Guépard* (flying the broad pennant of Captain Raymond Gervais de Lafond) and *Valmy,* the sloop *Élan,* and three submarines. The destroyers were large, handsome ships built with a war against Italy in mind, to threaten enemy sea lines of communication, protect their own sea lanes, attack the enemy's coastline, and defend the coast.[8] The British invasion gave the French navy, although greatly outnumbered, a rare opportunity to use these innovative warships in the manner for which they had been designed.

The Mediterranean Fleet, gravely weakened by the losses suffered off Crete, initially committed to the campaign a squadron, commanded by Vice Admiral King, consisting of the light cruiser *Ajax,* the antiaircraft cruisers *Coventry* and *Phoebe,* eight destroyers (*Kandahar, Kimberley, Jackal, Janus, Ilex, Isis, Hotspur,* and *Hero*), and the landing ship *Glengyle.* On the first day the British planned a commando assault to capture the bridge across the Litani River, the biggest obstacle on the coastal road between the Palestinian border and Beirut, but heavy surf forced a postponement. Admiral King returned the next night hoping for better conditions. The submarine *Caïman* spotted the British fleet and barely missed *Ajax* with a torpedo salvo. She thought she had *Barham* in her crosshairs.[9]

Meanwhile, *Guépard* and *Valmy,* alerted by *Caïman,* sortied from Beirut at 0700 to investigate. It was a beautiful morning with clear skies and a light breeze. By 0845 de Lafond's division had reached Ras Sarafend, six miles north of the Litani River, where it spotted masts poking above the west-southwest horizon. As these disappeared the French ships moved in to scout the activity ashore. They spotted an Australian column south of the river and opened fire. They lacked high-explosive ammunition, however, and, coming under counterfire from an Australian battery, the destroyers withdrew at 0922. *Guépard* expended forty-two rounds and *Valmy* just twenty during this episode.

De Lafond knew a powerful enemy flotilla was nearby, so he headed back up the coast. At 1145, just outside Beirut, the commanding admiral there ordered him to return south and scout the size of the enemy's naval squadron, without becoming engaged by a stronger force.

Meanwhile, King had heard that French warships had taken potshots at the Australians, and he rushed back to the scene with *Phoebe* and *Ajax.* By the time he arrived, de Lafond was long gone, so King ordered four destroyers to sweep north along the coast while he returned to Haifa. In addition to the submarine danger, the British admiral had experienced the destructive power of air attacks off Crete; also, the day before French Morane 406 fighters had shot down two Fulmars assigned to protect his forces and damaged several others.[10]

The French division had returned to Sidon when, at 1325, *Guépard* sighted destroyer masts to the southwest.[11] These belonged to *Janus*. *Jackal* followed about a mile off her starboard quarter and *Hotspur* a mile behind *Jackal*. *Isis* was operating inshore two miles south of *Hotspur*. Tothill sighted the French as they turned west at 1329. Under his rules of engagement the British commander could not fire first. Nonetheless, he rang up full speed and headed toward the intruders, without closing up his formation. Tothill was an experienced captain on a veteran ship that had fought off Norway and in surface actions against the Italians, including the Battle of Matapan. He anticipated there would be time to concentrate while the French closed range.[12] (See table 8.1.)

Table 8.1   Engagement off Sidon, 9 June 1941, 1335–1445

Conditions: Fair weather with brisk wind and small chop, good visibility
British ships— (Commander J. A. W. Tothill): DD: *Janus*D4 (F), *Jackal*D1, *Isis*, *Hotspur*
French ships— 3rd Scout Division (Captain Raymond Gervais de Lafond): DL: *Guépard*D1 (F), *Valmy*

De Lafond surprised Tothill, however, when his ships loosed their first salvo from sixteen thousand yards. *Guépard* judged that her rounds, marked by green splashes, fell four hundred yards under, while the *Valmy*'s red-dyed shells fell six hundred yards over. Both destroyers were on for deflection, and their second broadsides straddled. Nonetheless, *Janus* continued to close, while *Jackal* steamed to fall in astern and *Hotspur* remained farther back. *Janus* replied at 1335 from fifteen thousand yards. One of *Valmy*'s men later recalled, "The slender silhouettes of [the enemy] ships . . . were illuminated by momentary flashes, six here, four there. With greater anxiety than after our own salvos we mentally counted the time. Sharp cracking sounds, white geysers; they were far away. The enemy opened very short."[13] (See map 8.1, inset.)

The French, now shooting five rounds a minute, pressed west, while the straggling British line assumed a parallel heading. Then, at 1343, with the range at ten thousand yards, *Guépard* struck *Janus* three times. One shell blew a hole in the aft deck; another exploded outside the captain's sea cabin, killing everyone on the bridge except Tothill; and the third slammed into no. 1 boiler room, slaughtering crewmen and destroying the saturated-steam line. With steam escaping and no. 2 boiler out of action, *Janus* drifted to a stop. Then two more shells piled in, one of which exploded in no. 1 boiler room. Rolling on the swell, *Janus* dropped smoke floats and worked her guns under local control. *Guépard*, steaming west at twenty-two knots, projected a torpedo toward this target, at an estimated range of nine thousand yards.

At this juncture *Jackal* overhauled *Janus* and wrapped smoke around her stricken sister. *Jackal* then turned to port and at 1350 sent three torpedoes churning on a long run north. *Hotspur* remained out of effective range.

At 1354 the French ships ceased fire and simultaneously turned east. A few minutes later de Lafond sighted *Isis* speeding north to join the fight and, with the odds once again out of balance, and with half of his precious supply of ammunition already expended, the French captain turned north.

Jackal followed at full speed, zigzagging to present a difficult target. *Hotspur* came next, twenty-five hundred yards astern, while *Isis* trailed well off *Hotspur's* starboard quarter. *Jackal's* dogged perseverance impressed her enemy. "That bloodhound—*Jackal*—clung to us . . . shooting with perfect precision and regularity her six-fold salvos."[14] At 1414 the French altered course to the northeast, straight for Beirut, still twenty miles distant, and started to lay black funnel and white chemical smoke. However, this provided little concealment. With *Jackal* following thirteen thousand yards behind, de Lafond ordered his gunners to back her off with concentrated salvos. Shortly thereafter a 5.45-inch shell exploded on *Jackal's* upper deck, igniting a small blaze in the tiller flat (that is, the steering machinery room, over the rudder) and wounding one man. The French ceased fire at 1420 and increased speed to twenty-four knots.

At 1421 *Jackal's* gunfire finally told: a shell rattled into *Guépard's* crew quarters. This did little damage, but a few yards one way or the other would have been a different story. The French emitted more smoke and increased speed to thirty knots. However, the smoke failed to conceal, so at 1433 de Lafond turned again and flung a few salvos at *Jackal* before resuming course for Beirut. This maneuver succeeded in opening the range, and *Jackal* broke off the chase at 1446. She had expended 611 4.7-inch rounds. In addition to being hit once, *Guépard* had suffered minor splinter damage.

Kimberly towed *Janus* to Haifa, where she burned out of control until 0500 the next day. The Admiralty concluded that Tothill should have kept his force concentrated, though it conceded that the French "produced long range gunnery of an accuracy considerably above our destroyer standard." In fact, it was even more impressive in light of the limitations of the French weapons.[15]

On 10 June the 10th Destroyer Flotilla (*Stuart, Jaguar, Griffin,* and *Defender*) arrived to reinforce King's squadron, followed three days later by the light cruiser *Leander* and the destroyers *Jervis* and *Hasty.* Meanwhile, *Ajax, Stuart, Hotspur,* and *Kandahar* departed. De Lafond's small squadron remained active despite the growing odds against it. His destroyers conducted "tip and run" raids, trying to catch isolated British ships and getting in some licks against enemy ground forces.

On 14 June *Leander* and *Coventry* received word of *Guépard* and *Valmy* to the north. Accompanied by four destroyers, the Allied cruisers hurried to intercept, and by 1635 *Leander* had the enemy in sight. But the French ships fled to the protection of Beirut's 9.45-inch batteries before the cruisers could engage.

In the ground war, the Australian 21st Brigade captured Sidon on 15 June, whereupon its drive bogged down against stiffening resistance. German aircraft, meanwhile, flying from Rhodes, joined French planes, making King's coastal forays even more perilous. At 1703 on 15 June German Ju.88s severely damaged *Isis*. Two hours later a formation of sixteen French Glen Martins dropped two 500-lb bombs close alongside *Ilex* and opened her no. 1 boiler room to the sea. This knocked both destroyers out of action for more than a year.

First Encounter off Beirut

The British invasion enraged Admiral Darlan. His staff dissuaded him from dispatching the High Seas Force to Beirut with a convoy ferrying a weak brigade, the only mobile force in the whole Armée de l'Armistice, but on 11 June the destroyer *Chevalier Paul* sailed with eight hundred much-needed rounds of 5.45-inch ammunition to replenish the squadron's stocks. She passed Castellorizzo on 15 June, hugging the Turkish coast to make the dangerous passage around Cyprus at night. However, signals intelligence revealed that the Germans had granted permission for the mission. A reconnaissance aircraft duly spotted *Chevalier Paul* at 1815, and a flight of six Swordfish departed Cyprus to attack. At 0300 on 16 June they found the destroyer under the light of a bright moon and torpedoed her, at the cost of one aircraft. (See table 8.2.)

Table 8.2   First Encounter off Beirut, 16 June 1941, 0400–0415

Conditions: Calm sea, good weather and visibility
Allied ships— CL: *Leander* (NZ); DD: *Jervis, Kimberley*
French ships— 3rd Scout Division (Captain Raymond Gervais de Lafond): DL: *Guépard* (F), *Valmy*

Chevalier Paul radioed for help, and within an hour *Valmy* and *Guépard*, which had steam up, were under way. They had barely cleared the port, however, when *Leander, Jervis,* and *Kimberley* appeared, sailing up the coast. Leery of

French gunnery, *Kimberley* came to full speed and charged the French ships as both sides opened fire. De Lafond's orders were to avoid engaging a superior foe (he was nearly out of ammunition in any case), so he made smoke and retreated to Beirut. In the brief engagement the French destroyers expended seventy-eight rounds while the *Kimberly* claimed hits, but in fact neither side damaged the other. Once the Allied ships departed, hurried off by French aircraft, which unsuccessfully bombed *Kimberley, Guépard* and *Valmy* set out once again. But they arrived too late. *Chevalier Paul* sank at 0645. All they could do was rescue survivors (including the crew of the downed Swordfish).

Second Encounter off Beirut

Admiral Cunningham continued to reinforce King. On 17 June *Naiad*, with destroyers *Kingston, Jaguar,* and *Nizam,* joined his squadron. However, disturbed by the growing number of ships under repair and the lack of fighter support provided by the Royal Air Force, and faced with a stalemated ground campaign, Cunningham ordered King to remain in Haifa during daylight hours rather than risk German and French air attacks. He declared, "The Army must choose between naval support for [its] left flank and fighter protection for [its] troops."[16]

On 18 June *Élan* bombarded Allied positions along the coast. The large destroyer *Vauquelin* reached Beirut on 21 June carrying eight hundred 5.45-inch rounds, but British bombers damaged her in port the next day, and the French admiral decided his fleet should disperse at night when fighters could not provide cover. (See table 8.3.)

Table 8.3   Second Encounter off Beirut, 22 June 1941, 0145–0200

Conditions: Calm sea, fair weather, no moon
Allied ships—   CL: *Leander* (NZ), *Naiad*; DD: *Jaguar, Kingston, Nizam* (AU)
French ships—   DL: *Guépard*[D1], *Valmy*; DS: *Élan*

On the night of 22 June, *Guépard* and *Valmy* slipped their moorings. Steaming north-northwest at eight knots (to conserve fuel), de Lafond intended to pass the darkness loitering off Cape Ras Beyrouth. The ships had reached a point six miles north of the city when lookouts reported unexpected silhouettes looming out of the dark. He had run into a squadron of British warships coming down from the north. (An additional four destroyers, *Jervis, Havock, Hotspur,* and

Decoy, were deployed farther offshore on antisubmarine patrol.) As searchlights snapped on, the French destroyers increased speed and turned south. *Valmy's* captain remembered: "Shadows danced on the bridge. We exchanged brief words as the guns swiveled to compensate for our evasive maneuvers. Then the sound of enemy artillery rang out on multiple octaves, each sounding a unique chord as shells tore the air."[17]

As the French ships completed their turn, *Naiad,* only five thousand yards away, hit *Guépard.* The 5.25-inch round penetrated the French ship's aft magazine but failed to explode. In any case, the magazine was empty, as her crew had landed *Guépard's* ordinance just the day before. *Valmy* replied with two torpedoes at 0153. Then "at 0155, the action reached its climax: speed was twenty-eight knots, communications with *Guépard* had broken down. It was necessary to operate using our own judgment. . . . [It] showered orange stars. Searchlights perforated the night unceasingly."[18] *Leander* launched four torpedoes and *Jaguar* two more. The French ships hugged the coast so closely that the British overs exploded ashore and set the chaparral ablaze. At that moment *Guépard* and *Valmy* rounded Ras Beyrouth. French shore batteries opened fire in their support—and then, as suddenly as it had begun, the action was over. De Lafond's ships passed into the night without further damage. *Élan,* operating separately, ran aground trying to evade detection but eventually worked her way off and returned to Beirut.

This was the campaign's last surface action. On June 25 the British submarine *Parthian* sank the French submarine *Souffleur* off Beirut. The British continued to rotate ships in and out of the theater, giving crews a chance to rest. More aircraft became available, and the fleet began to enjoy support from "real" fighters, as opposed to the ineffective Fulmars. On 3 July Palmyra fell, and the Australians occupied Damur, south of Beirut, on 10 July. With the prospect of a rare victory in the air, morale began to rise. One of *Hotspur's* officers would recall, "In a way it was a pity to leave the Syrian coast. After Greece and Crete it was an excellent tonic to be doing something aggressive again."[19]

The French, however, battled grimly on. Darlan resurrected his scheme to lift four infantry battalions to Syria aboard *Strasbourg,* four cruisers, a division of destroyers, and another of torpedo boats sailing under a German aerial umbrella. On 24 June his representative outlined this proposal to the German armistice commission. The Germans were slightly taken aback by France's willingness to court a conflict at sea with Britain.[20] On 27 June signals intelligence alerted London to this plan, which would have had "momentous consequences for development of German-Vichy-British relations."[21] However, there was no evidence the High Seas Force ever began preparing for such a mission, and, as its destruction in a lost cause would have squandered the French state's most potent asset, it is possible Darlan was merely testing German reactions.

Guépard, Valmy, and *Vauquelin,* meanwhile, sailed to Salonika to embark a battalion that had arrived from France by rail. On 9 July British aircraft spotted the ships early on their return journey, still two hundred miles from Beirut. According to orders and rather than risk the lives of the hundreds of embarked soldiers, they made for Toulon instead. The French authorities finally asked for an armistice, and the fighting ended on 14 July.

Thus concluded what Admiral Cunningham described as an "irritating though necessary interlude in the midst of all our other commitments and responsibilities."He acknowledged that "taking all in all it must be stated that the Vichy destroyers were well and boldly handled."[22]

If Cunningham dismissed the campaign as an irritating interlude, it was, in fact, significant. Mussolini had been casting covetous eyes upon Tunisia since September 1940, but events in Syria demonstrated that Tunisia would not be an easy prize. The campaign was also important for what did not happen. If ever there was a moment when France stood on the cusp of history, it was in June 1941. On one side beckoned partnership in the Axis, on the other frustrating semi-neutrality. While it is true that by late June German attention was focused on Russia and that Hitler's desire for French involvement had diminished, the heads of the navy and air force, Admiral Raeder and Marshal Hermann Göring, supported *Strasbourg's* proposed sortie. Admiral Darlan decided by 30 June, however, that total war with Britain would not serve France's best interest. The permission granted Germany to use Syrian airfields had not generated the political and economic concessions expected and instead had led to the loss of an important colony. With the war's end date receding on the Russian steppes, the French navy settled down to a wait-and-see policy, hoarding its meager stocks of oil for the moment when a decisive intervention on the winner's side would gain for France a restoration of its fortunes.

9

The Convoy War Intensifies

Summer and Fall 1941

The code name for the commitment of German troops in Africa was Sunflower. Unconsciously, someone had hit upon the perfect symbol: a huge and showy flower at the end of a long and rather fragile stem.

—German historian Wolf Heckmann, *Rommel's War in Africa*

By the end of the Syrian campaign the weakened Mediterranean Fleet was no longer tasked with engaging and destroying the enemy's battle fleet. Instead, it had three missions: to"assist the army build up its strength in the Western Desert, maintain the large garrison in Tobruk and to damage Rommel's pipe-line by destroying shipping on the Italy–Libya sea route."[1]

Great Britain also faced critical strategic decisions at this time. Planners believed a paratroop attack against Malta was probable and that Soviet resistance would likely collapse. If that should happen, London expected German troops to attack Iraq from out of Turkey as early as November.[2] The failure of Battleaxe and the threat of fresh Axis initiatives made the prime minister eager for a new desert offensive."To this end, [Churchill] poured reinforcements into Egypt and brushed aside his military's advisers' reminders about the longstanding decision that the defence of the Far East, and particularly of Singapore, was the second priority after the defence of Britain itself, and before the Middle East."[3]

Entering its second year of war, the Regia Marina likewise faced multiple obligations. These included building up Italian and German forces in Africa for a renewed attack on Egypt, returning the battleships damaged at Taranto to action, and keeping the Sicilian Channel closed and Malta isolated. Despite the government's shuffling of the navy's top leadership after the Taranto raid, tension between Supermarina and the fleet command continued. In a study regarding the failure to intervene during the Tiger convoy, Vice Admiral Iachino observed that "if we remain absent every time the enemy ventures through the Sicilian Channel, it follows that our navy is unable to perform offensive tasks in the central Mediterranean and that [the fleet] should be exclusively reserved for the task of escorting convoys."[4] A year of warfare had depleted the prewar fuel reserves, and reverses like Matapan and the *Tarigo* convoy action had disclosed the enemy's disconcerting superiority in radar and night fighting. Finally, cooperation between the navy and air force remained dismal.

Map 9.1   The Convoy War Intensifies, August–December 1941

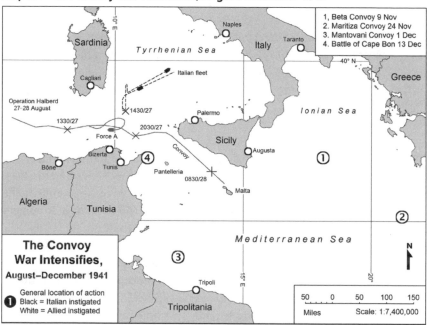

The international situation also affected the navy's calculations. The German invasion of the Soviet Union had in one stroke removed Italy's most promising future source of oil and handed Great Britain a powerful ally. As prospects for an early peace faded, commercial relations with Germany were proving unsatisfactory. The Reich was stingy in sharing technology like radar and its excellent marine diesel engines, and it expected much in return. Even Mussolini complained, "We may be willing to give up our shirts, but the Germans remove even pieces of hide."[5] (See map 9.1.)

In the first six months of 1941, 94 percent of the Axis materiel shipped to Libya arrived safely. From July traffic volume fell, but losses rose from 8,255 tons to 14,736 tons. Factors contributing to this turnabout included the transfer of X Fliegerkorps from Sicily, the reduction of pressure against Malta, and the corresponding increase in British air strength. Most importantly, however, Great Britain enjoyed a critical intelligence breakthrough in the summer of 1941. Under German pressure, Supermarina had introduced a machine cipher C38m in December 1940 for joint communications relating to naval transport matters, because the Germans believed "that the existing Italian cyphers were vulnerable."[6] British cryptologists broke C38m and on 23 June transmitted to the Middle East command details of a convoy of four giant liners carrying troops to Africa. Thereafter, "it was as a result of its reading of the C38m that [Britain] was able from July 1941 to give . . . advance notice of virtually every convoy and important independent ship that sailed with troops or supplies across the Mediterranean."[7]

Chart 9.1 Monthly Delivery of Materiel to Libya, 1941

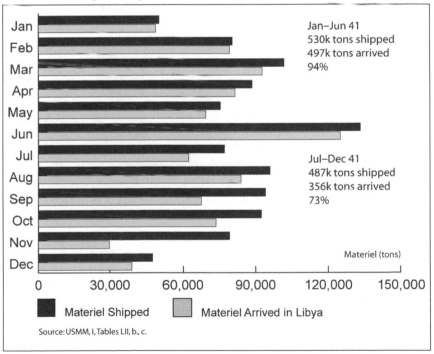

Jan–Jun 41
530k tons shipped
497k tons arrived
94%

Jul–Dec 41
487k tons shipped
356k tons arrived
73%

Materiel (tons)

Materiel Shipped   Materiel Arrived in Libya

Source: USMM, I, Tables LII, b., c.

The submarine *P33* scored the first mercantile success based on signal intelligence on 15 July 1941, sinking the Italian motorship *Barbarigo* (5,293 GRT). Other losses followed, the most serious of which were *Esperia* (11,398 GRT) on 20 August, by the submarine *Unique,* only eleven miles off Tripoli, and the liners *Neptunia* (19,475 GRT) and *Oceania* (19,507 GRT) on 18 September, by the submarine *Upholder.* In July the Axis lost 23,222 GRT of shipping and 21 percent of the material shipped to Africa; in August losses consisted of 31,007 GRT and 14 percent; and 62,431 GRT and 30 percent in September.[8] This toll infuriated the Germans, who complained the Italians were not doing enough to protect traffic.

Given the advantages enjoyed by the British, perhaps it is surprising that any convoys got through. However, the Axis forces also had factors working for them.

Cesare and *Doria* moved to Taranto in May, and in June *Littorio, Vittorio Veneto,* and *Duilio* joined them. The battle line's availability induced General Ugo Cavallero, Comando Supremo's chief of staff, to call for a combined navy/air force "mass action" against the British fleet as soon as possible. At the same time Supermarina replaced its operational head, Admiral Campioni, who was considered too old and had been almost isolated after the Matapan disaster; the new deputy chief of staff was Admiral Luigi Sansonetti, considered a smart and lucky leader. As Supermarina correctly calculated that the Mediterranean Fleet would avoid the central basin, given Rome's new battleships superiority, the only target for its projected mass action was Force H. Staff also contemplated a bombardment of Tobruk by *Doria* and the 3rd Division's heavy cruisers, synchronized with a ground offensive to capture the city.

The navy's fuel situation, however, had become embarrassing, and all that the Regia Marina and Regia Aeronautica could count on was Romanian production, about twenty-seven thousand tons a month. The lack of oil forced the navy to cancel plans, like a cruiser sortie into Spanish waters to hunt the British boarding vessels harassing that country's shipping. Malta, now the Regia Aeronautica's sole responsibility, enjoyed a return to the good old days of nuisance raids only, because of fuel limitations and because the "Italian air force could not afford to carry out large-scale operations, with the danger of heavy losses, as it received too few replacements from the domestic aircraft industry."[9]

Operation Substance

The invasion of Syria drew heavily upon the Mediterranean Fleet's resources. On top of that, the need to supply the beleaguered fortress of Tobruk and its garrison of nearly forty thousand men occupied the fleet's scarce destroyers in a grueling and dangerous routine. Because no convoy could be passed to Malta from the east, it became essential that the attempt should be made from the west, and in great strength if the convoy was to be fought through successfully.[10]

On 21 July 1941 Force H—*Renown, Ark Royal,* light cruiser *Hermione,* and six destroyers, supplemented by the battleship *Nelson,* three cruisers, and eleven destroyers from the Home Fleet—commenced Substance, the largest Malta operation since Excess in January. The operation's "object was to pass six freighters and a troopship from Gibraltar to Malta and simultaneously protect the westward passage of seven empty transports from Malta."[11] The Mediterranean Fleet, meanwhile, sortied from Alexandria on 22 July with *Queen Elizabeth* and *Valiant,* four light cruisers, two minelayers, and seven destroyers to confuse the enemy with a simulated convoy from the east.

Italian aircraft spotted warships south of the Balearics on 22 July, but the battle fleet remained in port, assuming that Force H was conducting another fly-off operation. It was too late to intervene with the three battleships at Taranto by the time a second aircraft discovered the convoy off Bône. Nonetheless, the Regia Aeronautica enjoyed some success. At 0942 on 23 July a "well-coordinated high- and low-level air attack" north of Bône scored a torpedo hit on the light cruiser *Manchester* that put her in the dock for seven months, and fatally damaged the destroyer *Fearless.*[12] That evening *Firedrake* fell victim to a high-level attack and required a tow back to Gibraltar.

Assisted by favorable weather, *MAS532* and *MAS533* intercepted the convoy near Pantelleria and created a commotion. The destroyer *Cossack,* the cruiser *Edinburgh,* and the fast minelayer *Manxman* opened fire when they heard an engine roar off the destroyer's port beam. Speeding through the heavy barrage, *MAS532* pressed in and torpedoed the freighter *Sydney Star* (11,219 GRT). Afterward the British report stated, "Their number is uncertain, perhaps a half dozen all told, although some ships thought it was more." The escort claimed it sank certainly one and maybe two boats, but in fact both escaped unharmed.[13] The convoy, including *Sydney Star,* reached Malta with fifty thousand tons of supplies. The islanders "lined the battlements on both sides of the harbor and cheered the vessels to their moorings."[14]

Having failed to stop the transports, Supermarina tried to hit them before they could unload. X MAS attacked Malta's Grand Harbor on the night of 25 July (following operations against Malta on 28 and 30 June that were aborted due to weapon defects and bad weather). However, British radar detected their mother ship, the sloop *Diana,* during the approach, and bad luck trying to storm the harbor—an explosion designed to blast a passage through a protective net caused the bridge over the entryway to collapse—turned the affair into a fiasco.

The commandos were killed or imprisoned, and the British captured one MAS boat, which an alert shore battery had disabled.[15]

Force H sortied again on 30 July to cover warships running personnel to Malta.

In August, in a far-flung operation, Imperial troops invaded Iran to oust the government and open another line of communications with the new Soviet ally. In the course of the attack a scratch Imperial flotilla consisting of the AMC *Kanimbla,* four sloops, *Shoreham, Falmouth,* the Australian *Yarra,* the Indian *Lawrence,* the corvette *Snapdragon,* a gunboat, an armed yacht, a trawler, river steamers, tugs, motorboats, and dhows took on the Iranian navy, whose major units, all Italian built, consisted of *Babr* and *Palang,* thousand-ton sloops mounting three 4-inch guns, and four 330-ton patrol boats each armed with a pair of 3-inch guns. On 25 August, in a surprise strike down the Shatt-el-Arab from Basra, a force including *Yarra* attacked Khorramshahr. *Yarra* confronted *Babr* and bombarded her under searchlight illumination until the Iranian's magazine exploded and she sank. Boarding parties then captured two patrol boats. Another strike, which included *Shoreham,* sailed upstream from Fao to hit Abadan, where *Shoreham* dispatched *Palang* in much the same fashion. The British also captured seven of the eight Axis merchantmen, totaling 44,400 GRT, docked at the two Iranian cities.[16]

On 22 August Force H, with one battleship, a carrier, a cruiser, and five destroyers, conducted Operation Mincemeat to support the fast minelayer *Manxman* in laying a field off Livorno and to launch an air raid against Tempio Pausania, in northern Sardinia. This time Supermarina, expecting another Malta convoy, ordered *Littorio, Vittorio Veneto,* four heavy cruisers, and nineteen destroyers to sea. Italian aircraft failed to catch Somerville's turn to the north. Force H accomplished its objectives, while Iachino burned precious fuel south of Sardinia in growing frustration.

Operation Halberd and the Failed Aero-Naval Mass Action

On 24 September Force H began another large Malta convoy movement, called Operation Halberd: nine transports covered by three battleships, *Prince of Wales, Rodney,* and *Nelson, Ark Royal,* the cruisers *Sheffield, Euryalus, Kenya, Edinburgh,* and *Hermione,* and eighteen destroyers. Mussolini and Comando Supremo's Cavallero saw this as another chance for the desired aero-naval mass action and concentrated forces accordingly, although Supermarina continued its usual policy of ordering Iachino to seek combat only if he enjoyed a decisive superiority.

On the Italian side there was initial uncertainty about the enemy's intentions, with a bombardment of Genoa considered a possibility. On 27 September, when reconnaissance spotted a convoy, the Italian fleet united, and twenty-eight torpedo bombers escorted by CR.42s winged south to attack the enemy. They had some success. An S.79 torpedoed *Nelson* in the bow at 1330: "There was a large 'crump,' the ship whipped considerably and a column of water rose approximately 15–20 ft high above the forecastle deck port side."[17] The battleship eventually settled eight feet by the bow and shipped thirty-five hundred tons of water. At this time the Italian fleet—*Littorio, Vittorio Veneto,* heavy cruisers *Trento, Trieste,* and *Gorizia,* light cruisers *Abruzzi* and *Attendolo,* and fourteen destroyers—was advancing south-southwest, with the cruisers ranging ahead, cleared for action. However, the weather began to deteriorate, with heat haze and gathering thunderheads complicating spotting and preventing the fighters Iachino expected from locating his force. At 1430, when he was just forty miles from the enemy, he reversed course.[18]

As Force H streamed east at sixteen knots, Iachino maneuvered to the northeast, trying to sort through confusing sighting reports and waiting for air support. He turned south again at 1700 after hearing there was only one enemy battleship. In fact, at 1530 Somerville had detached *Prince of Wales* and *Rodney* with two cruisers and six destroyers to confront the Italian fleet if needed. Thus Iachino would have enjoyed a large superiority in light forces as well as battleship parity had action followed. However, the Italian admiral turned away a final time at 1812 after a report made him suspect the British force was stronger than he had believed. Torpedo bombers delivered the day's final attack at 2030 and sank the transport *Imperial Star* (10,733 GRT).

Iachino received a chilly reception upon his return to Naples, but he kept his job after Italian agents at Algeciras reported that *Prince of Wales* and both *Nelson*-class battleships had been present that day, making it appear the British had planned a trap. As Iachino expressed it, "It was only by a happy intuition [that I] succeeded in avoiding an encounter with a vastly superior force."[19]

With the failure of the long planned aero-naval mass action and the exhaustion of prewar fuel stocks, the oil coming from Ploesti barely allowed the navy to conduct convoy operations while retaining a reserve for the scheduled bombardment of Tobruk.

Special Operations

The special weapons and underwater commandos of X MAS had failed to realize their potential over the war's first year due to temperamental equipment and some bad luck. The first four attempts to deploy the *Siluro a Lenta Corsa* (SLC), or "human torpedo" in August, September, and October 1940 failed due to defects or because the battleship targets had sailed on missions. The first success came on 26 March 1941, when six MTM explosive boats attacked Suda Bay and critically damaged the heavy cruiser *York* and the tanker *Pericles.*

Following this action an operation against Corfu on 5 April 1941 failed due to an alert defense. On 26 May defective SLCs scuttled a mission against Gibraltar. Finally, after abortive attacks against Malta in June and July, an operation against Gibraltar on 19 September succeeded. Although they were unable to penetrate the harbor to hit the battleships, three two-man teams sank the tanker *Fiona Shell* (2,444 GRT) in the roads and seriously damaged the freighters *Durham* (10,900 GRT) and *Denbydale* (8,145 GRT).[20] After this mission an engineer reported, "These craft . . . now constitute an absolutely efficient and trustworthy weapon, capable of achieving the most brilliant success in war."[21] It was fortunate for the British the Italians required so long to iron out the SLCs' bugs, as their successful use in the war's first months could have changed the dynamic of the Mediterranean war.

Enter the Kriegsmarine

In September, complaints by General Erwin Rommel, commander of the German Afrika Korps, led Berlin to conclude that the Italians "were not concentrating their forces on protecting the supply shipments to North Africa."[22] Feeling optimistic about progress in Russia, Hitler ordered the Kriegsmarine to dispatch six submarines as well as motor minesweepers and an S-boat flotilla to the Mediterranean. The first wave of German submarines slipped through the Straits of Gibraltar between 21 September and 5 October. They were to interdict traffic between Tobruk and Alexandria from a base at Salamis in the Aegean. However, their initial patrols sank only an estimated 4,091 tons of enemy shipping.[23] It was not a promising start, but Hitler determined, over the strong objections of Admiral Karl Dönitz, commander in chief U-boats, to steadily reinforce the Mediterranean, and the second wave of four boats headed south in November.

Force H, with *Rodney, Ark Royal, Hermione,* and seven destroyers, sortied on 14 October, and the *Ark Royal* flew off eleven Albacores and two Swordfish for Malta. On 10 November Force H put to sea again (with *Malaya* replacing *Rodney*) and delivered thirty-four of thirty-seven Hurricanes to Malta. On 13 November, while returning from this mission, *U-81* scored the Kriegsmarine's first major success in the Middle Sea when she hit *Ark Royal* with one torpedo.

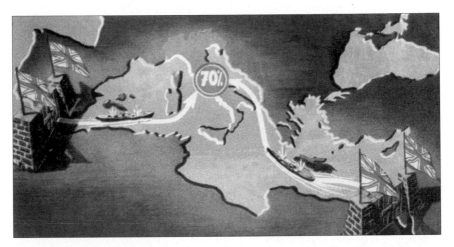

The Italian perspective. Italy received 70 percent of its imports from beyond the British-controlled chokepoints of the Straits of Gibraltar and Suez. *(Enrico Cernuschi collection)*

Prewar training. Italian destroyers laying smoke as viewed from a Duilio-class battleship. *(Andrea Tani/Enrico Cernuschi collection)*

More training. An Italian Turbine-class destroyer launching a torpedo during an exercise off Libya, summer 1939. *(Andrea Tani/Enrico Cernuschi collection)*

The Italian destroyer *Fulmine* at Venice during the summer of 1939. *(Andrea Tani/ Enrico Cernuschi collection)*

Italy's heavy cruisers of the 1st and 3rd divisions at the Battle of Calabria (*Maurizio Brescia collection*)

On 9 July 1940 at 1553 during the Battle of Calabria the Italian battleship *Cesare* opened fire on *Warspite* at a range of nearly twenty-nine thousand yards. (*Ufficio Storico della Marina Militare [USMM]*)

Cesare under fire. The top photo shows a near miss, on for deflection but short for range. The bottom photo records *Warspite*'s hit. The explosion is smaller than the splash and thus does not appear as dramatic. *(USMM)*

Malaya, Ramillies, and *Kent,* August 1940, steaming to conduct a bombardment of Bardia. *(Stephen Dent collection)*

The Battle of Cape Spartivento, 27 November 1940. An Italian heavy cruiser, with salvos dropping close astern. *(Andrea Tani/Enrico Cernuschi collection)*

Vittorio Veneto, probably 1941 at Naples. (*U.S. Naval Institute Photo Archive*)

Commander Francesco Mimbelli, commander of *Lupo* receiving the Iron Cross
First Class on 8 February at Piraeus from *Vizeadmiral* Erich Förset, the German
admiral commanding in the Aegean. Mimbelli was a successful leader who later
commanded Italian light forces in the Black Sea. *(Aldo Fraccaroli collection)*

Lupo standing off from *Città di Livorno* as she sinks. *(Aldo Fraccaroli collection)*

All the admirals, on the first anniversary of Italy's entry into the war, 10 June 1941. From left to right in the first rank, Admiral Domenico Cavagnari, former chief of staff; Grand Admiral Paolo Thaon di Revel, who led the navy during World War I; and incumbent chief of staff, Arturo Riccardi. *(Aldo Fraccaroli collection)*

The innovative French battleship *Richelieu*. Symbolic of the Marine Nationale's power and its travails, *Richelieu* escaped the Germans and fled to Dakar, rather than Plymouth, as the British had hoped. She was subject to several British attacks and was instrumental in defeating the attempt to seize Dakar. (*U.S. Naval Institute Photo Archive*)

HMS *Fortune*. Representative of the smaller, prewar destroyers that fought the brunt of the naval war against Italy, *Fortune* was a member of the 8th Destroyer Flotilla and served with Force H from August 1940 to February 1942. (*Stephen Dent collection*)

The Battle of Pantelleria, 15 June 1942. The Italian admiral, Da Zara, had lost track of the British convoy. The British commander had ordered his ships to sink the damaged stragglers *Burdwan* and *Kentucky*. Their gunfire ignited large fires, and Admiral Da Zara homed in on the smoke plumes. The source of the third plume is a mystery; British sources state it was an aircraft, but it seems too large and dense. *(U.S. Naval Institute Photo Archive)*

The gunfire of Da Zara's cruisers severely damaged the destroyer HMS *Bedouin*, veteran of many surface engagements against the Germans and Italians. An Italian SM79 torpedo bomber finished her off. *(U.S. Naval Institute Photo Archive)*

Mussolini decorating Lieutenant Commander Andrea Tani after the Pantelleria engagement. Mussolini had a special affection for this action, writing, "This clear cut victory was to the credit of Mussolini alone." *(Andrea Tani/Enrico Cernuschi collection)*

Strange bedfellows. Admiral Andrew Browne Cunningham, Admiral François Darlan, and General Dwight D. Eisenhower attending a ceremony in Algiers at the Tomb of the Unknown Soldier, 1 December 1942. Darlan was assassinated several weeks later. *(U.S. Naval Institute Photo Archive)*

Warships engaged in the Mediterranean

Royal Navy

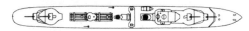

H Class destroyer (1936)
1,890 tons fl, 36kts, 4 x 4.7in/45-cal, 8 x 21in TT

J & K class destroyer (1938-40)
2,330 tons fl, 36kts,
6 x 4.7in/45-cal, 5 x 21in TT

Leander class light cruiser (1931-34)
9,200 tons fl, 32kts, 8 x 6in/50-cal, 8 x 4in/45-ca, 8 x 21in TT

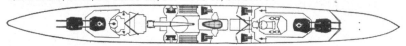

Southampton class light cruiser (1937-39)
11,650 tons fl, 32kts, 12 x 6in/50-cal, 8 x 4in/45-cal, 6 x 21in TT

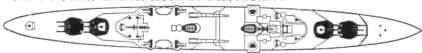

Marine Nationale

Guépard class large destroyers
3,200 tons fl; 35.5kts,
5 x 5.45in/40-cal, 6 x 21.7in TT

Regia Marina

Spica class torpedo boat (1936-38)
1,000 tons fl; 34kts, 3 x 3.9in/47-cal, 4 x 17.7in TT

Freccia class destroyer (1931-32)
2,110 tons fl, 38kts, 4 x 4.7in/50-cal, 6 x 21in TT

Zara class heavy cruiser (1931-32)
14,300 tons fl, 31kts, 8 x 8in/53-cal, 16 x 3.9in/47-cal

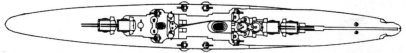

Abruzzi class light cruiser (1936)
11,575 tons fl, 34kts, 10 x 6in/55-cal, 8 x 3.9in/47-cal, 6 x 21in TT

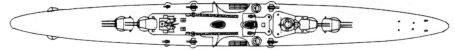

An Italian convoy cutting through rough seas during the winter of 1940/41, as seen from the torpedo boat *Cassiopea*. *(Andrea Tani/Enrico Cernuschi collection)*

Rear Admiral Luigi Biancheri on the bridge of the light cruiser *Garibaldi*, 21 August 1943. An energetic and respected commander, Biancheri personally led the landing party that recaptured the island of Castelorizzo from British commandos in February 1941. *(Aldo Fraccaroli collection)*

Germany's improvised fleet. *TA22*, formerly the Italian torpedo boat *Giuseppe Missori*, on the Dalmatian coast. Captured by Germany at Durazzo in September 1943, she served in the Kriegsmarine from December 1943 to June 1944, when an Allied air attack damaged her beyond repair. *(Storia Militare)*

The carrier sank the next day, only twenty-nine miles east of Gibraltar, principally due to poor damage control.

The five MTBs of the 3rd S-boat Flotilla reached La Spezia on 18 November after a trip through the Rhine–Rhône Canal disguised with dummy funnels as "harmless black tugs." They arrived at Augusta and, after an engine overhaul, reported as operational on 11 December. They began laying mines off Malta on 16 December.[24]

Meanwhile, the British sought to intensify the pressure on the African traffic by dispatching Force K, formed by two cruisers and two destroyers, to Malta on 21 October. "Its exploits during the next two months were to be an outstandingly successful exercise in the operational use of intelligence."[25]

Beta Convoy Battle

Supermarina quickly learned that surface ships had returned to Malta and temporarily suspended its convoys. Force K's first foray, on the night of 25 October, missed a squadron of Italian destroyers that were ferrying troops to North Africa.[26] However, deadlines imposed by the planned 21 November offensive against Egypt and Tobruk forced Supermarina to assemble an unusually large convoy, codenamed Beta, of seven ships, loaded with 13,290 tons of general cargo, 1,579 tons of ammunition, 17,281 tons of fuel, and 389 vehicles. The close escort consisted of six destroyers, while the distant escort included two heavy cruisers and four destroyers.

The convoy's route to Tripoli bent far to the east of Malta. Experience dictated the principal danger from the night portion of the passage would come from aircraft and that a surface interception was nearly impossible unless the enemy knew the convoy's exact route and speed. In the unlikely event a night encounter ensued, improved training and the recent introduction of primitive radar detection and jamming countermeasures gave Regia Marina staff some confidence the escort could handle the situation. Supermarina did not appreciate the evolving capability of British radar or the enemy's knowledge of the convoy's itinerary.

A Maryland "discovered" Beta on the afternoon of 8 November. Force K weighed anchor at 1730 and proceeded east-northeast at twenty-eight knots, planning to intercept at 0200. However, the ASV Wellington that was supposed to vector the British onto their target suffered radio and radar failures, and the mission nearly failed. Force K reached a point 135 miles east of Syracuse, where "we had, indeed, almost given up hopes of finding them, and were getting very near the time for turning homeward, when, at 0039, we suddenly raised a signal from *Aurora* reporting the enemy."[27] (See table 9.1.)

Table 9.1   Beta Convoy Battle, 9 November 1941, 0057–0140

Conditions: Wind, NNW, force 3; light cloud; clear with bright moon; moderate swell	
British ships—	Force K (Captain W. G. Agnew): CL: *Aurora* (F), *Penelope;* DD: *Lance, Lively*[D1]
Italian ships—	3rd Division (Rear Admiral Bruto Brivonesi): CA: *Trieste* (F), *Trento*
	13th Destroyer Squadron *Granatiere,* (F) *Fuciliere, Bersagliere, Alpino*
	10th Destroyer Squadron—Close Escort (Captain Ugo Bisciani): *Maestrale*[D2] (F), *Fulmine*[Sunk], *Euro*[D2], *Grecale*[D4], *Libeccio, Oriani*
	Convoy: *Duisburg*[Sunk] (GE 7,389 GRT), *San Marco*[Sunk] (GE 3,113 GRT), *Maria*[Sunk] (IT 6,339 GRT), *Rina Corrado*[Sunk] (IT 5,180 GRT), *Sagitta*[Sunk] (IT 5,153 GRT); Tankers: *Minatitlan*[Sunk] (IT 7,599 GRT), *Conte di Misurata*[Sunk] (IT 5,014 GRT)

Beta sailed on course 170 degrees at nine knots in two columns a half-mile apart. On the starboard side *Duisburg* led *San Marco* and *Conte di Misurata;* to port *Minatitlan* preceded *Maria* and *Sagitta,* while *Rina Corrado* brought up the rear between the two columns. *Maestrale* sailed at the convoy's head, while *Euro* and *Fulmine* guarded the starboard side, *Oriani* and *Libeccio* the port side, and *Grecale* the rear. The cruiser force zigzagged at twelve knots three to five miles astern, the direction considered most vulnerable to enemy attack.

Aurora approached, followed by *Lance, Penelope,* and *Lively,* maneuvering to a position down-moon on the convoy's starboard quarter. During this evolution *Fulmine* sighted the enemy but assumed they were Brivonesi's cruisers.

At 0050 the British column turned starboard to the east-northeast directly toward the convoy and reduced speed to twenty knots. Two minutes later *Aurora*'s lookouts spotted the cruisers looming vaguely in the darkness to port. Captain Agnew assumed they were more merchant ships following destroyers, and he decided to focus on the larger target dead ahead. Agnew's battle plan stressed the importance of early hits and distributed fire; also, the ships were to refrain from illumination. His plan represented an evolution of the original Admiralty doctrine, which specified: "The essence of night fighting is surprise followed by prompt action. . . . [I]f the most effective action is not taken immediately it is unlikely that there will be time to recover."[28] (See map 9.2.)

Map 9.2 Beta Convoy Action

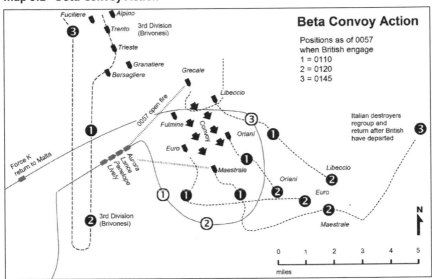

With the moon faintly silhouetting their target, *Aurora* laid her guns with Type 295 radar and opened fire at 0057, range fifty-seven hundred yards, followed seconds later by *Penelope* and *Lance*. The flagship's first three salvos staggered *Grecale*, and ignited large fires. *Penelope* aimed at *Maestrale*. *Lance* took on one of the cargo ships and then, after hitting from four thousand yards, shifted fire to *Fulmine*.

The convoy leader, *Maestrale*, reacted to the outburst of gunfire by turning away to port. Captain Bisciani, assuming the cruisers had his starboard quarter covered, was uncertain where the sudden attack had originated. He ordered smoke and then veered back to the southeast, keeping ahead of the convoy. *Libeccio* and *Oriani* remained on the unengaged side. Brivonesi's cruisers had just come about to their southeast heading, fifty-five hundred yards off the convoy's starboard quarter. *Bersagliere*, his lead destroyer, broadcast that the enemy bore 155 degrees. Brivonesi steered southwest and increased speed from twelve to eighteen knots.

At 0059 *Aurora* turned ninety degrees to run down the convoy's starboard side, unknowingly pulling away from Brivonesi's approaching cruisers. The merchant ships filled the air with antiaircraft fire and made no attempt to scatter or turn away. For the British it was pick and shoot. Four broadsides from *Aurora* set *Rina Corrado* aflame. *Lance* switched fire to *Grecale*, and at 0100 *Lively*'s first rounds devastated *Duisburg*.

At 0103 *Penelope* engaged *Fulmine* as that destroyer turned to make a torpedo attack. A 6-inch shell from the first salvo exploded on *Fulmine's* bridge, mortally wounding her captain and snuffing her offensive intention. At the same time *Trieste* opened fire seven thousand yards off *Lively's* starboard quarter."Accuracy of aim," an Italian report complained, "was difficult because the English ships, steaming southward in line ahead, were'end-on'to the cruisers' gunfire; also, in a short time the targets disappeared behind the smoke of the burning steamers and their destroyer's smoke screen."[29] No one in Force K realized that a pair of heavy cruisers was even present.

Lance launched a torpedo at 0104 and claimed a hit on *Minatitlan*. One minute later both *Penelope* and *Lively* landed flurries of shells on *Fulmine,* now just twenty-five hundred yards off their port beams. Heavily perforated below her waterline, the destroyer capsized and sank within minutes.

As *Fulmine* foundered, the heavy cruisers turned south, and Brivonesi ordered nineteen knots. The situation remained murky to the Italian admiral, and at 0108 *Trieste* fired star shell. Meanwhile, *Euro's* Commander Cigala Fulgosi, who had distinguished himself as *Sagittario's* captain, came hard to starboard toward the enemy line. Untouched, he closed to nearly two thousand yards, his torpedoes aimed and ready to fire. Then Bisciani ordered the destroyers to concentrate around his flagship on the convoy's port side. This caused Fulgosi to think the enemy must be on the port side and that he was stalking *Trieste.* Consequently he turned away, realizing his mistake only when *Lively* and then *Aurora* and *Penelope* engaged. The cruisers hit *Euro* six times, but their 6-inch shells passed through without causing major damage. *Maestrale* made smoke and circled the convoy's head to its port side. At 0108 *Aurora* targeted the Italian flagship; Bisciani lost his ability to influence the battle further when splinters cut *Maestrale's* radio antennas.

As *Libeccio, Oriani, Maestrale,* and *Euro* withdrew eastward to regroup the convoy continued on course, engaging imaginary bombers. One of *Penelope's* crew wrote, "The ships seemed to make no effort to escape, and it was all too easy; they burst into flames as soon as we hit them. A large tanker was like a wall of flame, and an ammunition ship gave a superb display of fireworks before she blew up with a tremendous explosion."[30] Agnew led his column to port around the convoy's head. By 0120 the British were heading east; at 0125 they began looping to the north to pass up the convoy's other side, setting one ship after another ablaze.

Brivonesi's cruisers were still coming south, working up to twenty-five knots. At 0123 *Lance* reported a large number of four-gun salvos falling around her. Agnew ordered *Penelope* to engage this"destroyer"one minute later, and she fired seven 4-inch salvos at *Trieste*. Then, as the British column turned to port and began to head north, they "disappeared behind the smoke of the burning steamers and their destroyers' smoke screen."[31] The heavy cruisers ceased fire at 0125 and turned north four minutes later, when Brivonesi conceived the notion of intercepting the enemy withdrawal. *Trieste* and *Trento* shot 207 8-inch and 82 3.9-inch rounds in twenty-three minutes and claimed one hit before the enemy vanished in the night.

Agnew ceased fire at 0140 as the British passed behind the convoy. Every ship in sight was burning. Concerned about the shortage of 6-inch ammunition at Malta (*Penelope*, for example, only fired 259 6-inch rounds), Force K headed home at 0205. The Italian destroyers finally "counterattacked" as a unit at 0207, making smoke and firing salvos, far too late for the enemy even to notice. At 0230 Force K passed twenty miles astern of Brivonesi's cruisers, which were still sailing north.

Force K had destroyed the convoy, roughed up the escort, and escaped harm except for splinter damage to *Lively*—near misses holed her funnel and a steam pipe on the starboard siren. To add to the Italian misery, the next morning the submarine *Upholder* torpedoed *Libeccio* as she was rescuing survivors.

The Beta action was one of the most brilliant British naval surface victories of the war, demonstrating superior doctrine, technology, and leadership, combined with luck, surprise, and inept opposition. Supermarina relieved both admirals involved. The escort commander, Bisciani, faced a commission of inquiry that eventually dismissed him without charges. Iachino intervened on behalf of Brivonesi, the cruiser admiral, and he subsequently commanded the naval base at La Maddalena. The Germans were furious and wanted to force the Regia Marina to accept German officers as advisors, even aboard Italian warships. Raeder reported to Hitler, "Today the enemy has complete naval and air supremacy in the area of the German transport routes. . . . [T]he Italians are not able to bring about any major improvements in the situation, due to the oil situation and to their own operational and tactical impotence."[32]

Crusader

General Claude Auchinleck, the British Middle East commander in chief, launched his meticulously prepared and long-delayed Crusader offensive on 18 November, preempting an Axis attack by three days. His objective was to quickly conquer Cyrenaica. London held such high expectations that on 18 October the chiefs of staff had advised the Middle Eastern commanders that they planned to exploit the situation by launching an invasion of Sicily on 9 December with four divisions being held in the United Kingdom."The assumption is that Italian morale will have collapsed as a result of a heavy defeat and that, in consequence, there may be a psychological moment for striking at Sicily simultaneously with an advance on Tripoli."[33] However, Auchinleck and Cunningham forestalled this Churchillian venture, which was fortunate, because Crusader degenerated into a slugfest that rapidly consumed painstakingly accumulated stocks of fuel and ammunition on both sides. The British finally reached El Agheila on 6 January and did not clear the last Axis enclaves at Sollum and Bardia until 17 January. By that time, their"blow was spent."[34]

After the Beta convoy debacle Supermarina experimented with small, scattered, simultaneous convoys, or single-ship sailings, as means of confusing the enemy and minimizing losses. Signals intelligence, of course, defeated such tactics. The Italians sailed an important four-ship convoy from Naples, escorted by heavy and light cruisers, on 20 November, but the British had already worked out its exact route. The submarine *Utmost* torpedoed *Trieste,* while a Swordfish torpedoed *Abruzzi;* with the escort so weakened, the convoy withdrew to Naples rather than risk a surface night attack. The Regia Marina also pressed warships into service as emergency transports and used submarines to land a few hundred tons of fuel and munitions directly at the front, enough to supply a mobile division for a day.

Maritza Convoy Action

On 23 November Italy had six one- and two-ship convoys at sea, revising tactics in the belief that more targets would spread the risk and reduce the damage. Force K sortied from Malta at 2330, instructed to seek a particularly important two-ship group carrying"what the Sigint [signals intelligence] had described as fuel cargo of decisive importance to the [German air force], although Captain Agnew, not being an Ultra [Allied cryptanalysis of the most sensitive Axis codes] recipient, believed he was acting on an aerial sighting."[35] Four hours later, Force B—*Ajax* and *Neptune* and destroyers *Kimberley* and *Kingston,* commanded by Rear Admiral H. B. Rawlings—departed Alexandria seeking the same target. Shortly after 0800 on 24 November, the submarine *Settembrini* sighted Force K, and Supermarina promptly ordered all ships back to port; however, the convoy the British were after, two small German steamers, proceeding at five knots from Piraeus to Benghazi escorted by two torpedo boats, failed to get the message; sailing in an area of German responsibility, it missed the recall order because it was broadcast on Italian frequencies.

At 1310 Agnew's ships reached the Piraeus–Benghazi route and began sweeping northwest in a line of bearing, each ship five miles apart. There were Axis aircraft in the air, but most ignored the British ships. At 1526 *Penelope* sighted smoke, and Agnew came to the north-northeast and closed at full speed. (See table 9.2.)

Table 9.2   *Maritza* Convoy Action, 24 November 1941, 1535–1630

Conditions: Low clouds with rain squalls	
British ships—	Force K (Captain W. G. Agnew): CL: *Aurora* (F), *Penelope*[D1]; DD: *Lance*, *Lively*
Italian ships—	Convoy Escort (Lieutenant Commander Mimbelli): TB: *Lupo* (F), *Cassiopea*[D1]
	Convoy: *Maritza*[Sunk] (GE 2,910 GRT), *Procida*[Sunk] (GE 1,842 GRT)

The convoy was 110 miles west southwest of Antikithera Island when, at 1535, Lieutenant Commander Mimbelli sighted Force K coming up fast. Having defended a convoy off Crete six months before, he had a good idea what to expect. The torpedo boats turned toward the attackers emitting smoke, while *Maritza* and *Procida* turned north-northwest. Two Ju.88s accompanying the convoy dive-bombed the squadron at 1540, but their bombs fell wide.[36]

The British destroyers deployed to *Penelope*'s port and starboard quarters to protect against air attack and assist if needed while *Aurora* stood by in support. At 1547 *Penelope* engaged from twenty-two thousand yards, forcing the escorts to chase salvos. Mimbelli hoped to delay the British and give the German air force time to mount a strike from Crete. Therefore *Lupo,* perhaps trading on her reputation as the luckiest ship in the Italian navy, made a dash toward the cruiser while *Cassiopea* maintained the smoke. At 1603 *Lupo* opened fire from fifteen thousand yards, and at ten thousand Mimbelli's ship launched a pair of torpedoes. *Penelope* easily avoided these and continued pressing forward, laying a heavy fusillade around the twisting torpedo boat. *Lupo* fired her last torpedoes and then withdrew in the face of *Penelope*'s relentless advance.

Penelope pushed the Italian escorts into a rainsquall to the northwest. By 1620 the range between the British cruiser and the slow steamers had dropped to four thousand yards. As crews hurriedly abandoned ship, *Penelope* commenced a steady, aimed bombardment that ignited both fuel-laden vessels. They collided, and at 1632 first one and then the other blew up. Satisfied with this result,

Force K returned to Malta. Force B, when it received word of the action, headed back to Alexandria.

Although the Italian escorts had fought more effectively than at night, they had lacked the firepower to affect the final outcome. In all, *Lupo* had expended 116 and *Cassiopea* 188 3.9-inch rounds. Splinters lightly damaged *Penelope* and *Cassiopea*. Because stocks of 4-inch shells were low in Malta, the British destroyers had held fire to conserve ammunition.

The risk involved in every sortie was demonstrated two days later. Admiral Cunningham, pressed by Churchill (who wired his naval commander on 23 November, "Stopping of these ships may save thousands of lives apart from aiding a victory of cardinal importance"), had sailed with the Mediterranean Fleet to support further sorties of Force K and Force B.[37] At 1625 on 25 November *U-331* penetrated the fleet's screen and torpedoed *Barham*. She capsized several minutes later and exploded, with the loss of 861 men. This was the German navy's second major success in the Middle Sea, and it appeared to vindicate Hitler's decision to send submarines there. However, these successes had a cost. By the end of December there were twenty-three German submarines in the Mediterranean, but three had been sunk transiting the Straits of Gibraltar and five during operations, prompting Dönitz to write, "It should, therefore, be investigated whether the value of operations in the Mediterranean and off Gibraltar and prospects of successes by U-boats outweigh those high losses."[38]

The Admiralty, meanwhile, calculating that it could multiply Axis losses by basing another surface strike group in Malta, pressured Cunningham to make it so. He replied, "I have hesitated to send further forces to Malta owing to the fuel situation but in view of the overriding necessity to stop enemy supply I am sending [Force B] tomorrow."[39]

Mantovani Convoy Action

The Italian convoys, which had returned to port at the time of *Maritza* incident, regrouped and set out again at the end of November in five separate one- and two-ship formations, supported by three cruisers, three destroyers, and a covering force consisting of *Duilio*, the light cruiser *Garibaldi*, and six destroyers. Force B had transferred to Malta, and with Force K, it sailed at 0500 on 30 November to intercept two convoys that had sailed from Brindisi and Taranto bound for Benghazi.

The combined force, commanded by Admiral Rawlings, took position south of the convoys' projected track at 2100 and waited for reports from an ASV Wellington to vector it in. At 2248 the aircraft radioed that a single ship with a destroyer escort bore fifty miles south. Rawlings detached Force K to develop this sighting while he stood north to search for the larger prize. However, one of the two convoys had already returned to port after losing a ship to air attack; the other eluded the British and reached Benghazi.

Homed in by the Wellington, Force K sighted the solitary Italian auxiliary *Adriatico* (1,976 tons and two 4.7-inch guns) at 0225 in bright moonlight. *Aurora* approached to fifty-five hundred yards and at 0304 scored one hit with her second broadside. She then stood by to give the crew a chance to abandon ship, but instead *Adriatico* returned fire. Following this courageous but futile display, *Aurora* pounded the small auxiliary and at 0340 left *Lively* to finish her off while the cruisers shaped a course of 300 degrees to take them beyond Axis air range before daylight.

At 1040 on 1 December, Force K, while steaming for Malta, received reports of a tanker and destroyer near Kerkenah Bank. Lacking specific orders or confirmation that aircraft had sunk the sighted ships, Agnew elected to steer Force K toward this contact. (See table 9.3.)

Table 9.3 *Mantovani* Convoy Action, 1 December 1941, 1800–1953

Conditions: Clear
British ships— Force K (Captain Agnew): CL: *Aurora* (F), *Penelope*[D1]; DD: *Lively*
Italian ships— Convoy Escort: (Captain Francesco Dell'Anno): DD: *Da Mosto*[Sunk]
Convoy: *Mantovani*[Sunk] (10,540 GRT)

Mantovani was bound for Tripoli, but intelligence based on Italy's compromised machine cipher, C38m, had disclosed her route. Three planes from Malta torpedoed the tanker at 1310, leaving her dead in the water. *Da Mosto* passed a line and began slowly towing *Mantovani* toward Libya; however, the air attacks continued, and after another hit at 1650 the tanker began to settle by the stern, seventy-five miles northwest of Tripoli.

At 1714 Force K spotted aircraft circling about twenty miles away and headed in that direction, sighting masts a half hour later. The aircraft, three Italian CR.42s, closed the British, but antiaircraft fire drove them off. *Da Mosto* was rescuing survivors when at 1800 her lookouts reported the unwelcome sight of enemy cruisers.

Aurora engaged *Da Mosto* at 1801 from sixteen thousand yards. *Penelope* hauled out of line and held fire so as not to spoil her sister's aim. *Da Mosto's* Commander Dell'Anno turned toward the enemy. At eleven thousand yards the destroyer emptied one set of tubes, made smoke, and reversed course, ducking into the protection of her own smoke. Her return fire was wide of the mark, falling five to seven hundred yards from *Lively* in tightly grouped patterns.

The cruisers continued forward, so *Da Mosto* emerged from her smoke, advanced to sixty-five hundred yards, and launched a second torpedo attack. Up until this point she had not been hit. With torpedoes away, she turned back toward her smoke screen, but at 1809 a 6-inch shell struck *Da Mosto's* aft magazine, and the detonation blew away the destroyer's stern. The cruisers turned back toward Malta at 1830, while *Lively* rescued survivors and then at 1953 dispatched *Mantovani* with a single torpedo.

The Battle of Cape Bon

The toll of ships lost and materials sent to the deep was one component of the Axis supply crisis. The other was the disruption caused by delayed or aborted sailings. Signals intelligence from German air force Enigma showed that the loss of *Maritza* "had placed German operations in 'real danger' and had necessitated the ferrying of fuel by all available aircraft and by Italian destroyers."[40]

Italy's first-generation light cruisers also carried gasoline to Africa. On 9 December the *Di Giussano* and *Da Barbiano* sailed, but air attacks forced them to abort their mission and seek shelter in Palermo. On 12 December, this time accompanied by the torpedo boat *Cigno,* they set forth once again, bound for Tripoli carrying 950 tons each of aviation fuel in cans loaded "in every available corner, even on the bridge" and nine hundred tons of other supplies.[41] Supermarina ordered them to assiduously avoid any engagements.

Despite advance notice of this important sailing, Force K remained in port to conserve fuel. Accordingly, Vice Admiral Malta proposed to attack the Italian cruisers at dawn with torpedo bombers. The 4th Destroyer Flotilla, en route from Gibraltar to Alexandria to reinforce the Mediterranean Fleet, likewise heard the news. Commander Stokes increased speed from twenty to thirty knots, hoping to intercept. (See table 9.4.)

Table 9.4   Battle of Cape Bon, 13 December 1941, 0323–0328

Conditions: Clear	
Allied ships—	4th Destroyer Flotilla (Commander G. H. Stokes): *Sikh* (F), *Maori, Legion, Isaac Sweers* (DU)
Italian ships—	4th Division (Vice Admiral A. Toscano): CL: *Alberico Da Barbiano*[Sunk], *Alberto Di Giussano*[Sunk]; TB: *Cigno*

The British destroyers hurried along the African coast, staying in French waters to avoid enemy minefields. At 0302, as they approached Cape Bon, look-outs spotted flashing lights and ship silhouettes that quickly disappeared behind the promontory. Altering course from east to southeast at 0316, *Sikh,* followed by *Legion, Maori,* and *Sweers,* rounded the cape in pursuit, although Stokes believed he had little chance of engaging. Admiral Toscano, meanwhile, heard "a noise of aircraft in the sky above our formation" and assumed British aircraft had fixed him. Mindful of his orders, he decided to abort his mission and executed a simul-taneous turnabout, which put *Cigno* far to the formation's rear.[42]

As Stoke's flotilla steadied on its new course, the British commander was surprised to see the Italian cruisers fine off his port bow. He only had time to steer slightly inshore to hide against the dark mass of Cape Bon's rocky prom ontory and to signal the ships behind that the enemy was in sight.

At 0323 *Sikh* edged starboard and fired four torpedoes at *Da Barbiano* from fifteen hundred yards. The run to target at this range was slightly over a minute. Toscano's lookouts had just spotted shapes off the port bow when they reported torpedo tracks as well.[43] There was no time to avoid, and within seconds the 4th Division's flagship erupted into flames as two of *Sikh's* salvo slammed into her hull. By this time *Legion* also had two torpedoes in the water, likewise aimed at *Da Barbiano.* The destroyers unleashed their 4.7-inch and machine guns; bullets shredded the gasoline cans lashed to the deck of both ships.

One of *Legion's* two torpedoes hit *Da Barbiano,* but the cruiser was already sinking. *Di Giussano* had time to fire three 6-inch salvos, but the rapidly con-verging destroyers were difficult targets, and the shells exploded ashore. Her captain ordered thirty knots. When *Legion* saw that she and *Sikh* were launching torpedoes at the same cruiser, she aimed her last six at *Di Giussano.*

At 0327 a torpedo hit *Di Giussano* amidships, along with two 4.7-inch shells and a stream of machine-gun fire. There was a massive explosion; the cruiser swerved fifteen degrees to port and began losing way.[44] *Maori,* the third ship, fired two torpedoes and claimed a hit on *Da Barbiano.*

Cigno had just reversed course when flames flared up ahead. As the Allied ships passed she launched a torpedo and opened fire, incorrectly claiming sev-eral scores. *Sweers* in turn targeted the torpedo boat, straddling her and launch-ing four torpedoes, which all missed. Allied destroyers continued south at high speed, leaving *Da Barbiano* sinking in a sea of flames and *Di Giussano* waging a losing fight against uncontrollable fires. Admiral Toscano, with more than nine hundred members of his division, died.

The Battle of Cape Bon was an embarrassing defeat. Ciano was moved to write, "What is happening in the Navy is baffling, unless what Somigli says is true, and that is, that our General staffs are obsessed by an inferiority complex that paralyzes all their activities."[45] Tactically, Toscano could not have picked a worse time to reverse course, although his real error was in coming about simultaneously rather than in line ahead, which would have allowed *Cigno* to continue leading.

The World Scene

Events in the Mediterranean had worldwide ramifications. The German liaison officer in Rome, Rear Admiral Eberhand Weichold, correctly noted that "the British command had long been carefully preparing for a second offensive in Cyrenaica. . . . This was done at the expense of other theaters of war. The defense of Malaya and Singapore had to bear the cost of the Cyrenaica offensive."[46] Likewise, the British naval forces facing the Regia Marina were greater by far than those facing the Imperial Japanese Navy. British global strategy had been seriously derailed by the requirements of fighting Italy and the failure to win meaningful victories against it.

America's entry into the conflict might have seemed beneficial for Great Britain, but this was to prove true only in the long term. The immediate consequences were negative. With Lend-Lease, active patrolling by the U.S. Navy in the Atlantic, and American occupation of important points like Iceland, Great Britain had accrued many of the advantages of American participation during 1941 and none of the negatives. With the attack on Pearl Harbor, however, this was no longer the case. Moreover, the furious Japanese offensive forced the British to defend another naval frontier. They suffered serious losses in East Asia, losses that up through 4 March 1942 included a battleship, a battle cruiser, two cruisers, and six destroyers. Hitler and Mussolini both were happy, and over the next nine months it seemed their satisfaction had good cause.

10

The Axis Resurgent

1942

Today [13 November 1941] the enemy has complete naval and air supremacy in the area of the German transport routes; he is operating totally undisturbed in all parts of the Mediterranean.

—Grand Admiral Raeder, *Fuehrer Conferences on Naval Affairs*

The New Year of 1942 found our naval situation in the Eastern Mediterranean depressing in the extreme.

—Admiral Cunningham, *A Sailor's Odyssey*

On 15 December 1941, as the Italo-German army withdrew from Gazala, its supply situation was so critical that Axis air forces in Libya had fuel for just one day's operations. Defeat loomed unless the Italian navy could fight a major convoy through to Tripoli. In this crisis Supermarina turned to the tactic used in the uncertain days of July 1940 and mustered the entire fleet to break the British blockade. Ciano upon hearing the plan cynically remarked, "All the ships and all the admirals at sea. May God help us!"[1]

The submarine *Upright* frustrated the first attempt, Operation M41, on 13 December, when she torpedoed the merchantmen *Fabio Filzi* (6,835 GRT) and *Carlo del Greco* (6,836 GRT) outside of Taranto. Two other freighters collided in the confusion caused by the attack. Then the submarine *Urge* penetrated *Vittorio Veneto*'s screen and torpedoed her on 14 December. Supermarina, with no time to dwell upon this depressing start, launched a repeat, Operation M42, two days later.

M42 included four motor ships—*Monginevro* (5,324 GRT), *Napoli* (6,142 GRT), *Vettor Pisani* (6,339 GRT), and the German freighter *Ankara* (4,768 GRT)—directly escorted by seven destroyers and one torpedo boat. *Duilio,* three light cruisers, and three destroyers provided the close covering force, while distant support included *Littorio, Doria,* and *Cesare,* heavy cruisers *Gorizia* and *Trento,* and ten destroyers. The freighters departed Taranto two hours before dusk on 16 December. Three were bound for Tripoli; *Ankara*'s final destination was Benghazi. (See map 10.1.)

Map 10.1 Axis Resurgent, November 1941–August 1942

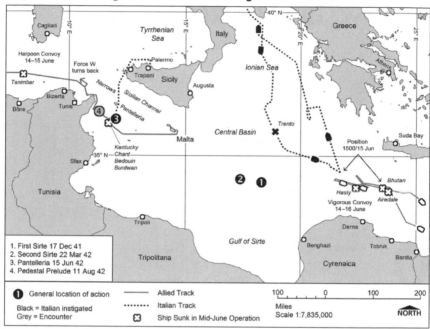

By chance, the British also had a convoy at sea. A fuel shortage was limiting the activity of the Malta-based warships. Thus, naval storeship *Breconshire* sailed from Alexandria on 15 December to replenish the island with five thousand tons of fuel oil. The escort group was commanded by the newly arrived Rear Admiral Philip Vian, who had led a destroyer flotilla in a night action against *Bismarck* and a cruiser force against a German convoy off Norway. It included the 15th Cruiser Squadron and the 14th Destroyer Flotilla. The next day Cunningham learned of the Italian convoy and ordered Vian to attack it after *Breconshire*'s safe arrival. Force K and the 4th Destroyer Flotilla sallied from Malta to reinforce Vian. Force B—light cruiser *Neptune* with destroyers *Jaguar* and *Kandahar*—followed later. Cunningham stayed in Alexandria with *Queen Elizabeth* and *Valiant*, because he lacked enough destroyers to screen them.

After receiving his instructions, Vian ordered three warships back to Alexandria: the antiaircraft cruiser *Carlisle*, too slow for a night action; *Kingston*, which had developed machinery defects; and *Hasty* to escort the pair. The remainder of Vian's squadron joined Force K at 0800 on 17 December. The combined flotilla endured a series of Italo-German air attacks throughout the afternoon, dodging torpedoes on six occasions. Vian knew there were Italian battleships at sea; an 1122 sighting placed them 150 miles north of his position. He turned west by southwest at 1400 to reduce the chance of contact as he awaited better information.

Admiral Iachino received intelligence at 1024 of a battleship (*Breconshire* had been disguised as a capital ship), two cruisers, and twelve destroyers steering west at twenty knots. He turned southwest and increased speed to twenty-four knots at 1145. At 1408 a scout plane reported the enemy steering 300 degrees at twenty-two knots. Unfortunately for Iachino, the aircraft, one of *Littorio's* Ro.43 floatplanes, got the heading wrong by sixty degrees: the enemy was farther south than the Italian admiral anticipated.

At 1700, after pressing south most of the day, with the heavy cruisers probing ten miles ahead of his battleships, Iachino slowed, concluding the enemy was too distant to engage before dark. Then, at 1730, lookouts reported smoke bursts on the eastern horizon. This was the British fleet repelling another air attack. Iachino turned in this direction, and as the sun disappeared, British masts poked into view. (See table 10.1.)

At 1742 *Naiad* reported a contact bearing 300 degrees, range seventeen miles. One British participant related,"We had been receiving reports all day of a strong Italian battle squadron at sea, but as the last position given for this force was some eighty miles to the north of us there seemed no danger . . . so we examined [these ships] with interest but without excitement. . . . As we watched, however, more masts appeared, among them the unmistakable control tower of an Italian eight-inch gun cruiser. . . . [T]here was a dim red glow from the leading Italian, like a cigarette end as the smoker draws on it in the dark and then a bunch of tall thin splashes came up round us."[2] At 1747 Vian's force simultaneously turned due south. A minute later the Italian battleships steered to follow, as did the cruisers of the 3rd Division, now five thousand yards south-southeast of Iachino's battleships.

At 1753 *Littorio* opened fire from thirty-five thousand yards—the longest-range opening salvo fired during the war using optical sights.[3] As *Breconshire, Decoy,* and *Havock* continued south Vian swung his four cruisers and remaining destroyers toward the enemy, engaging the 3rd Division and laying smoke to protect *Breconshire*. The 14th Flotilla briefly pulled ahead, intending to launch a torpedo attack, but at 1757 Vian recalled it, thinking such an action premature unless the Italians directly threatened the transport.[4]

Table 10.1 First Battle of Sirte, 17 December 1941, 1753–1804

Conditions: Poor weather and rough seas

Allied ships—	15th Cruiser Squadron (Rear Admiral P. L. Vian): CL: *Naiad* (F), *Euryalus*
	14th Destroyer Flotilla (Captain P. J. Mack): *Jervis* (F), *Kimberley, Kipling*[D1], *Nizam* (AU), *Havock, Decoy*
	Force K (Captain W. G. Agnew): CL: *Aurora* (F), *Penelope;* DD: *Lance, Lively*
	4th Destroyer Flotilla (Commander G. H. Stokes): *Sikh* (F), *Legion, Maori, Isaac Sweers* (DU)
	Convoy: Breconshire (9,776 GRT)
Italian ships—	Battleship Division (Admiral A. Iachino): *Littorio* (F), *Doria, Cesare*
	3rd Division (Rear Admiral Angelo Parona): CA: *Gorizia, Trento*
	9th Destroyer Squadron: *Oriani, Gioberti*
	10th Destroyer Squadron: *Maestrale*
	12th Destroyer Squadron: *Corazziere, Carabiniere*
	13th Destroyer Squadron: *Granatiere, Bersagliere, Alpino, Fuciliere*
	16th Destroyer Squadron: *Usodimare*

The Italian heavy cruisers and even the destroyers engaged, and their gun-fire proved uncomfortably accurate despite the range. *Gorizia* believed she had sunk a destroyer and *Maestrale* that she had hit another. A member of *Jervis*'s crew recalled "the 15in shells sounded like motor buses going overhead."[5] Splinters damaged several British ships, including *Kipling,* which suffered one death. Vian's cruisers maneuvered wildly to confuse the enemy aim, and in the process he "not only lost contact with the enemy but also for a time with his own ships."[6] Iachino facilitated Vian's efforts to break contact when, at 1804, he ordered a ninety-degree starboard turn, incorrectly believing that the British destroyers had launched torpedoes. At the same time the Italians ceased fire. Iachino then turned north at 1828; his mission was to protect the convoy sixty miles north of his position. He had reports of Force B's departure from Malta but judged that the escort and close support groups could deal with that threat. He was more concerned that Vian might circle around to attack the valuable merchantmen. Thus, he ordered the convoy to steer north for four hours while he protectively zigzagged along the enemy's line of approach, until 0200 on 18

December. At 0825 he rejoined the convoy and conducted it south until 1300, when he came about and shaped course for Taranto.

Vian, meanwhile, ordered his scattered ships to concentrate. Force K remained with *Breconshire*. Force B joined Force K at 0700 on 18 December, having failed to locate the enemy. *Breconshire* and her escort made Malta at 1500 on 18 December. Vian, with the 15th Cruiser Squadron and the 4th and 14th destroyer flotillas, patrolled north in three columns along the anticipated enemy track. At 0230 on 18 December, having sighted nothing, Vian broke off and steamed for Alexandria at high speed.

The Italian convoy split into two sections, with each ship escorted by two destroyers. *Ankara* made Benghazi on 18 December, but the three freighters bound for Tripoli ran into an air raid. Believing that mines might have been dropped, the freighters anchored ten miles outside port while they waited for sweepers to clear the way. Two Albacore torpedo-bomber squadrons attacked them and achieved a nonlethal hit on *Napoli*. At 1830 on 18 December, Forces B and K steamed from Malta hell bent to hit this target before the freighters could find refuge in Tripoli.

Neptune, Aurora, and *Penelope,* with *Kandahar, Lance, Havock,* and *Lively,* were twenty-three miles off Tripoli Harbor at 0300 on 19 December, steaming in line ahead at thirty knots. As they crossed the hundred-fathom line, still supposedly in safe waters, *Neptune*'s paravanes exploded a mine. As the other ships sheered off to port and starboard, *Neptune* backed into another mine, which wrecked her propellers. Then *Penelope* and *Aurora* touched off mines. Heavily damaged, *Aurora* struggled back to Malta at sixteen knots. *Penelope,* lightly damaged, stood by to assist *Neptune* when she drifted clear, but instead the flagship detonated a third mine. *Kandahar* tried to pass a tow, but she herself tripped a mine that blew away her stern. Finally, at 0400 a fourth explosion staggered *Neptune.* The cruiser capsized and sank within five minutes. Only one man from her crew of 763 was eventually rescued, by an Italian warship. On the morning of 20 December, *Jaguar* saved all but ninety-one of *Kandahar*'s men and then torpedoed the hulk.

British accounts typically trumpet the First Battle of Sirte as another example of their moral ascendancy. For example,"Undaunted by the disparity in strength, the British cruisers and destroyers moved in to attack, [but the Italians] soon drew off to the north."[7] Italians, in contrast, hail it as a victory that greatly raised morale:"It was one of the three or four turning points of the war for Italy.... [T]he route to Libya, red with the blood of Italian sailors, could now be considered open again."[8] Even the Kriegsmarine's Admiral Weichold acknowledged, "The convoy reached its destinations without losses. The task has been completed and the critical supply situation in North Africa has improved considerably."[9]

The mining of Force B and K, the Battle of Sirte, and the convoy's success-ful arrival were not the only Italian victories that night to stagger a Royal Navy already buffeted by the November losses of *Ark Royal* and *Barham* and the sink-ing of *Repulse* and *Prince of Wales* in the Far East.

Riding SLC submersible torpedoes, X MAS commandos penetrated Alex-andria Harbor on 19 December while the antitorpedo net was down to per-mit Vian's return. They sank *Queen Elizabeth* and *Valiant* in the harbor's shallow waters—although both were later refloated—and damaged the oiler *Sagona* (7,554 GRT) and destroyer *Jervis*. Finally, the Germans reconstituted their air forces on Sicily and by the end of December were subjecting Malta to heavy attack. On 5 January 1942 another major convoy, escorted by the Italian fleet, arrived safely at Tripoli. On 21 January Italian and German forces counter-attacked from El Agheila, and within weeks Rommel was again threatening Tobruk from the Gazala line.

The Pendulum Swings

Throughout the winter of 1942 Malta's situation progressively deteriorated. As early as 3 January the island's commander, Vice Admiral Wilbraham Ford, wrote to Cunningham, "I've given up counting the number of air raids we are getting. . . . Damnable to be so useless. Something must be done at once."[10] In fact, the Royal Navy remained absolutely committed to keeping Malta via-ble. "It had become 'The Verdun of the Naval War'—an outpost that it took dis-proportionate losses to maintain and resupply rather than a useful base."[11] On 8 January Operation MF2 shepherded transport *Glengyle* (9,919 GRT) to Malta and returned *Breconshire* to Alexandria without incident. Convoy operation MF3 sailed on 14 January. Vice Admiral Carlo Bergamini departed Taranto on the morning of 15 January with *Duilio,* two light cruisers, and seven destroyers, and Rear Admiral Angelo Parona left Messina with two heavy cruisers and five destroyers, but both failed to locate the British.[12] *P36* torpedoed the destroyer *Carabiniere* on 16 January as the force was homeward bound. The convoy landed twenty-one thousand tons of cargo on 19 January, the first substantial delivery of supplies in four months, although at the cost of destroyer *Gurkha* and one of the four transports, *Thermopylae* (6,665 GRT)—victims of German submarine and air attacks, respectively.

Convoy MF4 made Malta on 27 January, fighting through air attacks with-out damage to the escort or the sole transport, *Breconshire*. Convoy MF5, dis-patched in mid-February, however, was a complete failure. The escort consisted of *Carlisle,* one fleet destroyer, and seven destroyer escorts. Cover included the three light cruisers of the 15th Squadron and eight fleet destroyers. Air attacks damaged *Clan Campbell* (7,255 GRT), forcing her to turn back, and sank *Clan Chattan* (7,262 GRT) and *Rowallan Castle* (7,798 GRT).

Throughout this period, small convoys shuttled between Italy and North Africa. Major operations supported by *Duilio* included the movement of four transports that arrived in Tripoli on 24 January (although at the cost of ex-liner *Victoria* [13,098 GRT], sunk by torpedo bombers), six transports on 23 February, and four more on 9 March.

Despite the increasing fury of the Axis air offensive, Force K, with *Penelope* and five to six destroyers, remained at Malta, but it mostly escorted empty transports out from Malta and shepherded full ones in. On the night of 7 February it achieved a rare surface success when, west of Sicily, *Lively* and *Zulu* sank a pair of Italian coasters, *Aosta* (494 GRT) and *Grongo* (316 GRT). Vian sailed from Alexandria to intercept a reported convoy on 10 March. His three cruisers and nine destroyers could not locate the enemy, and during the return to base, *U-565* sank *Naiad*, his flagship, north of Mersa Matruh. Vian was fished from the sea, "cold and oily"; the submarine escaped.[13]

As food stocks dropped to critical levels, the British mounted a major convoy operation in mid-March in conjunction with a sortie by Force H to fly off Spitfires to bolster the island's air defenses.

On 20 March *Breconshire*, *Clan Campbell*, *Pampas* (5,415 GRT), and the Norwegian *Talabot* (6,798 GRT) departed Alexandria at 0700, accompanied by *Carlisle* and the 22nd Flotilla. Vian, with the 15th Cruiser Squadron and the 14th Flotilla, followed eleven hours later. The 5th Flotilla, consisting of seven Hunts, had sortied from the Egyptian base a day earlier to sweep for submarines in advance of the convoy's route and then to refuel at Tobruk before joining the escort. This group passed *U-652*, which torpedoed *Heythrop* at 1100 on 20 March and then escaped. *Eridge* attempted to tow the stricken ship to Tobruk, but *Heythrop* foundered at 1600.

The British took extensive measures to forestall air attacks on the convoy, including commando raids on airfields and demonstrations by the 8th Army.[14] These resulted in a quiet passage through the danger zone between Crete and Cyrenaica, but the Italian submarine *Platino* reported the convoy at 1420 on 21 March south of Crete. Supermarina concluded that a major Malta operation was under way and swiftly ordered two surface groups to intercept. Admiral Iachino led *Littorio* and four destroyers from Taranto at 0027 on 22 March, while three cruisers and four destroyers, under Rear Admiral Parona, left Messina at 0100. The Italians believed that their movements were unknown to the British, but while this was true of Parona's cruisers, signals intelligence and the submarine *P36* gave notice of *Littorio*'s departure.[15]

Vian's ships joined the convoy escort at 0600 on 22 March; *Penelope* and *Legion* arrived from Malta two hours later. Vian had received *P36*'s contact report at 0518, so he headed west by southwest, speed thirteen knots, to delay contact until evening "if practicable."[16] His orders were to "evade the enemy if possible until dark, when the convoy—dispersed if it seemed advisable—was to be sent on to Malta with the Hunt class destroyers, and the remaining warships were to attack the enemy."[17]

Axis air attacks commenced shortly after 0930 on 22 March as the British passed beyond fighter escort range. "The forenoon attempts were not dangerous, however, being only a few torpedo shots at long range by Italian S.79 aircraft."[18] Vian anticipated the enemy might intercept him during the afternoon, and in that event he intended to maintain smoke between them and the convoy and to employ his force in seven independent divisions, organized as follows:

First—*Jervis, Kipling, Kelvin,* and *Kingston*
Second—*Dido, Penelope,* and *Legion*
Third—*Zulu* and *Hasty*
Fourth—*Cleopatra* and *Euryalus*
Fifth—*Sikh, Lively, Hero,* and *Havock*
Sixth—*Carlisle* and *Avon Vale* to lay smoke
Seventh—the other five Hunts to escort the convoy.

A storm developed as the Italians pressed south, and heavy seas reduced the destroyers to twenty-two knots; one returned to Taranto with mechanical problems. Parona's cruisers passed east of *Littorio*'s track and by 1400 were fifty-five miles ahead of the battleship. The Italians had aerial reports to facilitate their contact, although as Parona dryly noted in his report, these were "not always in agreement."[19]

At 1422 *Gorizia*'s lookouts spotted flak bursts to the south-southeast, and *Euryalus* sighted Parona's division five minutes later. At the time the rising wind was blowing at twenty-five knots from the southeast. Visibility hovered below twenty thousand yards. (See table 10.2.)

Contact had come several hours before Vian had expected, and this presented the British admiral with a quandary. If the convoy was to avoid a morning run through the bomber-infested waters off Malta with minimal escort (there was not enough oil in the island to refuel the 15th Squadron and 14th Flotilla), it could not detour far from its direct course. Thus, Vian "could not afford to be entangled in operations at night far to the westward."[20] All he could do was implement his defensive plan and hope for the best. Parona's orders helped; these called for him to make visual contact and then "to communicate news without engaging."[21]

Table 10.2 Second Battle of Sirte, 22 March 1942, 1427–1858

Conditions: Gale building to hurricane, misty, extremely rough seas	
British ships—	15th Cruiser Squadron (Rear Admiral P. L. Vian): CL: *Cleopatra*[D2] (F), *Dido, Euryalus*[D1]
	Force K (Captain Angus Nicholl): CL: *Penelope* (F); DD: *Legion*[D1]
	Escort Group (Captain D. M. L. Neame): CLA: *Carlisle*
	22nd Destroyer Flotilla (Captain St. J. A. Micklethwait): *Sikh*[D1] (F), *Zulu, Lively*[D1], *Hero, Havock*[D4], *Hasty*
	14th Destroyer Flotilla (Captain A. L. Poland): *Jervis* (F), *Kelvin, Kingston*[D3], *Kipling*
	5th Destroyer Flotilla (Commander C. T. Jellicoe): DE: *Southwold* (F), *Beaufort, Dulverton, Hurworth, Avon Vale, Eridge*
Italian ships—	Group Littorio (Admiral A. Iachino): BB: *Littorio*[D1] (F)
	11th Destroyer Squadron *Ascari, Aviere, Oriani*
	Group Gorizia (Rear Admiral A. D. Parona): CA: *Gorizia* (F), *Trento* CL: *Bande Nere*
	13th Destroyer Squadron: *Alpino, Bersagliere, Fuciliere, Lanciere*

The convoy and escort division turned southwest, while *Carlisle* and *Avon Vale* trailed smoke. The strike force formed columns by division and headed west by northwest, also spewing white chemical and black funnel smoke. The wind drove the dense clouds ahead of the British warships directly toward the Italian cruisers.

Parona's force labored southwest in a line of bearing with *Gorizia* in the center, the destroyers to starboard, and *Trento* and *Bande Nere* to port. At 1429, as the British columns advanced toward him, Parona turned north, "to lead the cruisers toward the *Littorio* group."[22] Parona had from Iachino, a notoriously rigid commander, strict written instructions that were based on Iachino's expectation that the British would pursue. Trying to perfect the Gavdos action, he hoped to trap the enemy between the 3rd Division and *Littorio*.

Parona's cruisers engaged at 1435 from twenty-three thousand yards with their aft turrets. The heavy sea caused the ships to pitch and roll, and spray blew into their range finders. This, along with the smoke and long ranges, rendered accurate gunnery impossible, although Parona incorrectly claimed a hit on a *Dido*-type cruiser.[23]

The British divisions sailed in a large semicircle, turning northeast at 1433 to further spread the smoke, then northwest at 1456, when *Cleopatra* and *Euryalus* began to return fire against *Bande Nere* from twenty-one thousand yards. *Penelope's* Captain Nicholl wrote, "[We] began a long-range battle, and a number of shell splashes fell quite close to us. The smoke carried by a rising south-easterly wind was lying perfectly, completely screening the convoy from the enemy."[24] The British cruisers bracketed *Bande Nere*, and many shells fell around her, but none hit. For her part, *Bande Nere* straddled *Cleopatra* and *Euryalus*.

Due to the smoke few of the other British ships sighted the enemy, and only *Lively* discharged a few rounds. By 1513 all guns had fallen silent, and two minutes later Vian swung southwest to rejoin the convoy.

During this engagement, the convoy endured attacks from German Ju.88s. The Hunts and *Carlisle's* 4-inch guns foiled these in a barrage described as "impressive, resembling continuous pom-pom fire, even though heard at a distance of 8 to 10 miles."[25] The only damage occurred when *Carlisle* and *Avon Vale* collided while dodging bombs. However, as Vian aptly noted about these escorts, their "potentiality for rapid high angle fire far outran their capacity for storing the ammunition."[26] The convoy returned to its westerly heading at 1520. At 1535 Vian signaled Cunningham that he had driven off the enemy. He rejoined the convoy by 1630 and, because the Hunts had depleted their supply of antiaircraft ammunition, ordered the first and the smoke-laying divisions to join the close escort.

Parona's cruisers, meanwhile, had sighted *Littorio* at 1530. The weather continued to deteriorate, with the wind rising to thirty knots and whipping the spray into a low-lying mist. The Italians assumed a line of bearing, with Parona's division to the west-northwest of Iachino, and shortly after 1617 *Littorio's* lookouts spotted a *Dido*-type cruiser bearing 210 degrees. The battleship's floatplanes reported the convoy beyond the enemy cruisers. Iachino now possessed a fairly accurate picture of the enemy's strength and disposition. He immediately adjusted course to starboard and headed due west.

Vian learned that his signal to Cunningham had been premature at 1637, when *Zulu* reported four unknown ships eighteen thousand yards to the northeast. *Euryalus* confirmed, and the strike force, less the first division, which remained with the convoy, stood north by northeast and commenced spouting smoke.

A British history remarks,"It was probably the first time since the days of sail when to hold the 'weather gauge' was decisively important."[27] Admiral Iachino called it an "unpropitious atmosphere for a naval combat. . . . The visibility conditions were already very bad and continuously grew worse, aggravated by the presence of an immense extended mass of smoke."[28] Given that only two hours of daylight remained, the admiral elected to use his superior speed to position his force between the British and Malta and to attack the convoy from that direction. He did not believe there was time to duck behind the enemy into the teeth of the gale to gain the weather gauge, and he was leery of losing contact and then having to reestablish it once again if he did so. Likewise, Iachino decided not to split his force and risk defeat in detail. (See map 10.2.)

Map 10.2 Second Battle of Sirte, 1705–1840

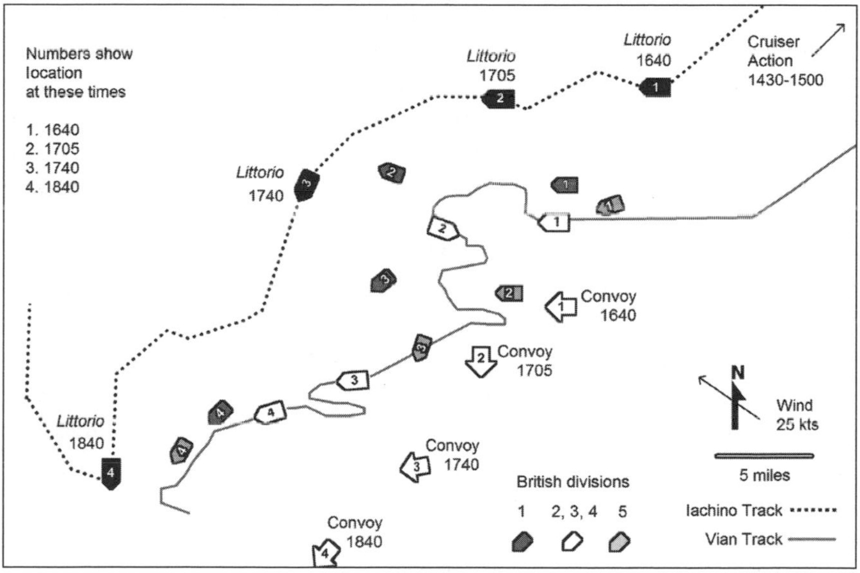

At 1643 the cruisers engaged. *Bande Nere* landed a round on *Cleopatra's* bridge with her second salvo, disabling the radar and radio and killing fifteen men. Shortly thereafter, a metal shard from a near miss killed another man. *Littorio's* guns rumbled into action from 18,800 yards and one-ton shells straddled *Euryalus,* peppering the cruiser with large splinters. Vian's division ducked into the smoke at 1648. *Dido's* Captain H. W. McCall later recalled, "The smoke was at that time extremely dense; 15-inch guns could be heard firing at no great distance, occasional large splashes were seen, and the positions of destroyers were obscure; so that a very exciting period ensued until we emerged from the smoke steering an easterly course at 1703."[29]

This exchange lasted until 1652, when poor visibility rendered further shooting pointless. Iachino slowly narrowed the range, however. At 1703 *Dido* discharged nine broadsides at either *Trento* or *Gorizia* and *Penelope* a few salvos at *Bande Nere*. Both cruisers incorrectly claimed hits. At 1703 *Littorio* engaged *Dido* until McCall sought the shelter of the smoke at 1712.

Micklethwait's fifth division—*Sikh, Lively, Hero,* and *Havock*—sailed roughly parallel south-southwest of the enemy until 1705, when it turned south, "to avoid punishment."[30] To the Italian lookouts this maneuver made it appear the British destroyers had launched torpedoes, and *Ascari* even reported tracks. Thus, at 1707 Iachino altered course twenty degrees starboard before coming back to 270. He ordered his three destroyers to counterattack, and under enemy fire, they launched torpedoes and then turned north. The convoy and its close escort pitched and plunged south-southwest, the rising gale on their port beam.

As the Italians were not significantly closing range, *Cleopatra* and *Euryalus* freshened the smoke, gradually looping southeastward and then west at 1714 and to southeast again at 1720, firing sporadically as gunlayers glimpsed targets.

At 1718 Iachino turned thirty degrees port to 240, then ten degrees back to starboard to 250, reducing speed to twenty knots. Parona's cruisers were falling into line behind the battleship. At 1720 *Littorio* near missed *Havock* from fourteen thousand yards. A perforated boiler cut the destroyer's speed to sixteen knots and forced her to limp south and join the convoy escort.

At 1727 *Littorio* targeted *Sikh* when she briefly poked her bow beyond the smoke. Then, at 1730, Vian decided to take the second, third, and fourth divisions "in search of two enemy ships not accounted for and which I thought might be working round in the rear."[31] This action was based on the British admiral's misappreciation of his opposition and his opinion of what they ought to be doing, although, with nightfall so near, Iachino had had no time for such a lengthy maneuver, even if it had commenced long before.

Vian's run east—which he later characterized as "a serious tactical error"—left Micklethwait's fifth division's three remaining destroyers facing the entire Italian formation.[32] At 1731 Iachino, now heading south by southwest, began to close range and reengaged. Micklethwait turned north, replying to *Littorio*'s 15-inch projectiles with 4.7-inch and 4-inch shells, in, as he called it, a "somewhat unequal contest."[33] Then the destroyers veered back south, spewing billows of wind-whipped smoke. At 1735 Vian reversed course and plunged blindly back through his own smoke. Iachino was now nearly thirty thousand yards away from the British flagship. The convoy itself was twenty-five thousand yards south of *Littorio.*

Poland's first division, with *Legion* tagging along, had made for the convoy as ordered, and when the second Italian attack developed he contented himself with making smoke. Poland's first taste of battle came at 1745, when he beheld mist-filtered gun flashes to the northwest. The convoy commander on *Breconshire,* apparently fearing air attacks more than a battleship falling upon his merchantmen, resumed a southwesterly course at 1745.

Micklethwait forestalled the Italians with threatened torpedo attacks, but at a cost. After the battleship straddled *Sikh* at 1748 from twelve thousand yards he ordered the convoy to immediately turn south, and as *Littorio* slowly drew ahead, he fired two torpedoes "in order to avoid sinking with all torpedoes on board and in the hope of making the enemy turn away."[34]

At 1752 Iachino ceased fire, because he could see nothing to shoot at. With the seas on their port beam the Italian ships pitched and rolled—the heavy cruisers as much as twelve degrees and the light cruiser by as much as twenty-seven degrees. It was worse for the destroyers. Nonetheless, Iachino was slowly blocking the convoy from its destination, and at 1759, with the situation appearing critical, Vian made the general signal, "Prepare to fire torpedoes under cover of smoke."

At 1803 *Cleopatra,* returning to the battle zone, engaged *Littorio* from thirteen thousand yards and at 1806 discharged three torpedoes. *Littorio* jogged northwest to avoid these. As the battleship disappeared in smoke, neither the other British cruisers nor the two destroyers accompanying the flagship could launch torpedoes. Vian then turned east again, obsessed by the enemy cruisers he believed he had lost track of. He later justified this action: "While it was evident that the battleship and some cruisers were attempting to pass to leeward of the smoke, it was equally evident that the enemy's most effective course of action was to pass to windward (east) of it and that all this force was not with the battleship so that some cruisers might be taking this course of action."[35] Vian steamed away from the enemy until 1817. At 1808 Poland overheard an alarming message from Micklethwait that placed the Italians only sixteen thousand yards north of the convoy. This prompted him to turn northwest.

Micklethwait was alarmed because his fifth division remained the only British force between Iachino and the convoy. At 1819, with the range at six thousand yards, he jogged northward to lay more smoke. Iachino steered 280-degrees until 1820, when he came to 220, turning to 180 at 1827. Poland was trying to help, but a torpedo-bomber attack at 1823 delayed him. Finally, at 1834 Poland spotted *Littorio* just twelve thousand yards away.

The Italian column had resumed fire at 1831. Poland turned his ships west in line abreast replying with sixteen guns under central control. A member of *Legion's* crew would recall, "Looking through my gunlayer's telescope, we seemed to be right alongside the battleship."[36] The British commander reported the Italian return fire as erratic.

At 1841 with the range at six thousand yards, Poland swung starboard (*Legion,* the southernmost ship, went to port, because she had already trained her tubes to starboard). As *Kingston* turned *Gorizia* hit the destroyer hard in her boiler room, igniting a fire and temporarily bringing her to a halt.[37] The Italians were blazing away with every gun that could bear. Nonetheless, the first division began launching torpedoes at 1844. *Jervis* launched five of her nine, the weather preventing a full salvo; *Kipling* discharged all five, *Kelvin* four of five (she had fired one earlier in error), *Legion* all eight; and *Kingston* fired three of five, because the hit just received had damaged two tubes. The Italian spotters saw *Legion* disappear in a forest of two-hundred-foot-high geysers as a 15-inch salvo spouted around her and were astonished to see her emerge on the same course and speed, apparently undamaged. Iachino turned 110 degrees to starboard and reduced speed from twenty-two to twenty knots to avoid this attack. Lookouts spotted one torpedo passing ahead of *Littorio,* and others bubbled between the Italian ships.

As Poland's destroyers charged, Vian's three divisions were rushing west with *Dido* and *Penelope,* and *Zulu* and *Hasty* following some distance astern of *Cleopatra* and *Euryalus.* The lead cruisers supported Poland by engaging *Littorio,* and the battleship returned their attentions. *Euryalus's* captain recorded, "Then, at 6:41 PM, the battleship *Littorio* spotted *Euryalus* through a gap in the smoke screen. I saw flashes from her fifteen-inch guns rippling down her side as she fired a salvo at us. . . . An age seemed to pass before her shells arrived with a deafening crash, as they plunged into the water all round us, engulfing the ship in columns of water masthead high. We'd been straddled. . . . *Euryalus* shuddered and shook and then rocked so violently that I thought the topmast would come down, while fragments of shell screamed through the air to bury themselves in our ship's sides."[38]

At 1851 Iachino turned north-northwest and increased speed to twenty-six knots. With darkness rapidly descending, he did not want to linger in torpedo waters and chance a last-minute disaster. In fact, at 1855 the fifth division attempted a torpedo attack from eight thousand yards. *Lively* launched eight torpedoes, but *Sikh* and *Hero* held fire, not having a clear shot. *Littorio* barked back with her aft turret. The blast set her floatplane ablaze and caused the British to credit themselves with having inflicted a serious hit. Then a 15-inch shell landed beside *Lively* and pierced her hull and superstructure, with splinters causing some flooding. In turn, also at 1855, a 4.7-inch shell struck *Littorio* on her starboard aft deck. This parting shot was the only hit the British achieved during the entire battle.

By 1858 both sides had ceased fire. The Italians had fired 1,492 rounds, while the British cruisers had replied with more than 1,600 and the destroyers 1,300, as well as thirty-eight torpedoes.[39] The convoy was untouched, but the British had suffered damage to six warships. During the surface action the escort had successfully fought off twenty-eight air attacks, which, up to about 1800, consisted of German Ju.88s and then Italian S.79 and German He.111 torpedo aircraft. In the process, however, it had expended most of its remaining ammunition.

The weather continued to deteriorate as Iachino put about for home. *Scirocco* foundered the next morning, as did *Lanciere*, which had inadvisedly sailed to reinforce *Littorio* on 22 March. Their pumps could not keep up with flooding caused by the heavy seas and the need to follow a proscribed course; when electricity failed, the destroyers rapidly sank. Only eighteen from their combined complement of 471 men survived. *Bande Nere* and *Geniere* suffered heavy storm damage but made port. On 1 April, the submarine *Urge* would torpedo and sink *Bande Nere* while she was sailing north to make repairs.

At 1940 Vian turned back to Alexandria, less *Penelope* and *Legion* and the damaged *Havock* and *Kingston*, which all headed for Malta. Sailing through the teeth of the rising gale, the British ships also experienced weather damage, although not on the scale suffered by the Italians. The convoy dispersed and headed for Malta at each ship's best speed, accompanied by *Carlisle* and the Hunts. The convoy master knew that he was painfully behind schedule, and he did not care to complete the rest of the journey at the best speed of the slowest ship, *Clan Campbell*. But, given the horrible weather and the fact most escorts had little ammunition remaining, a concentrated force might have fared better than proved the case.

Due to the detour forced by the surface action, even the fastest merchant ships, each escorted by only a Hunt or two, remained at sea the next morning and came under heavy air attack. *Talabot* and *Pampas*, hit by two dud bombs, made Grand Harbor between 0900 and 1000 on 23 March. *Breconshire* was heavily bombed at 0920 and forced to anchor near Marsaxlokk when efforts to tow her to Grand Harbor failed, and German aircraft sank *Clan Campbell* twenty miles short of the island. A near miss damaged *Legion*. She was beached and subsequently towed into Malta. *Southwold*, while patrolling offshore to guard *Breconshire*, struck a mine and sank on 24 March. Unrelenting air attacks destroyed *Legion*, *Breconshire*, *Talabot*, and *Pampas* on 26 March and most of the

25,900 tons of cargo and oil they carried. A British wartime account paints this disaster in a heroic hues: "Sailors and soldiers, with divers in the flooded holds, working night and day regardless of bombs, saved much of the invaluable cargo and many precious tons of oil fuel from the *Breconshire*."[40] In fact, Maltese longshoremen refused to unload the ships during air attacks, and the governor was very slow to order soldiers to undertake the task. The ships sat in harbor several days before they were sunk, and in all that time only 807 tons were unloaded. Subsequently, troops salvaged another thirty-three hundred tons—all in all, a disappointing return for the effort expended.[41]

Admiral Cunningham described the Second Battle of Sirte as "one of the most brilliant actions of the war, if not the most brilliant."[42] The Admiralty assessment, however, was considerably less enthusiastic, stating that "the providential escape of the March convoy, [was] mainly due to weather."[43] In fact, Italian performance in the Second Battle of Sirte does not suffer in comparison to that of others in similar engagements. Germans warships twice attacked British convoys in the Arctic Ocean. In the first instance, on 1 May 1942, four old and underarmed escorts easily fended off three large, modern German destroyers. During the Battle of the Barents Sea on 31 December 1942, a British destroyer flotilla feinted torpedo attacks for three hours to repulse two German heavy cruisers and six large destroyers.[44] The action off Samar in October 1944 provides another example of the difficulty of penetrating smoke and torpedo-armed escorts, even under favorable conditions, to get at, in that case, a group of escort carriers.

In fact Iachino conducted an intelligent action under extremely difficult conditions. Plunging with his precious battleship through an enemy smoke screen, with large numbers of torpedo-armed warships waiting on the other side, entailed risks that no other competent commander—British, German, Japanese, or American—would have dared take. Although Iachino ran out of time before he could actually engage the merchantmen, the Italians shot much better than the British, suffered negligible battle damage, and forced the convoy to detour south and ultimately to scatter. This meant that even the fastest merchant ships had to face another morning of air attacks, which otherwise would not have been the case. Also, because the British escorts fired off most of their antiaircraft ammunition while the fleet units fought the surface engagement, the extra air attacks that the battle made possible were particularly effective. Iachino did not cover himself in glory, but he accomplished his mission.

Spring 1942

On 3 April Admiral Cunningham hauled down his flag. "He left behind little more than light forces . . . and [his fleet's] remnants clung on to a shrinking portion of the eastern basin. It was a force which enjoyed little scope for initiative and, with Malta's desperate hour at hand, even less in the months to come."[45] Acting Admiral Henry Harwood, a Churchill favorite since his victory over *Graf Spee* in December 1939, replaced Cunningham on 22 April.

Also in April, Axis air forces savaged Malta, dropping more bombs than during any other month and forcing the Royal Navy to finally withdraw its surface forces after losing destroyers *Lance*, *Gallant*, and *Kingston*, a minesweeper, three submarines, a tanker, and several smaller vessels. *Penelope* escaped in such poor condition that she earned the nickname "HMS *Pepperpot*." Small Italian convoys crisscrossed the Mediterranean regularly, suffering light losses to submarines. The U.S. Navy entered the Mediterranean war, lending the aircraft carrier *Wasp* to fly off Spitfires to Malta on 20 April and 9 May. Italian destroyers, MAS boats, and German S-boats thickened the minefields surrounding Malta. The 3rd S-boat Flotilla, now fourteen boats strong, laid twenty-four fields from 16 December through the middle of May. They saw little of the British, sinking a motor launch and a trawler. *S31* struck a mine just off Valletta on 10 May, while *S34* fell victim to a shore battery on 17 May. The rest of the flotilla transferred to Derna on 21 May.

On 27 April Germany decided that the land war held priority over the naval war and transferred most Luftwaffe units operating from Sicily to Libya. On 21 May the Axis command postponed Operation Herkules, an Italo-German operation to capture Malta with paratroop and amphibious forces. Italy considered the conquest of Malta essential to victory, but it was not a German priority. In a conference with Raeder on 15 June 1942, Hitler acknowledged the operation's importance but proceeded to list all the reasons it was infeasible, including the Eastern Front situation, a lack of transport planes, and distrust of Italian troops. He also rationalized, "The British efforts to get convoys through to Malta from the east and from the west testify the plight of the island. These convoys, by the way, give us an opportunity to inflict much damage on the enemy."[46]

While the German air force was supporting the land war, Malta experienced a period of relative calm. Throughout May seven hundred tons of bombs fell on the island, just a tenth of the April total and most of those in the first ten days of the month, before the island received heavy reinforcements of Spitfires.[47]

On 11 May Harwood, in his first major initiative, dispatched the 14th Flotilla from Alexandria to intercept an Italian convoy reported to be en route to Benghazi. This proved disastrous when German aircraft pounced on the destroyers south of Crete and sank *Lively, Kipling,* and *Jackal. Jervis* returned to Alexandria, crammed with 650 survivors. Other than this ill-fated episode, the Mediterranean Fleet kept largely to port. Carrier forces from Gibraltar made ferry runs to Malta on 18 May and 9 June.

On 26 May Axis forces attacked the 8th Army's Gazala Line. After a see-saw struggle, Panzer Army Africa captured Tobruk on 21 June. By 30 June Rommel had approached El Alamein, only sixty miles west of Alexandria. This was the consequence of six months of continuous Axis domination of the central Mediterranean, during which Italy transported 441,878 tons of material to North Africa, suffering losses, principally due to British submarines, of only 6 percent.[48]

By June, despite reduced air harassment, Malta's powers of resistance were ebbing fast. The civilian population was down to a daily diet of twelve to fifteen hundred calories. Malta's governor estimated that starvation would force surrender within two months.

To succor the island the British planned a simultaneous double-convoy operation from Alexandria and Gibraltar, following the pattern successfully pioneered in 1941. The western operation consisted of five steamers and one tanker the Admiralty codenamed Harpoon, while the operation from the east, which included eleven merchant ships, was called Vigorous. The escort for Vigorous, under Admiral Vian's command, totaled eight light cruisers, twenty-six destroyers, four corvettes, two minesweepers, and the ex-target ship *Centurion* in disguise as a modern battleship—the Mediterranean Fleet's greatest display of strength since 1941, made possible by the Eastern Fleet's loan of four cruisers and ten destroyers.

Supermarina knew a large convoy operation was in the works, and air attacks against Taranto in early June led to the deduction that the enemy would make its major effort in the eastern basin.[49] British intelligence "from reading the messages from the network of Axis agents . . . knew how much the enemy knew." However, the fact that the principal Italian navy code remained secure meant that "against the ever present threat of intervention by the Italian fleet it was not possible to rely on advance notice."[50]

Vigorous sailed on 12 June. A destroyer captain later wrote, "The ring of warships round the convoy was a heartening sight and represented a tremendous volume of A-A [antiair] fire power."[51] It lost only two ships, one to bomb damage and the other to straggling, as it approached the dangerous waters between Crete and Libya. On 14 June massive antiair barrages deflected seven Axis air attacks at the cost of one freighter. At 1430 that same afternoon at Taranto, Admiral Iachino weighed anchor, planning to intercept the enemy at 0930 the next morning. He had *Littorio* and *Vittorio Veneto*, heavy cruisers *Gorizia* and *Trento*, light cruisers *Garibaldi* and *Duca d'Aosta*, and twelve destroyers.

Admiral Harwood, in his first major test, found himself making crucial decisions based on insufficient information leavened with hope. At 1825 aircraft reported two battleships and four cruisers clearing the Gulf of Taranto. At 2315, in response to a query from Vian whether he should face battleships with his cruisers, Harwood ordered the convoy commander to press on until 0200 and then reverse course. Vian duly brought his force about at the appointed time, but in the midst of this awkward maneuver six boats from the Derna-based 3rd S-boat Flotilla, which had been stalking the convoy since sunset, struck. *S54* clipped *Newcastle* in the bow with a torpedo, inflicting six months' worth of damage, and *S55* sank the destroyer *Hardy*.

At 0525 Harwood ordered Vian to return to his original west-northwest course. He hoped to hamstring the enemy using Beaufort torpedo bombers and newly arrived American B-24s, as well as a submarine picket line that lay across their course.

A night torpedo attack by four "Fishingtons" (torpedo-armed Wellingtons) from Malta failed. However, Beauforts attacking from Malta at 0610 torpedoed *Trento* and claimed damage to the battleships, just as they were passing the submarines, none of which could get into position to attack. At 0905 eight B-24s from Egypt delivered a high-level attack and claimed a dozen hits on both battleships. Just as the B-24s were winging off, Beauforts, also from Egypt, came in low; they claimed at least one hit on a battleship (the Americans, still in a position to observe, said it was a cruiser). In fact, the only result of both attacks was a bomb that bounced off *Littorio*'s A turret. At 0828, when reconnaissance reported the Italians still coming, Harwood ordered Vian "to reverse course, in the hope that he would meanwhile receive reports of success, as the air and submarine attacks on the Italians developed." This delayed the convoy, and continued air attacks damaged *Birmingham*, sank the Hunt *Airedale*, and further depleted reserves of antiair ammunition.[52]

At 1151 Harwood ordered Vian to reverse course a fourth time, once again toward Malta, after he received the exaggerated reports of the 0900 attacks. Vian, however, who did not receive this order until 1315, knew the Italian fleet was still pressing onward, and placing little confidence in the airmen's claims, he held steady for Alexandria. By the time aircraft reported that the enemy battleships were withdrawing, the British had neither the time nor ammunition to make a run for Malta. On the way back to harbor *U-205* torpedoed and sank *Hermione*, while Italian air attacks led to the loss of the Australian destroyer *Nestor*. The Italians, however, did not escape unharmed. The submarine *Umbra* dispatched the already damaged *Trento,* while a Fishington torpedoed *Littorio* and put her into dock for nearly three months.

Battles do not always require direct combat. The Vigorous convoy battle was one of the Italian fleet's major victories. The threat of battleships (a threat established by Iachino in March) created the conditions that allowed Axis air and light surface forces to repeatedly attack, and the threat of battleships ultimately caused this massive convoy to turn away—something airpower alone never accomplished.

Harpoon

Coming from the other end of the Mediterranean, the Harpoon convoy consisted of five merchant ships and one tanker. Force X, the direct escort, included the antiaircraft cruiser *Cairo,* five fleet destroyers of the 11th Flotilla, four Hunts of the 12th Flotilla, four minesweepers, and six motor launches. Force W with *Malaya,* carriers *Argus* and *Eagle,* three light cruisers, and eight destroyers, under the command of Vice Admiral Alban T. B. Curteis, provided distant support. The fast minelayer *Welshman* operated independently, and a tanker, accompanied by two corvettes, participated to refuel the escort.

The shortage of oil and the effort against Vigorous reduced the force available to attack Harpoon. "As the British were getting underway, the Italians were shutting down the boilers on their larger ships to save fuel."[53] Supermarina could intervene with only a light cruiser division and a destroyer squadron under Rear Admiral Alberto Da Zara, who departed Cagliari at 1620 on 13 June in response to a report of two British ships north of Tunisia. When the report proved false, Da Zara put into Palermo and awaited events.

By 0800 on 12 June Harpoon's various components united east of Gibraltar and headed toward Malta at twelve knots. They enjoyed smooth sailing, as Axis aircraft did not spot them until 13 June.

The 14th day of June dawned "bright and clear . . . with hardly a cloud in the sky."[54] At 1030, seventy miles north-northwest of Bône, Italian dive-bombers struck. A half hour later Italian torpedo bombers and high-level bombers attacked together. Torpedoes sank the Dutch freighter *Tanimbar* (8,619 GRT) and damaged the cruiser *Liverpool,* which had to be towed back to Gibraltar by a destroyer, escorted by another.

Twice more Axis air forces attacked, without success, although "the *Argus* escaped several torpedoes from the Savoias only by her handiness under helm."[55] Upon reaching the Sicilian narrows at 2015, Force W turned back, and the convoy, accompanied by Force X, commenced its final dash to Malta. An hour later

Map 10.3 Battle of Pantelleria, First Phase, 0530–0730

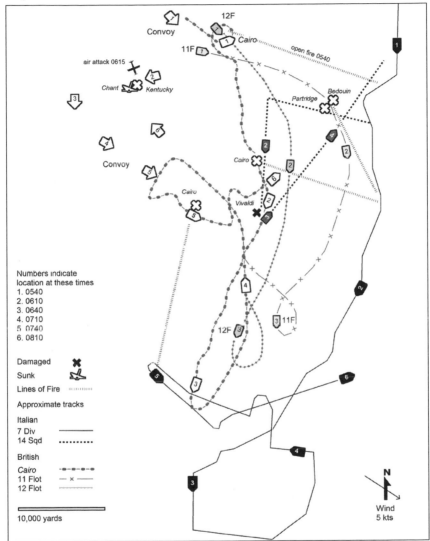

Numbers indicate
location at these times
1. 0540
2. 0610
3. 0640
4. 0710
5. 0740
6. 0810

Damaged
Sunk
Lines of Fire
Approximate tracks

Italian
7 Div
14 Sqd

British
Cairo
11 Flot
12 Flot

10,000 yards

N

Wind
5 kts

the 7th Division departed Palermo, accompanied by two destroyer squadrons. Da Zara had orders to engage south of Pantelleria at dawn on 15 June. En route mechanical problems forced two of his seven destroyers to return to Palermo, but he pressed on nonetheless. A British submarine spotted the Italian warships, but the naval commander at Malta, Vice Admiral Ralph Leatham, calculated they would be joining Iachino, and Admiral Curteis kept Force W on course for

Gibraltar, feeling he needed both of his surviving cruisers to screen the vulnerable carriers.

The last air attack against Harpoon occurred at 2105 as darkness fell. Thereafter, the convoy hugged the Tunisian coast. Lookouts, suffering perhaps from frayed nerves, reported parachute flares to seaward, sparking worry that surface forces were hunting them. One destroyer imagined signals from shore as it rounded Cape Bon, and at 0112 the 11th Destroyer Flotilla engaged the wreck of a British destroyer stranded the year before. *Marne*'s captain even claimed that he saw "the fall of shot ahead of his ship at this time."[56]

At 0520 the British convoy, sailing southeast at twelve knots twenty-five miles southwest of Pantelleria, received an unwelcome radio report from a covering Beaufighter that two enemy cruisers and four destroyers bore off their port beam just fifteen miles away. Harpoon's freighters proceeded in two columns, with the *Cairo* in front. The destroyers sailed ahead—the 11th Flotilla to starboard, the 12th Flotilla to port—and the minesweepers brought up the rear. Da Zara placed his 10th Destroyer Squadron ahead of his two cruisers. The 14th Squadron, which was several knots slower, trailed; Da Zara intended it to operate independently. (See map 10.3)

The two fleets sighted each other almost simultaneously at 0530 in the growing light of dawn. Hardy ordered the 11th Flotilla's fleet destroyers to cut in front of the formation from the unengaged side while the Hunts and *Cairo* made smoke. He wrote: "My immediate intention was to gain time and to fight a delaying action in the hope that an air striking force could be sent from Malta."[57] (See table 10.3.)

At 0540 *Eugenio di Savoia* opened fire from eighteen thousand yards and straddled *Cairo* with her second salvo. As geysers erupted around its ships, the convoy turned away to starboard, while the 11th Flotilla bore toward the enemy at high speed.

Da Zara rang up thirty-two knots at 0544, hoping to draw ahead of his opponents, and ordered his gunners to target Scurfield's destroyers, mistaking them for cruisers. Within four minutes the 14th Squadron's Captain Castrogiovanni radioed that due to engine problems on *Malocello*, his best speed was twenty-eight knots. Da Zara, not considering it practical to fight his cruisers at this speed, ordered Castrogiovanni to peel off and attack the convoy. At 0554 the 14th Squadron turned sharply to starboard and headed west by northwest as the other Italian units continued south.

Castrogiovanni faced a wall of smoke, and almost immediately *Blankney*, followed by her three flotilla mates, surprised him by bursting from the muck and crossing his bow, guns blazing. At 0558 the Italians claimed a hit on the third enemy ship in line. Meanwhile, the 11th Flotilla crossed astern at longer range. The 14th Squadron engaged both enemy formations, as well as the convoy, but at 0600, considering it impossible to continue under such intense fire, *Vivaldi* and *Malocello* turned to port, firing two torpedoes each toward the nearest merchant ship, which was only sixty-three hundred yards away.

Table 10.3 Battle of Pantelleria, 15 June 1942, 0542–1420

Conditions: Wind Force 2 from the northwest

Allied ships—	Force X (Captain C. C. Hardy): CLA: *Cairo*[D2]
	11th Destroyer Flotilla (Commander B. G. Scurfield): *Bedouin*[Sunk] (F), *Partridge*[D3], *Marne*, *Matchless*, *Ithuriel*[D1]
	12th Destroyer Flotilla (Lieutenant Commander P. F. Powlett): DE: *Blankney* (F), *Badsworth*, *Middleton*, *Kujawiak* (PO)
	Minesweepers (Lieutenant Commander A. E. Doran): *Speedy* (F), *Hythe*, *Hebe*[D1], *Rye*
	Convoy: *Chant*[Sunk] (5,601 GRT), *Burdwan*[Sunk] (5,601 GRT), *Troilus* (7,422 GRT), *Orari* (10,350 GRT); Tanker *Kentucky*[Sunk] (9,308 tons)
Italian ships—	7th Division (Rear Admiral Alberto Da Zara): CL: *Eugenio di Savoia*[J1] (F), *Montecuccoli*[D1]
	10th Destroyer Squadron (Captain Riccardo Pontremoli): *Ascari* (F), *Oriani*, *Premuda*
	14th Destroyer Squadron (Captain Ignazio Castrogiovanni): *Vivaldi*[D4] (F), *Malocello*

Even before this attack, the 11th Flotilla, deployed in a widely spaced line of bearing, broke into the clear off the starboard quarter of Da Zara's cruisers. *Bedouin* opened fire with her guns at maximum elevation, but Italian 6-inch projectiles outmatched British 4.7-inch rounds in hitting power and accuracy. One after the other shells rapidly shredded the large destroyer's superstructure. Captain Scurfield later recalled, "One of the first things to go was the mast, and with it the wireless. I knew the bridge had been hit. . . . [M]ost of the signalmen and 'rudolf' men on the flag-deck were either dead or wounded." Concerned that his ship might sink, Scurfield turned the vessel to starboard and ordered an officer to fire torpedoes. "During the turn we were hit several times, but the torpedoes were fired when the sights came on. After swinging past the firing course the ship came to a standstill." Although Scurfield later wrote the range was five thousand yards, the distance to the enemy cruisers was in fact three times that. In total, twelve 6-inch shells perforated *Bedouin,* although several did not explode.[58]

The Italian cruisers divided their fire. At 0600 a 6-inch projectile landed on *Cairo*'s fore superstructure. She replied with her 4-inch guns, "though without much hope of harming the enemy."[59] The British flagship maintained a course roughly parallel to Da Zara and chased salvos. A 6-inch shell slammed into *Partridge* and damaged her engines. At 0602, as she lost headway, *Partridge* too sent torpedoes on an equally long range and low percentage chase.

As the warships battled, eight Italian dive-bombers appeared overhead, and with only the minesweepers to oppose them, they delivered an effective attack. *Chant* suffered a direct hit and quickly sank. Two bombs straddled *Kentucky,* and the concussion cracked a steam line to the main generator. *Kentucky* was a modern American ship with an elaborate electrical system and complex engine room; her newly installed British crew could not make the repairs required to get the otherwise undamaged ship under way. This forced *Hebe* to take her in tow.

Da Zara, slowly drawing ahead of the British formation, continued south as *Marne, Matchless,* and *Ithuriel* swept past their drifting flotilla mates. *Marne* and *Matchless* engaged *Oriani* and *Ascari,* while *Ithuriel* sparred with *Montecuccoli.* The Italian history describes their gunfire as intense.[60] A projectile struck *Montecuccoli* in the officers' quarters, wounding eight men, while *Eugenio di Savoia* suffered light damage from a hit to her hull near the waterline that killed two men. Splinters from near misses peppered *Ithuriel.*[61]

At 0615 Captain Hardy ordered his three remaining fleet destroyers to concentrate on *Cairo.* When *Ithuriel* received the order she was only eight thousand yards from *Montecuccoli* and under "a heavy and accurate fire."[62] She broke off, but *Marne* and *Matchless* continued to parallel the cruisers.

As the main action continued, a second battle raged farther north. After turning south Castrogiovanni's two destroyers made smoke, sniped at the merchant ships as they appeared through gaps in the screen, and engaged the 12th Flotilla, which was ahead to port on a parallel course. From the British perspective, the Italian squadron kept popping in and out of view. The Italians believed they were fighting six enemy vessels eight to nine thousand yards away, with—it seemed to them—some success. At 0612 lookouts reported an explosion on the bow of an enemy destroyer and claimed that she dropped out of line. Then at 0620 a shell detonated in *Vivaldi*'s forward boiler room; within five minutes she was burning and dead in the water. Castrogiovanni ordered *Malocello* to flee, but instead she circled *Vivaldi* with smoke and stood by. The squadron commander sent a dramatic message to Da Zara that he would fight to the last: "Long live the king!" This got Da Zara's attention, and he dispatched Pontremoli's 10th Squadron to

Castrogiovanni's aid. Da Zara rationalized that if the destroyers were reunited into one group they "could also constitute a serious threat to the convoy."[63]

In fact, the battle passed *Vivaldi* by. An intense fire in the vicinity of the engine room defied efforts to control it, but the destroyer soon generated enough steam to get one turbine turning, and this allowed the 14th Squadron to start limping northeast.

A prominent consideration for the Italians was the presence of a twenty-five-mile-long, north-south mine barrage called "7 AN" east of the battle zone. As Castrogiovanni headed toward this barrier's northern end, Pontremoli decided to join him, by first striking southeast toward the southern end, then sailing due north along 7 AN's eastern side and meeting Castrogiovanni above the barrage. This circular route consumed time and valuable fuel, and it left *Vivaldi* exposed for nearly two hours, had the British been interested in finishing her off.

Meanwhile, Da Zara continued trying to come at the convoy from the southwest. He kept his distance, however, as he was leery of torpedoes from out of the smoke and because longer ranges favored his 6-inch guns over the more numerous British 4.7- and 4-inchers. Despite Hardy's 0615 order to concentrate, *Marne* and *Matchless* continued to parallel Da Zara, swapping salvos in an exchange described as, "accurate, though neither succeeded in hitting."[64]

By 0640 Da Zara was south of *Cairo*. After an hour of sustained gunfire, his magazines were running low on HE ammunition. In the face of intense British counterfire, he turned his cruisers due south to open range and then decided to turn east, the direction he knew the enemy eventually had to go. As he explained, "[My] purpose was to prevent the convoy from slipping past to the east by winding around its head and thus force it to reverse course once again."[65] Hardy observed his maneuver and reversed course to close the convoy.

As *Cairo* headed north-northeast the 7th Division circled to starboard and crossed its own track. By 0720 Da Zara was back on a northwesterly course, heading toward the British. The swirling smoke and mist to the northwest obscured the Italian admiral's appreciation of the situation; in fact, the convoy was steering southeast, directly toward him. At 0734, when Captain Hardy caught sight of enemy cruisers, he signaled the convoy commander to make a 180-degree turn while the *Cairo* and the destroyers commenced laying smoke.

Once again the two forces swapped salvos on parallel courses. Da Zara did not like the situation. His two cruisers faced eight enemy ships; his magazines were depleted. Within three minutes, with the convoy once more hidden from view, he hauled about to the southeast. At 0740 a 6-inch AP round struck *Cairo* on the starboard side. The shell penetrated an oil tank, and the engine room began to flood, but pumps kept up with the water, and the shell did not explode.

Da Zara veered east-northeast at 0752 and held this course until 0810, when he turned southeast. The battle was drifting toward 7 AN, and the admiral decided to round the barrier's southern extremity and then head north. Because the convoy was closer to the northern end, he concluded that this is where Hardy would go and that he, Da Zara, could be there to greet him.[66]

The British lost sight of the enemy by 0830, at which point Hardy came about to find the convoy. *Partridge* had restored power and taken *Bedouin* in tow. *Partridge* advised Hardy that she intended to make for Gibraltar, but Hardy ordered her to join the convoy, "as I considered that this gave me the best chance of giving him protection."[67]

By 0930 the Harpoon convoy was steering southeast once again. *Troilus*, *Orari*, and *Burdwan* remained undamaged; *Hebe* was still towing *Kentucky*. Fighters from Malta had finally appeared overhead. However, due to *Kentucky*'s condition, the general speed was only six knots. Hardy considered delegating the tow to *Ithuriel* but concluded he could not tie up a valuable destroyer while Italian warships remained a threat. Then, at 1020, as the convoy slowly plodded eastward, an attack by Ju.88s and Ju.87s arrived just after one shift of fighters left for Malta and before the next arrived. Near misses disabled *Burdwan*. The convoy was still 150 miles short of Malta, a long day's journey at six knots, and even at that speed *Kentucky* was slowly dropping astern. Reviewing the situation, Hardy made a difficult decision, weighing the effort expended to defend the convoy, the fact he had fighter cover, and the operation's importance. "I decided to cut my losses and at [1042] ordered *Badsworth* and *Hebe* to scuttle *Burdwan* and *Kentucky* at the same time ordering the remaining merchant ships to proceed at their utmost speed."[68]

As this transpired Da Zara ordered *Oriani* and *Ascari* to rejoin him, leaving *Permuda* and *Malocello* with *Vivaldi*. He arrived north of 7 AN at 0935, but the only enemy he discovered was a Beaufort, which attacked his ship. He radioed the Sicilian air command for news. Then, after the two destroyers rejoined him, he started searching. In fact, at 1037, as Da Zara began a half-hour jaunt to the north, the convoy was thirty-five miles southwest of his position steering southeast.

Finding nothing, Da Zara turned southwest at 1110. Hardy had split his force, and the two undamaged freighters were almost forty miles south by southwest of the Italians. The Sicilian air command had failed to radio Da Zara any news of its attacks. *Hebe* and *Badsworth* were dutifully pumping 4-inch shells into *Kentucky* and *Burdwan*, to little effect. They did, however, ignite fires that cast huge smoke plumes into the sky. At 1123 *Eugenio* sighted smudges far on the southwestern horizon. Da Zara turned in that direction, and by 1145 he could clearly see three spreading columns of black smoke.

By 1215 the Italians saw warships around the burning vessels. At 1235 Da Zara ordered the destroyers to finish off the cripples while the cruisers engaged a ship they identified as a Tribal-class destroyer, actually *Hebe*. As the mine-sweeper fled east, she suffered one light hit. *Bedouin*, still under tow by *Partridge*, was farther east.[69] At 1241, hearing gunfire from over the horizon, Captain Hardy hauled around with *Cairo, Marne, Matchless,* and *Ithuriel* to support the ships he had left behind. Hardy reported that he sighted the enemy off his starboard bow, but Da Zara did not notice the British formation. Instead, he identified the most important targets as two *Jervis*-type destroyers, *Partridge* and *Bedouin*.[70] Hardy steamed northwest until 1300, when, "having covered the *Badsworth, Hebe,* and *Hythe,* I decided I could no longer afford to steam away from the convoy which was then about fifteen miles distant."[71] *Oriani* and *Ascari* were shelling *Kentucky* from thirteen thousand yards, "provoking enormous fires," when Da Zara recalled them.[72] He had turned his guns from *Hebe* and at 1253 swung to attack *Partridge* and *Bedouin*. He opened fire at 1259 and claimed at least one hit. *Partridge,* meanwhile, cast off her tow and circled *Bedouin* with smoke. As the British destroyers disappeared into this muck Da Zara ceased fire and came southeast and then south, seeking to reestablish contact.

At 1325 a violent explosion marked *Bedouin*'s location. An S.79 torpedo bomber had found the stricken destroyer and put a torpedo into her engine room. She capsized to port, taking twenty-eight members of her crew down with her.

The Italians took off after *Partridge,* with the cruisers pursuing to starboard and the destroyers to port. At 1343, as they passed seventy-three hundred yards away, *Oriani* torpedoed *Kentucky,* reporting that the weapon hit on the bow but deflagrated instead of exploding.[73] Da Zara engaged *Partridge* at 1345 but had the impression the British ship was pulling away, although Captain Hardy reported her top speed as only eighteen knots. At 1420 Da Zara decided to suspend the chase and turned northeast for home. Five minutes later the Italian division repelled a British air attack.

The cruisers returned to Naples. *Premuda* towed *Vivaldi* into Pantelleria's tiny harbor. The Harpoon convoy, however, faced one last trial. The British history comments, "After the day's happenings it was perhaps not surprising that misunderstandings should arise as to the precise channel [into Malta's Grand Harbor] to be swept and the order in which ships should arrive. The *Badsworth* and the Polish *Kujawiak* . . . and the *Orari, Matchless* and *Hebe* all struck mines."[74] *Vivaldi* and *Malocello* had laid the barrage the previous month, using Swedish-

made mines and recently introduced German electronic countermeasures that
blinded the shore radars. Only *Kujawiak* sank, but it was a bad end to a costly
venture; fifteen thousand tons of stores made it ashore, but this was precious
little, considering the scale of the two operations and the losses suffered."From
atop the bastions on both sides of the harbor, thousands of islanders who had
come to cheer the convoy in, watched in grim silence."[75]

Many British accounts treat this action as another example of Italian timidity.
"Tactically the Italian admiral had failed to act with the boldness to make the
destruction of the convoy complete."[76] In fact, Da Zara's 7th Division had sunk
one fleet destroyer, badly damaged another, damaged a light cruiser, a destroyer,
and a minesweeper, and finished off two crippled merchant ships. In turn, one
ship in the Italian force had suffered significant damage. By any measure, it was
a good day's work.

Advance to El Alamein

On 20 June Axis tanks broke through Tobruk's defenses. That same evening
Malta's governor went on the radio to announce that edible rations were being
cut to four ounces a day.[77] On 21 June Admiral Harwood sent a signal to the
Admiralty: "Tobruk has fallen and situation deteriorated so much that there
is a possibility of heavy air attack on Alexandria in near future, and in view of
approaching full moon period I am sending all Eastern Fleet units south of the
Canal to await events."[78]

However, the pitiless requirements of logistics intervened. The Axis armies
proved incapable of advancing beyond the point reached in early July at the El
Alamein bottleneck, although convoys continued running to North Africa, suffering only minor interference from British submarines and aircraft.

On 7 July Comando Supremo officially cancelled the operation to invade
Malta. A recently introduced class of Italian motorized barges (*motozattere*)
scheduled to carry troops for this operation instead joined German MFPs in
transporting supplies from Italy directly to Marsa Matruh, near the front lines.
The first such "mosquito" convoy arrived on 21 July, followed by another on 24
July. The British fleet's abandonment of Alexandria for Haifa and Suez made such
operations feasible. The British tried to counter with destroyer bombardments
of Marsa Matruh. The first, on 11 July, included the Hunts *Beaufort, Dulverton,
Eridge,* and *Hurworth,* which also sank the German freighter *Sturla.* On 19 July
Vian, with two cruisers and four fleet destroyers, repeated the bombardment.
Aldenham and *Dulverton* had an inconclusive engagement the same day with
German S-boats operating out of Derna. Nonetheless, four more barge convoys

reached Marsa Matruh up through 10 August. Chasing barges was dangerous, as demonstrated by the fate of the Hunt *Eridge,* which fell victim to X MAS special attack craft on 29 August.

Prelude to Pedestal

London began planning the next Malta convoy operation even before Harpoon and Vigorous ended. The Admiralty concluded that insufficient strength had caused the failure of the mid-June operations."Next time they would have to be given priority over all other demands, for on the success or failure of 'Pedestal' . . . would hang the fate of Malta and hence in all probability of the Nile valley."[79] From 14 to 19 July *Eagle* flew off thirty-one Spitfires to replace the wastage suffered by Malta's fighter forces, while *Welshman* made a solitary run to the island, arriving on 16 July having eluded in the thick weather efforts by Italian surface forces, submarines, and aircraft to intercept her. From 20 to 22 July *Eagle* sent another twenty-eight Spitfires to Malta. Also, on 20 July British submarines returned to the island.

Once again, Italian intelligence knew an operation was pending and commenced counter-preparations, including refreshing the minefields the Allies would have to pass through and laying some completely new ones.

The first clash of the Pedestal operation occurred when the destroyers *Badsworth* and *Matchless* escorted the empty transports *Orari* and *Troilus* from Malta back to Gibraltar. All four ships had suffered damage during Harpoon and also from incessant air raids during their two-month stay in Malta, but the dockyard had patched them up enough to permit a breakout attempt. They were painted with Italian recognition colors, and this ruse kept them from being reported as enemy ships their first day at sea. At the beginning of the second day they encountered *Malocello* near Cape Bon. This destroyer, accompanied by *MAS533*, was laying a minefield in French territorial waters south of the cape. (See table 10.4.)

At 2200 *Malocello* sighted a shaded light to the south-southeast. She turned west, inshore, and reduced speed to twelve knots. The sighting resolved itself into two freighters and two destroyers, but Commander Tona assumed it was either a French or Italian force that his instructions had failed to mention. He decided to continue his mission and—he hoped, given his load of mines—avoid notice. *MAS552* and *MAS553*, present to assist *Malocello* in positioning the mines, also spotted the convoy.[80]

Heading north to round Cape Bon, the British force passed the Italian destroyer; at 2225 *Matchless* detected *Malocello* forty degrees off her port

Table 10.4 Prelude to Pedestal, 11 August 1942, 2225–2245

Conditions: Night	
British ships—	(Lieutenant-Commander J. Mowlem): DD: *Matchless* (F); DE: *Badsworth*
Italian ship—	(Commander Pierfrancesco Tona): DD: *Malocello*

quarter. She fired two rounds, which splashed about four hundred yards behind target. *Malocello* replied with two salvos from her forward guns. The convoy turned east as *Malocello* increased speed and came to port to open her arcs of fire. Then *Matchless* illuminated the Italian ship with her searchlight and fired star shells. From the Italian point of view, the lights went out and the enemy ceased fire and continued on their way. The Italian ship also held fire. The time was 2245, and she proceeded to lay her mines. Commander Mowlem saw what looked like a French minesweeper and believed she had given the proper recognition signal. Considering the patched-together nature of his force, he had no interest in a sea battle. (See table 10.4.)

Ironically, this inconsequential engagement was the only time large surface ships came in contact during Pedestal—the war's biggest Malta convoy operation.

Pedestal

The story of the Pedestal convoy can be quickly summarized. The British navy's situation had deteriorated to the point where it could mount just one operation from the west. The Mediterranean Fleet, sailing out of Port Said and Haifa, mounted a dummy convoy that went as far as Alexandria before turning back. The western convoy was "Harpoon over again on a larger scale."[81] The Admiralty collected three aircraft carriers (*Victorious, Indomitable,* and *Eagle*), two battleships (*Nelson* and *Rodney*), seven cruisers, and twenty-four destroyers to escort fourteen merchant ships. Two fleet oilers protected by four corvettes, eight additional destroyers escorting the carrier *Furious,* and eight submarines completed the Allied order of battle. It was a massive commitment at this point in the war, although the suspension of the Arctic convoys following the PQ17 debacle, and the loan of American battleships, permitted the Admiralty to draw from the Home Fleet.

Using all fuel available, Supermarina assembled a surface strike force of three heavy cruisers, three light cruisers, and eleven destroyers to intercept Pedestal.

The plan was for them to intervene in the waters south of Pantelleria at dawn on 13 August. It was to be the Battle of Pantelleria perfected. The British were likewise prepared to refight Pantelleria, but this time they planned to meet the enemy with four light cruisers and twelve destroyers.

Before the carrier/battleship force turned around at the Skerki Channel it endured four air attacks, including one of a hundred planes. *U-73* sank *Eagle*. Luftwaffe and Regia Aeronautica aircraft heavily damaged *Indomitable* and lightly damaged *Victorious*. Aircraft hit one merchantman, which had to proceed independently and was later sunk, and an Italian aerial torpedo fatally damaged the destroyer *Foresight*.

Pedestal's true tribulations began an hour after the support force turned back. The Italian submarine *Axum* fired a spread of torpedoes that hit three ships— *Nigeria* (the flagship of the escort force commander), *Cairo*, and the tanker *Ohio*. *Nigeria* withdrew, *Cairo* sank, and *Ohio* continued. Next a night air attack accounted for two merchantmen, and an Italian submarine torpedoed light cruiser *Kenya*. However, as bad as this was, Italian MS and MAS motor torpedo boats proved even deadlier, inflicting fatal damage on light cruiser *Manchester* and sinking four merchantmen outright, damaging a fifth. A surface intervention would have filled Pedestal's cup of woe, but it never occurred.

Rear Admiral Parona's 3rd Division and Da Zara's 7th Division, with a strong contingent of destroyers, were steaming to intercept. However, shortly before midnight, six hours before contact, Mussolini recalled Parona. The reason usually given for this decision was that only eighteen elderly Cr.42s were available to protect the strike force against British torpedo bombers. But in fact, that evening the Italian air force reported that a *Nelson*-class battleship and a cruiser had joined the escort (the planes had actually spotted the light cruiser *Charybdis* and the destroyers *Eskimo* and *Somali*). Supermarina concluded that Parona's force had no chance in clear weather, as forecast for the next day, against a battleship's big guns and heavy armor; after an emotional debate between Commander Roselli-Lorenzini, who advocated interception at all costs, and the admiral on duty, Parona's cruisers were recalled. The commander literally slammed the door when he left the situation room and was reassigned to a submarine.[82]

Next morning Axis air attacks inflicted more punishment. Eventually five merchant ships, including the oft-damaged *Ohio*, reached Malta with thirty-two thousand tons of supplies and fifteen thousand tons of oil.

The Pedestal battle was the largest aero-naval victory won by Axis forces during the Mediterranean war. The German contribution was important, but the majority of the forces involved were Italian, and they inflicted the bulk of the damage. However, Supermarina's failure to attack with the 7th and 3rd cruiser divisions proved decisive. Italy was fighting an enemy that could afford to expend cruisers and carriers and suffer losses of two-thirds of its merchantmen and still describe the results as a "magnificent crash through of supplies" that would have "an important influence on the immediate future of the war in the Mediterranean."[83] The five ships that made port, the oil and supplies that landed, were not enough to release Malta's population from their starvation rations, but they were enough to keep the island going. On 17 August Rear Admiral Franco Maugeri, head of Italy's naval intelligence, recorded in his diary, "And Malta has resumed functioning despite all the losses we inflicted."[84]

11

The Allies Resurgent

Torch to Tunis

It was clear from the start that the landing of American forces in the Mediterranean was an event of great strategic significance, destined to modify and, in fact, to reverse the balance of military power in this sector.

—Benito Mussolini, *My Fall*

In late summer 1942 the Axis partners viewed the war situation with satisfaction. On 4 August, after a briefing by Comando Supremo, Ciano wrote, "The prospects are good because English reinforcements are slower than had been foreseen while our reinforcements, especially the Germans . . . are arriving regularly. Operations in Russia are developing well. [Comando Supremo] thinks that Russia will probably be detached from the Allied camp, after which Great Britain and American will be obliged to come to terms."[1]

However, Rommel's 30 August offensive to break the British lines at El Alamein failed. He claimed the problem was a lack of fuel, that only 954 tons had arrived in the month before his attack; actually, August deliveries had amounted to 20,037 tons—and this despite the return of bombers and submarines to Malta and signals intelligence that allowed the British to specifically target tankers. Reasons for the German failure could more credibly be ascribed to Rommel's fatigue, British strength, and the decrypt of communications outlining Rommel's offensive intentions. Even Field Marshal Albert Kesselring, the German commander in chief South, later wrote, "The Comando Supremo and C.-in-C. South had moved heaven and earth to assemble an adequate provision of petrol. . . . The defeat may be attributed to causes of a more psychological nature."[2]

In the war against shipping, British forces sank nineteen Axis merchantmen of over five hundred tons in July and August 1942. For nearly every one, signals intelligence provided "either the location in port or anchorage, or the timing or routing of the final voyage, in good time for the operational authorities to reconnoiter and attack." To put this in perspective, however, sixty merchant-men of more than 1,000 GRT arrived in an African port from Italy during this two-month period, as well as twenty-five cargo-loaded submarines and fifty-three MZ barges. Italy also maintained from the western ports to the eastern ports a vigorous coastal traffic that saw fifteen vessels of over 100 GRT arrive at Benghazi, eighteen dock at Tobruk, and twenty-six unload at Marsa Matruh.[3] (See chart 11.1.)

Chart 11.1   Monthly Delivery of Materiel to Libya, 1942

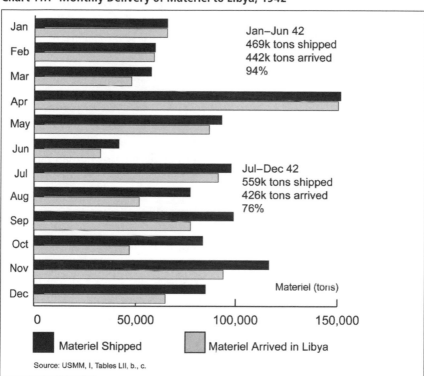

The major naval event between Operation Pedestal in August and Operation Torch in November occurred on 14 September, when British troops raided Tobruk intending to cripple its capacity as a supply port. However, the oper-ation backfired, principally because, as at Castelorizzo, the British underesti-mated their Italian opponents, who "acted with speed and resolution."[4] The Axis took 576 prisoners, while shore batteries and aircraft sank the antiaircraft cruiser *Coventry*, destroyers *Sikh* and *Zulu*, three MTBs, and two MLs.

Late summer 1942 may have been the high point of Rome's naval war against Great Britain. However, after having observed the Regia Marina for two years, Japan's naval attaché in Rome, Captain Mitunobu Toyo, recorded comments in his diary that struck at the heart of Italy's continuing naval dilemma: "The Italian navy and air force are sound, man for man, plane for plane, and ship for ship. [However,] there is no collaboration between the navy and the air force. Everyone is fighting on their own. This seems absurd to me. . . . About night combat the Italian navy reminds me of the Japanese navy of ten years ago."[5]

Map 11.1 Allies Resurgent, November 1942–May 1943

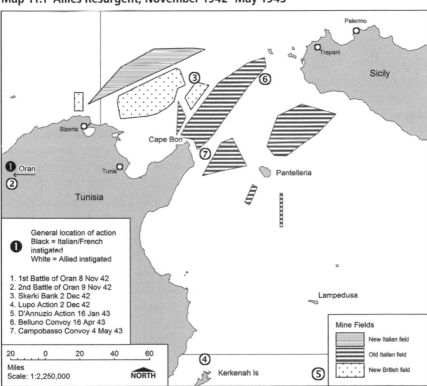

The British did not try to fight another large convoy through to Malta, but the fast minelayer *Welshman* and submarines shuttled in enough fuel, food, and ammunition to keep the island viable. The fleet remained exiled in Haifa and Suez, but a flotilla of Hunts and MTBs returned to Alexandria in

August to reinforce the watchful eye focused on Admiral Godfroy's squadron still ensconced there. Meanwhile, during this period of relative calm, the 15th Cruiser Squadron rotated its ships to Massawa for maintenance in a salvaged ex-Italian floating dock.

On 23 October the British 8th Army attacked the Italo-German forces in Egypt and on 4 November propelled Rommel into full retreat. This battle of El Alamein is often described as one of the war's turning points, but it was events on the other side of the Mediterranean that banished the Axis from Egypt for good. (See map 11.1.)

Torch

Major expeditionary forces from Great Britain and the United States entered the Mediterranean theater on 8 November 1942. This operation—codenamed Torch—represented a compromise between American leaders, facing the political need to deploy troops against Germany before the end of 1942, and the British, who were horrified by U.S. plans to seek a lodgment in France in that year.

The plan specified widely separated landings at three points in Morocco and two in Algeria. The British, under Admiral Andrew B. Cunningham, who was back in the Mediterranean in command of naval operations after a stint in Washington, D.C., directed naval activity within the Mediterranean and the escort of convoys to and from the United Kingdom, while the Americans conducted Moroccan operations and escorted the U.S. convoys. The U.S. Joint Chiefs of Staff feared Germany might compel Spain to close the straits and thus "desired an alternative land line of communications running from Casablanca to Oran."[6] This was the principal reason the Allies did not risk a landing closer to Tunisia, the objective that mattered most.

The buildup was impossible to hide. The Italians suspected a descent on French North Africa, but Berlin, biting on British disinformation, expected a large Malta convoy or a landing in southern France, or even Tripoli. The French were caught napping. Despite the examples of Dakar, Syria, and Madagascar, Vichy "considered [it] inconceivable that a landing meant to initiate a second front would be made any place else than in Axis-occupied territory."[7] From summer 1942 Admiral Darlan had concluded the Allies would win the war after all, and he planned to transfer Pétain and the fleet to North Africa at the appropriate time. However, he did not appreciate how deeply the Allies distrusted him; in late October the American consul led him to believe that a descent on Algeria and Morocco would not occur until February 1943.

Torch involved over four hundred warships. The eastward passage of "more than 340 vessels" within a few hours through the Straits of Gibraltar clearly demonstrated the advantage of Allied sea power, expressed by an ability to draw upon worldwide resources to reinforce any theater at will.[8] To guard against intervention by France's High Seas Force or the Italian battle fleet, Force H, under Vice Admiral Neville Syfret, deployed *Duke of York* and *Renown,* carriers *Formidable* and *Victorious,* three light cruisers, and fifteen destroyers.

First Battle of Oran, 8 November 1942

The Allies improvised a plan to capture the critical ports of Oran and Algiers intact. At Oran two British sloops, *Walney* and *Hartland,* ex–U.S. Coast Guard cutters loaded with four hundred men from a "hurriedly trained" battalion of the U.S. 1st Armor Division, received the mission of penetrating the harbor, discharging their troops, and preventing vastly superior French forces from demolishing the facilities.[9] (See table 11.1.)

Table 11.1 First Battle of Oran, 8 November 1942, 0315–0755

Conditions: Light fog, calm seas
British ships— CL: *Aurora;* DD: *Brilliant, Boadicea*[D?]; DE: *Calpe;* DS: *Walney*[Sunk], *Hartland*[Sunk]
French ships— 7th Destroyer Division (Commander de Féraudy): *Typhon*[D1], *Tornade*[Sunk], *Tramontane*[Sunk]; PS: *La Surprise*[Sunk]

Screened by two smoke-making motor launches, these brave vessels approached Oran harbor at 0300 on 8 November. They missed the boom on their initial pass and circled to try again, broadcasting instructions in French to hold fire. In response, a rocket arced overhead and searchlights probed the channel. *Walney* crashed the boom at 0315. A shore battery and a pair of docked submarines engaged as she entered the channel. Then *Walney* encountered the sloop *La Surprise* sailing in the opposite direction and attempted to ram. In response the sloop opened fire and destroyed the cutter's bridge. As damage and casualties mounted, *Walney* reached her assigned dock, to find it occupied by the destroyers *Epervier* and *Tramontane.* They blasted the cutter at point-blank range. With three-quarters of her nearly 250 crewmember and passengers dead or wounded, and abandoned by the survivors, *Walney* blew up and capsized at 0445. (See map 11.2.)

Map 11.2 First Battle of Oran, 8 November 1940

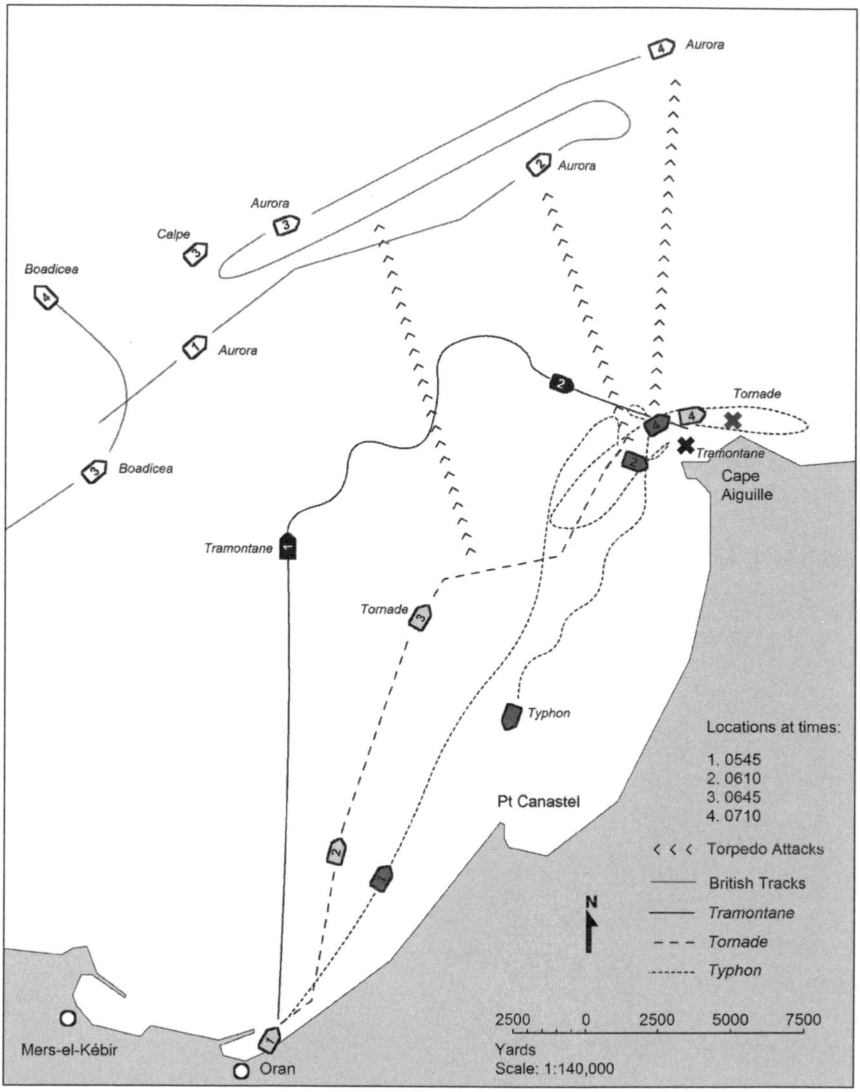

Hartland's experience was similar. She found *Typhon* occupying her position. The French destroyer's searchlight revealed a strange vessel flying a large American flag, and she immediately fired upon it with her 5.1-inch and 37-mm guns. "Shells bursting inside her hull brought [*Hartland*] to a standstill[,] turning her mess deck, on which the troops were waiting, into a shambles."[10] With half her complement dead, the survivors abandoned ship at 0410; *Hartland* drifted, fiercely on fire and wracked by explosions, until she finally sank at 1025.

After *La Surprise* passed *Walney*, she emerged into the roads and then turned west to investigate enemy landings reported at Les Andalousee. There she encountered British destroyers bombarding shore targets. At 0640 the sloop attacked the destroyer *Brilliant* from 3,700 yards with her single 3.9-inch gun. *Brilliant* returned her fire and gravely damaged *La Surprise*, which sank at 0730. Fifty-five French sailors, including the captain, died.

At 0445 the French command ordered *Tramontane* to attack enemy forces reported in Arzew Bay. She sailed up-channel conveying the orders to *Typhon* and *Tornade*. They followed after some minutes, but in the thick smoke roiling up from *Hartland*, *Tornade* struck the mole, damaging her bow. *Epervier*, completing a five-month refit, was not ready for sea and remained in port. Thus, the French destroyers headed toward Arzwe individually.

At 0542 *Tramontane*, which only had three guns operational, sighted a ship off her port bow and signaled a challenge. It was *Aurora*, still skippered by Captain W. G. Agnew. The veteran light cruiser replied with a well-aimed salvo from six thousand yards that struck the French destroyer's number 3 mount. Then a shell knocked out number 1 mount just as it opened fire. Metal fragments swept *Tramontane*'s bridge and killed or severely wounded the captain, several officers, and other men. Mount 2 engaged briefly before being silenced in its turn when splinters cut down the crew.

The executive officer took command, and the French destroyer turned northeast, zigzagging to confuse *Aurora*'s deadly aim. Number 3 mount briefly fired over open sights, then fell silent for lack of ready ammunition. By this time, *Aurora* was riddling the destroyer's superstructure with its 40-mm pom-poms. *Tramontane* fled southeast toward Cape Aiguille, where she ran aground on rocks offshore.

Typhon, cutting through a glassy sea and light fog, observed *Tramontane*'s plight. At 0610 she aimed two torpedoes at *Aurora* from ten thousand yards and then came alongside her sister ship. After taking aboard many survivors, she passed a tow, under *Aurora*'s watchful eye.

Meanwhile, having patched her bow, *Tornade* gingerly headed into the bay, making twelve knots. She had British warships in sight from 0615. At 0645 *Boadicea* made a signal, which the French ship ignored, whereupon *Boadicea* opened fire. *Tornade* immediately replied and holed the British destroyer on the starboard side with a 5.1-inch round that burst in the forward 4.7-inch shell room. Fragments ignited a number of ammunition boxes, and while these did not explode, the damage knocked *Boadicea* out of action for a month.[11] She turned away behind smoke. At 0650 *Calpe* joined the action; her salvos fell close, and splinters shattered one of *Tornade's* searchlights. The French ship turned and risked a burst of speed to confuse *Calpe's* aim. She then sent six torpedoes toward *Aurora* on long-range runs. As *Tornade* approached Cape Aiguille, *Typhon* suspended her rescue efforts and, shooting at *Calpe,* circled around to fall in behind *Tornade.*

At 0710 *Typhon* launched a torpedo at *Aurora* from twelve thousand yards. The cruiser's reply straddled *Tornade,* and the next salvo hammered her with three hits, the most damaging exploding in *Tornade's* engine room. Five minutes later another cluster of 6-inch shells detonated on the French destroyer, two below the waterline and another that disabled number 4 mount. As more hits followed *Tornade* lost way and began to list to starboard. At 0720, as she drifted onto the rocks just north of Cape Aiguille, her captain ordered the crew to abandon ship.

Tornade's fate released *Typhon* to operate independently. She continued east past Cape Aiguille. Then at 0719, short of torpedoes, with half her ammunition expended, her decks crowded with *Tramontane's* survivors, and *Aurora* paralleling her course to the north, *Tornade* reversed course. Zigzagging violently and emitting smoke, the destroyer fled southwest at high speed. A 6-inch shell struck her fore funnel, killing three men, but she made port at 0755 without further damage. *Typhon* had expended 220 5.1-inch rounds in this unequal combat. *Tornade* capsized and sank at 0825. She lost twelve men and *Tramontane* twenty-eight.[12]

On 9 November, the reprovisioned *Typhon* and *Epervier,* the latter hastily made fit for sea, sallied from the harbor at twenty-three knots hoping to escape north. One of *Typhon's* officers wrote, "The sea was beautiful, and a slight mist gave us the hope to pass undetected."[13] However, at 0930 a British reconnaissance plane began to shadow them. At 0950, as they passed Cape Aiguille, the French squadron could see four minor warships to port, a convoy in the distance, and an aircraft carrier and its escort ahead. There was clearly no passage in such a crowded sea. *Aurora,* patrolling off Cape Ferrat to the northeast, spotted the French flotilla and began steaming in their direction. *Jamaica,* patrolling to the northwest, likewise turned to intercept. (See table 11.2.)

Table 11.2 Second Battle of Oran, 9 November 1942, 1000–1120

Conditions: Good weather, glassy seas
British ships— CL: *Aurora, Jamaica*
French ships— DL: *Epervier*[Sunk], DD: *Typhon*[D1]

At 1020, boxed in by the enemy cruisers, *Epervier* reversed course to return to Oran. However, *Aurora* engaged at 1023 from ten thousand yards. *Jamaica*, eight thousand yards to the west, also opened fire. *Epervier* replied and quickly straddled *Aurora*, while *Typhon* targeted *Jamaica*. For ten minutes the French warships fired as they ran south, making for Cape Aiguille. Then at 1033 one of *Aurora*'s tight salvos landed, damaging *Epervier* in the engine room, boiler room, and bridge. As she rapidly lost way, *Typhon* circled her, laying smoke. At 1045 *Typhon* aimed three torpedoes at *Aurora* and then rounded Cape Aiguille, which screened her from the deadly light cruiser. Her captain wanted to return and assist *Epervier*, but "the English cruiser reappeared [from behind Cape Aiguille] and again began shooting with astonishing precision so that *Typhon* could avoid her shells only with difficulty despite zigzagging at a speed of thirty knots."[14]

Typhon turned south toward the Cape Canastel battery. At 1115 she launched her last three torpedoes. *Aurora* followed until 9.45-inch rounds from the battery began splashing around her. The French ship, which had only suffered splinter damage, scuttled in Oran Harbor's narrow entrance at 1135. *Epervier* grounded herself on Cape Aiguille. She suffered twelve killed, nine missing, and thirty-one wounded.[15]

Admiral Cunningham dismissed the French efforts in these two engagements, reporting that "*Aurora* . . . polished off her opponents on each occasion with practiced ease" (although he complained that "the performance of *Jamaica* in expending 501 rounds to damage one destroyer was less praiseworthy.")[16] In fact, outnumbered, outgunned, and out of practice, the French ships valiantly performed what they perceived as their duty. It was their misfortune to go up against what was perhaps the best-shooting ship in the Royal Navy.

Algiers

The plan to prevent the French from sabotaging Algiers called for two old British destroyers, *Broke* and *Malcolm*, to penetrate the harbor and land three companies of U.S. Rangers. They had trouble locating the harbor entrance, however, and came under fire from shore batteries. *Malcolm* sustained a hit in her boiler room and wisely withdrew. *Broke* finally forced the boom at 0520, an hour and a half behind schedule. After trading shots with a minesweeper and a submarine as they passed heading out to sea, the destroyer discharged her troops at the wrong location. "Apart from desultory sniping, however, the next hour was comparatively quiet."[17] Then one shore battery began to harass *Broke*, and at 0915 her captain decided to withdraw, leaving most of the American troops stranded in the city. The shore battery pummeled the old destroyer as she exited the harbor;

she eventually foundered under tow. The Rangers surrendered, but their captivity was brief. Although the Allied landings had been poorly executed, they luckily faced little opposition, and Admiral Darlan, who was in the city to attend a sick son, ordered a cease-fire on the morning of 10 November.

Morocco

American forces attacking Morocco encountered the greatest resistance. The battleship *Jean Bart* traded main-battery salvos with the American battleship *Massachusetts*. The Casablanca assault faced a sortie by a French cruiser and nine destroyers, which had the landing craft under fire before being deflected by U.S. warships from the fire support group. The French navy suffered heavily in the subsequent Battle of Casablanca, losing four destroyers to American gunfire and suffering severe damage to the cruiser and three more destroyers. The city resisted longest, holding out until 11 November. French submarines barely missed *Massachusetts* and several cruisers. They lost, however, eight boats in port, at sea, or scuttled. Overall the French navy lost 462 men.[18]

The Axis response to the landings came too late to jeopardize their success. The German navy had concentrated its S-boats at Trapani, waiting for a Malta convoy. Up through 14 November German aircraft sank the sloop *Ibis,* two troop transports, a landing ship, and two merchant ships totaling 55,305 GRT. They damaged the carrier *Argus* and the monitor *Roberts.*[19] There were fifteen German submarines in the Mediterranean on 1 November 1942, reinforced by another six boats during the month, all west of Algiers. They sank the destroyers *Martin* and *Isaac Sweers,* three merchant ships totaling 37,183 GRT, and a transport. Twenty-one Italian subs operating east of Algiers accounted for the antiaircraft auxiliary *Tynwald* and one steamer of 13,482 GRT. These losses were bearable, given the scale of the forces deployed. In return, Allied antisubmarine forces sank five German submarines and damaged six.

Toulon and Rejoining the Allies

The Vichy government disavowed Darlan's cease-fire order of 10 November, while privately assuring him that he retained Marshal Pétain's confidence. Hitler's confidence, however, had vanished, and on 11 November Germany and Italy invaded southern France unopposed. To avoid the defection of the High Seas Force the Germans agreed to respect the naval base at Toulon if the commander, Admiral Jean de Laborde, promised to defend it against Allied or dissident attacks.

Satisfied that Darlan had Pétain's secret blessing (and confronted with overwhelming force), French leaders in North Africa agreed to cooperate with the Allies under Darlan's leadership, rather than that of the Allied candidate, General Henri Giraud, an army commander who had escaped German captivity. They presented this accord to the Supreme Allied commander, General Dwight D. Eisenhower, on 13 November, and he accepted the deal in the interest of securing French cooperation. On 14 November Admiral Darlan announced that he was high commissioner of France in Africa, "in the name of the Marshal under duress."[20]

Explaining his unpopular decision, Eisenhower radioed, "Existing French sentiment here does not remotely agree with prior calculations. . . . The name of Marshal Pétain is something to conjure with. . . . [Everyone] agrees that only one man has an obvious right to assume the Marshal's mantle in North Africa. He is Darlan."[21] Churchill choked but had to go along, telling Parliament, "[The Americans] do not feel the same way about Darlan as we do. He has not betrayed them. He has not broken any treaty with them. He has not vilified them. . . . They do not hate him and despise him as we do over here."[22]

Darlan wanted the High Seas Force to sail to Algeria. This would have preserved France's greatest asset and cemented his personal position. Although the naval forces in Morocco, Algeria, and Dakar accepted Darlan's authority, Admiral de Laborde, whom Cunningham described as a "charming but idiotically obstinate man," was a rival who instead sought his government's permission to sail as an Axis cobelligerent immediately following the Torch landing.[23] Admiral Godfroy in Alexandria likewise rejected Darlan's call.

The situation in France degenerated as Marshal Pétain withdrew from political life and many ministers resigned. The Vichy government ceded to the Germans 158 merchant ships of 646,000 GRT. Then, after Berlin had wrung from France all it could, it turned against Toulon.

German tanks crashed the immense base's main gate at 0425. But by the time troops arrived at *Strasbourg*'s dock, it was 0600. "Explosions sounded all over the ship, as gun after gun was blown up. The reduction gears on the turbines had been cut with an oxyacetylene torch, and other important machinery parts blasted with hand grenades. The sea cocks were opened, and the *Strasbourg*, which drew 10 meters, settled on an even keel until her top decks were four meters under."[24] In total, the navy scuttled a quarter-million tons of warships. The Germans seized only four destroyers in dry dock, which, over the Kriegsmarine's protest, Hitler assigned to the Italians in January 1943. Only four submarines escaped. (See table 11.3.)

Table 11.3 French Forces at Toulon, November 1942

High Seas Force (Admiral J. de Laborde): BB: *Strasbourg;* CA: *Algérie, Dupleix,*
  Colbert; CL: *Marseillaise, Jean de Vienne;* DL: *Guépard, Verdun, Tartu,*
  Volta, Vauquelin, Kersaint, L'Indomptable, Gerfaut, Vautour, Cassard; DD:
  Bordelais, Le Mars, La Palme

Training Squadron (Vice Admiral André Marquis): BB: *Provence;* CVS:
  Commandant Teste; DD: *Mameluk, Casque;* TB: *L'Adroit, Baliste,*
  La Bayonnaise, La Poursuivante, and ten submarines

Deactivated: BB: *Dunkerque;* CA: *Foch;* CL: *La Galissonnière;* DL: *Tigre, Lynx,*
  Panthère, Lion, Valmy, Aigle, Vauban, Mogador; DD: *Lansquenet,*
  Le Hardi, Foudroyant, Siroco, Bison, Trombe, and ten submarines

---

Thus France fulfilled the pledge originally given by Darlan to Churchill and the British government in June 1940. Honor was preserved, but at great cost. The fleet's destruction freed the Germans "from a diplomatic constraint and enabled [them] to impose fresh pressures on France—probably Hitler's real motive."[25] Meanwhile, French authorities in North Africa lacked the power and respect they would have commanded had the fleet sailed when Darlan asked.

The Race to Tunis

Once the Allies had occupied Algeria, the race for Tunis began. The German assessment correctly concluded that "Tunisia always was and still is the decisive key position in the Mediterranean." However, the Germans erred when they supposed, "It is a simple task to supply our Armoured Army, since our lines are short."[26]

The first German troops deplaned in Tunis on 9 November. The colony's substantial garrison ignored orders from Vichy to cooperate with the Germans and instead withdrew to the hills. The British occupied Bône, 115 miles west of Tunis, on 12 November. The first Italian ships docked in Tunisia the same day. German and British spearheads clashed seventy miles west of Tunis on 17 November. By 28 November the Allies had scratched their way to a point fifteen miles short of their objective. The German commander warned he could hold on only if "reinforcements were sent 'on a scale quite different from hitherto.'"[27] The 10th Panzer Division's first armored elements docked the next day, immediately went into action, and finally pushed the British back.

The need to provision the new Tunisian bridgehead came on top of Italy's continuing requirements to supply Libya and maintain its considerable coastal

and inter-island traffic. For example, three-quarters of Sicily's monthly require-
ment of 200,000 tons of coal arrived by sea. The Axis could muster about thirty-
seven large steamers and tankers grossing 150,000 tons for this new obligation.
The windfall of seized French shipping eased the problem, but only about
100,000 tons was immediately serviceable.[28]

During these critical weeks, as the campaign hung in the balance, the Allied
command did little to impede the stream of Italian shipping in the Sicilian
Channel. Submarines accomplished nothing, while Allied air forces concentrated
on ground operations. Cunningham did not request air attacks against naval
targets until 19 November. He delayed re-forming Malta's Force K, three light
cruisers and four destroyers under Rear Admiral A. J. Power, until 27 November
due to concerns about air support.[29] Believing that Bône was too exposed, he did
not establish there Force Q, three light cruisers and two destroyers under Rear
Admiral C. H. J. Harcourt, until 30 November. However, once they were established, the naval strike forces had an immediate impact.

On 1 December the Regia Marina had four convoys en route to Africa. One
was Convoy B, which departed Naples for Bizerta at 1430 on 30 November with
six steamers (two German) and an escort of four torpedo boats, later reinforced
by three destroyers and another torpedo boat. Convoy C, the steamers *Veloce*
and *Chisone* escorted by three torpedo boats, left Naples for Tripoli at 2300 on
30 November. Convoy G sailed from Palermo for Tunisia at 0900 on 1 December
with the tanker *Giorgio* escorted by a destroyer and torpedo boat. Convoy H followed an hour behind Convoy G, also bound for Bizerta and consisted of four
transports loaded with 1,766 troops, thirty-two vehicles, four tanks, twelve
88-mm guns, and 698 tons of supplies. It was escorted by three destroyers and
two torpedo boats.

Signals intelligence from C38m and Luftwaffe Enigma provided the British
details of these movements, and at 1730 on 1 December Force Q sallied on its
first mission.[30] The convoy needed to be sighted and reported by aircraft, and
as this was being accomplished, Italian intelligence decrypted Allied signals
and thus learned enemy warships were at sea. Supermarina determined that
Convoys H and G were the most threatened and that the enemy could intercept Convoy H as soon as 0010 on 2 December. Moreover, aircraft from Malta
had already attacked Convoy G and set *Giorgio* afire. Under these circumstances
Supermarina decided Convoy H lacked time to retreat and that it would be better to let it proceed. (See table 11.4.)

Table 11.4 Battle near Skerki Bank, 2 December 1942, 0038–0130

Conditions: Night, cloudy, fair, calm seas	
British ships—	Force Q: (Rear Admiral C. H. J. Harcourt): CL: *Aurora* (F); CL: *Sirius, Argonaut;* DD: *Quiberon, Quentin*
Italian ships—	Convoy Escort: (Captain Aldo Cocchia): DD: *Da Recco*[D4] (F), *Camicia Nera, Folgore*[Sunk]; TB: *Clio, Procione*[D2]
	Convoy: *KT1*[Sunk] (GE 850 GRT), *Aspromonte*[Sunk] (IT 976 GRT), *Puccini*[Sunk] (IT 2,422 GRT), *Aventino*[Sunk] (IT 3,794 GRT)

Captain Cocchia, the escort commander, had just sent *Procione* ahead to sweep for mines when he learned that enemy warships threatened his force. There had already been intimations of trouble. Aircraft buzzed overhead, and flares periodically floated down along their course. Despite Supermarina's intention that the convoy maintain a tight and tidy formation, Cocchia decided to alter course three miles to the south—the maximum distance believed safe, due to unmarked minefields in that direction. He ordered a simultaneous ninety-degree turn at 0001 to the south-southeast, resuming a course of west-south-west at 0017.

This evolution proved unfortunate. *Puccini* did not hear the 0017 order and rammed *Aspromonte*. Worse, the small German transport *KT1*, which, due to her lack of a radio, was supposed to follow *Puccini,* missed the 0001 turn and ended up far to the northwest.

Thus, Convoy H was scattered when, just ten minutes later, Harcourt's ships came riding down its original course at twenty knots. *De Recco,* sailing west-southwest, led a straggling column consisting of *Aventino, Clio,* and *Aspromonte*. *Puccini* and *Folgore* followed six thousand yards behind *De Recco* in line abreast, steering south-southwest. *Camicia Nera* was three thousand yards north of *Puccini*. *Procione,* her paravanes streaming [to sweep mines], was six thousand yards south of *De Recco*. *KT1* plowed her solitary way seven thousand yards northwest of *De Recco*. These last three vessels were all headed west-southwest.

Harcourt approached in order *Aurora, Sirius, Argonaut, Quiberon,* and *Quentin*. At 0038 the lead cruisers engaged *KT1* from eighteen hundred yards, and their first broadsides caused the coal-burning transport—and her load of munitions—to explode. As *Argonaut* and *Quiberon* targeted a ship to the southeast—either *Procione* or *De Recco*—Cocchia ordered the escort to counterattack. (See map 11.3)

Map 11.3 Battle near Skerki Bank, 2 December 1943

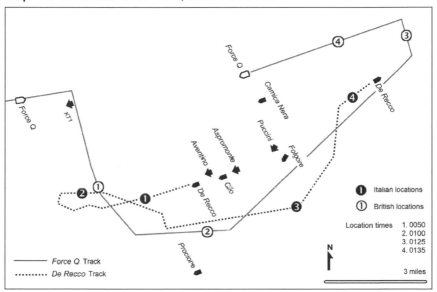

Harcourt circled *KT1*'s burning wreck to strike the rest of the convoy. At 0039, while *Aurora* targeted a false contact to the northeast, *Argonaut* loosed a broadside and a torpedo at *KT1* in passing. Two minutes later she engaged *Camicia Nera*, which was advancing to launch torpedoes. *Aurora* also aimed at the enemy destroyer, mistaking her for a merchant ship. The Italian turned and loosed six torpedoes between 0043 and 0045 at an estimated range of twenty-two hundred yards. As she retired north, salvos splashed closely around her.

At 0046 *Aurora* targeted *Aspromonte* nine hundred yards to port and *Aventino* four thousand yards distant. *Argonaut* also had *Aventino* in her sights. Meanwhile, *Sirius* engaged *Folgore* and *Clio*.

Folgore steered toward the British line even before Cocchia ordered a counter-attack. At 0047 she aimed three torpedoes to port at *Aurora* at a range she under-estimated as fifteen-hundred yards. Then, while disengaging, *Sirius* illuminated with her searchlight a transport. *Folgore* made a hard swing to port and at 0050 discharged her other three fish toward the searchlight. She erroneously claimed two hits. As *Folgore* withdrew south-southwest, *Argonaut* ranged in, and at 0052, nine 5.25-inch shells devastated the Italian destroyer, causing a large fire and extensive flooding. *Folgore* continued at twenty-seven knots, but she assumed a twenty-degree list and at 0116 capsized to starboard, losing 126 men.

Procione fouled her paravane cable when the shooting started, and it was fifteen minutes before she sighted *Sirius* two thousand yards off her starboard bow. The British cruiser already had a broadside on its way, and at 0053 a flurry of shells ravaged the torpedo boat, slaughtering the forward gun crew. *Procione*'s captain maneuvered to disrupt the enemy's aim and then withdrew southwest. He never opened fire, because, "advancing to the attack we deemed it inopportune to reveal our position . . . and after breaking off we were unable to give timely orders to the guns given the breakdowns of the fire control and telephone networks."[31]

Clio made smoke and fired at British searchlights and muzzle flashes, while *Da Recco* sought to launch torpedoes.

At 0055 *Quiberon* left the formation and maneuvered independently against *Clio*. The torpedo boat's return fire bracketed the British destroyer but failed to hit. Meanwhile, *Sirius* and *Argonaut* had *Puccini* in their sights; at 0058 *Argonaut* propelled one torpedo at this target and two minutes later another toward *Aventino*, which was on her port beam, burning. At 1102 *Sirius* likewise discharged a torpedo at *Aventino*. This unfortunate merchantman, which was loaded with munitions, blew up and sank.

At 0106 *Ouiberon*, cutting through waters filled with survivors, engaged *Puccini*. At 0112 *Quentin* swung into formation behind *Quiberon*, and together they pummeled *Puccini* and set her ablaze. At the same time *Aurora* had *Aspromonte* in her crosshairs, about eight thousand yards away. At 0121, with this target sinking, the three cruisers turned their guns on *Clio*, ahead and to starboard. Although *Clio* endured their concentrated gunfire for five minutes, she slipped away undamaged.

By 0130 *Da Recco* had closed to within forty-five hundred yards of the enemy, but her torpedo attack failed, and a concentrated fusillade from *Sirius*, *Quiberon*, and *Quentin* slaughtered 118 members of her crew and left her dead in the water. *Pigafetta* finally towed her to port. Following this execution the British column completed its wide loop around the convoy and set course for Bône.

Harcourt's force had sunk or critically damaged every merchant ship and suffered only splinter damage in return. Force Q did not make it back to base unscathed, however. German aircraft surprised it at 0630 fifty miles short of Bône and inflicted slight damage on *Quiberon*, and an aerial torpedo sank *Quentin*.

Camicia Nera scuttled *Puccini*, the last surviving transport, at 1500, after salvage proved impossible. Nearly twenty-two hundred Axis sailors and troops had lost their lives in this attack. According to Admiral Cunningham, "Our submarines next morning reported large areas covered in debris and thick oil with numbers of floating corpses in lifebelts."[32]

This battle was a major failure for the Regia Marina. After two and a half years of combat, it was unacceptable that such a critical and heavily escorted convoy had been wiped out. It is particularly noteworthy that the escort had failed to inflict any damage—especially having launched so many torpedoes at such close ranges. Some Italian historians consider this unlikely, but the hard truth is that the attack hit a disorganized convoy, which had made an uncoordinated response.[33] Little progress had been made in improving nighttime torpedo accuracy, one of the Regia Marina's greatest, if least known, failings of the war, in part because, accepting reports that incorrectly claimed successful strikes, the navy did not realize how great the problem was.

The revived Force K departed Malta at 1600 that same day. One officer later remembered, "There had been no air raids since we had arrived at Malta, and we were not attacked as we left the island. . . . What a welcome change this was from conditions the year before."[34] Force K's target was Convoy C, steamers *Veloce* and *Chisone*, escorted by torpedo boats *Lupo, Aretusa,* and *Ardente,* en route to Tripoli.

At 2330, fleet Albacores from Malta torpedoed *Veloce.* Loaded with benzene, this unfortunate vessel blazed up like beacon and attracted Force K as it was nearing Kerkenah Banks. As the veteran torpedo boat *Lupo* stood by to rescue survivors, the rest of Convoy C proceeded inshore, aware that an enemy surface force was nearby. (See table 11.5.)

Table 11.5 Destruction of *Lupo*, 2 December 1942, 2346–2355

Conditions: Night, clear, no moon	
British ships—	14th Destroyer Flotilla (Captain A. L. Poland): *Jervis* (F), *Javelin, Nubian, Kelvin*
Italian ships—	Convoy Escort (Lieutenant Commander Giuseppe Folli): TB: *Lupo*[Sunk]
	Convoy: *Veloce*[Sunk] (5,451 GRT)

Force K closed, and at 2346 *Jervis* lofted a star shell, "which illuminated the whole scene. The destroyer and the sinking merchant ship were the only vessels visible in the area." *Jervis* then snapped on her searchlight and opened fire from only two thousand yards, catching the enemy completely by surprise. The initial salvos shredded *Lupo*'s bridge. "Within three minutes, hot, glowing circles appeared on her superstructure and hull from the hits that she was sustaining."[35] *Javelin, Nubian,* and *Kelvin* followed, pounding their helpless target, which never fired a shot in reply. Only a dozen of *Lupo*'s men survived. The balance of the convoy, however, escaped into Kerkenah Banks' dangerous shallows.

Encouraged by these successes, Cunningham reinforced Force Q with the cruiser *Dido* and began sending a pair of cruisers and destroyers on nightly sweeps. However, just three days later he complained to Admiral Pound, "The enemy are building up too and we do not seem to be able to interrupt his sea communications to Bizerta and Tunis. Our submarines, for some reason, have been unsuccessful. . . . The air from Malta, with the exception of one good Albacore strike, do not appear to be having much luck in sea strikes."[36] In part, this was because Supermarina had switched to heavily escorted daylight convoys and had laid new minefields that sent Force Q on a long detour to reach its hunting grounds. When the minefields were completed, Supermarina reinstituted night convoys. The other factor was that surface strikes were most effective when they caught the enemy unprepared. The delay in deploying Force K and Force Q proved critical: "Had their operations begun but a few days earlier, and had they prevented or delayed the arrival of the armoured elements of 10th Panzer Division, the Allies would have broken through to Tunis."[37]

Patrolling without specific objectives was always dangerous. On 14 December the Italia submarine *Mocenigo* clipped *Argonaut* with a pair of torpedoes, one at the bow and one at the stern, and sent her to the dockyard for nearly eleven months.[38]

The Route of Death

A significant development in the Mediterranean war was the increased scale of American participation. On 4 December 1942 U.S. Army Air Forces B-24s flying from Egypt attacked Naples and sank the light cruiser *Attendolo* and severely damaged *Montecuccoli, Eugenio,* and four destroyers. Concluding that Naples was too exposed, Supermarina withdrew the battle fleet to La Spezia and the 3rd Division's cruisers from Messina to La Maddalena. With only the 8th Division remaining in southern waters, the Regia Marina lost its ability to intervene in the decisive area, although, as even the British history acknowledged, "the Italians would have been hard put to it to find the fuel for even a few cruisers on active operations."[39]

As December continued, Allied aircraft and submarines finally began to hurt Axis shipping. During this month forty-five merchant ships or tankers departed Italy for Africa, but only twenty-nine arrived. Italian destroyers likewise made forty-five transport runs. The end of the year saw Axis armies holding on in Tunisia but retreating in Tripolitania. Imperial troops captured El Agheila in mid-December and reached Buerat, more than halfway to Tripoli. Because it was proving impossible to supply armies in both Tunisia and Tripolitania, Mussolini decided to evacuate Libya, as Tunisia was more important to the Axis war effort.[40] This decision temporarily increased Axis coastal traffic, and destroyers from Malta began hunting along the Tunisian shoreline each night, even without specific intelligence.

On the night of 8 January *Nubian* and *Kelvin* reported sinking three motor sailing vessels off the Kuriat Islands, but they had actually engaged floating barrels of gasoline dropped by a small Italian convoy, which reached Tripoli safely. More deadly was a minefield laid by *Abdiel* that sank the destroyer *Corsaro* and damaged *Maestrale* the next night northeast of Bizerta. The deadly and largely silent mining efforts conducted by both sides determined the geography of the convoy war. By early December massive Italian fields fenced in a fifty-mile-wide corridor supposedly safe from surface intervention between Sicily and Tunisia. However, the fast British minelayers *Abdiel* and *Welshman* slipped into the corridor, a tricky and dangerous business, and laid counter fields. Besides *Corsaro*, these fields sank the corvette *Procellaria* on 31 January, the torpedo boat *Uragano* and the destroyer *Saetta* on 3 February, *Ciclone* on 7 March, and the destroyers *Malocello* and *Ascari* on 24 March. Short on minesweepers, the Italians soon gave up trying to sweep these fields, and by March the route between the Aegades and Tunisia was "reduced to the point where, for a distance of forty miles, the ships had to pass through a narrow 'alley' that was . . . scarcely more than a mile wide."[41]

D'Annuzio Action

On 15 January *Perseo* set out with the motorship *D'Annunzio* from Tripoli for Lampedusa under gale conditions that gave Supermarina reason to believe they would escape detection. At 0230 on 16 January, however, *Perseo* reported an enemy aircraft stalking the force. *Nubian* and *Kelvin* were not far behind, and they intercepted at 0320, fifty miles south of Lampedusa. On this day *Kelvin* was experiencing machinery problems that limited her speed to twenty-three knots.[42] (See table 11.6.)

At 0319 the Italian warship spotted a silhouette forty-five hundred yards away, and a moment later a star shell burst in the sky. Gunfire followed quickly. *Perseo* reported, "We observed no less than three, but more probably four enemy units without being able to establish the type."[43] Pitching on the wild sea, the torpedo boat could answer only with her stern mount. At 0324 a shell disabled this gun and ignited the ready ammunition. At 0326 *Nubian* and *Kelvin* targeted

Table 11.6 *D'Annuzio* Action, 16 January 1943, 0321–0350

Conditions: Night, moderate gale, large waves, white foam crests
British ships— Force K: DD: *Nubian, Kelvin*
Italian ships— Convoy Escort (Lieutenant Saverio Marotta): TB: *Perseo*[D2]
Convoy: *D'Annunzio*[Sunk] (4,537 GRT)

D'Annunzio and quickly set her ablaze. *Perseo* came about and at 0335 launched two torpedoes from twenty-two hundred yards and then withdrew. When this attack failed, the ship returned and at 0345 discharged her last two. Shortly afterward, the crew "heard a peculiar explosion in the direction of the enemy ship."[44] At 0350 *Perseo* withdrew to Lampedusa, believing she had connected with her last salvo.

The British destroyers, concentrating on the merchantman, failed to notice *Perseo*'s torpedo attacks. *Kelvin* shot five torpedoes at *D'Annunzio* and scored with one, sinking the merchantman. *Nubian* rescued ten survivors from the three hundred men aboard.

The Royal Navy's persistent antishipping patrols helped balance the air forces' continuing lack of success during January. "Nearly 1,700 R.A.F. and at least 180 U.S.A.A.F. sorties are recorded as spent by the 'Torch,' Malta, and Middle East air forces in searching for and attacking shipping during January; yet, largely because of bad weather, the air success of any note on the Tunisian route was long in coming." Allied air forces spent almost as much effort bombing enemy ports of arrival (968 sorties) and departure (203 sorties); U.S. aircraft delivered 55 percent of these missions.[45] Extensive minefields and antisubmarine patrols kept British submarines out of the Sicilian narrows.

Between 0015 and 0045 on 20 January, *Javelin* and *Kelvin* jumped a convoy departing Tripoli consisting of the minesweepers *RD31, 36, 37,* and *39*—old, ten-knot ships displacing two hundred tons and armed with single 3-inch guns; auxiliary minesweepers *Cinzia* (71 GRT), *Guglielmo Marconi* (304 GRT), and *Angelo Musco* (69 GRT); the small tankers *Irma* (305 GRT) and *Astrea* (136 GRT); and the barge *Santa Barbara*. *RD36* tried to delay the British, but the destroyers quickly overwhelmed her and then rampaged through the convoy, sinking every vessel. *Kelvin* expended three hundred rounds and *Javelin* five hundred. The same night *Nubian, Pakenham,* and the Greek *Vasilissa Olga* dispatched the small transport *Stromboli* (206 GRT).

On 23 January the British 8th Army entered Tripoli unopposed. The retreating Italians had blocked the port with ships filled with metal debris and concrete.

General Bernard Montgomery, commander of the 8th Army, unjustly complained that there was "dilatoriness" in clearing this wreckage, criticism that ultimately cost Harwood his job as Commander in Chief Levant.[46]

Accelerating Attrition

In February the Regia Marina maintained its efforts to supply Tunisia. By this time escorts—particularly destroyers, which were also valuable as minelayers and fast troop transports—were becoming scarce. On the other hand, the French shipping requisitioned in November offset mercantile losses to a considerable extent. The number of Allied air sorties against the supply traffic and ports dropped due to the need to support ground troops during the Axis mid-February Kasserine offensive. The British introduced MTBs into Bône, but these had little success. (See table 11.7.)

Table 11.7 Number/Tonnage of Axis Merchant Ships over 500 GRT Lost in the Mediterranean[47]

	Surface	Air	SS	Other/Shared	Total
January	4/7,757	9/41,088	11/28,561	10/40,490	34/117,896
February		15/45,090	11/44,790	4/4,885	30/94,765
March		18/62,453	16/39,872	2/9,156	36/111,481
April	3/7,487	15/59,566	10/35,492	5/13,678	33/116,223
May	1/3,566	30/89,628	4/10,733	4/8,807	39/112,734

By March, the USAAF was accounting for two-thirds of the increasing tonnage sunk by aircraft. A raid by twenty-four B-17s on Palermo on 22 March was particularly effective, destroying seven ships of 11,500 tons. Forces Q and K continued to seek targets but with little success and some danger, as demonstrated on 12 March when *S55* torpedoed the destroyer *Lightning* from Force Q as she was returning to base.

At the time of the Torch landings ten S-boats remained in the 3rd Flotilla. Up until their success with *Lightning,* the flotilla had concentrated on minelaying. It occasionally joined Italian warships as escorts but never had to defend a convoy against surface attack.

By April 1943 fuel and munitions available to the Axis ground forces in Tunisia were running low, as the rate of large merchant vessels "sunk in passage or in port rose to 50 per cent as compared with less than 20 per cent in February."[48] In response, the Axis used smaller craft and barges, which were harder to find and thus sink, as well as easier to unload.

In a typical operation, the steamship *Belluno,* carrying a cargo of munitions, and her escort, the torpedo boats *Tifone* and *Climene,* sailed from Naples for Tunisia on 15 April. The force made Trapani and picked up the torpedo boats *Cigno* and *Cassiopea,* which were to scout for British MTBs, a pair of which had ambushed an Italian convoy near Cani Rocks on 1 April and damaged two ships. The augmented force left Trapani at 0100 on 16 April.

The convoy was barely under way when, at 0238, *Cigno* spotted shapes nine thousand yards south. These belonged to *Pakenham* and *Paladin.* The British, acting on signals intelligence, were sweeping north at twenty knots in search of the convoy and detected the Italians visually at 0242. (See table 11.8.)

Table 11.8 *Belluno* **Convoy, 16 April 1943, 0248–0315**

Conditions: Night, good weather, quarter moon, calm seas
British ships— (Captain J. S. Stevens): *Pakenham*[Sunk] (F), *Paladin*[D1]
Italian ships— (Lieutenant Commander Carlo Maccaferri): *Cigno*[Sunk] (F), *Cassiopea*[D4]

Cigno steered toward the contact, switching on her fighting lights (small lights used in combat to facilitate recognition) and making recognition signals. *Pakenham* likewise lit her fighting lights and came to starboard, toward the enemy, while *Paladin* continued north in a flanking move.

Range closed quickly as the two flagships barreled toward each other. By this time Maccaferri had identified the intruders as British destroyers. At 0248 *Cigno* opened fire from twenty-five hundred yards. A 3.9-inch shell from the first salvo exploded on *Pakenham's* stern, destroying the deckhouse, igniting a small fire, and disabling the aft torpedo tubes. At the same time *Cassiopea,* heading north-northwest on a converging course, engaged *Paladin* from forty-five hundred yards. At the sound of gunfire *Bellano* and her escorts came hard about for Trapani, in accordance with their orders.

Cigno hit *Pakenham* again at 0250; a shell penetrated the British destroyer's lower deck, igniting a serious fire and causing Captain Stevens to order the aft magazine flooded. The range had become point-blank, and machine guns rattled, filling the air with colored tracers. At 0253 *Pakenham* blasted *Cigno* in her forward boiler, just aft of the bridge. A great cloud of smoke and steam enveloped the torpedo boat. As *Cigno* drifted to a stop she aimed torpedoes at *Pakenham* but missed. At 0258 *Pakenham* returned the favor with her forward tubes, and two minutes later a torpedo exploded on *Cigno* amidships, breaking her in two.

Cigno's stern section sank rapidly, but her forward half remained afloat, and its 3.9-inchers continued taking potshots at the enemy as *Pakenham* turned north to engage *Cassiopea*. Shortly after 0300 a Parthian round from *Cigno*'s sinking fore section detonated on *Pakenham*'s waterline, flooding her engine room and bursting the main boiler tubes. *Pakenham* took on a fifteen-degree list to port, and escaping steam forced the engine room's evacuation. As electric power failed *Pakenham* slid to a stop, with fires flickering along her length.

Cassiopea had only suffered splinter damage up to this point, but at 0302 *Paladin* raked her with an effective burst of 2-pounder rounds, jamming the rudder and sparking a small fire astern and a more serious one forward. The Italian's two stern mounts fired back, and at 0306 she uncorked a torpedo from twelve hundred yards. This blow failed to connect, although her crew claimed success because at 0308 *Paladin* extinguished her searchlights and ceased fire.

In fact, *Paladin* was taking evasive action. Because Italian shells tended to explode and fragment when they hit the water, they often caused splashes large for their size and, based on this evidence, *Paladin*'s captain, concluding his opponent was a *Regolo*-class cruiser, broke off to the southeast. Meanwhile, *Pakenham* had restored power and headed north, hitting *Cassiopea* from four thousand yards. *Cassiopea* replied with her stern guns until 0313, when she tagged *Pakenham* on the British ship's quad 40-mm mount. *Pakenham*, which had lost nine men in this intense action, ceased fire and followed *Paladin*. The severely damaged *Cassiopea* was content to see the enemy go.

The British destroyers withdrew south but at 0400, with no feed water for her boilers, *Pakenham* lost power again and *Paladin* took her in tow. When at dawn Italian fighters buzzed the crippled ship, Vice Admiral Malta concluded that an attempt to save *Pakenham* might lead to the loss of both vessels. At 0800 he ordered *Paladin* to scuttle *Pakenham* with torpedoes.[49]

For her part, *Cassiopea* was in serious trouble, adrift without power and with a large fire forward. However, the fire burned itself out by 0500, and *Climene* towed her the short distance back to Trapani. *Cassiopea* was six months under repair. *Cigno* lost 103 men. *Bellano* returned to sea at 0545 that day and landed her cargo at its destination.

This action was one of the few times an Italian escort fought off a superior British surface group in a night engagement. In their inquest, the British concluded they had faced fleet destroyers and had sunk both. They attributed *Pakenham*'s loss to an unfortunate hit and acknowledged that the crews of the two ships lacked experience. Although chance played its part and every hit can be considered unfortunate, experience seemed the major factor. Both torpedo boats were seasoned veterans, while the British destroyers had come from the quiet waters of the Indian Ocean. That the Italians saw the British first and hit first was significant. Finally, *Paladin*'s decision to retreat due to an imagined threat was unusually cautious. However, to describe as successful an action wherein the Italians preserved a one-ship convoy from attack at the cost of one escort sunk and another seriously damaged indicated the degree of Britain's night combat superiority.

By May Tunis was clearly doomed. The Axis aerial bridge to Africa had reversed direction and was flying troops and specialists back to Italy. However, Hitler's directive was to resist as long as possible, and so the dangerous, mostly one-ship, operations continued. On 3 May the freighter *Campobasso*, which had been waiting at Pantelleria for the right conditions, sailed at 1900 for Tunis, following a convoluted course necessitated by the labyrinth of minefields she had to traverse.

Campobasso Convoy

British destroyers, alerted by signals intelligence, waited along the convoy's expected route. At 2325 *Perseo*'s German-made Metox radar detector picked up enemy emissions; a message from Supermarina that the convoy had been found quickly followed. Star shell lofted overhead ten minutes later when the ships were seven miles east of Kelibia, on Cape Bon. Shell fire hit *Campobasso* almost immediately, and she burst into flames. Aboard the torpedo boat, one crewman later recalled, "Remembering the previous 15 January action everyone knew what would happen; immediately the torpedo boat turned toward the enemy to launch."[50] (See table 11.9.)

Table 11.9 *Campobasso* Convoy, 3–4 May 1943, 2340–0100

Conditions: Night, wind force 4
British ships— Force K: DD: *Nubian, Petard, Paladin*
Italian ships— Convoy Escort: TB: *Perseo*[Sunk]
Convoy: *Campobasso*[Sunk] (3,566 GRT)

At 2344 *Perseo* put her two starboard torpedoes into the water, range seven hundred yards, and, heading northwest, made full speed for Cape Bon. At 2348

Campobasso exploded in a giant fireball, exposing *Perseo* in the glare. Star shells burst overhead, and the torpedo boat began maneuvering wildly to avoid the enemy salvos that followed. At 2352, however, she suffered a rudder defect, and a minute later, before manual steering could be engaged, two shells slammed into the ship, followed by rounds that hit her bridge and engine spaces. As hot steam swirled on deck the engines stopped. The British destroyers swarmed as close as five hundred yards, hitting with their main batteries and antiaircraft weapons. At 2358 Lieutenant Commander Marotta ordered his men to abandon ship.

Against expectations, *Perseo* remained afloat nearly an hour. On the rafts, crew members joked that the ship's armor—hundreds of accumulated coats of paint—was proving sound.[51] However, the magazine finally exploded, and the torpedo boat sank stern first at 0100. She lost 133 men with eighty-three rescued; seventy-three of *Campobasso's* crew died, and only thirty were rescued.

By this time Tunis harbor was so "crowded with the protruding masts of sunken ships that one prisoner thought it looked 'almost like a forest.'"[52] The Allies expected the Axis to mount an evacuation, and remembering their own operations undertaken from France and Greece under the stress of enemy air superiority, the British named their plan to block this anticipated rescue "Retribution." From 9 May ten to twelve destroyers patrolled each night off Cape Bon, with a similar number of coastal craft inshore. The destroyers sported superstructures painted royal red to facilitate aerial recognition after friendly aircraft attacked several times—a telling indicator of the margin of air superiority the Allies had finally gained and one reason why Supermarina decided that any last-minute, large-scale evacuation would have "ended vainly in a useless slaughter of ships and men."[53] Thus the Axis made only small, scattered attempts to flee Africa by sea, and the blockading warships netted just eight hundred men. The Allies captured 238,000 Germans and Italians, including noncombatants.[54]

The fall of Tunisia ended the three-year struggle to control Africa and opened the direct passage through the Mediterranean. On 26 May the first Gibraltar–Alexandria convoy since early 1941 docked in Egypt. One historian summarized this event's impact on the Allied war effort: "Naval Staff estimated that it would bring us at least a fifty per cent saving of shipping bound for the Middle East and about a twenty per cent saving of ships sailing to and from India."[55] Overall, the gain amounted to about a million tons of shipping, while many warships and aircraft were freed for other duties, such as amphibious operations.

The French situation also stabilized. Initially, North Africa teetered on the verge of civil war, with many dissatisfied that Vichy leaders remained in charge. However, a young Frenchman assassinated Darlan on 24 December 1942, in "a plot involving both monarchists and Gaullists."[56] The naval forces reorganized, and in February 1943 the best ships, like the *Richelieu*, the most modern cruisers, and large destroyers headed to American shipyards for refits, updated electronics, and more antiaircraft weapons. On 12 May Admiral Godfroy in Alexandria finally decided to end his prolonged isolation and rejoin the Allies. The naval forces in the Antilles, facing the prospect of civil war and an American blockade, did the same on 4 July. On 1 June Charles De Gaulle arrived in Algeria and asserted his authority over the navy. This resulted in a purge of officers like Vice Admiral François Michelier, who commanded French forces in Morocco, and the navy's final split with the lingering remains of the Vichy state.

The Italian Armistice

The Italians have made heavy sacrifices in a hard and bloody war, and have thereby proved that it is not weakness or fear in themselves that have been the mainsprings of [the armistice]. For the individual Italian, who possess a special, often an exaggerated, feeling of honor, the defection from his ally was doubtless extremely painful.

—Admiral Weichold, writing postwar,
quoted in *Hitler's Admirals*

Even before the conclusion of the Tunisian campaign members of Italy's leadership contemplated defeat. When Tripoli fell on 23 January 1943, Admiral Maugeri, now head of Italy's naval intelligence, recorded in his diary, "Who could have thought it possible a year ago when we reasonably had hopes of conquering? . . . [But] our situation now seems clear and sharp to me: we have lost the war." A week later, upon the occasion of General Vittorio Ambrosio's promotion to Comando Supremo's chief of staff, Ciano wrote, "under present conditions, I don't think even a Napoleon Bonaparte could work miracles."[1] Mussolini hoped that a separate peace with the Soviet Union would save his regime. The Germans, with potentially decisive weapons like jet aircraft, missiles, and true submarines, in the pipeline remained committed to total victory.

Messina Convoy

Even after the loss of Africa, Italy still maintained a vital maritime traffic along its coasts and with its islands, which the British, continuing to rely upon signals intelligence, took every opportunity to disrupt.

In response to intelligence that a convoy had departed Taranto bound for Messina, *Jervis* and *Vasilissa Olga* sortied from Malta on 1 June. The flotilla commander, Captain A. J. Pugsley, who was not privy to Ultra, would recall, "We had hardly got well away before a report came in that a small convoy had been sighted, southbound along the 'foot' of Italy. . . . A hurried consultation of the chart and a stepping-off of distances with the dividers and I knew that there would just be time enough to intercept the convoy, 'give it the works' and get back under air cover by daylight."[2] (See table 12.1.)

Table 12.1 Messina Convoy, 2 June 1943, 0134–0315

Conditions: Clear night, calm seas	
Allied ships—	14th Destroyer Flotilla (Captain A. J. Pugsley): *Jervis* (F), *Vasilissa Olga* (GK)
Italian ships—	Convoy Escort (Lieutenant Commander Marino Fasan): TB: *Castore*[Sunk]
	Convoy: *Vragnizza*[D3] (1,513 GRT), *Postumia*[D3] (595 GRT)

Pugsley's flotilla ran to the convoy's farthest possible position and then turned back along its estimated track. At 0134 off Cape Spartivento they sighted two small steamers. The destroyers altered course and approached undetected. Upon their word, an ASV Wellington dropped flares. "The fire gongs clanged and the ship reeled as the 4.7s opened up at a range of 2,000 yards. The first shots hit the merchantman squarely. There was a dull red glow as the shells burst inside her."[3]

After eight salvos, the British flagship shifted fire to *Postumia*. Then *Castore*, which had been leading the convoy, counterattacked, sending shells whistling overhead. *Jervis* immediately targeted the escort and claimed first-salvos hits, forcing *Castore* to lay smoke and turn away. The Allied destroyers chased into the muck to within a mile of shore but lost contact. The aircraft, however, continued to drop flares, and in their light Pugsley finally saw *Castore* rounding back, aiming her torpedoes. "Leading [*Vasilissa Olga*] past her on an opposite course, once again the guns found their mark before the enemy could make any effective reply."[4] Shells wrecked *Castore*'s steering gear, and she finally sank offshore at 0315.[5] Pugsley's flotilla also claimed the destruction of the merchant ships, but in fact, although damaged, they reached Messina, their destination.

Jervis only expended 142 4.7-inch rounds and one torpedo. On the high-speed return journey *Vasilissa Olga* suffered a boiler breakdown that left her dead in the water for an hour. Nonetheless, the two arrived at Malta undamaged at 1335 on 2 June.

Sicily

Following their expulsion from Africa, the German and Italian high commands expected the Allies to strike across the Mediterranean by invading Sicily, Sardinia, or Greece. In fact, at the Casablanca Conference in January 1943, following "some of the most arduous negotiations ever to occur between the two allies," they decided to invade Sicily. This choice was driven by convenience and the need to completely clear the sea lanes through the Sicilian Channel; it was also seen as a way to placate Stalin's demands for a second front. However, "there was no agreement on the matter of the Mediterranean verses cross-Channel strategy, no agreement on what to do beyond Sicily, no agreement even that knocking Italy out of the war was the immediate objective of the Anglo-American strategy."[6]

After the capture of Pantelleria in June and with growing indications that Sicily was the enemy's next target, it seemed time for the Regia Marina to hazard the battle fleet, against the Allied juggernaut. Although continually battered by air strikes, the fleet could deploy *Vittorio Veneto* and *Littorio,* along with three light cruisers and eleven destroyers. The problem was that in order to intervene, this squadron needed to steam five hundred miles under enemy-dominated skies—a twenty-five-hour journey at twenty knots. Upon reaching the decisive zone, the survivors would face four battleships, two fleet carriers, six light cruisers, and eighteen destroyers. Based at Taranto the Regia Marina had *Doria* and *Duilio* (both recently reactivated), a light cruiser, and a destroyer. The British waited with the modern battleships *King George V* and *Howe,* and six destroyers, should the untrained Italian crews venture to sea. On top of this the Allies had nine cruisers and 104 destroyers supporting the amphibious fleet. An American historian asked, "Would any modern navy, except the Japanese, have sought battle under like conditions?"[7] (See map 12.1.)

When the Allies mounted their massive amphibious assault against Sicily on 10 July, the only Axis naval resistance came from submarines and motor torpedo boats. The submarines sank two LSTs, five merchant ships, and a tanker, at the cost of three German and nine Italian boats.[8] The MTBs accomplished less: "The few serviceable [German] boats sailed a handful of torpedo missions, all frustrated by strong defences."[9] The Allies won their beachheads and progressed inland.

Facing the prospect of having the Adriatic cut off from the west coast, the Regia Marina decided to reinforce the Taranto squadron with a fast intruder unit, the new cruiser *Scipione Africano.* She departed La Spezia on 15 July and reached the Straits of Messina at 0200 on 17 July, after a stopover in Naples forced by a British sighting. While steaming on the last leg of her dangerous journey, she

Map 12.1 The Italian Armistice, September 1943

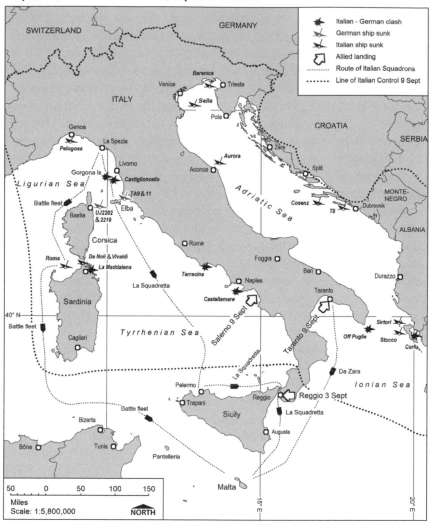

encountered four British MTBs off Reggio. The Allied commander reported, "I was caught completely napping. We were lying with engines stopped . . . in a flat calm with a full moon to the south silhouetting us nicely. . . . We never dreamed that a cruiser would be able to get down there unseen through all our patrols."[10] As *Scipione* steamed straight for them, working up to thirty knots, the boats maneuvered in pairs to get on each side of the enemy's bow. The two boats to the west, *MTB260* and *313*, fired three close-range torpedoes. *Scipione*'s captain reported, "The torpedoes had not touched the water when, at my order, all of *Scipione's* weapons, cannons and machine guns, opened fire on them, a fire so precise and violent as to amaze even me, though I knew the ship's capabilities."[11] On the east side *MTB316* was preparing to launch when a 5.3-inch salvo demolished her and slaughtered the entire crew. The cruiser burst through the enemy line at thirty-six knots and continued south. *MTB315*, launching two torpedoes that passed astern, followed for a time before withdrawing.

All British torpedoes missed, although they claimed a hit, while *Scipione* took credit for sinking three of the four boats. In fact, *MTB260* and *313* were lightly damaged. *Scipione* made Taranto without further incident at 0940 that morning.

On 22 July Palermo surrendered, and by the 23rd only the island's northeastern third remained in Axis hands. Sicily's imminent fall had major political repercussions. On 25 July, King Victor Emmanuel III ordered Benito Mussolini arrested, following a rare meeting of the Italian Fascist Grand Council. The king immediately formed a new government under that ambitious survivor, Field Marshal Pietro Badoglio. Badoglio proclaimed that the war would continue, even as his government tentatively contacted the Allies. The Germans had no doubt that Mussolini's fall foreshadowed a separate peace and acted accordingly. On 28 July *Grossadmiral* Dönitz ordered that "if Rome is occupied the German Navy will immediately secure the Italian Fleet units in La Spezia, Taranto, and Genoa . . . the Commanding Officer of Submarines, Italy, shall station submarines off La Spezia making sure, however, that the Italians do not become aware of this. . . . They will destroy the large ships of the Italian Navy if the latter should leave without our approval."[12]

Supermarina knew that the new government was sounding out the Allies but continued to mount minor operations, for political as much as military reasons. The Italian liaison officer with the Germans wrote, "The employment of the Navy for offensive missions was the minimum proof of goodwill to continue the war, which the Germans anxiously sought."[13] On 4 August *Eugenio di Savoia* and *Montecuccoli* sortied to strike Allied shipping at Palermo. Early on the morning of 6 August, just an hour from their destination, the cruisers encountered the American subchaser *SC503* escorting a water barge. The American boat challenged, worried that she had encountered a pair of friendly but trigger-happy destroyers, whereupon both Italian ships opened fire. After three salvos *SC503* turned her 12-inch searchlight upon herself, and then upon the enemy, to convey that she was friendly. This had the desired effect, as the cruisers abruptly ceased fire and changed course. The Italians believed they had encountered a corvette leading torpedo boats; the commander, Rear Admiral Romeo Oliva, reported, "At 0434 considering as a result of the encounter with enemy torpedo boats and likely air reconnaissance that the surprise on which the mission depended had been lost. . . . I decided not to proceed."[14]

Thinking Oliva had come close to success, Supermarina launched a follow-up raid with *Garibaldi* and *Duca d'Aosta,* under Rear Admiral Giuseppe Fioravanzo's command. These ships departed Genoa on 6 August and staged through La Maddalena the next day. However, as they approached Palermo at 0200 on 8 August, a radar-equipped German aircraft warned of enemy warships near the target. Supermarina ordered Fioravanzo to continue, assessing the sighting as four merchant vessels, but Fioravanzo had already turned away. Had he continued he would have run into the U.S. light cruisers *Philadelphia* and *Savannah* and destroyers *Bristol* and *Ludlow.* The Regia Marina's new chief of staff, Admiral Raffaele De Courten, who was half-German and had been the naval attaché in Berlin, sacked Fioravanzo and continued to mount cruiser sweeps from Taranto, mainly to lay mines.

On 17 August, with the conquest of Sicily complete, De Courten decided that when the Allies moved against the mainland the fleet would commit itself in "a heroic gesture for the honor of the nation and the Navy."[15] As Supermarina drew up plans the odds remained poor, but at least *Roma* had rejoined the fleet, the steaming distance was only 350 miles, and recent exercises had demonstrated the ability to control fighter aircraft from battleships with ship-to-plane radio links. However, on 3 September, still unbeknownst to the navy's leadership, representatives of General Eisenhower and Badoglio signed an armistice document not only ending Italy's participation in the Axis but declaring Italy's intention to cooperate with the Allies. The same day, British forces crossed the Straits of Messina.

The Armistice

That evening Badoglio briefly met the chiefs of staff and advised them that armistice negotiations were under way. He did not reveal that the deal was already done. In part Badoglio based this extraordinary discretion on the advice of General Ambrosio, the plan's principal architect. Ambrosio hoped that the Germans would, when faced by the deal he had crafted, retreat to the north, that the army or SS would depose Hitler, and that the Third Reich would collapse like the second one had in 1918. Such a scenario would make heroes of Badoglio and Ambrosio and spare Italy a bloody separation from its adamant ally.

However, the scenario did not unfold as the army's warlords wanted. During the protracted negotiations German troops had been pouring into Italy, and at the last moment Badoglio attempted to delay the armistice. Eisenhower would have none of that, however, and on 8 September, just ninety minutes before the American general went on the air and announced Italy's surrender, Badoglio informed the king and the navy that an armistice had been signed. Some of the king's council recommended that Italy renege, but the king confirmed Badoglio's actions, and shortly thereafter the marshal went on the air and reluctantly affirmed the deal. At that moment, the Regia Marina had in its fleet the major ships listed in table 12.2.

Table 12.2 Status of the Regia Marina, 8 September 1943

Type	Operational	Under repair	Under construction
New battleship	3		1
Old battleship	2	1	
Aircraft carrier			2
Heavy cruiser		2	
Light cruiser	9		4
Fleet destroyer	15	12	8
Old destroyer	3		
Torpedo boat	17	2	14
Old torpedo boat	14	10	
Corvette	20	4	31
Sloop	1		
Fleet submarine	34	31	18

At 0500 the next morning Badoglio, Ambrosio, and the king fled Rome without ordering resistance against the Germans as the Allies had expected. Although caught by surprise, Supermarina ceased hostilities and instructed units to concentrate in bases under Italian control, rather than the ports specified in the armistice document. The battle fleet had already raised anchor at 1700 on 8 September to attack the Salerno invasion beaches. De Courten telephoned the fleet commander, Admiral Carlo Bergamini, and convinced him to sail to La Maddalena rather than scuttling, as Bergamini wanted.

Because the king had ordered De Courten to accompany him on his flight from Rome, the deputy chief of staff, Vice Admiral Sansonetti, remained at headquarters, despite the uncertain conditions. The failure to implement a coordinated response to the armistice most impacted Italy's army, which melted away, but it affected the navy as well. For example, at 0200 on 9 September the Italian 11th Army in Greece signed a truce with the local German command. This included the Italian warships at Piraeus and Suda Bay, which were under its jurisdiction. The order was soon extended to the Albanian base of Durazzo. The warships thus handed over proved useful to the Germans in their forthcoming Aegean and Adriatic campaigns.[16]

Action off Bastia

Elsewhere, fighting between the erstwhile allies had already erupted. At Bastia, in Corsica, German navy troops seized the harbor at midnight and damaged the torpedo boat *Ardito* (slaughtering seventy members of her crew), the freighter *Humanitas* (7,980 GRT), and a MAS boat. The torpedo boat *Aliseo*, skippered by Commander Fecia di Cossato, who wore the Iron Cross Second Class and the Knight's Cross for his successes as a submarine commander in the Atlantic, cast off just in time and was able to slip out of port. *Aliseo* then stood offshore and awaited instructions.

Italian troops counterattacked early that morning and drove the Germans from their positions. The Italian port commander radioed *Aliseo* and instructed di Cossato to prevent the German ships from withdrawing. (See table 12.3.)

Table 12.3 Action off Bastia, 9 September 1943, 0700–0845

Conditions: Light mist, calm seas
German ships— SC: *UJ2203*[Sunk] (2,270 tons), *UJ2219*[Sunk] (280 GRT); MFP: *F366*[Sunk], *F387*[Sunk], *F459*[Sunk], *F612*[Sunk], *F623*[Sunk]; ML: *FL.B.412*[Sunk]
Italian ships— (Commander Fecia di Cossato): TB *Aliseo*[D2]; DC: *Cormorano*

At dawn a light fog hung along the shore. *Aliseo*'s lookouts saw enemy vessels emerge one by one from the mist at the port's narrow mouth and swing north, hugging the coast.

The German flotilla was superior to *Aliseo* in every respect except speed. Both escorting subchasers had 88-mm guns, while each barge was armed with one 75-mm and either a 37-mm or 20-mm gun. Nonetheless, *Aliseo* closed range as the subchaser *UJ2203* opened fire, followed by other German units as they bore. The torpedo boat zigzagged and withheld fire until 0706, when she was eight thousand yards from the German column. Then, for the next twenty-five minutes, she ran north paralleling the German line and firing rapidly. At 0730 an 88-mm shell hit *Aliseo* in her engine room. Emitting a great cloud of steam she drifted to a halt, but her crew rapidly repaired the damage and plugged the holes to minimize flooding, and she was able to get under way.

Renewing the action, *Aliseo* overhauled the German formation by 0815 and turned west, quickly closing the enemy. The shorter range improved her accuracy; 3.9-inch shells slammed into *UJ2203* and several of the barges. At 0820 *UJ2203* exploded, killing nine men and sending an enormous column of smoke into the air. *Aliseo* shifted her fire to *UJ2219,* and ten minutes later she too exploded and sank.

Meanwhile, the column of motor barges, maintaining an intense fire, began to break up as each craft fled on its own. Machine-gun shells riddled *Aliseo*'s fire-control director, forcing her guns to continue under local control. But with the ranges nearly point-blank, this hardly mattered. "The Captain continued to maneuver to shorten the range. We locked onto a group of three motor barges. We were so close we were able to duel with machineguns. We were hit profusely with 20 mm projectiles, but they failed to inflict serious damage."[17]

By 0835 *Aliseo* had sunk three barges. At 0840 she engaged two more, which were loaded with ammunition. These boats were being shelled by Italian shore batteries at Marina de Pietro and by the Italian corvette *Cormorano,* which had just arrived. Caught three ways, they ran themselves ashore.

With ammunition nearly expended, Di Cossato ceased fire at 0845. Between 1000 and 1050 *Aliseo* pulled twenty-five Germans from the water, but 160 lost their lives. Di Cossato then set a course for La Spezia until ordered instead to Elba, arriving there that afternoon.

Other Actions

In other clashes, German artillery sank the Italian minelayer *Pelagosa* off Genoa and the corvette *Berenice* off Trieste.[18] The incomplete cruiser *Giulio Germanico* repulsed an attempt by German troops to seize the town of Castellamare di Stabia in the Gulf of Naples. However, the most serious event occurred at La Maddalena, where German commandos attacked the naval base at noon on 9 September and captured the commander, Rear Admiral Bruto Brivonesi, of Beta convoy fame. This left no Italian-controlled port in the western Mediterranean capable of receiving the battle fleet.

At 1225, off Cape Santa Maria di Leuca, in southern Puglie, *S54* and *S61* with the barge *F478* sank two Italian auxiliary minesweepers. At 1430 *Scipione* arrived and forced the German motor torpedo boats to scuttle the MFP and flee.

At Rhodes Italian forces captured the German steamship *Taganrog*. German R-boats clashed with the Italian submarine chasers *VAS234* and *235* off the Gorgona Islands. Near Terracina the corvettes *Folaga, Ape,* and *Cormorano* engaged five German MFPs, sinking *F345* and forcing the other four ashore. At Castiglioncello, German minelayers eliminated two Italian auxiliaries and captured the minelayer *Buffoluto* after a long gunfire exchange.

Then, at 1535, twenty-eight Do.217 bombers armed with the recently introduced FX-1400 guided bomb attacked the battle fleet, sinking Bergamini's flagship *Roma*, killing nearly fourteen hundred men, including the admiral, and lightly damaging her sister, *Italia* (the former *Littorio*). At the same time *Duilio* and *Doria*, the cruisers *Cadorna* and *Pompeo*, and the destroyer *Da Recco* departed Taranto. Originally believing the Germans intended to occupy the port, Vice Admiral Da Zara planned to scuttle his squadron, but the area commander convinced him to sail instead for Malta and, as long as the ships remained under Italian control, to respect the armistice.

Clashes between the Regia Marina and German forces continued. At 1650 the destroyers *Vivaldi* and *Da Noli* attacked a German R-boat and three MFPs in the narrows between Corsica and Sardinia and drove the barges ashore. The shore batteries at Bonifacio, which Italian Blackshirts had turned over to the Germans that morning, counterattacked and damaged both destroyers. *Da Noli* then ran into a mine and sank. A German bomber hit *Vivaldi* that same day, and she foundered on 10 September.

That night, navy-manned coastal batteries at Piombino sank three German MFPs from a force of ten after their embarked troops attacked the port. The next day the German torpedo boats *TA9* and *TA11* seized four Italian subchasers that were entering Piombino Harbor. At 2045, *TA9* and *TA11* attacked the Italian shore batteries. The guns returned fire and sank *TA11*, the four subchasers, and the ex-French steamer *Carbet* (3,689 GRT). *TA9* escaped heavily damaged and was paid off (that is, taken out of service) later that month.[19]

On 10 September at 0930 Da Zara's force appeared off Malta and entered Grand Harbor. That same morning the reduced battle fleet, now under the command of the 7th Division's Admiral Oliva, came in sight of a British force that included *Warspite, Valiant,* and seven destroyers. A destroyer carrying Admiral Cunningham and General Eisenhower met the Italian fleet off Bizerte at 1500. After requesting permission, Captain T. M. Brownrigg of Cunningham's staff boarded the new flagship *Eugenio*. Eisenhower's naval aide noted that "as Brownrigg and Smith were seen to board [the cruiser] and all appeared serene, the tension was relaxed, and from gun turrets came smiles and cameras."[20]

The battle fleet entered Malta on the morning of 11 September. Admiral Oliva rejected another suggestion by his second in command to scuttle the fleet in Grand Harbor. That afternoon Cunningham and Da Zara, the senior Italian officer present, met; the British admiral's courtesy to his ex-enemy gratified the Italians. That evening, however, Cunningham sent his oft-quoted dispatch, "Be pleased to inform their Lordships that the Italian Battle fleet now lays at anchor under the guns of the fortress of Malta." This signal failed to mention that the ships remained armed and under Italian control. In fact, three days later Cunningham wrote in a letter that "[the Italian fleet] is alright at the moment but I smell trouble coming. I am quite convinced that all the ships are prepared to scuttle should things not be to their liking."[21]

Meanwhile, another Italian fleet was at sea without a port to enter. This was a group of corvettes and torpedo boats nicknamed *La Squadretta*, or little fleet. It had originally headed for Elba, but when events drove it south, Supermarina ordered it to make for Palermo. It arrived there at 1000 on 12 September, much to the surprise of the American commander, who signaled, "Be pleased to inform Their Lordships that Palermo lies under the guns of an Italian Fleet."[22]

The most notable aspect of the actions of the individual Italian commanders is that they were ignorant of the armistice conditions and did not enjoy Supermarina's guidance, which made its last broadcast at 1709 on 10 September, after the authorities in Rome came to terms with the Germans. In this light there was a surprising degree of cooperation between the castaway admirals at Malta and the Allied authorities. For example, the destroyers *Legionario* and *Oriani* left Malta on 13 September to transport munitions and an American OSS detachment from Algiers to Ajaccio, Corsica, to assist French and Italian troops fighting there.[23]

Small-scale actions between the Germans and Italians continued, although at a lower intensity. Major losses suffered by the Italians included the gunboat *Aurora*, the motorship *Leopardi*, crowded with hundreds of civilian passengers, and the steamer *Pontinia*, captured by *S54* and *S61* on 11 September. These resourceful S-boats then ambushed the destroyer *Sella*, emerging from behind *Pontinia*'s lee, torpedoing her from only ninety yards. Their report tersely stated, "One minute later sank without trace. Steamer under command of prize crew was left to pick up survivors."[24] On 14 September a German air attack badly damaged the torpedo boat *Giuseppe Sirtori* off Corfu. In the Adriatic the torpedo boats *Stocco*, *Sirtori*, and *Cosenz*, as well as some freighters, tankers, and minor vessels, fell victim to German aircraft on 24, 25, and 27 September, respectively. Still, the Regia Marina rescued twenty-five thousand Italian troops from the Balkans during September without Allied support. In the two weeks between 11 and 23 September, Italian forces sank eight German MFPs and seven small auxiliaries.

The Italian navy's core remained intact despite the lack of national direction, the fluid and dangerous situation, and the mixed feelings, if not loyalties, of many officers and men. Finally, on 23 September, Admiral De Courten and Admiral Cunningham signed an agreement at Taranto that provided for naval cooperation between the kingdom of Italy and the United Nations. Table 12.4 indicates the fates of the fleet's operational units during this period.

Table 12.4 Fate of Italian Units after the Armistice

Type	Sunk	Scuttled	Captured	Interned	Joined Allies*
Battleship	1	0	0	0	5
Cruiser	0	0	0	1	8
Destroyer	3	0	2	3	11
Torpedo boat	0	2	8	0	24
Corvette	1	0	1	0	19

* includes some vessels under repair

Germany Grabs a Fleet

It might have seemed that the armistice would end significant naval combat in the Mediterranean, but this did not happen. Hitler, after some doubts and against the advice of many of his military advisors, concluded that Germany needed to become a Mediterranean power, and so the Kriegsmarine improvised a naval force to supplement the light forces—eighty-eight MFPs, ten Siebel ferries, and fifty smaller landing craft already based throughout the Mediterranean.

The German occupation of so many Italian bases and shipyards had resulted in a windfall of captured vessels, although, with the exception of the old torpedo boats and destroyers handed over in the Aegean, most required considerable work before they could serve. These warships were to form the backbone of Germany's ongoing resistance in the Middle Sea. (See table 12.5.)

A Fleet Fades Away

Even after the accord of 23 September, the Allies distrusted their former enemy. In part this was the residue of thirty-nine months of active enmity and

Table 12.5 German Navy Deployment in the Mediterranean, 9 September 1943

Type	Western Mediterranean	Eastern Mediterranean
Torpedo boats	2	1
Submarines	13	4
MTBs (S-boats)	11+1 under repair	6
Auxiliary subchasers	16	8
Motor minesweepers	27+1 under repair	7
Minelayers	2	2
Fighter-direction ship	1	0
Transports	3	1
Auxiliary minesweepers	26	15
Other auxiliaries	5	0

propaganda; in part it was caused by the fact that some Italians, including naval units, chose to fight alongside the Germans. *Vittorio Veneto* and *Italia* rusted in the Suez Canal's Bitter Lakes from 19 October 1943 until 5 February 1947 as hostages to Italy's conduct. The cruisers *Abruzzi* and *Duca d'Aosta*, on the other hand, sailed to Freetown, Sierra Leone, on 26 October 1943. From there, joined later by *Garibaldi*, they searched the central Atlantic for German raiders and blockade runners until March 1944.

Some Regia Marina destroyers patrolled the Albanian and Greek coasts engaging German shore batteries and MTBs during the spring of 1944. Italian destroyers, torpedo boats, corvettes, submarines, and above all, MTBs, conducted 370 special night missions, landing and recovering commandos, agents, and former prisoners of war along the Italian and Balkan coasts. During these dangerous patrols the navy lost a submarine and five MTBs.

The Allies appreciated Italy's naval special forces. Although X MAS had operated as the major unit of Mussolini's navy, a Royal X MAS conducted operations, both alone and in conjunction with British forces. The most noteworthy, at least in terms of propaganda value, were the destruction of the hulked heavy cruiser *Bolzano* at La Spezia on 22 June 1944 and an attack against the carrier *Aquila* at Genoa on 19 April 1945.

The principal activity of the Regia Marina during the war's last twenty months, however, was escort duty. "Italian ships almost exclusively performed the duties of protecting and escorting the convoys bringing supplies to the

Anglo-American armies in Italy." Italian ships "carried out 2,644 escort missions for 1,525 convoys made up of 10,496 ships." Italian cruisers and destroyers also logged nearly 370,000 miles as fast transports, carrying 317,000 men.[25]

Finally, one of the major activities of the Italian navy consisted of training other Allied forces. Because of their experience, Italian submarines in particular made excellent "aggressors" in exercises. At one time or another, four cruisers, five destroyers, six escort vessels, and forty submarines participated in these activities in the Mediterranean, Atlantic, Red Sea, and Indian Ocean.

13

Germany's War

1943–45

The immense strength radiated by the Fuehrer, his unwavering
confidence, and his far sighted appraisal of the Italian situation,
have shown how insignificant we are compared to him, and how
fragmentary is our knowledge of the situation. The man who
thinks he can do better than the Fuehrer is an imbecile.

—*Grossadmiral* Karl Dönitz, quoted by Raymond de Belot in
Struggle for the Mediterranean

itler's decision to hold southern Italy and the Aegean required that the
Reich become a Mediterranean power. The Kriegsmarine, demonstrating an impressive talent for improvisation, proceeded to fight four largely
self-contained campaigns: in the Aegean, which lasted until October 1944; in
the Adriatic and in the western Mediterranean, both of which endured to the
end of the war; and the sea-denial campaign, which ended by September 1944.
Their intensity can be measured by the fact that nearly 40 percent of the large
warship losses German suffered in sixty-eight months of total war in all theaters occurred in the Mediterranean during the twenty months these campaigns
lasted. (See map 13.1.)

The Aegean Pre-Armistice

Before the Italian armistice, German forces occupied the Aegean islands of Milos,
Lemnos, Chios, and Skiros, as well as nearly all of Crete. The German navy's
presence had started with four coastal defense flotillas, based at Piraeus (12th
Flotilla, formed July 1941), Salonika (10th Flotilla, August 1941), Crete (13th
Flotilla, November 1941), and Lemnos (11th Flotilla, May 1942). These consisted
of small, requisitioned vessels, each mostly fitted with a light antiaircraft weapon.
They were ill-suited for defense against Allied submarines, and so on 3 January
1942 the naval command formed the 21st Uterseebootsjager Flotilla, a motley
collection of vessels generally armed with at least one 88-mm gun and multiple

Map 13.1 Germany and the Mediterranean, September–May 1945

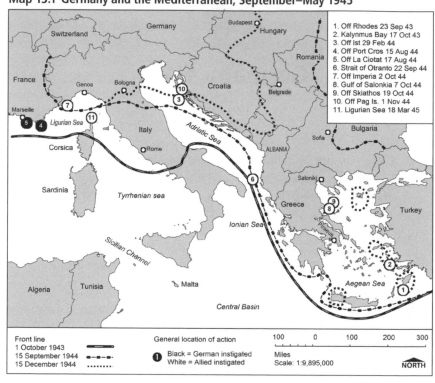

1. Off Rhodes 23 Sep 43
2. Kalynmus Bay 17 Oct 43
3. Off Ist 29 Feb 44
4. Off Port Cros 15 Aug 44
5. Off La Ciotat 17 Aug 44
6. Strait of Otranto 22 Sep 44
7. Off Imperia 2 Oct 44
8. Gulf of Salonkia 7 Oct 44
9. Off Skiathos 19 Oct 44
10. Off Pag Is. 1 Nov 44
11. Ligurian Sea 18 Mar 45

Front line
1 October 1943
15 September 1944
15 December 1944

General location of action

Black = German instigated
White = Allied instigated

100   0   100   200   300
Miles
Scale: 1:9,895,000
NORTH

antiaircraft weapons. These craft included an ex-Russian icebreaker (*UJ2105*), an ex-British trawler (*UJ2101*), ex-Swedish and British yachts (*UJ2102* and *UJ2107*), ex-Greek minelayers (*UJ2106, UJ2110,* and *UJ2103*), an ex-Norwegian whaler (*UJ2104*), and the salvaged ex-British minesweeper *Widnes* (*UJ2109*). Five wooden schooners dubbed *GA41–45* and armed with 88-mm guns also served as escorts. This narrow-water fleet escorted interisland traffic and guarded the important connection with the Black Sea. Germany's sole destroyer in the Mediterranean, the ex-Greek *Vasilefs Georgios*, renamed ZG3 (*Hermes*), commissioned in May 1942. After successful duty in the eastern Mediterranean she transferred to the central basin in April 1943. Her principal accomplishment was the sinking of the British submarine *Splendid* on 21 April. Allied aircraft damaged her on 30 April off Tunisia, in an attack that sank the Italian destroyers *Pancaldo* and *Pigafetta;* she was scuttled in Africa on 7 May. Other Aegean units present in September 1943 included two minelayers—*Bulgaria* (1,108 GRT) and the modern ex-Yugoslavian seaplane tender *Drache* (1,870 tons, two 4-inch guns and sixteen knots), as well as five motor minesweepers (R-boats) of the 12th Flotilla, sixteen *Marinefährprahm* (MFP) barges, two S-boats at Salamis, and miscellaneous small units, along with five submarines.[1]

Improvise and Dare: The Aegean 1943

Immediately after the Italian armistice, Kriegsmarine staff concluded that the Aegean islands were vulnerable and had little defensive value. Hitler, however, vetoed Dönitz's request to evacuate, explaining, "The attitude of our allies in the south-east, and likewise Turkey's attitude is determined exclusively by their confidence in our strength. Abandonment of the islands would create the most unfavourable impression."[2] A German withdrawal would have also granted the Allies easy access to Russia via the Black Sea. Therefore, Germany disarmed the Italian troops on Crete, occupied the small Italian-held islands in the Cyclades, and seized the six Regia Marina destroyers and torpedo boats in Grecian ports, commissioning five of them by the end of October as the 9th Torpedo Boat Flotilla. (See table 13.1.)

Table 13.1 Large German Warships Commissioned in the Aegean Sea
(Ex-Italian unless otherwise indicated)

Name	Original name	Type	Service date	Fate
ZG3	*Vasilefs Georgios* (GK)	DD	5/42	Scuttled 7/5/43
TA10	*La Pomone* (FR)	TB	7/4/43	Sunk 23/9/43 surf
TA14	*Turbine*	DD	28/10/43	Sunk 15/9/44 air
TA15	*Crispi* ex-*TA17*	DD	20/10/43	Sunk 8/3/44 air
TA16	*Castelfidardo*	TB	14/10/43	Sunk 2/6/44 air
TA17	*San Martino* ex-*TA18*	TB	28/10/43	CL 18/9/44 air
TA18	*Solferino*	TB	25/7/44	Sunk 19/10/44 surf
TA19	*Calatafimi*	TB	13/9/43	Sunk 9/8/44 sf
UJ2109	*Widnes* (BR)	DC	16/1/43	Sunk 17/10/43 surf

Fates: air—by air forces; CL—constructive loss; surf—by surface forces; sf—by special forces.

Hitler's decision to hold the Aegean clashed with Churchill's long-standing dream of drawing Turkey into the war and rolling up Germany's position in southeastern Europe.[3] The British had a plan to seize the Aegean but, when the opportunity arrived the demands of the Italian campaign prevented its full implementation. In the end, pushed by Churchill's famous signal to "improvise and dare," the Levant command tried to conquer the archipelago with a destroyer flotilla, six submarines, and eighteen launches or landing craft. It also deployed two Spitfighter, two Beaufighter, and two bomber squadrons, and the 234th Infantry Brigade, Malta's former garrison, which was in the area for a rest from the privations of that island's siege.[4] (See map 13.2.)

Map 13.2 Aegean Campaign, September–November 1943

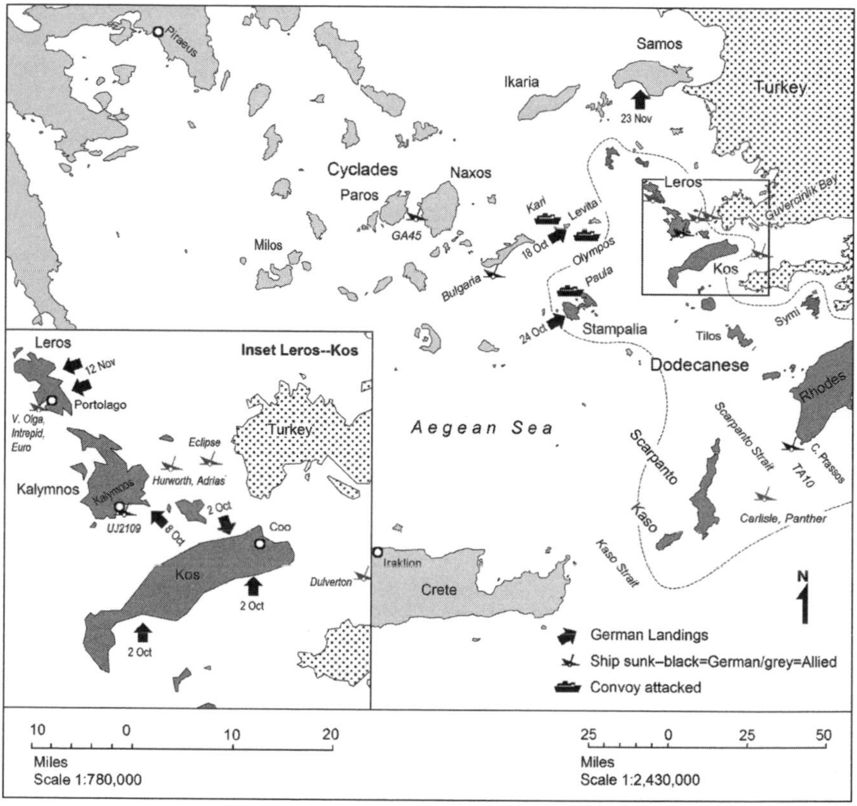

Rhodes was the real prize, because of its size and location. On 9 September two British agents parachuted onto the island to encourage the governor, Admiral Campioni, and his thirty-thousand-man garrison to resist the seventy-five hundred Germans stationed there. Fighting had already broken out but, as an Italian naval officer complained to one of the agents, the Italian troops "were not good and were shockingly led."[5] Campioni balked at the enticements of his ex-enemies and instead surrendered to the Germans on 11 September. They eventually handed him over to Mussolini, who had the admiral shot for treason in May 1944.

The failure to seize Rhodes should have ended the Aegean adventure. Instead, the British flung scratch forces ashore on Castelorizzo on 11 September and then on the larger islands of Kos on 14 September (which had the only air-field outside of Rhodes), Leros on 17 September (site of a major Italian naval base), Kalymnos, Samos, Symi, and Stampalia. The Italians were generally coop-erative, if demoralized and confused, but this attitude was not universal. The cap-tain of *MAS522*, for example, defected to the Germans on 18 September, taking with him Allied agents and an Italian general he was supposed to be ferrying from Samos to Ikaria. Moreover, on 11 September Hitler ordered the execution of captured Italian officers who fought the Germans. This order was routinely obeyed, and large-scale atrocities also occurred, such as the massacre of thou-sands of men of the Acqui Division on Kefallonia, in the Ionian Sea.[6]

The campaign that unfolded demonstrated the interrelationship of air, naval, and amphibious forces in narrow waters. The Germans had air and the Allies naval superiority, but neither completely dominated. Sea power struck the first heavy blow on 18 September, when the destroyers *Faulknor, Eclipse,* and the Greek *Vasilissa Olga* intercepted a small convoy north of Stampalia: the German cargo ships *Pluto* (3,830 GRT) and *Paula* (3,754 GRT), escorted by *UJ2104* (715 tons). The destroyers approached from down-moon at high speed, and at 0017 they surprised their quarry, quickly setting *Paula* afire. She exploded and sank within five minutes. *UJ2104*, armed with an 88-mm gun and a pair of 20-mms, was the next target. After being pounded by 4.7-inch shells she drifted off, barely afloat, and eventually stranded. *Vasilissa Olga* damaged *Pluto,* and *Faulknor* fin-ished her with a torpedo. Italian troops captured the 131 survivors who swam to Stampalia. German air superiority, however, kept Allied warships away during the day. The British tried to equalize the situation from the beginning by deploying two Spitfire squadrons on Kos, but the Luftwaffe bombed the field daily starting on 18 September and had largely eliminated the enemy fighters by month's end.

On the night of 22 September the destroyers *Eclipse, Faulknor,* and *Fury* fer-ried twelve hundred troops to Kos. On their return south they patrolled for enemy traffic—the *Eclipse* via Scarpanto Strait and the others via Kaso Strait. (See table 13.2.)

Ten miles south of Rhodes, *Eclipse* sighted *TA10*, on her first combat mis-sion, and the steamer *Donizetti* (2,428 GRT), packed with 1,584 Italian prison-ers. Attacking shortly after 0100, *Eclipse* quickly dispatched *Donizetti*, which sank with no survivors, and then crippled *TA10*, killing five crewmen. Rescue vessels

Table 13.2 Action South of Rhodes, 23 September 1943, 0100

Conditions: Night, three-quarter moon, moonrise at 0117
British ship—   DD: *Eclipse*
German ship— TB: *TA10*[D4]

towed the torpedo boat into Prassos Bay, on Rhodes, where Allied aircraft finished her off two days later.

The need to base Allied warships at Cyprus or Alexandria limited their endurance on station. Attempts to use Leros as a forward naval base proved costly when German aircraft sank the destroyers *Intrepid* and *Vasilissa Olga* there on 26 September and the Italian destroyer *Euro* on 1 October. By that date the Germans, having brought in reinforcements from Russia and France, had seventy-five fighters, eighty-five long-range bombers, and sixty-five dive bombers in the area.[7]

On 1 October the Germans commenced Operation Eisbär (Polar Bear) to capture Kos. From Iraklion sailed the transport *Citta di Savona* and MFPs *F336* and *F338*, escorted by *UJ2109;* from Suda transports *Catherine Schiaffino* (1,591 GRT), *Kari* (1,925 GRT), and *Trapani* (1,855 GRT), with *F123, F129, F308, F370, F496,* and *F532,* escorted by *UJ2101* and *UJ2102;* from Piraeus transports *Ingeborg* (1,160 GRT) and *F497,* the minelayers *Drache* and *Bulgaria,* with *UJ2110* and *UJ2111;* and from Naxos *R34, R194, R210, GA41, GA42, GA44, GA45,* and two converted motor fishing boats, *KFK2* and *KFK3.* By coincidence, the British fleet destroyers were absent, having been ordered to escort the battleships *Howe* and *King George V,* which were bound for Suez on their way to the Far East. Three Hunts were patrolling in Kaso Strait, but command ordered them to Alexandria to refuel, despite reports of a convoy off Naxos, which it assumed was bound for Rhodes.[8]

Every German vessel arrived safely. The MFPs landed the assault wave and shuttled back to the transports for more men. The surprised garrison put up a feeble resistance, and by the evening of 3 October Kos had fallen. The Germans captured 1,388 British troops, 3,145 Italians (after shooting sixty-six officers), and vast stocks of ammunition, fuel, and provisions. They lost only fourteen men. Afterward, the Middle East commander, General Maitland Wilson, reported that there had been "no intelligence at our disposal which would have led us to foresee that the enemy would be able to collect and launch at such short notice an expedition of the magnitude which made the assault on Cos."[9]

The British responded to this disaster by reinforcing the Levant Fleet with four light cruisers of the 12th Squadron and three P-class destroyers, which sailed for Alexandria on 4 October. Eisenhower, although concerned about dispersing his forces, reluctantly loaned the British six squadrons of USAAF P-38 fighters, capable of operating north of Rhodes.

On 7 October just before dawn, the submarine *Unruly* sighted a convoy consisting of *Olympos* (5,216 GRT, carrying an infantry battalion), *F308, F327, F336, F494, F496, F532*, and the escort *UJ2111* (ex-Italian *Tramglio* 667 GRT)—bringing reinforcements for the Leros invasion. *Unruly*'s torpedo attack failed, but she surfaced and expended fifty-four shells, damaging the transport and one of the barges. As dawn broke *UJ2111* pinpointed the submarine and drove her under, but just over the horizon *Sirius, Penelope,* and the destroyers *Faulknor* and *Fury* had picked up *Unruly*'s report. They intercepted the Germans south of Levita forty minutes later. While the destroyers sank *Olympos*, which had been straggling, the cruisers closed to point-blank range and demolished the barges and *UJ2111*. The subchaser's captain wrote in his report, "With all of our weapons silent, and under constant enemy fire, I give the order 'Open sea-cocks. Everybody abandon ship.'" However, the sea-cocks were blocked by heavy marine growth coating the ship's hull, so that "the ship remains floating in the water for about another two hours burning and exploding."[10] Only the badly damaged *F496* survived. Four hundred men perished. Later that morning German aircraft caught *Penelope* on her run south and hit her with a bomb that passed through her port side without exploding. That same day the Germans occupied Kalymnos, just south of Leros. On 8 October *Unruly* dispatched *Bulgaria*, loaded with 285 troops, with two torpedoes. The next day the cruiser *Carlisle*, accompanied by the destroyers *Panther, Petard, Rockwood,* and *Miaoulis,* were withdrawing south after a night of patrolling when, during a brief gap in their fighter protection, a strong force of Ju.87s attacked; the dive-bombers sank *Panther* and crippled *Carlisle,* ending her career. However, late arriving P-38s tore into the German formation and claimed the destruction of seventeen enemy planes. On 11 October, much to the Levant command's distress, Eisenhower recalled the P-38s. Levita fell on 18 October to a commando force that landed from seaplanes.

With the loss of Kos and the recall of the P-38s, British warships had to keep well clear of the battle zone by daylight or risk destruction. The impact on morale was captured by an anecdote told by the captain of one of the Hunts. Upon arriving on the bridge he observed his signalman inflating his lifebelt. When asked why, the sailor replied, "Air protection, sir. This is the only [expletive] air protection we shall get in this area."[11] To offset the lack of daytime transport, the Levant command pressed two British and four Italian submarines into service as supply vessels.

The Germans, facing supply bottlenecks of their own, attempted to transfer shipping from the Adriatic to the Aegean, but this effort failed. Ten vessels tried to run the Straits of Otranto, but only two made it to Piraeus. Surface warships captured two and sank two (including *Argentina*, captured, and *Olimpia*, sunk on 15 October), while submarines and aircraft accounted for one each and Yugoslav partisans another. One just disappeared.[12]

On the night of 15 October British warships searched for a convoy reported headed toward Kalymnos but found nothing; the next morning, however, the convoy fell afoul of the submarine *Torbay*. She torpedoed the steamer *Kari*, loaded with five hundred troops (of whom 320 were rescued), and damaged *Trapani*. Alerted by this contact, destroyers sallied that evening from Guvercinlik Bay, an isolated Turkish anchorage the British use of which Berlin and Istanbul had ignored to keep Turkey at peace. (See table 13.3.)

Table 13.3 Kalymnos Bay, 17 October 1943

Conditions: Night, calm, moonset 1022
Allied ships—   DD: *Jervis, Penn*; DE: *Hursley*[D2], *Miaoulis* (GK)
German ship— DC: *UJ2109*[Sunk]

The convoy had reached Kalymnos Harbor when the Allied flotilla arrived. While *Jervis* and *Penn* stood off, *Hursley* and *Miaoulis* entered the bay, illuminated, and engaged the German ships. They sank *F338* and *UJ2109* and badly damaged the freighters *Santorini* and *Trapani*. A German 4-inch shell struck *Hursley* in the port side and blasted a four-by-three-foot hole in her hull.[13] Despite her damage, *Trapani* unloaded her cargo that day. The next night *Sirus* and *Penn* returned and bombarded the transport until she capsized in shallow water. However, on the British ships' return to base, German aircraft roughed up *Sirius* hitting her with a 250-kg bomb and scoring four near misses.

The back-and-forth attrition continued as each side landed reinforcements and supplies by night and suffered air attacks by day. Although British signal intelligence was providing considerable details of enemy operations, the Germans slowly gained the upper hand. *Drache* laid on 22 October a minefield that sank the British destroyers *Hurworth* and *Eclipse* and left the Greek Hunt *Adrias* a constructive loss. The Germans captured Stampalia on 24 October. On 30 October a 500-kg bomb knocked *Aurora* out of the campaign.

By early November only destroyers remained to confront the Leros invasion convoy, which the participants nicknamed the "Children's Crusade"—
a miscellany of infantry landing boats, auxiliaries, and small warships. It departed
the Greek mainland on 5 November, and intelligence traced its movement "in
great detail and with little delay." Beaufighters attacked several times but did little damage in the face of a strong fighter escort. On the night of 7 November
the destroyers *Penn* and *Pathfinder* surprised the convoy's leader, *GA45*, as it
debouched from the Naxos–Paros Strait. The auxiliary sacrificed itself while the
rest of the convoy fled back the way it had come. After this close call, which
caused a two-day postponement, the little armada continued only by day with
aerial protection until it reached its staging areas on Kalymnos and Kos.[14] *Petard*,
Rockwood, and the Polish Hunt *Krakowiak* shelled Kalymnos Harbor on the night
of 10/11 November with fifteen hundred rounds, but they missed the small craft
sheltering there, and *Rockwood* was heavily damaged by an Hs293 glider bomb.
Faulknor, Beaufort, and the Greek *Pinos* attacked Kos, with similarly poor results.

On 11 November invasion groups departed Kalymnos and Kos carrying elements of the 22nd Air Landing Division. The western convoy from Kos had *F123,
F129, F331,* and two infantry landing boats; it was escorted by *R210, UJ2101,*
and *UJ2102.* The eastern convoy from Kos and Kalymnos had *F370, F497,* twelve
small boats, and two infantry landing boats, and it was escorted by *R195* and
UJ2110. The 9th Torpedo Boat Flotilla, with *TA14, TA15, TA17,* and *TA19,* sailed
in support, on its first operational mission.

British aircraft reported two barge groups at 0120 on 12 November, but no
destroyers sortied, because the Levant Command failed to appreciate the significance of the sighting and was leery about risking minefields without good
cause.[15] Thus, the Germans proceeded without opposition; the western convoy's escort even captured the British minesweeper *BYMS72* en route. In other
actions, *MTB307* encountered *TA14* off Kalymnos at 0330 and came under fire,
while *ML456* found the eastern convoy at 0500 while on patrol and was damaged by *R195* when she approached to investigate.

Even with an unopposed passage, however, the invasion nearly failed. Italian
shore batteries repulsed the western landing. *TA14* and *TA15* led it on a second
attempt but broke off after the batteries began hitting the landing craft. A last
try that afternoon failed despite the gunfire support of all four torpedo boats
when *TA17* took a shell in her boiler room. The eastern group also met tough
resistance, but just enough troops made it ashore to gain a precarious lodgment,
which the Germans reinforced that day by dropping a battalion of paratroopers. Over the succeeding nights the British shuttled in reinforcements, and their
destroyers chipped in with brief shore bombardments—fifty-seven rounds by

Faulknor, Beaufort, and *Pindos* on 12 November, and ninety rounds by *Echo* and *Belvoir* on 14 November. The Allied destroyer patrols failed in their main task to control the nighttime waters surrounding Leros and prevent the Germans from landing reinforcements of their own. They suffered one loss, when an Hs293 glider bomb sank *Dulverton* at 0145 on 13 November east of Kos.

Ashore, German troops once again outfought their enemies, and the Allies capitulated on 16 November. The Germans captured 3,200 British troops and 5,350 Italians. This decided the campaign. Just one week later, Samos, the last of the Allied-held islands, surrendered after *TA15* and *TA19,* along with units of the 21st UJ Flotilla, landed troops to accept the surrender of twenty-five hundred Italians.

The Aegean campaign had cost the Allied navies eight destroyers, two submarines, and ten smaller ships; and five cruisers, four destroyers, and eleven other ships were seriously damaged. It was an embarrassing and bitter defeat for the British; the Germans had proved unexpectedly adept at conducting an island-hopping, amphibious campaign with an improvised fleet and more resolute in accepting risk than the Royal Navy at the campaign's climax.

The Aegean 1944

After Germany ejected the British from the Aegean, Dönitz came to better appreciate the island-strewn sea's value. Naval plans to develop a fortified submarine base at Lemnos or Salonika foundered on transportation bottlenecks, but even as late as February 1944 the grand admiral argued that "a well fortified Lemnos directly in front of the Dardanelles would be of the greatest strategic value."[16]

Escort duties occupied Germany's Aegean surface forces. By late winter, eight British, Dutch, and Greek submarines crowded the narrow sea. Unfortunately, one of their victims on 8 February 1944 was *Petrella* (4,785 GRT), loaded with 3,173 Italian prisoners of war, of whom 2,600 drowned. Bombers sank *UJ2124* on 1 February 1944 and *TA15* on 8 March. On 1 June Allied planes jumped an important Cretan convoy consisting of three freighters escorted by *TA16, TA17, TA14,* and *TA19,* three UJ boats, and two R-boats. After losing *UJ2101* and *UJ2105* and suffering heavy damage to two freighters and *TA16,* the Germans suspended convoys to Crete and maintained contact by small craft only. The British were anxious to eliminate the 9th Torpedo Boat Flotilla, whose ships, for all their age, were Germany's most useful vessels in the area; on the night of 17 June commandos penetrated Portolago (Leros) Harbor and mined *TA14* and *TA17.* Two days later Allied fighter-bombers damaged *TA19.* Overall, the Allies sank thirty-eight steamers in the Aegean, totaling 72,100 GRT, between the end of September 1943 and August 1944.[17]

In September 1944 Soviet advances into the Balkans threatened to isolate Greece. On 5 September the Germans began withdrawing from portions of Crete and some of the Aegean islands. For this task the Kriegsmarine, reinforced by shipping driven from the Black Sea, utilized fifty-two merchant vessels and more than two hundred caiques and landing craft. The imperative to evacuate as many troops as possible escalated on 12 September when Romania came to terms with the Allies.

One year after their defeat the British retained a strong interest in the Aegean; they now feared Soviet domination of the Dardanelles and Balkans, and they were anxious to prevent the communists from grabbing power in Greece. However, the British command concluded that forces locally available were insufficient to exploit the German withdrawal. Fortunately, a flotilla of seven escort carriers, which had been supporting the southern France invasion, had assembled in Malta. Although ultimately bound for the Indian Ocean, they had time to intervene in the Aegean on their way; they formed the core of Force 120, which also included seven cruisers, nine fleet destroyers, and eleven Hunts.

Force 120 sailed on 9 September and initially operated south of Crete. On the night of 12/13 September the destroyers *Troubridge* and *Tuscan* intercepted a small convoy on the Candia–Santorin route and sank the transport *Toni* (638 GRT). Fighters from the escort carriers covered the strike force's withdrawal. On 15 September the British seized Kithera, off the Peloponnesus, as an advance destroyer base. That night the light cruiser *Royalist* and the destroyer *Teazer* sank *KT26* and *UJ2171* off Cape Spada. On 17 September *Aurora* went chasing after a report of the minelayer *Drache* near Milos. The German made port before the cruiser could arrive but was forced to spend the day chasing *Aurora's* sporadic salvos until escaping that night through a back channel.[18] This, however, was a temporary reprieve, as British aircraft sank her on 22 September. Between 9 September and 24 September aircraft also accounted for *TA14*, *UJ2142*, *R178*, *KT18*, and the steamer *Orion* (707 GRT). Aircraft sank the last two German submarines in the Aegean on 25 September. Allied submarines, meanwhile, were active, including the French *Curie*, which torpedoed the steamer *Zar Ferdinand* (1,994 GRT) on 2 October and a patrol vessel the next night.

Handicapped by the destruction of their largest escorts, Germany's Naval Group South decided to reinforce the 9th Torpedo Boat Flotilla with three Adriatic torpedo boats. (See table 13.4.)

TA37, *TA38*, and *TA39* sailed from Trieste on 20 September, accompanied by *S30* and *S36*. Early on 22 September, after the German warships had exited

Table 13.4 Encounter in the Strait of Otranto, 22 September 1944, 0550–0630

Conditions: n/a
British ships— DE: *Belvoir, Whaddon*
German ships— (Lieutenant Commander Werner Lange): TB: *TA37, TA38, TA39*

the Strait of Otranto, they encountered a pair of British Hunts. At 0550 the Hunts opened fire, but the Germans had a three-knot speed advantage and by 0630 they had drawn out of range, reaching the safety of the Corfu Channel an hour later.

This flotilla anchored at Piraeus on 24 September and quickly proved its worth, escorting convoys and sowing mines on 30 September and 2, 3, and 5 October. *TA38* and *TA39* even fought a minor action on 6 October, destroying the British motor launch *ML1227*. Its next encounter with British warships, however, proved more difficult. (See table 13.5.)

Table 13.5 Action in the Gulf of Salonika, 7 October 1944, 0100

Conditions: night, three-quarter moon
British ships— DD: *Termangant, Tuscan*
German ships—TB: *TA37*[Sunk]; DC: *UJ2102*[Sunk]; PB: *GK62*[Sunk]; ML: *Zeus* (2,423 GRT)

A major evacuation route ran from Piraeus to Salonika. The island of Euboea sheltered most of the passage, but a portion crossed the Gulf of Salonika. On the night of 7 October the minelayer *Zeus*, formerly the Italian auxiliary cruiser *Francesco Morosini*, was carrying 1,125 men across the gulf, escorted by *TA37*, *UJ2102*, and the patrol boat *GK62*. The destroyers *Termagant* and *Tuscan*, which had slipped into the northern Aegean after minesweepers cleared the Kinaros Channel, intercepted the convoy shortly after midnight. *Zeus* escaped, but the destroyers sank all three escorts. *TA37* lost 103 men in this action.

On 10 October Soviet troops cut the rail line between Athens and Berlin. Germany evacuated Piraeus on 12 October, and British paratroopers descended on Athens airport that same day. The Kriegsmarine's last days in the Aegean were predictably bloody. *TA38* was scuttled following bomb damage, and *TA39* ran into a mine off Salonika. *TA18* was the last surviving major warship. She had entered service only on 25 July and was of doubtful combat value, having been cannibalized for spare parts following her capture the year before. (See table 13.6.)

Table 13.6 Action off Skiathos, 19 October 1944, 2340

Conditions: Night, no moon
British ships— DD: *Termangant, Tuscan*
German ship— TB: *TA18*[Sunk]

On the evening of 19 October *Termagant* and *Tuscan* found *TA18* in the Gulf of Salonika south of Vólos. The British destroyers beat up the German ship with their combined gunfire and drove her aground. Greek partisans subsequently captured and shot most of the surviving crew.

By the end of October Germany had lost twenty-nine merchant ships, five torpedo boats, a minelayer, an R-boat, and three submarine hunters. The remaining German ships—an S-boat, three R-boats, and three auxiliaries—were scuttled when Germany evacuated Salonika on 31 October. The Kriegsmarine had evacuated 37,138 troops, losing only 380 men in the process. The air force had flown out an additional 30,740. Hoping for better days, Germany left garrisons on Crete (11,828 Germans and 4,737 Italians), Milos (620 Germans), Rhodes (6,356 Germans and 4,097 Italians), Leros (1,102 Germans and 809 Italians), Kos (3,228 Germans and 611 Italians), Tilos (266 Germans), Kalymnos (193 Germans), and Alimia (14 Germans).[19]

On October 31 the escort carriers continued their voyage east. Only the 14th Destroyer Flotilla (consisting of four K- and J-class vessels) and eight Greek Hunts remained, harassing the isolated and increasingly malnourished German garrisons to the end of the war.

The Adriatic Campaign

The Adriatic served Germany as a vital highway between the Balkan and Italian theaters. For example, on 1 November 1943 the German high command "demanded 100,000 tonnes of supplies monthly by ship to meet the running demand and the winter requirements of the Army units along the Dalmatian and Albanian coasts, since rail and land transport alone was inadequate." While supplies went south, resources flowed north: "An estimated 50 percent of Germany's oil, all of its chrome, 60 percent of its bauxite, 24 percent of its antimony, and 21 percent of its copper were procured from Balkan sources." Thus, Germany needed to secure the Adriatic Sea to guard its Balkan flank. The Kriegsmarine's first task was to evict partisans from the northern islands. Starting on 13 November, the minelayer *Kiebitz* (the ex-Italian auxiliary *Ramb III*), along with Siebel ferries and other light craft, escorted by the old antiaircraft

Map 13.3 Adriatic Campaign, February–November 1944

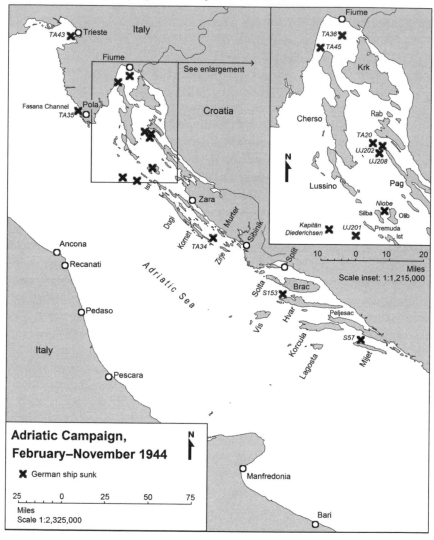

cruiser *Niobe* (ex-Yugoslavian *Dalmacija*) and *TA21,* launched a series of assaults against Krk, Cherso, and Lussino.[20] (See map 13.3.)

The British, meanwhile, finding Bari too distant to support MTB operations along the Dalmatian coast, joined the partisans holding Vis Island in mid-November and based the 20th and 24th MTB flotillas there. On 21 December the motor torpedo boats achieved their first major success when *MTB226* and

298 snuck up on *Niobe,* which was stranded off Silba Island, and blasted her with three torpedoes, also sinking a tug that was trying to pull her off.

Despite such interference, the Germans followed their conquest of the northern islands with landing operations on the middle archipelago, assaulting Korcula on 23 December, Solta on 12 January 1944, Brac on 13 January, and I Ivar on 19 January. Most of these landings involved battalion-sized forces delivered by MFPs, motor sailboats, and other auxiliaries.

Table 13.7 Large German Warships Commissioned in the Adriatic Sea (All ex-Italian)

Name	Old name	Type	Service date	Fate
TA20	Audace	old TB	21/10/43	Sunk 1/11/44 surf
TA21	Insidioso	old TB	8/11/43	Sunk 5/11/44 air
TA22	Missori	old TB	3/12/43	CL 25/6/44 air
TA34	T7/96F	old TB	9/9/43	Sunk 24/6/44 surf
TA35	Dezza	old TB	9/6/44	Sunk 17/8/44 mine
TA36	Stella Polare	TB	13/1/44	Sunk 18/3/44 mine
TA37*	Gladio	TB	8/1/44	Sunk 7/10/44 surf
TA38*	Spada	TB	12/2/44	Scuttled 10/13/44
TA39*	Daga	TB	27/3/44	Sunk 10/16/44 mine
TA40	Pugnale	TB	17/10/44	Scuttled 1/5/45
TA41	Lancia	TB	7/9/44	CL 17/2/45 air
TA42	Alabarda	TB	30/1/45	Sunk 21/3/45 air
TA43	Sebenico/Beograd	DD	22/2/45	Scuttled 1/5/45
TA44	Pigafetta	DD	14/10/44	Sunk 17/2/45 air
TA45	Spica	TB	6/9/44	Sunk 13/4/45 surf
TA48	T3/78T	old TB	16/10/43	Sunk 20/2/45 air
UJ201	Egeria	DC	28/1/44	Sunk 29/2/44 surf
UJ202	Melpomene	DC	24/4/44	Sunk 1/11/44 surf
UJ205	Colubrina	DC	14/1/44	Sunk 27/3/44 air
UJ208	Spingarda	DC	6/5/44	Sunk 1/11/44 surf

*Transferred to Aegean 20 September 1944
Fates: air—by air forces; CL—constructive loss; surf—by surface forces

The British 24th Destroyer Flotilla sailed out of Bari, and in January and early February its vessels patrolled the middle and upper Adriatic, sinking *S153* off Hvar on 12 January and bombarding Durazzo on 15 January, Korcula on 16 and 18 January, Recanati and Pedaso on 1 February, and Korcula again on 4, 12, and 27 February. At the same time, the Kriegsmarine was commissioning modern torpedo boats to serve as capital ships to its Adriatic mosquito fleet. On 12 February *TA37* and *TA38* entered service. In total the Kriegsmarine launched and commissioned nineteen small destroyers and corvettes in the Adriatic from the Italian armistice to the end of the war. (See table 13.7.)

The German command also concentrated in the Adriatic the six S-boats available in the eastern Mediterranean. They were used mainly in escorting, laying mines, and disrupting partisan traffic along the Dalmatian Archipelago.

In late February 1944 the French 10th Light Squadron, the large destroyers *Le Terrible, Le Malin,* and *Le Fantasque* reinforced the 24th Flotilla. The speed and power of these ships made them the perfect intruder units for striking targets in the northern Adriatic under the cover of darkness. At 1345 on 29 February they departed Manfredonia, upon receiving intelligence that a German convoy had sailed from Pola bound for Piraeus hardly an hour before. The convoy consisted of the motor ship *Kapitän Diederichsen,* ex-Italian *Sebastiano Venier,* and a strong escort. The escorting torpedo boats were on their second operation. (See table 13.8.)

Table 13.8 Battle off Ist, 29 February 1944, 2144–2210

Conditions: Night, one-quarter moon, set 2313
French ships— 10th Light Squadron (Commander Pierre Lancelot): DL: *Le Terrible* (F), *Le Malin*
German ships— 11th Security Flotilla (Lieutenant Commander Jürgen von Kleist): TB: *TA37*[D3] (F) *TA36*[D2]; DC: *UJ201*[Sunk], *UJ205*; MMS: *R188, R190, R191*
Convoy: *Kapitän Diederichsen*[Sunk] (6,311 GRT)

The French destroyers were passing Ist when, at 2135, *Le Terrible's* radar detected ships 18,600 yards north. The French came to thirty knots, and nine minutes later, with the range down to 8,750 yards, *Le Terrible* engaged the freighter while *Le Malin* targeted the nearest escort. The German war diary entry describes the suddenness of the attack. "Proceeding with the minesweepers 3,000–4,000-m ahead of the torpedo boats. Around 2145, west of Ist Island, a strong gunfire was opened against us, probably from three enemy destroyers that were approaching along the shore. After the second salvo *TA37* was hit and after the third or fourth salvo our vessel burst into flames."

The Germans responded with smoke and returned fire, Commander Lancelot's flagship hit *Kapitän Diederichsen* at 2148, when the range was down to forty-five hundred yards. She fired torpedoes, and at 2157 one exploded against the freighter, which, burning fiercely, drifted to a halt. *Le Malin* continued northwest and confronted *UJ201*, which had been trailing the formation. Shells ripped into the German corvette even as another torpedo salvo splashed into the water. One struck and detonated *UJ201*'s magazine, disintegrating the unfortunate ship; there were no survivors. In the melee the destroyers also lightly damaged *TA36* while a well-placed round that exploded in *TA37*'s engine room had cut her speed to ten knots.

With the freighter and *TA37* burning, Lancelot hauled around and headed south at high speed. He had spotted the low silhouettes of the motor minesweepers and, believing they were S-boats, worried that a torpedo might disable one of his ships deep in unfriendly waters.[21]

TA36 and *UJ205* stood by and rescued the freighter's crew. *Kapitän Diederichsen* remained afloat, but attempts to tow her failed, and she sank at 1145 the next morning. *TA37*, however, made Pola under tow.

On 8 March British destroyers shelled Korcula again. *Le Terrible* and *Le Fantasque* raided into the northern Adriatic 2–4 March and then, on the night of 7 March, bombarded Zante in the Ionian Sea. These powerful warships attacked three Siebel ferries and an MFP on 19 March. They sank *SF273* and *SF274* and crippled the other two, suffering light damage from 20-mm return fire. After this mission the French destroyers rotated to the Aegean, where they shelled Kos on 2 May and sank the small tanker *Giuliana* (350 GRT) on 16 June, although the tanker's escort of four R-boats escaped.

On 17 March a German flotilla consisting of *TA36, TA20, TA21, UJ205,* and *Kiebitz* sailed to lay a mine barrage east of San Giorgio. *TA36* sank in an old Italian minefield off Fiume, but the rest continued their mission.

Through the summer of 1944 Yugoslavian partisans gained territory and strength, while German surface forces suffered steady attrition. The Dalmatian Islands were frequent battlegrounds, subject to British commando raids, such as against Hvar on 11 and 12 July. *MGB659, 662,* and *MTB670* destroyed *TA34* on 24 June off Murter, while Allied aircraft shot up *TA22* off Trieste the same night. Aircraft badly damaged *TA21* on 9 August off Istria's Salvore Point. *TA35* became a constructive loss on 17 August after striking a mine in Fasana Channel. On 19

August British MTBs sank *S57* in Mijetski Channel, between Mijet and Peljesac, along with most of the vessels from the convoy she had been escorting.

In September the Germans began evacuating the southern Dalmatian Islands. British coastal craft pounced on this traffic, and MTBs destroyed two small coastal convoys off Vir on the night of 11 October. The heavy units of the German 2nd Escort Division—*UJ202, UJ208, TA20,* and *TA21,* operating out of Fiume—were active in this period, with the two corvettes completing ten and the torpedo boats six and four operations, respectively. These warships shelled partisan positions and, because of their heavy weapons, were dangerous for MTBs to confront. However, in October the torpedo boats were forced to suspend operations due to the effects of burning low-quality fuel oil.

Partisan advances forced further evacuations. Early on 31 October small craft lifted a German regiment from Zara to Sibenik. There the Germans gathered four MFPs, thirteen landing craft, and two large "storm" boats (*Große Sturmboote*) to lift the troops to Fiume the next day. Four S-boats were to have provided escort, but an air attack sank *S158* and damaged *S156.* Thus, *UJ202* and *UJ208* sailed from Fiume at 1600 to cover the convoy, followed by *R187* a half hour later. At 1900, *TA20* got under way after solving her fuel system problems, but *TA21* had to remain in port. The Adriatic command also dispatched *TA40, TA45,* and *Kiebitz* to Fiume, but they arrived too late to participate.

That same day a British flotilla consisting of two Hunts, three MTBs, three MGBs, and a motor launch departed Ist to land a party of coast watchers on the north end of Rab. (See table 13.9.)

Table 13.9 Ambush off Pag Island, 1 November 1944, 1950–2300

Conditions: Night, full moon, deteriorating weather, building swells
British ships— (Captain Morgan Giles): DE: *Wheatland* (F), *Avon Vale*[D1]
German ships— 2nd Escort Flotilla (Lieutenant Commander Wilhelm Thorwest): TB: *TA20*[Sunk] (F); DC: *UJ202*[Sunk], *UJ208*[Sunk]; MMS: *R187*

The British shore party had just cast off at 1950 when the MTBs sighted *UJ202* and *UJ208* steaming south down the Kvarneric Passage, the main channel between Cherso and Rab. The German corvettes had reached the northern tip of Pag Island when, at 2015, radar registered contacts to port. *UJ202* fired two star shells, whereupon the Hunts, each taking a separate target, opened fire. Shells detonated on *UJ202*'s bridge and radio room and knocked her 3.9-inch main gun, her forward 20-mm quadruple machine guns, and her aft 37-mm guns out of action almost immediately. She turned to port and responded as best she could, but the rapid-firing and hard-hitting Hunts overwhelmed her, and she sank by 2100. *UJ208* also suffered immediate and devastating damage, losing all her forward guns. She foundered at 2030. *R187* observed her flotilla mates engaging an unseen enemy and turned east, escaping into the night.

The British were rescuing survivors when, at 2230, radar picked up *TA20* approaching from the north. *R187* had maintained radio silence to prevent detection, leaving *TA20* to be caught off guard. The Hunts hit the torpedo boat's bridge with their first salvos, slaughtering her officers and destroying the fire-control systems. The veteran warship sank rapidly. Hampered by worsening weather, the British pulled only ninety survivors from the water; more than two hundred Germans perished in this action. *R187* met the convoy coming from Sibenik and led them north, reaching Fiume on 2 November without loss.[22]

Throughout the winter and into the spring of 1945, the Kriegsmarine kept to the upper Adriatic. A shortage of fuel and a suffocating Allied air and sea superiority limited the time German ships spent at sea. However, the Germans continued to undertake operations to the limits of their abilities. For example, six German explosive boats attacked the British light cruiser *Delhi* at Split on 12 February 1945. The boats needed to undertake a two-hundred-mile approach, during which two dropped out for mechanical reasons. They found the city lit up and the protective nets down. A guard post raised the alarm as they penetrated the harbor, but one boat managed to ram a landing craft alongside *Delhi*, and the ensuing explosion moderately damaged the cruiser.[23]

The Allies destroyed Germany's last operational destroyer-sized warships during the war's final weeks. *MTB670* and *697* torpedoed *TA45* in the Gulf of Fiume on 13 April 1945, while *TA43* scuttled at Trieste on 1 May. The final mission of the eight surviving S-boats involved sailing from Pola to Ancona crammed with hundreds of men who preferred to surrender to the British rather than to Yugoslavian partisans.

The Tyrrhenian and Ligurian Campaigns

From September 1943 to the end of the war the Kriegsmarine, assisted by Mussolini's Fascist Italian republic's small navy (Marina Nazionale Repubblicana), harassed Allied forces and tenaciously defended a vigorous coastal traffic of 1.5 to 2 million tons a month in the Tyrrhenian and Ligurian seas.[24]

In October 1943 the German navy commissioned two captured Italian torpedo boats in the western Mediterranean. These conducted their first operation in December, and by February 1944 there were enough units to form the 10th Torpedo Boat Flotilla. (See table 13.10.)

During the fall and winter of 1943 larger Allied warships escorted convoys, while coastal forces fought in the front lines in the Tyrrhenian and Ligurian seas. The Anglo-American mosquito fleet enjoyed some success as when U.S. PT boats torpedoed the German auxiliary minelayer *Juminda* (ex–*Elbano Gasperi 742 GRT*) on 23 October and boats sank *UJ2206* on 3 November. Nonetheless, their activities barely dented the flow of German traffic.[25]

The first major post-armistice amphibious operation in the Mediterranean, the Allied assault at Anzio, occurred on 22 January. The Allies obtained tactical surprise and lost only one minesweeper on the first day. The Kriegsmarine offered scant resistance, as most of its assets were engaged on escort duties farther north, but it did mount a defensive minelaying operation out of La Spezia, taking heart in the fact that "the place chosen by the enemy for the landing shows again that he intends to proceed step by step and is not willing to take a risk with one daring coup."[26] After the first day, resistance ashore and aloft stiffened. The Germans succeeded in containing the beachhead. This tied up surface assets, as the Allied navies were obliged to supply and support cut-off corps with ground fire and so provided a concentrated target for Axis counterattacks.

German Torpedo Boats

The German 10th Torpedo Boat Flotilla operated out of Genoa and La Spezia, laying minefields, patrolling, conducting coastal bombardments, and escorting convoys. For example, they conducted nine minelaying sorties during April and four in May 1944, in addition to bombarding Bastia on 22 April. On 25 April, during one of these missions, *TA23* sank in a mine field laid by the Italian torpedo boat *Sirio*. Because the Anzio stalemate occupied the larger warships, MTBs provided the Allies' main opposition to these German activities, although poor weather and ineffective tactics limited their effectiveness through the winter of 1943/44.

With better weather, the radar-equipped U.S. PT boats enjoyed some productive operations. On 24 May three PTs attacked two corvettes and, putting eleven torpedoes into the water, sank *UJ2223* and damaged *UJ2222*, which limped back to port but was never repaired. Three nights later the PTs bagged *UJ2210*. On 31 May PTs fought an inconclusive action with *TA29* and *TA30*. Three PTs ambushed *TA26* and *TA30* on 15 June seventeen miles west of La Spezia and sank both with a spread of six torpedoes.[27] *TA25* fell victim to another PT attack on 21 June while engaged in mining operations. Finally, American bombers

Table 13.10 Large German Warships Commissioned in the Ligurian Sea and Southern France (Ex-Italian unless otherwise indicated)

Name	Old name	Type	Service date	Fate
TA9	Bombarde (FR)	TB	5/4/43	27/9/43 decommissioned
TA11	L'Iphigenie (FR)	TB	5/4/43	Sunk 11/9/43 shore batt
TA23	Impavido	TB	9/10/43	Sunk 25/4/44 mine
TA24	Arturo	TB	7/10/43	Sunk 18/3/45 surf
TA25	Ardito	TB	8/12/43	Sunk 21/6/44 surf
TA26	Intrepido	TB	16/1/44	Sunk 15/6/44 surf
TA27	Auriga	TB	29/12/43	Sunk 9/6/44 air
TA28	Rigel	TB	23/1/44	Sunk 4/9/44 air
TA29	Eridano	TB	6/3/44	Sunk 18/3/45 surf
TA30	Dragone	TB	15/4/44	Sunk 15/6/44 surf
TA31	Dardo	DD	17/6/44	20/10/44 decommissioned
TA32	Premuda/Dubrovnik	DD	18/8/44	24/4/45 scuttled
UJ2221	Vespa	DC	16/11/43	24/4/45 scuttled
UJ2222	Tuffetto	DC	20/2/44	CL 24/5/44 surf
UJ2223	Marangone	DC	20/2/44	Sunk 24/5/44 surf
UJ2224	Strolaga	DC	18/4/44	Sunk 8/9/44 air
UJ2226	Artemide	DC	12/7/44	24/4/45 scuttled
UJ2227	Persefone	DC	15/10/44	24/4/45 scuttled
UJ6081	Camoscio	DC	9/9/43	Sunk 17/8/44 surf
UJ6082	Antilope	DC	9/9/43	Sunk 15/8/44 surf
UJ6085	Renna	DC	?/?/44	Sunk 4/9/44 air
SG14	Matelot Leblanc (FR)	DS	5/6/43	Sunk 24/8/43 air
SG15	Rageot de la Touche (FR)	DS	3/10/43	Sunk 22/5/44 sub
SG20	Papa (FR)	TB	17/10/43	CL 01/11/43 mine
SG21	Amiral Sénès (FR)	DS	28/3/44	Sunk 15/8/44 surf

Fates: air—by air forces; CL—constructive loss; surf—by surface forces; shore batt—by shore batteries destroyed *TA27* in port on 9 June. In July the 10th Flotilla, reduced to just *TA24*, *TA28*, and *TA29*, conducted five mining operations and one shore bombardment in addition to ten reconnaissance sorties. Its vessels had inconclusive encounters with Allied MTBs on the nights of 28 June and 15, 19, and 25 July.

On 15 August 1944 the 10th Flotilla had four ships in service—*TA24*, *TA28*, *TA29*, and *TA31*—with *TA32* working up. On this day the Allies conducted their fifth major amphibious assault in the Mediterranean, on the French Rivera coast. (See table 13.11.) The 10th Flotilla did not attempt to intervene, but corvettes based at Toulon fought two small but sharp battles against U.S. Navy units.

Table 13.11 Major Allied Warships Deployed for Operation Anvil, 15 August 1944

Type	USA	Britain	France	Greek	Total
Battleship	3	1	1	0	5
Cruisers	8	11	5	0	24
CVE	2	7	0	0	9
Destroyers	59	29	19	4	111

The U.S. destroyer *Somers* detected the German corvettes *UJ6081* and *SG21* south of Île du Levant. At 0440, when it seemed their course would threaten the invasion transports, *Somers* passed them astern and opened fire from 4,750 yards. (See table 13.12.)

Table 13.12 Action off Port Cros, 15 August 1944, 0440–0722

Conditions: Night, light mist, wind five knots from ESE, new moon, calm sea
U.S. ship—   (Commander W. C. Hughes): DD: *Somers*
German ships— DC: *UJ6081*[Sunk], *SG21*[Sunk]

Somers belted *SG21* with her opening salvos and set her ablaze; the sloop burned and periodically erupted with small explosions until after dawn. The American destroyer then chased down *UJ6081*, which had a top speed of eighteen knots; by 0520, ten salvos had left her dead in the water. *UJ6081* rolled over and sank at 0722. *Somers* had expended only 270 rounds and suffered no casualties during this brief, well-fought action.[28]

Two nights later a naval special operations force, including the American destroyer *Endicott* and two British river gunboats, *Aphis* and *Scarab*, appeared off

La Ciotat, between Marseilles and Toulon, to feint a landing. At 0555 the corvette *UJ6082* and the large subchaser *UJ6073*, formerly the motor yacht *Nimet Allah*, engaged British gunboats and forced them to flee. (See table 13.13.)

Table 13.13 Action off La Ciotat, 17 August 1944, 0430–0830

Conditions: Night, good weather, slight swells, 30 percent moon
Allied ships—   (Captain Harry C. Johnson): DD: *Endicott*[D1]; GB: *Aphis*, *Scarab*
German ships— DC: *UJ6082*[Sunk], *UJ6073*[Sunk]

Endicott arrived at 0620 in response to the gunboats' call for help. She attacked *UJ6073*, even though jammed breech blocks had disabled three of her four mounts. In the first minutes, two 5-inch shells detonated in the ex-yacht's engine room, and *UJ6073* quickly lost way. One German shell hit *Endicott* and caused minor flooding.

At 0648 *UJ6082* launched two torpedoes, forcing *Endicott* to evade. The destroyer replied with two torpedoes of her own. When *UJ6082* combed its tracks, *Endicott* closed to fifteen hundred yards and raked the corvette's deck with machine guns. *UJ6082* gamely returned fire for a few minutes until 5-inch rounds exploded near her stack and bridge. *UJ6082*'s crew started abandoning ship at 0717. *UJ6073* sank at 0709, while *UJ6082* finally capsized at 0830.[29]

In the following weeks the Allies overran southern France, but their resources did not permit an offensive over the Alpine passes into Italy. Thus, the front line froze east of Monaco along the Franco-Italian border, preserving Germany's enclave on the Ligurian Sea for another eight months.

The Allies established a formation called "Flank Force Mediterranean," under French command, to suppress German naval activity and "keep the coastal batteries along the Italian Riviera stirred up."[30] The French contributed Cruiser Division 3, under Rear Admiral Philippe Auboyneau; it consisted, at one time or another, of the light cruisers *Georges Leygues*, *Montcalm*, *Gloire*, *Emile Bertin*, *Jeanne d'Arc*, and *Duguay-Trouin*, as well as seven destroyers. The U.S. Navy rotated the cruisers *Brooklyn* and *Philadelphia* and various destroyers through this force. There were also one American and two British MTB squadrons and swarms of minesweepers, subchasers, and patrol craft. The British maintained the 5th Destroyer Flotilla at Livorno. Overall, it was more than enough force to dominate a two-hundred-mile stretch of enemy-held coast and harass coastal batteries. Nonetheless, the German 10th Torpedo Boat Flotilla remained active, as when it shelled Allied positions near the Arno Estuary on the night of 30–31 August.

On the evening of 1 October, the U.S. destroyer *Gleaves* was on patrol off San Remo, Italy. When news arrived that Allied aircraft had bombed three vessels farther up the coast, Captain Klee steered his ship to investigate. (See table 13.14.)

Table 13.14 Encounter off Imperia, 2 October 1944, 0020–0035

Conditions: Night, overcast, strong winds
U.S. Ship—   (Commander W. M. Klee): DD: *Gleaves*
German ships— 10th Torpedo Boat Flotilla (Commander Wirich von Gartzen): TB: *TA24*[D1] (F), *TA29*[D1]; DD: *TA32*

That same evening *TA24, TA29,* and *TA32,* the latter two loaded with ninety-eight mines, sailed from Genoa toward San Remo, intending to deposit their cargo offshore. The German force had just passed Imperia when, at 2313, lookouts spotted a large warship eleven thousand yards southwest. This was *Gleaves,* which was also tracking the Germans. At 2319 the American destroyer turned parallel and opened fire.

Gleaves' first salvo landed fifty yards from *TA24.* The Germans maneuvered as the next sent geysers spouting near *TA29.* At 2324 von Gartzen ordered a simultaneous turn to starboard, but *TA29,* her rudder control affected by the cargo of mines, rammed *TA24.* The German ships managed to separate and retreated toward Genoa, opening fire against the American destroyer at 0235. Klee assumed that German shore batteries had him in their crosshairs, and at 2339, when radar detected two aircraft only three miles away, *Gleaves* made smoke and broke contact. The gunfire continued until 2345. The American ship had expended eighty rounds and eight star shells.

The German torpedo boats made port by 0315. They thought they had fought a French light cruiser. In his report Klee concluded that he had attacked three merchant ships. He had observed two of them explode while under fire and believed them sunk or seriously damaged.[31] In fact, he had missed a excellent opportunity to put the 10th Flotilla out of business.

Despite such intense and risky operations and heavy attrition, the Kriegsmarine still had three torpedo boats, two minelayers, five UJ-boats, four V-boats, ten R-boats, and thirty-five MFPs and Siebel ferries and other armed barges in the Ligurian Sea at the beginning of 1945. They were supported by six MAS boats of the Marina Nazionale Repubblicana. The disparity of the Allied forces deployed against them was a tribute to the Kriegsmarine's ability to tie up Allied resources that could have found better employment elsewhere.

On the night of 17 March 1945, the last three operational ships of the 10th Torpedo Boat Flotilla conducted an offensive mining operation northwest of Corsica. This led to the Mediterranean war's final surface naval battle. After dropping 132 mines, the flotilla united for the return to Genoa, with *TA24* and *TA29* preceding the larger *TA32*. They were twenty miles north of Cape Corse when Allied shore radar at Livorno noted their presence. Four Allied destroyers were patrolling in the vicinity: the French *Basque* and *Tempête*, and the British *Meteor* and *Lookout*. (See table 13.15.)

Table 13.15 Battle of the Ligurian Sea, 18 March 1945, 0300–0420

Conditions: Night, rainsqualls, moonset 0002
British ships— DD: *Meteor, Lookout*[D1]
German ships— 10th Torpedo Boat Flotilla (Commander Wirich von Gartzen): TB: *TA24*[Sunk] (F), *TA29*[Sunk]; DD: *TA32*[D1]

Tempête's captain, the senior officer, ordered the British ships to intercept the intruders while he led the slower French vessels southeast to cover a convoy nearing Cape Corse.

Lookout established radar contact at 0301. The German column was sailing north at twenty knots. The British destroyer approached at high speed and opened fire at 0310 from five thousand yards. Two minutes later she swung around and launched torpedoes. *Lookout*'s radar-directed gunfire slammed into *TA24* and *TA29*. *TA29* dropped out of the line, while the other two ships fled north. *Lookout* let them go, concentrating on the cripple. She circled *TA29*, firing continuously from as close as two thousand yards. *TA29* grimly fought back; her gunners almost hit the destroyer numerous times, but *Lookout*'s only damage came when a burst of 20-mm shells struck some smoke floats and ignited a small fire. Riddled by more than forty shells, *TA29* sank at 0420.

Meteor, meanwhile, closed, and at 0352 her radar fastened on the other German ships. She opened fire at eight thousand yards, hitting *TA24* almost immediately. *Meteor* followed up with a salvo of torpedoes, and one smacked *TA24*, which exploded and sank at 0405. *TA32*, although also damaged, escaped after firing a few broadsides and an ineffective torpedo barrage.[32]

Convoys and U-boats

After Operation Torch, huge Allied convoys began passing the Straits of Gibraltar. The fifty American UGS convoys that transited the Mediterranean from the Italian armistice to December 1944 averaged sixty-nine ships each, for example. Their size and frequency demonstrated how greatly the Allies had expanded their effort in the Mediterranean and what freedom of navigation on the Middle Sea meant to the war effort. These American convoys also made an illuminating contrast to the Royal Navy's Malta convoys, which had averaged slightly less than 3.5 ships over sixty-one operations in thirty months.[33]

These megaconvoys provided German forces something that had hitherto been lacking in the Mediterranean—an abundance of targets. However, they were also well protected, and German attempts to fight a war against shipping failed. The Mediterranean was a difficult environment for submarines in any case, and by 1943 Allied antisubmarine doctrine and weapons had become very sophisticated.

The last German submarine success in the Mediterranean occurred on 18 May 1944, when *U-453* sank one ship from a convoy being escorted by, ironically, four Italian torpedo boats and two corvettes. The Italians subjected the submarine to a prolonged hunt before passing the chase to a pair of British destroyers, which ultimately sank her. In many respects the story of *U-453* encapsulates the German experience in the Mediterranean.

U-453 departed Kiel on 12 November 1941 for La Spezia, arriving on 17 December after sinking a Spanish tanker en route. *U-453* damaged a hospital ship on 7 April 1942, on her second patrol. The following patrols were unproductive until, on 20 January 1943, during her ninth patrol, she sank the Belgium *Jean Jadot* (5,859 GRT) from convoy KMS7. On her eleventh patrol she damaged a British tanker and sank the steamship *Shahjehan* (5,454 GRT), on 6 July 1943. On *U-453*'s twelfth patrol she missed a battleship and on her thirteenth laid a minefield off Brindisi. The fourteenth patrol, also a minelaying expedition, proved more effective, accounting for the British destroyer *Quail* and the minesweeper *Hebe*. The next patrol to bring results was number sixteen, when, operating off the Syrian coast, *U-453* claimed to have rammed four small sailing vessels, of which Allied records confirm two. On 30 April 1944, *U-453* set forth on her eighteenth and final patrol. On 18 May she attacked convoy HA43 and sank the British steamer *Fort Missanabie* (7,147 GRT). The Italian escort started the hunt, and finally, on 20 May 1944, *U-453* surfaced after being depth charged and fought it out on the surface with the British destroyers *Liddesdale, Tenacious,* and *Termagant*. They sank her and captured her crew, less three men who died.[34]

The power of the Allied convoys also frustrated the Luftwaffe. For example, two submarines and sixty-nine aircraft attacked a heavily escorted convoy of sixty-five ships that passed the Straits of Gibraltar on 9 May 1944. The escort shot down nineteen planes, at no cost to itself or the convoy.

Ultimately, the German navy conceded to the Anglo-Americans free use of the Middle Sea. The Allies could land anywhere they wanted, if they felt the effort was worth it. However, when the Axis armies in Italy surrendered on 2 May 1945, the Germans still maintained active naval forces and held some coastline. Their ability to prolong this campaign, fought far from the German heartland in the face of such superior forces, was a remarkable accomplishment.

In summary, the depth of Germany's commitment to the Middle Sea and its cost can be measured by examining the ships sunk there (see table 13.16). Counting only major surface warships, Germany lost sixty-two vessels, or 39.2 percent of all such ships sunk during the war. The Americans sank twenty-five ships and the British twenty-one. Most of the rest were scuttled.

Table 13.16 Major German Surface Warships Lost in the Mediterranean

Cause	BR	US	GK	IT	YU	N/A	Total
Aircraft	8	20					28
Mined				2		1	3
Scuttled/interned/ accident						12	12
Shore batteries				1	1		2
Submarines			1				1
Surface actions	11	5					16
Total	19	25	1	3	1	13	62

Conclusion

It is only the politicians who imagine that ships are not earning their keep unless they are madly rushing about the ocean.

—Admiral Pound, 28 December 1942
letter to Admiral Cunningham

Flawed assessments and disappointed expectations set the early course of the Mediterranean conflict. In June 1940 Great Britain correctly appreciated that it was engaged in a war to the death against the Axis and advertised this fact to the world when it attacked the French at Mers-el-Kébir. London erred, however, when it also concluded there was a quick solution to the conundrum presented by Italy's entry and France's exit from the war, and that that was to knock Rome out with a hard blow delivered by the only weapon it possessed for the job, the Royal Navy. Naturally, Italy's appreciation was much different, although equally wrong. Rome believed it had entered a short war, a holding action really, and did not grant the battle Britain sought but instead tried to fight its own actions, appropriate to the war it wanted to wage—actions in which it would have many advantages and few risks. Neither got what it wanted.

The bitter naval war that ensued demonstrated the tactical application of sea power and its relationship to both the land war and grand strategy. It demonstrated that any nation waging war in the Mediterranean littoral had to use the sea and dispute the enemy's use to the best of its abilities. This may seem obvious when North Africa was the battleground and supplies could only come from over water, but it was just as true when the Italian and Balkan peninsulas became seats of war in 1943. The unfolding of the naval war demonstrated that to use the sea, combat had to be accepted—generally on the enemy's terms—but that even so, sea denial was a difficult task and lasting victory came only through the exercise of sea control. Because Italy lacked the long-range warships and airpower required to dispute Allied domination of the Mediterranean's western and eastern basins, and because the Allies lacked the staying power to routinely break Rome's blockade of the central basin or to sever the sea lanes to Libya, neither side could decisively exercise sea control in the enemy's waters. Thus the North African fighting dragged on for three years—longer than any European land campaign of World War II, save the Russian conflict. Then, after the Italian armistice, Germany fiercely defended its Mediterranean bridgeheads to gain time to bring its secret, war-winning weapons on line, or for a Fredrick the Great–type miracle to occur, effectively using the Aegean, Adriatic, Tyrrhenian, and Ligurian seas and prolonging the maritime campaign to the war's end.

The Scorecard

More surface actions were fought in the Mediterranean by more participants than anywhere else in the war (see table C.1).

Table C.1 Surface Engagements by Ocean/Sea

Atlantic (including English Channel)	49
Arctic	8
Baltic & Black	5
Indian	14
Pacific	36
Mediterranean (including Red Sea)	55

The surface engagements described in this work were fought by the nations given in table C.2.

The loss of major surface warships (from battleships to large escorts) to enemy action provides one way to measure performance. The Italians sank thirty-three Allied warships and lost eighty-three in the Mediterranean and Red seas from 10 June 1940 through 8 September 1943 (seventy to the British and their allies and thirteen to the Americans). In this period German forces sank an additional forty-three Allied warships. The warships sunk by Italy totaled 145,800 tons and by the Germans 169,700, for a total of 315,500. The British dispatched 161,200 tons of Axis warships and the Americans 33,900, for an Allied total of 195,100.[1]

Table C.2 Surface Engagements by Belligerent

Great Britain	50
Italy	36
France	
Marine Nationale	1
Vichy	7
Free French	1
Germany	11
United States	3
Greece	2
Australia	9
New Zealand	2
Netherlands	2

The Germans accounted for 57 percent of Allied losses, whereas the British, with minor help from the Polish, Greek, and Dutch navies, accounted for 83 percent of Italian warship losses. German aircraft and submarines proved more effective than their Italian counterparts. German aircraft sank 30 percent of the Allied total loss, compared to only 9 percent for Italian aircraft. German submarines sank 21 percent, compared to 7 percent for Italian submarines. In the categories of special weapons, surface actions, mine warfare, shore batteries, and capture, the Italians accounted for 28 percent of the Allied total, compared to 5 percent for the Germans.

The differences in the Italian and German tallies suggest certain conclusions. First, the Regia Aeronautica did not develop the weapons and tactics needed to participate adequately in the naval war. Had the Regia Marina controlled its aerial assets and developed an efficient reconnaissance force and the torpedo-bomber squadrons envisioned in the mid-1930s, Italy would have fought more effectively at sea. Next, Italian submarines were less deadly than their German counterparts mostly because of unrealistic training and flawed doctrine. Finally, while the Italian navy suffered more damage in naval surface actions than it inflicted, the vast majority of this damage was incurred at night, in a few actions fought in defense of traffic. Chart C.1 further illustrates this point.

Allied warships were more effective ship killers than were Italian or German vessels. British warships accounted for twenty-three major Italian and nine German warships, while the U.S. Navy sank two Germans and the French one.

Chart C.1   Ships Sunk and Damaged in Surface Actions, 1940–45,
             Mediterranean and Red Sea

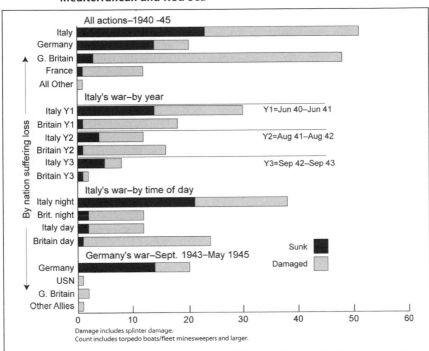

The Royal Navy only lost three major warships—all destroyers—as the result of Italian surface action (excluding a cruiser and three destroyers sunk by Italian and German MTBs). The difference revolved around when the action was fought. The British nighttime superiority was based upon better training and doctrine, radar, and an ability to pick the time of action and so achieve surprise. Moreover, the Regia Marina achieved dismal results with its ship-launched torpedoes due to inferior doctrine, training, and fire control.

Italian performance, however, improved as the war progressed. The Regia Marina inflicted more damage than it suffered during the war's second year, and it fought effectively during the day when sea control was exercised, sinking one and damaging twenty-three British ships while suffering two sunk and ten damaged. Finally, while many factors affected German effectiveness in surface actions fought following the Italian armistice, the final tally—fourteen large German warships sunk and six damaged versus the light damage Kriegsmarine vessels inflicted on four Allied warships in return—reflects favorably on Italian performance in the same type of nocturnal clashes in defense of traffic.

The Regia Marina

The Regia Marina survived as an effective force, unlike the other Axis navies. That the kingdom of Italy sought an armistice instead of fighting to the bitter end helped, but the fact remains that after thirty-nine months of war Italy still possessed a significant fleet capable of intervention, and that fleet was still running convoys to the islands and along the coasts. When the Ligurian-based battle squadron received the unexpected news of the armistice on 8 September, boilers had been fired and the fleet was prepared to expend itself on a do-or-die strike against the Salerno landings.

The Regia Marina not only survived but largely accomplished its missions. Up until May 1943 it closed the direct passage through the Mediterranean to all but eight freighters in three massively protected convoys (Collar, Excess, and Tiger, between November 1940 and May 1941). This forced Great Britain to build and supply an army in Egypt the hard way, around the Cape of Good Hope,

Chart C.2   Impact of the Mediterranean Strategy, British Imports and Tonnage Lost

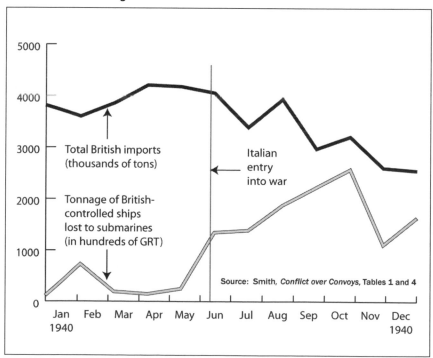

Total British imports (thousands of tons)

Tonnage of British-controlled ships lost to submarines (in hundreds of GRT)

Italian entry into war

Source: Smith, *Conflict over Convoys*, Tables 1 and 4

rather than though the Straits of Gibraltar—a journey of forty days for a fast convoy, and 120 days for a slow one. The tying up of shipping and naval resources by this and the Mediterranean campaign itself had two direct and measurable outcomes. Britain's imports collapsed and never recovered, while German submarines ran wild.[2] (See chart C.2.)

Chart C.3   Personnel and Materiel Escorted or Carried by the Regia Marina, June 1940–8 September 1943

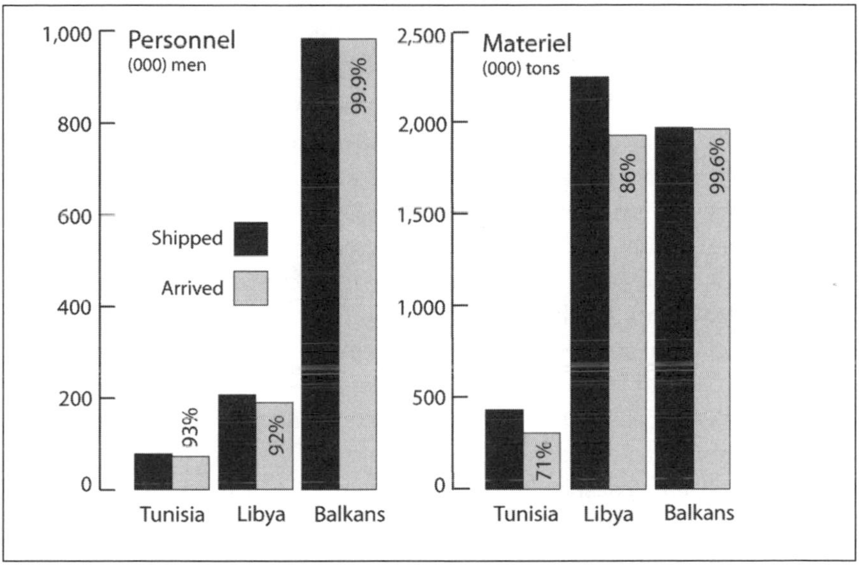

With regard to Italy's mercantile war, the chart C.3 demonstrates that over the course of its war, 98 percent of the men and 90 percent of the material that set forth from Italian ports for Libya, Tunisia, or the Balkans arrived safely.

The nature of its operations and the priorities set by the navy's political leadership required the Regia Marina to operate in a defensive posture defending these convoys in an environment where air support, doctrine, technology, and intelligence favored the Allies. Italy's navy certainly had its failures and suffered its defeats. But these should not obscure its victories. Overall, it performed the jobs it was tasked to do. It was a successful service, considering its lack of oil or of an integral air component and the caliber of the opposition it faced.

France

In 1939 the Marine Nationale was the world's fourth-largest fleet, equipped with modern and innovative warships. After France's defeat the navy remained intact and served as the Vichy regime's principal expression of power and prime guarantor of its precarious independence. When Germany occupied Vichy France, the heart of the navy destroyed itself, out of loyalty to its unique and powerful sense of honor. During the balance of the war the Marine Nationale's remnants served the Allied cause. It is significant that when the navy, in any of its avatars, had an opportunity to fight, it fought well. It beat the British off Syria and Dakar and the Germans in the Adriatic, and it earned the grudging admiration of its opponents, even in defeat off Oran and Casablanca.

Such devotion to what the British, Americans, and even the Germans considered an unworthy cause demonstrated that if French motivations remained mysterious to friend and foe alike, they were strong enough to endure the motherland's defeat, its occupation, and more than two years of political twilight. Many writers describe the Vichy French government as collaborationist or traitorous, which implies that it was bound to act in Britain's interests. Pétain, however, regarded France's welfare as paramount. The key to evaluating the French navy's performance and resilience is to appreciate that France acted, always, in what it perceived to be its own best interests. The situation from June 1940 to the end of 1942 left little space for defying the Germans. The most remarkable aspect about the French navy during the Vichy period is that it did not become an Axis cobelligerent, despite British provocation and German pressure. This fact demonstrated where France saw its own true interests to lie.

The Royal Navy

The Royal Navy's deeds in the Mediterranean fill a proud chapter in that service's glorious history. The Beta Convoy battle, the action off Sfax, the Battle of Cape Bon, and the action off Skerki Bank were some of the most aggressive and successful surface actions ever fought. Individual ships like the light cruiser *Aurora* compiled records that would be the envy of any warship, at any time, in any service. The irony, however, is that despite these examples of excellence and the Royal Navy's superiority in intelligence, doctrine, technology, and resources, London, when it adopted its Mediterranean strategy in the summer of 1940, chose a campaign the navy was unable to win.

Wars are complicated processes, with subtle interconnections that defy easy analysis; however, by this strategic decision Britain beggared itself fighting what turned out to be a three-year-long war of attrition at the end of a supply line that ran twelve thousand miles around Africa. The Royal Navy's victories were mostly in sea denial, not the sea-control victories it required. Nor did American intervention break the deadlock. After an inconclusive, three-year seesaw campaign in Libya and Tunisia, the Allies required four major amphibious operations to advance the front line gradually across the Mediterranean and partially clear its northern shores. The war in the Middle Sea lasted fifty-nine months; by contrast, in northern Europe the Allies thrust from Normandy into the heart of Germany in just ten months. When the Soviets raised the red flag on the Reichstag on 1 May, a stubborn trickle of German shipping still plied the Middle Sea. When troops of the U.S. Fifth Army finally reached the Brenner Pass—the Mediterranean Theater's northern frontier—on 6 May 1945, they discovered that their comrades of the Seventh Army had already driven through Germany and had arrived there two days before them.

The Kriegsmarine

The Kriegsmarine fought thirteen surface actions in the Mediterranean between 9 September 1943 and 2 May 1945, and while it avoided defeat in two instances, it failed to win a single victory. In fact, the Germany's record of defending convoys in night actions was worse than Italy's. However, Germany did not have to rely upon do-or-die convoys, as Italy was forced to at certain points in the war. The narrow waters permitted the Germans to conduct a guerrilla war, and the Allies, despite all the resources at their disposal, never eliminated German maritime traffic. Given the technology of the time, perhaps it was impossible to stop a determined foe who was willing to accept losses. In any case, the Kriegsmarine did what was required—it fought a littoral war, shielded against a landing in Istria and Liguria that would have cut off the Reich's Italian army, and sustained a vital maritime traffic, as well as its island garrisons. It survived in the Middle Sea until the end of the war, despite overwhelming Allied naval and air power and, in so doing, was instrumental in preventing the Reich from ever being threatened from the south.

The U.S. Navy

The U.S. Navy was the last major force to enter the theater. Its efforts are commonly associated with the Pacific, the war against shipping in the North Atlantic, and the cross-channel invasion; however, its Mediterranean commitment was large. Including the Torch operation, the USN participated in five major amphibious landings. The American convoys that transited the Mediterranean after 1942 dwarfed in size everything that had come before. In addition, by lending warships to the Royal Navy's Home Fleet the USN allowed Great Britain to release ships for its Mediterranean operations in the summers of 1942 and 1943.

By May 1945 the U.S. Navy, despite massive forces deployed in the Pacific and heavy commitments in the Atlantic, was the Mediterranean's dominant naval power, and it has remained so ever since.

Conclusion

In summary, the Italian navy fought hard, and overall it fought well; the French demonstrated resolve and honor and proved a formidable foe when occasion forced it to fight. The British were workmanlike at their worst and brilliant at their best, but their focus on the Mediterranean was a strategic mistake that worked to Germany's benefit until the last day of the European war. The Germans conducted a remarkable and seldom-recognized rear-guard action and defied Allied attempts to deny them use of the Middle Sea. The Americans came to the Mediterranean late, but they ultimately came in great strength, though unfortunately, in their choice of amphibious objectives, they did not display the strategic boldness they had demonstrated in the Pacific campaign.

Nearly seventy years after Italy declared war, giant tankers and container ships ply the Mediterranean. What has changed since 1940 is that the economies of the littoral states are even larger. Egypt minds the Suez Canal, and Malta is independent, but Great Britain still possesses Gibraltar and bases at Cyprus. There has been conflict on the Middle Sea since 1945. Great Britain and France attacked the Suez Canal in 1956, and France warred in Algeria. The United States struck Libya in 1982 and 1986. Israel and its neighbors have fought four general wars, which included several naval battles. American, British, and Italian warships and submarines stalked their Soviet counterparts for fifty years, never crossing the threshold into open conflict. Meanwhile, as always, the Marine Nationale largely went its own way.

Today, the Middle Sea remains one of the planet's decisive choke points. Despite the end of the Cold War, it is crowded with warships from many nations. Although it is hard to imagine the circumstances that could result in another major naval war, the possibility remains as long as the region is so well armed and all the Mediterranean nations have so much at stake in their free use of the sea.

Abbreviations

AA	antiair
AP	armor piercing
ASV	air surface vessel (radar)
ASW	antisubmarine warfare
BR	British
CDN	Canadian
D1	superficial or splinter damage
D2	moderate damage with combat or maneuvering ability not significantly impaired
D3	significant damage with combat or maneuvering ability impaired
D4	major damage with combat or maneuvering ability eliminated
DP	dual purpose
FL	full load (displacement)
FS	flagship
GE	German
GK	Greek
GRT	gross registered tons

HA	high angle
HE	high explosive (or high effect)
HMSO	Her Majesty's Stationery Office
IFF	Identification Friend or Foe
MHQ	*Military History Quarterly*
NO	Norwegian
NZ	New Zealand
OSS	(U.S.) Office of Strategic Services
PO	Polish
RCN	Royal Canadian Navy
RN	Royal Navy
RO	Rumanian
RSI	*Repubblica Sociale Italiana* (Italian Social Republic)
SAP	semi-armor-piercing
SB	shore battery
SO	Soviet
US	United States
USAAF	United States Army Air Force
USMM	*Ufficio Storico della Marina Militare*
USN	U.S. Navy
X MAS	Tenth Light Flotilla, or *Decima Flottiglia* MAS

Ship Types

AMC	armed merchant cruiser
BB	battleship
BC	battle cruiser
BM	monitor
CA	heavy cruiser
CB	coastal battleship (obsolete)
CL	light cruiser
CLA	antiair light cruiser
CV	aircraft carrier
CVE	escort carrier

DD	destroyer
DC	corvette/sloop
DF	frigate
DE	destroyer escort
DL	large destroyer (French *contre-torpilleur*)
DS	sloop
GB	gunboat
LST	landing ship, tank
MAS	*motoscafi armati siluranti* or *motoscafi anti sommergibili* (Italian motor torpedo boat)
MFP	*Marinefährprahm* (German armed barge or "F" lighter)
ML	minelayer or motor launch
MMS	motor minesweeper
MS	minesweeper
MS	*motosiluranti* (large Italian motor torpedo boat)
MTB	motor torpedo boat
MTM	*motoscafo turismo modificato* (Italian explosive motorboat)
MZ	*motozattere da sbarco* (Italian armed barge or "F" lighter)
OBB	old battleship
PB	patrol boat
PC	submarine chaser (USN)
PT	patrol torpedo boat (USN)
R-boat	*raumboote* (German motor minesweeper)
S-boat	*schnellboote* (German motor torpedo boat or "E" boat)
SC	submarine chaser
SS	submarine
TA	*torpedoboote auslandisch* or foreign torpedo boat
TB	torpedo boat
UJ-boat	*unterseebootsjäger* (German submarine chaser)
VAS	*vedette antisommergibili* (Italian submarine chaser)
V-boat	*vorpostenboote* (German patrol boat)

Notes

Introduction

1. Enrico Ricciardi, *Mediterraneo 1940–43* (Parma: Ermanno Albertelli, 2004), 21.

2. Andrew B. Cunningham, *Sailor's Odyssey* (London: Hutchinson, 1951), 260.

3. Anglo-centric histories include Bernard Ireland, *The War in the Mediterranean 1940–1943* (London: Arms and Armour, 1993), and Donald Macintyre, *The Battle for the Mediterranean* (New York: W. W. Norton, 1965). Italo-centric histories include James J Sadkovich, *The Italian Navy in World War II* (Westport, Conn.: Greenwood, 1994), and Marc' Antonio Bragadin, *The Italian Navy in World War II* (Annapolis, Md.: Naval Institute, 1957). More balanced works include Raymond De Belot, *The Struggle for the Mediterranean 1939–1945* (Princeton, N.J.: Princeton University Press, 1951), and Jack Greene and Alessandro Massignani, *The Naval War in the Mediterranean 1940–1943* (London: Chatham, 1998).

4. Bartimeus, *East of Malta, West of Suez* (Boston: Little Brown, 1944), 13.

5. Samuel E. Morison, *Operations in North African Wars October 1942–June 1943* (Boston: Little Brown, 1984), 189.

6. Peter Smith, *Destroyer Leader* (London: New English Library, 1974), 59.

7. Lisle A. Rose, *Power at Sea: The Breaking Storm 1919–1945* (Columbia: University of Missouri Press, 2006), 132.

8. Cajus Bekker, *Hitler's Naval War* (New York: Doubleday, 1978), 243.

9. B. H. Liddell Hart, *The German Generals Talk* (New York: Quill, 1979), 158.

10. Hans Frank, *S-Boats in Action in the Second World War* (Annapolis, Md.: Naval Institute Press, 2007), 79.

11 Warren Tute, *The Reluctant Enemies* (London: Collins, 1990), 145.

12. Michael Simpson, ed., *The Cunningham Papers*, vol. 1, *The Mediterranean Fleet, 1939–1942* (Aldershot, England: Ashgate, 1999), 557.

13. Bernard Brodie, *A Guide to Naval Strategy*, (Princeton, NJ: Princeton University Press, 1944), 2.

14. Christopher Page, ed., *The Royal Navy and the Mediterranean*, vol. 1, *September 1939–October 1940* (London: Frank Cass, 2002), xi.

Chapter 1. The Eve of War: June 1940

1. W. O. Blanchard, "Seventy Years of Suez," *Scientific Monthly* 50 (April 1940): 301.

2. Joseph S. Roucek, "The Geopolitics of the Mediterranean, II," *American Journal of Economics and Sociology* 12 (July 1953): 72.

3. Quoted in James J. Sadkovich, "The Indispensable Navy: Italy as a Great Power, 1911–43," in *Naval Power in the Twentieth Century*, ed. N. A. M. Roger (Annapolis, Md.: Naval Institute Press, 1996), 70.

4. Reynolds M. Salerno, *Vital Crossroads: Mediterranean Origins of the Second World War 1935–1940* (Ithaca, N.Y.: Cornell University Press, 2002), 181.

5. John Gooch, *Mussolini and His Generals* (New York: Cambridge University Press, 2007), 512.

6. Pietro Badoglio, *Italy in the Second World War* (Westport, Conn.: Greenwood, 1976), 15.

7. Gooch, *Mussolini and His Generals*, 516. Other Italian leaders had their doubts. On 1 June King Victor Emmanuel III told Galeazzo Ciano, Mussolini's son-in-law and Italy's foreign minister, "The country is going to war without enthusiasm. . . . Those who talk of a short and easy war are fools." Galeazzo Ciano, *The Ciano Diaries 1939–1943* (Safety Harbor, Fla.: Simon, 2001), 258.

8. Cunningham, *Odyssey*, 227; and Gerhard Schreiber et al., *Germany and the Second World War*, vol. 3, *The Mediterranean, South-East Europe, and North Africa 1939–1941* (Oxford: Clarendon, 1995), 111.

9. See Douglas J. Forsyth, *The Crisis of Liberal Italy: Monetary and Financial Policy, 1914–1918* (London: Cambridge University Press, 1993), 167. Also Gooch, *Mussolini and His Generals*, 12.

10. Quoted from MacGregor Knox, *Mussolini Unleashed 1939–1941* (London: Cambridge University Press, 1982), 81, 110.

11. See the discussion in James J. Sadkovich, "Understanding Defeat: Reappraising Italy's Role in World War II," *Journal of Contemporary History* 24 (January 1989): 32–33. Also I. C. B. Dear and M. R. D. Foot, *The Oxford Companion to World War II* (Oxford: Oxford University Press, 1995), 584–85.

12. Gooch, *Mussolini and His Generals*, 518.

13. Salerno, *Vital Crossroads*, 201.

14. Angelo Iachino, *Tramonto di una grande marina* (Verona: Alberto Mondadori, 1966), 155.

15. Giuseppe Fioravanzo, "Italian Strategy in the Mediterranean, 1940–43," U.S. Naval Institute *Proceedings* 84 (September 1958): 66.

16. Iachino, *Tramonto,* 299–300.

17. Ibid., 156.

18. Reynolds M. Salerno, "The French Navy and the Appeasement of Italy, 1937–39," *English Historical Review* 112 (February 1997): 78.

19. Ibid., 100. Also see Martin Thomas, "At the Heart of Things· French Imperial Defense Planning in the Late 1930s," *French Historical Studies* 21 (Spring 1998): 342.

20. Ibid., 98.

21. F. H. Hinsley et al., *British Intelligence in the Second World War: Its Influence on Strategy and Operations* (New York: Cambridge University Press, 1979), vol. 1, 200.

22. Page, *Royal Navy and the Mediterranean,* vol. 1, 7.

Chapter 2. The Defeat of France

1. Franco Maugeri, *From the Ashes of Disgrace* (New York: Reynal and Hitchcock, 1948), 4. Nonetheless, he felt that war was a mistake and that "the masses of Italy were totally unready and unwilling to bear the terrible miseries and sacrifices of modern war." Badoglio was harsher: "It was a pitiable spectacle. Herded like sheep between the officials and the riff-raff of the Fascist Party, the crowd had orders to applaud every word of the speech. But when it was over, the people dispersed of their own accord in complete silence." Pietro Badoglio, *Italy in the Second World War: Memories and Documents* (Westport, Conn.: Greenwood, 1976), 20. Of course, had Italy won, memories would have been different.

2. Hinsley et al., *British Intelligence,* vol. 1, 205.

3. Simpson, *Cunningham Papers,* vol. 1, 48–51. These intentions are stated in a series of letters to the Admiralty written between 6 and 9 June.

4. Paul Auphan and Jacques Mordal, *The French Navy in World War II* (Westport, Conn.: Greenwood, 1976), 98.

5. Page, *Royal Navy and the Mediterranean,* vol. 1, 125.

6. Simpson, *Cunningham Papers,* vol. 1, 70.

7. Giuseppe Fioravanzo, *La Marina Italiana nella Seconda Guerra Mondiale,* vol. 4, *Le Azioni Navali in Mediterraneo Dal 10 Giugno 1940 al 31 Marzo 1941* (Rome: Ufficio Storico Della Marina Militare, 1976), 87–90.

8. Frédéric Stahl, "Le Royale à l'assault de Gênes," *Navires et Historie* 44 (October/November 2007): 32.

9. Auphan and Mordal, *French Navy,* 99.

10. Henri Darrieus and Jean Queguiner, *Historique de la Marine française 1922–1942* (St. Malo: l'Ancre de Marine, 1996), 113.

11. Greene and Massignani, *Naval War in the Mediterranean,* 54.

12. Darrieus and Queguiner, *Marine française,* 114–15.

13. Hinsley et al., *British Intelligence,* vol. 1, 209.

14. See S. W. Roskill, *Churchill and the Admirals* (New York: William Morrow, 1978), 150; and Correlli Barnett, *Engage the Enemy More Closely: The Royal Navy in the Second World War* (New York: W. W. Norton, 1991), 211–12.

15. Hinsley et al., *British Intelligence,* vol. 1, 209. The quote refers to the situation of a year earlier.

16. Barnett, *Engage the Enemy,* 212.

17. Simpson, *Cunningham Papers,* vol. 1, 56.

18. Page, *Royal Navy and the Mediterranean,* vol. 1, 29.

19. ADM 234/317, Battle Summaries, No. 1, *Operations against the French Fleet Mers-el-Kébir (Oran) 3rd–6th July, 1940,* para. 1.

20. Simpson, *Cunningham Papers,* vol. 1, 87.

21. Calvin W. Hines. "The Distorted Danger: Winston Churchill and the French Dreadnoughts," in *Naval History: The Seventh Symposium of the U.S. Naval Academy,* ed. William B. Cogar (n.p.: Scholarly Resources, 1988), 267.

22. ADM 234/317, *Mers-el-Kebir,* para. 2.

23. Michael Simpson, ed., *The Somerville Papers: Selections from the Private and Official Correspondence of Admiral of the Fleet Sir James Somervile, G.C.B., G.B.E., D.S.O.* (Aldershot, England: Scolar, 1996), 90.

24. Ibid., 95.

25. Ted Biggs, http://hmshood.com/crew/remember/TedFlagship.html#Ch16.

26. Anthony Heckstall-Smith, *The Fleet That Faced Both Ways* (London: Anthony Blond, 1963), 69.

27. There are different versions of this meeting. This account is based on Auphan and Mordal, *French Navy,* 130–31. ADM 234/317, *Mers-el-Kebir,* para. 12 states, "Admiral Gensoul says crews are being reduced and the [*sic*] threatened by enemy would go to Martinique or U.S.A.; but this is not quite our position. Can get no nearer. This was received in the "Hood" at 1729. As it did not comply with any of the conditions laid down, the air striking force was ordered to fly off, and the battleships stood in towards the coast."

28. Biggs, http://hmshood.com/crew/remember/TedFlagship.html#Ch16.

29. British historians call Gensoul arrogant and uncooperative and blame him for failing to give his government the ultimatum's full details. For example, "The possibility of avoiding a resort to force was, unhappily, greatly reduced by the wording of the message in which Gensoul communicated the British proposals to the French Admiralty." S. W. Roskill. *The War at Sea 1939–1945,* vol. 1, *The Defensive* (London: HMSO, 1954), 243. See Philippe Lasterle, "Could Admiral Gensoul

Have Averted the Tragedy of Mers-el-Kébir?" *Journal of Military History* 67 (July 2003): 836–44, for a refutation of this logic.

30. Page, *Royal Navy and the Mediterranean,* vol. 1, 37.

31. Heckstall-Smith, *Fleet That Faced Both Ways,* 102.

32. Jean-Jacques Antier, *Les grandes Batailles Navales de la Seconde Guerre mondiale: Le drame de la Marine française* (Paris: Omnibus, 2000), 205–6.

33. J. P. Bezard, "Mers el Kebir," *Naval Review* 67 (July 1979): 196.

34. Raymond Dannreuther, *Somerville's Force H* (London: Aurum, 2005), 31.

35. Bezard, "Mers el Kebir," 196.

36. Darrieus and Queguiner, *Marine française,* 142.

37. Simpson, *Cunningham Papers,* vol. 1, 102.

38. Biggs, http://www.hmshood.com/crew/remember/tedflagship.htm#Ch16.

39. Page, *Royal Navy and the Mediterranean,* vol. 1, 50.

40. Simpson, *Somerville Papers,* 108.

41. Auphan and Mordal, *French Navy,* 125.

42. Heckstall-Smith, *Fleet That Faced Both Ways,* 98.

43. Green and Massignani, *Naval War in the Mediterranean,* 60.

44. Winston S. Churchill, *The Second World War,* vol. 2, *Their Finest Hour* (Boston: Houghton Mifflin, 1949), 212. The prime minister was new to his position. He also wanted to send a message to the "appeasers," like Lord Halifax or Neville Chamberlain. See Lasterle, "Could Admiral Gensoul Have Averted the Tragedy of Mers el- Kébir?" 839.

45. "Battle of Oran Is Challenge of War to Bitter End," *New York Times,* 6 July 1940.

46. Ciano, *Diaries,* 273.

47. Page, *Royal Navy and the Mediterranean,* vol. 1, 96.

48. Ciano, *Diaries,* 273.

49. *Fuehrer Conferences on Naval Affairs, 1939–1945* (London: Chatham, 2005), 115.

50. Heckstall-Smith, *Fleet That Faced Both Ways,* 58.

Chapter 3. Italy's Parallel War: June and July 1940

1. Hinsley et al., *British Intelligence,* vol. 1, 206.

2. Ibid., 210.

3. Enrico Cernuschi, "L'attivita crittografica dell marine inglese e italiana prima e durante la Seconda Guerra mondiale: un bilancio," unpublished manuscript.

4. See Enrico Cernuschi and Vincent O'Hara, "In Search of a Flattop: The Italian Navy and the Aircraft Carrier 1907–2007," in *Warship 2007* (London: Conway Maritime, 2007), 80.

5. Regarding war plans see Gooch, *Mussolini and His Generals,* 487. For port capacities, Renato Mancini. "Í Porti della Libia" *Storia Militare* 53 (February 1998): 24.

6. Page, *Royal Navy and the Mediterranean,* vol. 1, 22.

7. Hermon G. Gill, *Royal Australian Navy 1939–1942* (Adelaide: Griffin, 1957), 166.

8. Page, *Royal Navy and the Mediterranean,* vol. 1, 24.

9. Ibid., 22–23.

10. Simpson, *Somerville Papers,* 116.

11. Cunningham, *Odyssey,* 258–59.

12. ADM 234/323, Battle Summaries, *No. 8, Mediterranean Operations Operation M.A.5, 7th to 15th July, 1940,* "Action off Calabria of 9th July 1940," 44.

13. Simpson, *Cunningham Papers,* vol. 1, 71.

14. Cunningham, *Odyssey,* 259. Also: "The right range for any ship of the Mediterranean Fleet, from a battleship to a submarine, to engage an enemy ship with gunfire is POINT BLANK (nowadays 2,000 yards or less)." S. W. C. Pack, *The Battle of Matapan* (New York: Macmillan, 1961), 36.

15. Fioravanzo, *Azioni Navali,* vol. 4, 122.

16. ADM 199/1048, *Naval Actions in the Mediterranean,* "Action off Calabria," *Neptune* letter no. 3513, 14 July 1940, para. 8.

17. ADM 199/1048, *Neptune* letter, para. 12.

18. The quote is from Pack, *Matapan,* 39. The signal is from ADM 199/1048, enclosure 16 to Mediterranean letter no. 0112/00212/16. Record of Signals Received by the Commander-in-Chief, 4.

19. Francesco Mattesini, *La battaglia di Punta Stilo* (Rome: Ufficio Storico, 2001), 71.

20. ADM 199/1048, Signals Received, 6.

21. ADM 199/1048, 14th Destroyer Flotilla, "Narrative of Action with Enemy Forces on 9th July 1940," 2.

22. Fioravanzo, *Azioni Navali,* vol. 4, 124.

23. ADM 199/1048, "Action off Calabria, 9th July 1940," Commanding Officer HMS *Warspite* Narrative, 1.

24. ADM 199/1048, *Neptune* letter, para. 21: "I was anxious to conserve ammunition."

25. ADM 199/1048, "Action off Calabria, 9th July 1940," Commanding Officer HMS *Malaya* Narrative.

26. Ibid.

27. ADM 199/1048, *Neptune* letter, para. 17.

28. ADM 199/1048, HMS *Decoy* Report on Action off Calabria on 9th July, 2.

29. ADM 199/1048, Captain (d) 14th Destroyer Flotilla, 2.

30. ADM 199/1048, Captain (d) 10th Destroyer Flotilla, HMAS *Stuart,* 2.

31. ADM 199/1048, HMS *Hasty* Narrative of Action off Calabria 9th July 1940, 1.

32. ADM 234/323, Battle Summaries, *No. 8,* 54.

33. Roskill, *Churchill and the Admirals*, 150. Also see Simpson, *Cunningham Papers*, 169: "[Churchill] actually stated that he considered you were too pussy-footed in your dealings with Godfroy at the time of Oran."

34. Ricciardi, *Mediterraneo*, 23.

35. Fioravanzo, *Azioni Navali*, vol. 4, 151.

36. "Report of an Action with the Italian Fleet off Calabria, 9th July 1940," *London Gazette*, Supplement, 27 April 1948, 2.

37. For examples, see Nathan Miller, *The War at Sea: A Naval History of WWII* (New York: Charles Scribner's Sons, 1995), 116; Martin Stephen, *The Fighting Admirals: British Admirals of the Second World War* (Annapolis, Md.: Naval Institute Press, 1991), 69; P. K. Kemp, *Key to Victory: The Triumph of British Sea Power in WWII* (Boston: Little, Brown, 1957), 93; Roskill, *The Defensive*, 299; and Julian Thompson, *The War at Sea: The Royal Navy in the Second World War* (Osceola, Wisc.: Motorbooks International, 1996), 58.

38. Simpson, *Cunningham Papers*, vol. 1, 101.

39. Ibid., 110.

40. Gill, *Australian Navy 1939–1942*, 187.

41. Ibid., 188.

42. Fioravanzo, *Azioni Navali*, vol. 4, 172.

43. Ibid., 173.

44. Ibid., 174; and Gill, *Australian Navy 1939–1942*, 191.

45. See http://www.bbc.co.uk/ww2peopleswar/stories/12/a5815712.shtml.

Chapter 4. No Quick Peace: August–December 1940

1. Gooch, *Mussolini and His Generals*, 512.

2. Simpson, *Somerville Papers*, 145.

3. Page, *Royal Navy and the Mediterranean*, vol. 1, 100.

4. Churchill, *Their Finest Hour*, 397–98.

5. Quote from Bragadin, *Italian Navy*, 33. Orders from Fioravanzo, *Azioni Navali*, vol. 4, 187. Paladini suffered a heart attack in August.

6. ADM 199/2378, *Preliminary Narrative for the War at Sea*, vol. 1, *January–December 1940*, 123; and Simpson, *Cunningham Papers*, vol. 1, 142.

7. See Macintyre, *Battle for the Mediterranean*, 31, or Knox, *Mussolini Unleashed*, 149. These opinions were based on Admiral Cunningham's statement in his memoirs that he turned south at dusk; however, he actually turned south nearly three hours before sunset. Cunningham, *Odyssey*, 272.

8. Fioravanzo, *Azioni Navali*, vol. 4, 196–99.

9. Ibid., 198–99. For the expectation of a British retreat see Archivio dell'Ufficio Storico della Marina Militare, Rome, Fondo MARICOSOM, Busta 32, Fascicolo

510, "Studio del S.T. D.M. Rolla per un eventuale piano d'azione contro le forze navali inglesi del Mediterraneo Orientale e successivo sviluppo per lo sbarco di truppe nazionali inn Alessandria d'Egitto," 25 August 1940.

10. Charles De Gaulle, *War Memoirs: The Call to Honour, 1940–1942* (New York: Viking, 1955), 92.

11. Peter C. Smith, *Action Imminent* (London: William Kimber, 1980), 134.

12. Anthony Martienssen, *Hitler and His Admirals* (New York: E. P. Dutton, 1949), 116.

13. Arthur J. Marder, *Operation Menace* (Oxford: Oxford University Press, 1976), 95.

14. Ibid., 149. Also ADM 234/444, *H.M. Ships Damaged or Sunk by Enemy Action 3 Sept. 1939 to 2 Sept. 1945, "Resolution,* 25th September 1940."

15. ADM 234/444, *"Barham* 25th September." The short may have been a 9.45-inch shell.

16. Darrieus and Queguiner, *Marine française,* 190.

17. Simpson, *Somerville Papers,* 154.

18. Martin Thomas, "After Mers-el-Kebir, the Armed Neutrality of the Vichy French Navy," *English Historical Review* (June 1997): 665.

19. Simpson, *Cunningham Papers,* vol. 1, 154.

20. Cunningham, *Odyssey,* 278.

21. Fioravanzo, *Azioni Navali,* vol. 4, 208. *Airone* estimated *Ajax's* speed as fourteen knots and her headings as 130 degrees, then 70 degrees, and then 110 degrees, indicating the ship was zigzagging. *Alcione* estimated the target speed as nineteen knots. The Italian torpedo boats carried just two single tubes per side.

22. Compare the experiences of *Ariel's* sister ship, *Lupo,* which absorbed eighteen 6-inch shells off Crete on 21 May 1941. Presumably rounds hitting beneath the waterline caused rapid and massive flooding.

23. Fioravanzo, *Azioni Navali,* vol. 4, 207.

24. The Italian inquiry suspected that *Aviere* fired the shot that crippled *Artigliere. Aviere's* captain, Carlo Tallarico, was relieved a few days later. See Luciano Bigi, *Una vita in marina* (Milan: Fondazione Italo Zetti, 2003), 183–84.

25. Simpson, *Cunningham Papers,* vol. 1, 167.

26. Greene and Massignani, *Naval War in the Mediterranean,* 98.

27. Bragadin, *Italian Navy,* 39–40.

28. Cunningham, *Odyssey,* 278; and Greene and Massignani, *Naval War in the Mediterranean,* 39.

29. Iachino, *Tramonto,* 224. Also see Schreiber et al., *Germany and the Second World War,* 419.

30. ADM 234/325, Battle Summaries, *No. 10, Mediterranean Operations 4th to 14th November, 1940 Air Attack on Taranto, 11th November 1940,* 36. The air raid was originally to include *Eagle* and a total of thirty aircraft. However, *Eagle* missed the operation due to mechanical defects. Some of her aircraft transferred to *Illustrious,*

but *Illustrious* lost several aircraft to accidents in the days before the raid. Decisive results were not anticipated, and the British made no provisions to exploit the excellent results they obtained. See Angelo N. Caravaggio, "The Attack at Taranto: Tactical Success, Operational Failure," *Naval War College Review* 59 (Summer 2006), for an analysis of these points.

31. Fioravanzo, *Azioni Navali*, vol. 4, 259.

32. Gill, *Australian Navy, 1939–1942*, 235.

33. ADM 234/325, Battle Summaries, *No. 10*, 37.

34. Churchill, *Their Finest Hour*, 481.

35. Simpson, *Cunningham Papers*, vol. 1, 192.

36. Simpson, *Somerville Papers*, 184.

37. Dannreuther, *Somerville's Force H*, 22.

38. Fioravanzo, *Azioni Navali*, vol. 4, 326. The British navy's fighting instructions likewise required avoiding a superior enemy.

39. "Action between British and Italian Forces off Cape Spartivento on 27th November, 1940," *London Gazette*, Supplement, 5 May 1948, 2802.

40. Fioravanzo, *Azioni Navali*, vol. 4, 278.

41. ADM 234/326, *Italian Account of the Action off Cape Spartivento, 27th November 1940*, 4.

42. "Cape Spartivento," *London Gazette*, 2804.

43. ADM 234/325, Battle Summaries, *No. 9, Action off Cape Spartivento, 27th November, 1940*, 6.

44. Fioravanzo, *Azioni Navali*, vol. 4, 286.

45. "It is in our interest to prolong the shooting at maximum range trying to hit the enemy before he can hit us, in order to create a favorable tactical balance of forces such that will assure our success in the later close range phase of the fighting. For the same reasons the enemy's interest is to close range as soon as possible; that means that in the first phase of the battle our ships will have to fire from their stern sectors, and for us, the battle will seem like a disengagement action." Archivio Centrale dello Stato, Rome, Ministero della Marina, "Direttive e Norme per l'impiego della Squadra nel conflictto attuale," January 1941, part 1, 10.

46. For the Holland quote, "Cape Spartivento," *London Gazette*, 2804. For the *Berwick* hit, see Smith, *Action Imminent*, 298. This was one of the longest-range hits obtained by a heavy cruiser during the war. Compare the shooting of Allied and Japanese cruisers at Java Sea on 27 February 1942 or at Kormandorski Islands on 26 March 1943.

47. ADM 234/325, Battle Summaries, No. 9, 7.

48. ADM 234/326, *Italian Account*, 9.

49. ADM 234/325, Battle Summaries, No. 9, 8.

50. Simpson, *Somerville Papers*, 197.

51. ADM 234/326, *Italian Account*, 6.

52. "Cape Spartivento," *London Gazette,* 2807.

53. Iachino, *Tramonto,* 228.

54. Archivio Ufficio Storico Marina Militare, Fondo MARICOTRAF, Busta 6, Fascicolo 4 "Corrispondenza tra Maristat-Ispettorato per l'Aviazione della R. Marina e il Comando Superiore M.M. a Tobruch sulla ricognizione aerea contro il traffico inglese tra l'Egitto e Creta."

55. *Fuehrer Conferences,* 155.

56. Bradagin, *Italian Navy,* 15.

57. Kevin Smith, *Conflict over Convoys* (London: Cambridge University Press, 1996), 249. Imports remained depressed for the rest of the war.

58. Ibid., 250.

59. Ciano, *Diaries,* 333.

Chapter 5. Enter the Germans: Winter 1941

1. Churchill, *Their Finest Hour,* 555–56.

2. Schreiber et al., *Germany and the Second World War,* 200.

3. *Fueher Conferences,* 141.

4. See Stanley G. Payne, *Franco and Hitler* (New Haven, Conn.: Yale University Press, 2008), 100–103. Also, Schrieber et al., *Germany and the Second World War,* 239.

5. See I. S. O Playfair, *The Mediterranean and Middle East,* vol. 1, *The Early Successes against Italy (to May 1941)* (Uckfield, England: Naval and Military, 2004), 316. One of the ships for Greece stranded in a gale.

6. Hinsley et al., *British Intelligence,* vol. 1, 385.

7. ADM 234/335, Battle Summaries, No. 18, *Mediterranean Convoys 1941,* 5.

8. Simpson, *Cunningham Papers,* vol. 1, 270.

9. Schreiber et al., *Germany in the Second World War,* 658; Bollettno d'Archivio dell'Ufficio Storico della Marina Militare, settembre 2008.

10. Bragadin, *Italian Navy,* 67. The sunken freighters were subsequently raised.

11. Dannreuther, *Somerville's Force H,* 78.

12. Roskill, *Churchill and the Admirals,* 53 and 59.

13. Greene and Massignani, *Naval War in the Mediterranean,* 145.

14. Federico F. Oriana, *Giuseppe Oriana: Ufficiale e gentiluomo* (Rome: Supplemento alla Rivista Marittima, July 2008), 17–20. Also, Franklin D. Roosevelt Presidential Library and Museum, Great Britain Diplomatic Files, box 35, Military Situation 1 March 1941.

15. Winston S. Churchill, *The Second World War,* vol. 3, *The Grand Alliance* (Boston: Houghton Mifflin, 1950), 659. Also see Guido Ronconi, "L'operazione "Abstention" in Egeo," *Storia Militare* (May 2001): 4–15, and (June 2001): 23–34.

16. Simpson, *Cunningham Papers,* vol. 1, 299.

17. Ibid., 327.

18. Ibid., 294.

19. And damaged several others. See Jürgen Rohwer, *Allied Submarine Attacks of World War II* (Annapolis, Md.: Naval Institute Press, 1997), 131–32.

20. Walter Ansel, *Hitler and the Middle Sea* (Durham, N.C.: Duke University Press, 1972), 133.

21. Schreiber et al., *Germany in the Second World War,* 663.

22. Ronald Seth, *Two Fleets Surprised: The Story of the Battle of Cape Matapan* (London: Geoffrey Bles, 1960), 20.

23. Cunningham, *Odyssey,* 325. Also see Hinsley et al., *British Intelligence,* vol. 1, 405.

24. Hinsley et al., *British Intelligence,* vol. 1, 405.

25. Aldo Fraccaroli, "Il combattimento navale de Gaudo," *Storia Militare* 88 (January 2001): 5.

26. Ibid., 6.

27. "Battle of Matapan," *London Gazette,* Supplement, 31 July 1947, 3598.

28. Ibid. One historian asserts that by running before the enemy the British admiral "strained morale in his squadron" and that "a powerful force of British cruisers running away was so unusual it was only a matter of time before someone on the Italian side smelled a rat." Martin Stephen and Erich Grove, *Sea Battles in Close-Up* (Annapolis, Md.: Naval Institute Press, 1993), 54.

29. George Stitt, *Under Cunningham's Command* (London: George Allen and Unwin, 1944), 53.

30. Fraccaroli, "Il combattimento navale de Gaudo," 10.

31. "Battle of Matapan," *London Gazette,* 3598.

32. Fioravanzo, *Azioni navali,* vol. 4, 437.

33. Greene and Massignani, *Naval War in the Mediterranean,* 151.

34. Iachino reported the first salvo was fired from 23,000 meters (25,150 yards). Pridham-Wippell reported it as 32,000 yards. Fioravanzo, *Azioni navali,* vol. 4, 438, "Battle of Matapan," *London Gazette,* 3599.

35. Stitt, *Under Cunningham's Command,* 55.

36. Cunningham made much of the fact that *Gloucester* was supposedly only capable of twenty-four knots; "however, the sight of an enemy battleship had somehow increased the *Gloucester*'s speed to 30 knots." Cunningham, *Odyssey,* 327. Pridham-Wippell's report to Cunningham noted that her safe speed, not her maximum speed, was twenty-four knots. In a crisis, she was as fast as the other cruisers.

37. Fioravanzo, *Azioni navali,* vol. 4, 438.

38. Greene and Massignani, *Naval War in the Mediterranean,* 152.

39. Pack, *Matapan,* 44.

40. Seth, *Two Fleets Surprised,* 84.

41. Stitt, *Under Cunningham's Command,* 60. This was Britain's first successful aerial torpedo strike in the Mediterranean against a surface warship under way.

42. "Battle of Matapan," *London Gazette,* 3596.

43. Seth, *Two Fleets Surprised,* xv.

44. "Battle of Matapan," *London Gazette,* 3899.

45. Archivio Ufficio Storico Marina Militare, Cartella 26, "Messaggi in arrivo comando in capo squadra navale."

46. Correspondence, 31 October 1992, Vito Sansonetti to Enrico Cernuschi.

47. Cunningham, *Odyssey,* 332; and Stitt, *Under Cunningham's Command,* 66.

48. British reports state a smaller ship led the Italian formation, followed by two larger ships. The Italians state that *Zara,* not *Alfieri,* led the formation. The record of night combat is filled with mistaken identifications and optical illusions; the evidence of survivors supercedes the evidence of observers.

49. Cunningham, *Odyssey,* 332. British histories record it was *Fiume* thus highlighted. The account in *Azioni Navale,* vol. 4, 483, states that "[*Zara*] was suddenly caught in the beam of a searchlight. It was that of the *Greyhound.*"

50. Seth, *Two Fleets Surprised,* 135.

51. See http://www.gunplot.net/matapan/matapan.html.

52. S. W. C. Pack, *Night Action off Cape Matapan* (Annapolis, Md.: Naval Institute Press, 1972), 86. Pack provides a representative summary of British accounts. According to these, *Warspite* and *Valiant* initially engaged *Fiume. Barham* was just completing her turn from course 240 to 280 degrees and records that she targeted the lead ship in the enemy column before shifting to the second ship. Thus, British histories relate that she initially fired on *Alfieri.* If this were true, then *Zara* would have enjoyed at least thirty seconds of freedom from main-battery fire. Fioravanzo, *Azioni Navali,* vol. 4, 483, asserts that a large-caliber broadside hit the *Zara* immediately following illumination. *Barham* was that broadside's likely source.

53. See http://www.bbc.co.uk/ww2peopleswar/stories/13/a2274013.shtml.

54. Seth, *Two Fleets Surprised,* 153.

55. Gill, *Australian Navy 1939–1942,* 313.

56. Fioravanzo, *Azioni Navali,* vol. 4, 491.

57. E. Bagnasco and M. Brescia, *Cacciatorpediniere Classi "Freccia/Folgore" "Maestrale" "Oriani" Parti Seconda e Terza* (Parma: Ermanno Alvertelli, 1997), 28.

58. Fioravanzo, *Azioni Navali,* vol. 4, 494.

59. Seth, *Two Fleets Surprised,* 155.

60. Ibid. *Stuart's* Captain Waller smoked a pipe.

61. Pack, *Matapan,* 146.

62. Pack, *Night Action,* 96.

63. Pack, *Matapan,* 150.

64. Bragadin, *Italian Navy*, 97, for example. Also Sadkovich, *Italian Navy*, 132—"sheer dumb luck."

65. I. S. O. Playfair, *The Mediterranean and Middle East*, vol. 2, *The Germans Come to the Help of Their Ally (1941)* (Uckfield, England: Naval and Military, 2004), 70; and Roskill, *The Defensive*, 431.

66. Iachino, *Tramonto*, 245.

Chapter 6. The Red Sea: 1940–41

1. See Enrico Cernuschi and Vincent O'Hara, "The Breakout Fleet: The Oceanic Programmes of the Regia Marina, 1934–1940," in *Warship 2006* (London: Conway Maritime, 2006). At its most grandiose, this fleet would have consisted of three battleships, a carrier, twelve scout cruisers, thirty-six destroyers, and thirty submarines.

2. Hinsley et al., *British Intelligence*, vol. 1, 202.

3. See Gill, *Australian Navy 1939–1942*, 133.

4. *Galvani* is credited for sinking the Indian sloop *Pathan* off Bombay on 23 June, but in fact *Galvani* operated near the Gulf of Oman on this date, and *Pathan* likely fell victim to a floating mine. See Jürgen Rohwer, *Axis Submarine Successes of World War II* (Annapolis, Md: Naval Institute Press, 1999), 257; and Pier Filippo Lupinacci, *Le operazioni in Africa Orientale* (Rome: Ufficio Storico Della Marina Militare, 1976), 40ff.

5. R. F. Channon, "Red Sea Incident," *Naval Review* 82 (October 1994): 408.

6. Christopher Langtree, *The Kellys: British J, K and N Class Destroyers of World War II* (Annapolis, Md.: Naval Institute Press, 2002), 106. Bragadin, *Italian Navy*, 24, states that one of *Torricelli*'s last shells struck *Khartoum* at 0600 and that a splinter caused the torpedo to explode, making enemy action, not an accident, the cause of *Khartoum*'s loss. This version is repeated in British sources, most notably Paul Kemp, *The Admiralty Regrets: British Warship Losses of the 20th Century* (Phoenix Mill, England: Sutton, 1999), 122. "During the engagement *Khartoum* sustained one hit from a 10 cm shell which burst near the after bank of 21 in torpedo tubes. A splinter caused the air vessel of a torpedo to explode."

7. "T.P.A." "The Red Sea," *Naval Review* 30 (November 1942): 295.

8. Lupinacci, *Le operazioni in Africa Orientale*, 95; Admiralty C.B. 3001(42), *Progress in Naval Gunnery* (Gunnery and Anti-Aircraft War Division, Naval Staff, 1942), 59.

9. Lupinacci, *Le operazioni in Africa Orientale*, 96.

10. See *Progress in Naval Gunnery*, 59.

11. S. D. Waters, *The Royal New Zealand Navy* (Wellington: War History Branch, 1956), 91.

12. Lupinacci, *Le operazioni in Africa Orientale*, 99.

13. Some reports deny that *Nullo* hit *Kimberley*; however, the official appreciation of damage inflicted, ADM 234/444, "*Kimberley* 21st October 1940," states that two

shells hit the destroyer, the second "hitting the shield of number 1 mounting and smashing the range and director receiver."

14. Simpson, *Cunningham Papers,* vol. 1, 507.

Chapter 7. A Close-Run Thing: Spring 1941

1. Cunningham, *Odyssey,* 338.

2. Bragadin, *Italian Navy,* 356.

3. Cunningham, *Odyssey,* 340.

4. For example, according to their reports *Jervis* opened fire at 0220, *Janus* at 0222, and *Nubian* at 0210. *Mohawk* has it that *Jervis* commenced fire at 0205. This account uses the flagship's clock as the base line. See "Report of an Action against an Italian Convoy on the Night of the 15th/16th April, *1941,*" *London Gazette,* Supplement, 12 May 1948, 2915.

5. Ibid.

6. Admiralty, *Progress in Gunnery 1942,* 55.

7. "Report of an Action against an Italian Convoy," *London Gazette,* 2915.

8. Ibid., 2914.

9. Bagnasco and Brescia, *Classi Freccia/Folgore Maestrale Oriani,* 78.

10. Admiralty, *Progress in Naval Gunnery, 1942,* 54.

11. Simpson, *Cunningham Papers,* vol. 1, 345.

12. Cunningham, *Odyssey,* 347.

13. Playfair, *The Germans Come to the Help of Their Ally,* 111.

14. See Joseph Caruana, "The Demise of Force 'K,'" *Warship International* 43(1) (2006): 99.

15. See chapter 10.

16. "Transportation of the Army to Greece and Evacuation of the Army from Greece, *1941,*" *London Gazette,* Supplement, 19 May 1948, 3042.

17. Ibid., 3053, for Pridham-Wippell's intentions. A. G. Prideaux, "With 'A.B.C.' in the Med," part 2, *Naval Review* 65 (July 1977): 272, for quote.

18. Ibid., 3055.

19. Simpson, *Somerville Papers,* 265.

20. Ibid., 263.

21. Bragadin, *Italian Navy,* 108.

22. Churchill, *Grand Alliance,* 223.

23. Simpson, *Cunningham Papers,* vol. 1, 332.

24. Hinsley et al., *British Intelligence,* vol. 1, 415.

25. Stephens, *Fighting Admirals,* 99.

26. "The Battle of Crete," *London Gazette,* Supplement, 24 May 1948, 3107.

27. Ralph Bennett, *Ultra and Mediterranean Strategy: The Never-Before-Told Story of How Ultra First Proved Itself in Battle, Turning Defeat into Victory* (New York: William Morrow, 1989), 59.

28. Langtree, *Kellys,* 112.

29. Enrico Cernuschi, *La Notte del Lupo* (Rome: Rivista Maríttima, 1997), 27.

30. Ibid., 28. Also ADM 234/444, *Orion* 22nd May, 1941.

31. Frank Wade, *A Midshipman's War: A Young Man in the Mediterranean Naval War 1941–1943* (Victoria, Canada: Trafford, 2005), 55.

32. Cernuschi, *Lupo,* 28.

33. Ansel, *Hitler and the Middle Sea,* 332.

34. Wartime accounts such as appear in Bartimeus, *East of Suez,* 121, that the Germans lost four thousand men and the entire convoy, were deliberate propaganda. In the war situation report of 22 May to President Roosevelt, claims were much more modest.

35. Greene and Massignani, *Naval War in the Mediterranean,* 170.

36. British accounts state,"On its way to the Kithera Channel Admiral King's force was bombed continuously; the *Naiad* had two turrets put out of action and her speed reduced." Playfair, *The Germans Come to the Help of Their Ally,* 137. Also Simpson, *Cunningham's Papers,* 431–32. King radioed for assistance and stated *Naiad* was seriously damaged. The entry for *Naiad* in Admiralty 234/444, *H.M. Ships Damaged or Sunk by Enemy Action,* does not mention any problem with her turrets, only that splinters had extensively damaged her stem. Circumstantial evidence indicates *Naiad* was torpedoed. A British memoir recounts,"One air-launched torpedo passed harmlessly under our stern. Another had punched a hole thought our stem without exploding"; when at Alexandria for temporary repairs,"with the help of the repair ships we set about welding a great plate over the huge hole for'd." Max Arthur, *The Navy 1939 to the Present Day* (Coronet Books, London, 1998), 78–81. In another account a crewmen on *Leander* recalled"watch[ing] *Naiad* enter Haifa with something new, technicolour camouflage. Her usual black, grey and light grey pattern was now augmented for'ard with a huge splash of red where her repairs had yet to be finally painted. She'd been torpedoed off Crete, [and] hastily repaired in dock at Alexandria." Jack Harker, *Well Done Leander* (Auckland: Collins, 1971), 150–51. If indeed *Naiad* had been torpedoed, then *Sagittario* may deserve credit, as the Luftwaffe had expended its last six aerial torpedoes on 21 May and no Italian torpedo bomber or submarine claimed any attack in that area on that day.

37. Simpson, *Cunningham Papers,* vol. 1, 416; and Churchill, *The Second World War,* vol. 3, *The Grand Alliance* (Boston: Houghton Mifflin,1950), 256.

38. See Schreiber et al., *Germany and the Second World War,* 549–50.

39. Prideaux,"With 'A.B.C.' in the Med,"part 2, 273.

40. P. F. Lupinacci, *La difesa del traffico con l'Albania, la Grecia e l'Egeo* (Rome: Ufficio Storico della Marina Militare, 1965), 148–49.

41. Iachino, *Tramonto,* 247.

42. A. G. Prideaux, "With 'A.B.C.' in the Med," part 3, *Naval Review* 65 (October 1977): 356–57.

43. Jürgen Rohwer and G. Hummelchen, *Chronology of the War at Sea 1939–1945* (Annapolis, Md.: Naval Institute Press, 2006), 72.

Chapter 8. France Defends the Empire

1. Simpson, *Somerville Papers*, 51.

2. *Fuehrer Conferences*, 188.

3. Simpson, *Somerville Papers*, 233–34.

4. Ibid., 236.

5. Thomas, "After Mers-el-Kebir," 663.

6. Robert L. Melka, "Darlan between Germany and Britain 1940–41," *Journal of Contemporary History* 8 (April 1973): 69.

7. Hinsley et al., *British Intelligence*, vol. 1, 424.

8. John Jordan, "2400-tonnes Series: The four-funnelled *Contre-torpilleurs* of the pre-war Marine Nationale," in *Warship 1994* (London: Conway Maritime, 1994), 98.

9. Antier, *Batailles Navales*, 115. British accounts relate that two torpedoes were seen crossing ahead of *Phoebe* at 0300, an hour before the landing.

10. Christopher Page, ed., *The Royal Navy and the Mediterranean*, vol. 2, *November 1940–December 1941*, Naval Staff Histories (London: Frank Cass, 2002), 122.

11. Times generally differ in battle narratives, even from ship to ship in the same force. This account follows *Valmy*'s times. Add seven minutes to ten minutes for the corresponding times given in British accounts.

12. See Stitt, *Under Cunningham's Command*, 226.

13. Pierre Guiot, *Combats Sans Espoir: Guerre Navale en Syrie–1941* (Paris: La Couronne Littéraire, no date), 73.

14. Ibid., 77.

15. Simpson, *Cunningham Papers*, vol. 1, 493. "The relatively low muzzle-velocity of 725m/s of the short, 40 calibre gun meant a flight time of 17.6 second over 9000m, making it difficult to hit a fast-maneuvering target of comparable size." See Jordan, "2400-tonnes Series."

16. Simpson, *Cunningham Papers*, vol. 1, 485.

17. Darrieus and Quéguiner, *Marine française*, 275.

18. Ibid.

19. Gill, *Australian Navy 1939–1942*, 380.

20. Melka, "Darlan between Britain and Germany 1940–41," 75.

21. F. H. Hinsley, *British Intelligence in the Second World War*, abridged ed. (New York: Cambridge University Press, 1993), 86.

22. Cunningham, *Odyssey*, 398; and Simpson, *Cunningham Papers*, vol. 1, 493.

Chapter 9. The Convoy War Intensifies: Summer and Fall 1941

1. Page, *Royal Navy and the Mediterranean,* vol. 2, 158.

2. Hinsley et al., *British Intelligence,* vol. 2, 277.

3. B. H. Liddell Hart, *History of the Second World War* (New York: Putnam, 1970), 182.

4. Iachino, *Tramonto,* 252.

5. Ciano, *Diaries,* 366.

6. Hinsley et al., *British Intelligence,* vol. 1, 22 fn.

7. Ibid., 283–84.

8. Schreiber et al., *Germany and the Second World War,* 716.

9. Ibid., 708.

10. Roskill, *The Defensive,* 521.

11. ADM 234/335, Battle Summaries, no. 18, *Mediterranean Convoys 1941,* 11.

12. Kemp, *Admiralty Regrets,* 151.

13. ADM 234/335, *Mediterranean Convoys 1941,* 14.

14. Charles A Jellison, *Besieged: The World War II Ordeal of Malta, 1940–1942* (Hanover, N.H.: University Press of New England, 1984), 125.

15. See J. Caruana, "Decima Flotilla Decimated," *Warship International* 28(2) (1991): 178–86.

16. Gill, *Australian Navy 1939 1942,* 383 86.

17. Simpson, *Somerville Papers,* 311.

18. See Greene and Massignani, *Naval War in the Mediterranean,* 188–89.

19. Iachino, *Tramonto,* 257.

20. See Marco Spertini and Erminio Bagnasco, *I mezzi d'assalto della Xa Flottiglia MAS* (Parma: Ermanno Albertelli, 2005), 38–49, for a summary of operations.

21. Valerio J Borghese, *Sea Devils: Italian Navy Commandos in World War II* (Annapolis, Md.: Naval Institute Press, 1995), 129.

22. Schreiber et al., *Germany in the Second World War,* 711.

23. Lawrence Paterson, *U-Boats in the Mediterranean 1941–1945* (Annapolis, Md.: Naval Institute Press, 2007), 32.

24. Hans Frank, *German S-Boats in Action in the Second World War* (Annapolis, Md.: Naval Institute Press, 2007), 76–77.

25. Hinsley, *British Intelligence,* vol. 2, 287.

26. Ibid., 319.

27. John Winton, ed., *The War at Sea: The British Navy in World War II* (New York: William Morrow, 1968), 145.

28. ADM 239/261, *The Fighting Instructions, 1939,* clause 432, section 8.

29. Page, *Royal Navy and the Mediterranean,* vol. 2, 192.

30. Winton, *War at Sea,* 146.

31. Page, *Royal Navy and the Mediterranean*, vol. 2, 192.

32. *Fuehrer Conferences*, 240.

33. Simpson, *Cunningham Papers*, vol. 1, 519.

34. I. S. O. Playfair, *The Mediterranean and Middle East*, vol. 3, *British Fortunes Reach Their Lowest Ebb* (September 1941 to September 1942) (Uckfield, England: Naval and Military, 2004), 96.

35. Hinsley et al., *British Intelligence*, vol. 2, 320.

36. Page, *Royal Navy and the Mediterranean*, vol. 2, 201.

37. Simpson, *Cunningham Papers*, vol. 1, 535.

38. Paterson, *U-Boats in the Mediterranean*, 51.

39. Simpson, *Cunningham Papers*, 537.

40. Hinsley, *British Intelligence*, abridged ed., 195; also vol. 2, 322–23. Greene and Massignani, *Naval War in the Mediterranean*, 198, state that gasoline fumes on one destroyer were so strong that the crew had to wear gas masks.

41. Bragadin, *Italian Navy*, 142.

42. Page, *Royal Navy and the Mediterranean*, vol. 2, 217.

43. Greene and Massignani, *Naval War in the Mediterranean*, 199.

44. Giorgio Giorgerini and Augusto Nani, *Gli incrociatori italiani 1861–1964* (Rome: Ufficio Storico Della Marina Militare, 1964), 487.

45. Ciano, *Diaries*, 418. Somigli, a former deputy chief of staff sacked after Taranto was a Ciano protégé and made this often-quoted remark to paint his rivals in an unfavorable light.

46. G. H. Bennett and R. Bennett, *Hitler's Admirals* (Annapolis, Md.: Naval Institute Press, 2004), 119–20.

Chapter 10. The Axis Resurgent: 1942

1. Ciano, *Diaries*, 416.

2. A. G. Prideaux, "With 'A.B.C.' in the Med," *Naval Review* 66 (January 1978): 49.

3. *Yamato* opened fire at 34,000 yards at Leyte Gulf: "At 0658 the First Battleship Division commenced firing with the fore turrets at the range of thirty-one kilometers." Matome Ugaki, *Fading Victory* (Pittsburgh, Pa.: University of Pittsburgh Press, 1991), 492.

4. Page, *Royal Navy and the Mediterranean*, vol. 2, 221.

5. Greene and Massignani, *Naval War in the Mediterranean*, 202.

6. Schreiber et al., *Germany and the Second World War*, 723.

7. Roskill, *The Defensive*, 535.

8. Bragadin, *Italian Navy*, 151.

9. Schreiber et al., *Germany and the Second World War*, 723.

10. Jellison, *Besieged*, 150.

11. Eric Grove, *Sea Battles in Close-Up: World War II* (Annapolis, Md.: Naval Institute Press, 1993), vol. 2, 99.

12. The British concealed the results of the Alexandria attack for several weeks. However, by 15 January 1942 Italian naval intelligence had confirmed that X MAS had damaged both enemy battleships.

13. Philip Vian, *Action This Day* (London: Frederick Muller, 1960), 84.

14. Playfair, *British Fortunes Reach Their Lowest Ebb,* 164.

15. Hinsley et al., *British Intelligence,* vol. 2, 347.

16. ADM 234/353, Battle Summaries, no. 32, *Malta Convoys 1942,* 5.

17. Playfair, *British Fortunes Reach Their Lowest Ebb,* 164.

18. ADM 234/353, *Malta Convoys 1942,* 5.

19. Giuseppe Fioravanzo, *Le Azioni Navali in Mediterraneo dal 1 Aprile 1941 al'8 Settembre 1943* (Rome: Ufficio Storico Della Marina Militare, 1970), vol. 5, 202.

20. ADM 234/353, *Malta Convoys 1942,* 6.

21. Fioravanzo, *Azioni Navali,* vol. 5, 204 fn.

22. Ibid., 202.

23. One of *Littorio*'s Ro.43s reported a cruiser heading south escorted by a destroyer trailing a long plume of smoke. This, of course, was Vian's "smoke division."

24. Julius Thompson, *The War at Sea: The Royal Navy in the Second World War* (Osceola, Wisc.: Motorbooks International, 1996), 182.

25. ADM 235/324, *Malta Convoys 1942,* 6.

26. Vian, *Action this Day,* 89.

27. S. W. Roskill, *The War at Sea 1939–1945,* vol. 2, *The Period of Balance* (London: HMSO, 1956), 53.

28. Fioravanzo, *Azioni Navali,* vol. 5, 210.

29. ADM 234/325, *Malta Convoys 1942,* 8.

30. Ibid.

31. "The Battle of Sirte of 22nd March, *1942,*" *London Gazette,* Supplement, 18 September 1947), 4375.

32. Vian, *Action This Day,* 90.

33. Roskill, *Period of Balance,* 53.

34. ADM 234/325, *Malta Convoys 1942,* 9.

35. "The Battle of Sirte of 22nd March," *London Gazette,* Vian report, para. 53.

36. Thompson, *War at Sea,* 184.

37. *Trento* also claimed credit for this hit. See Fioravanzo, *Azioni Navali,* vol. 5, 223.

38. Winton, *War at Sea,* 224.

39. Greene and Massignani, *Naval War in the Mediterranean,* 221, lists the Italian totals as *Littorio,* 181 15-inch, 445 6-inch, and 21 3.5-inch; *Gorizia,* 226 8-inch and

67 4-inch; *Trento,* 336 8-inch and 20 4-inch; *Bande Nere,* 112 6-inch; and *Aviere,* 84 4.7-inch.

40. Bartimeus, *East of Malta, West of Suez,* 199.

41. Jellison, *Besieged,* 163; also J. A. Whelan, *Malta Airman* (Wellington: Historical Publications Branch, 1950), 23.

42. Ireland, *War in the Mediterranean,* 120.

43. Playfair, *British Fortunes Reach Their Lowest Ebb,* 183.

44. See Vincent P. O'Hara, *German Fleet at War, 1939–1945* (Annapolis, Md.: Naval Institute Press, 2004), 130–50.

45. Simpson, *Cunningham Papers,* vol. 1, 470.

46. *Fuehrer Conferences,* 285.

47. Jellsion, *Besieged,* 205.

48. Bragadin, *Italian Navy,* 356.

49. Reports from the American army attaché in Egypt were the source of Italy's information.

50. Hinsley, *British Intelligence,* abridged ed., 205.

51. A. F. Pugsley, *Destroyer Man* (London: Weidenfeld and Nicolson, 1957), 117.

52. Quote is from Vian, *Action this Day,* 97. Also see ADM 234/358, *Malta Convoys 1942,* 31–33.

53. Sadkovich, *Italian Navy,* 258: "Italian battleships needed 100 tons and cruisers 24 tons daily just to maintain steam."

54. ADM 234/358, *Malta Convoys 1942,* 17.

55. Playfair, *British Fortunes Reach Their Lowest Ebb,* 302.

56. "Mediterranean Convoy Operations," *London Gazette,* Supplement, 11 August 1948, 98.

57. Ibid.

58. Winton, *War at Sea,* 226–27.

59. ADM 234/353, *Malta Convoys, 1942,* 22.

60. Fioravanzo, *Azioni Navali,* vol. 5, 297.

61. Alberto Santoni and Francesco Mattesini, *La partecipazione aeronavale tedesca alla Guerra nel Mediterraneo* (Rome: Ateneo e Bizzarri, 1980), 216: "*Partridge, Bedouin* e *Ithuriel* vennero colpiti dal fuoco degli incrociatori italiani, riportando alcuni danni."

62. ADM 234/353, *Malta Convoys, 1942,* 22.

63. Fioravanzo, *Azioni Navali,* vol. 5, 297–98.

64. ADM 234/353, *Malta Convoys, 1942,* 22.

65. Fioravanzo, *Azioni Navali,* vol. 5, 300.

66. Ibid., 302.

67. "Mediterranean Convoy Operations," *London Gazette,* 4499.

68. Ibid., 4500.

69. Ibid. *Partridge's* captain was making to the west at this time (according to his original intention) because *Bedouin* had failed, against expectation, to get an engine started.

70. Fioravanzo, *Azioni Navali,* vol. 5, 307.

71. "Mediterranean Convoy Operations," *London Gazette,* 4500.

72. Fioravanzo, *Azioni Navali,* vol. 5, 307.

73. Axis aircraft finally dispatched *Kentucky* and probably *Burdwan.* Captain Hardy mocked the enemy for finishing the job he had assigned to *Hebe* and *Badsworth:* "Enemy torpedo bombers most conveniently attacked and sank *Burdwan* and *Kentucky*" ("Mediterranean Convoy Operations," *London Gazette,* 4500). The interpretation that Da Zara somehow mishandled the cripples has been repeated as late as 2006: "All Da Zara needed to do was hook up the two destroyers to *Kentucky* and tow her back to Pantelleria." Sam Moses, *At All Costs* (New York: Random House, 2006), 73.

74. Playfair, *British Fortunes Reach Their Lowest Ebb,* 307.

75. Jellison, *Besieged,* 219.

76. Macintyre, *Battle for the Mediterranean,* 157.

77. Jellison, *Besieged,* 220–21. This excludes bread and locally grown foodstuffs.

78. G. Hermon Gill, *Royal Australian Navy 1942–1945* (Adelaide: Griffin, 1968), 97.

79. Playfair, *British Fortunes Reach Their Lowest Ebb,* 316.

80. Peter Smith, *Pedestal: The Convoy That Saved Malta* (Manchester: Crecy, 1999), 92.

81. ADM 234/353, *Malta Convoys 1942,* 37.

82. See Sadkovich, *Italian Navy,* 295; Bragadin, *Italian Navy,* 211–12; Fabio Tani, *Memorie,* unpublished manuscript. Commander Lorenzini become the navy's chief of staff in 1970.

83. Winston Churchill, *The Second World War,* vol. 4, *The Hinge of Fate* (Boston: Houghton Mifflin 1950), 455.

84. Maugeri, *Ashes of Disgrace,* 83.

Chapter 11. The Allies Resurgent: Torch to Tunis

1. Ciano, *Diaries,* 510.

2. Albert Kesselring, *Kesselring: A Soldier's Record* (New York: William Morrow, 1954), 152. Also see Jack Greene and Alessandro Massignani, *Rommel's North African Campaign: September 1940–November 1942* (Cambridge, Mass.: Da Capo, 1999), 215. Tonnage and arrivals from Gino Jori, "I rifornimenti dal mare alle forze italo-tedesche ad El Alamein per la ripresa dell'attacco all'Egitto (2 luglio–2 settembre 1942," *RID* (February 1986), table 1.

3. For the impact of signal intelligence, Hinsley et al., *British Intelligence,* vol. 2, 423; for Axis arrivals, Jori, "I rifornimenti dal mar," tables no. 1 and 3; for Italian losses, Playfair, *British Fortunes Reach Their Lowest Ebb,* 327.

4. I. S. O. Playfair, *The Mediterranean and Middle East,* vol. 4, *The Destruction of the Axis Forces in Africa* (Uckfield, England: Naval and Military, 2004), 23.

5. Luigi Bolla, *Perchè a Salò* (Milan: Bompiani, 1982), 149–50.

6. Harry S Butcher, *My Three Years with Eisenhower: The Personal Diary of Captain Harry C. Butcher, USNR Naval Aide to General Eisenhower, 1942 to 1945* (New York: Simon and Schuster, 1946), 83.

7. Auphan and Mordal, *French Navy,* 210.

8. ADM 234/359, *Operation "Torch" Invasion of North Africa November 1942 to February 1943,* 9.

9. Ibid., 14.

10. Ibid., 38.

11. ADM 234/444, *Boadicea,* 8th November, 1942.

12. Marc Saibène, *Les Torpilleurs de 1500 Tonnes du Type Bourrasque* (Rennes: Marines Editions, 2001), 118–23.

13. Darrieus and Queguiner, *Marine française,* 331.

14. Ibid.

15. Barbara Brooks Tomblin, *With Utmost Spirit: Allied Naval Operations in the Mediterranean, 1942–1945* (Lexington: University of Kentucky Press, 2004), 77.

16. "The Landings in North Africa," *London Gazette,* Supplement, 23 March 1949, 1511. *Jamaica*'s poor results were attributed to "excessive use of helm wheel, which made it practically impossible to hold range or line." Michael Simpson, *The Cunningham Papers: Selections from the Private and Official Correspondence of Admiral of the Fleet Viscount Cunningham of Hyndhope,* vol. 2, *The Triumph of Allied Sea Power 1942–1946* (Aldershot, England: Ashgate, 2006), 91.

17. ADM 234/359, *Operation "Torch,"* 29.

18. See Vincent P. O'Hara, *The U.S. Navy against the Axis: Surface Combat 1941–1945* (Annapolis, Md.: Naval Institute Press, 2007), 138–50.

19. Rohwer and Hummelchen, *Chronology,* 210.

20. Auphan and Mordal, *French Navy,* 246.

21. Dwight Eisenhower, *Crusade in Europe* (New York: Doubleday, 1948), 109.

22. Churchill, *Hinge of Fate,* 574.

23. Simpson, *Cunningham Papers,* vol. 2, 56.

24. Auphan and Mordal, *French Navy,* 257.

25. Anthony Clayton, "A Question of Honour? Scuttling Vichy's Fleet," *History Today* (November 1992): 37.

26. *Fuehrer Conferences,* 300.

27. Bennett, *Ultra and Mediterranean Strategy,* 193.

28. Alan J. Levine, *The War against Rommel's Supply Lines, 1942–1943* (Westport, Conn.: Praeger, 1999), 80.

29. At Malta on that date there were five complete and three partial fighter squadrons, one bomber/reconnaissance squadron, portions of three torpedo-bomber squadrons, and two bomber squadrons. See Playfair, *Destruction of the Axis Forces,* 204.

30. Hinsley et al., *British Intelligence,* vol. 2, 495.

31. Aldo Cocchia, *La difesa del traffico con 'Africa Settentrionale dal 1 ottobre alla caduta della Tunisia* (Rome: Ufficio Storico Della Marina Militare, 1964), vol. 8, 161.

32. Cunningham, *Odyssey,* 505.

33. Based on *Folgore's* report, Enrico Cernuschi believes that *Folgore* torpedoed *Quentin* in the Italian destroyer's second attack and that the torpedo holed the British ship but did not detonate until that morning, when she was returning to port at high speed. He reaches this conclusion based on the fact that German records show no attacks by torpedo aircraft that morning. The only recorded action is a bombing attack by three Ju.88s of I./KG 54. They claimed a near miss on a destroyer north of Zembretta Island, nearly a hundred miles from where *Quentin* was attacked. He further states the submarine *P219* surfaced during the battle and fired a torpedo, which, although it missed, was considered by the Admiralty as the possible source of *Quentin's* loss.

34. Wade, *Midshipman's War,* 182.

35. Ibid., 183.

36. Simpson, *Cunningham Papers,* vol. 2, 60.

37. Hinsley et al., *British Intelligence,* vol. 2, 496.

38. See Rohwer, *Axis Submarine Success;* 240. Playfair, *Destruction of the Axis Forces,* 206 credits aircraft torpedoes.

39. Playfair, *Destruction of the Axis Forces,* 211.

40. Ibid., 230.

41. Bragadin, *Italian Navy,* 242.

42. Langtree, *Kellys,* 156.

43. *Perseo* report, "Danni inflitti al nemico," 22 April 1943.

44. Ibid.

45. Playfair, *Destruction of the Axis Forces,* 241–42.

46. Simpson, *Cunningham Papers,* vol. 2, 72.

47. Extracted from Playfair, *Destruction of the Axis Forces,* 251, 417.

48. Hinsley et al., *British Intelligence,* vol. 2, 607.

49. See ADM 199/2068, *Inquiry Operation Headache,* and Vincent P. O'Hara and Enrico Cernuschi, "Battle with No Name," *World War II* (March 2006): 36–41.

50. Enrico Cernuschi, correspondence to author, based on interview with Carmelo Zippitelli

51. Ibid.

52. Rick Atkinson, *An Army at Dawn: The War in North Africa, 1942–1943* (New York: Henry Holt, 2002), 516.

53. Bragadin, *Italian Navy,* 250.

54. Dear and Foot, *Oxford Companion to World War II,* 818.

55. Roskill, *Period of Balance,* 443.

56. C. Huan,"The French Navy in World War II,"in *Reevaluating Major Naval Combatants of World War II,* ed. James J. Sadkovich (New York: Greenwood, 1990), 93.

Chapter 12. The Italian Armistice

1. Maugeri, *From the Ashes of Disgrace,* 101; and Ciano, *Diaries,* 577.

2. Pugsley, *Destroyer Man,* 142.

3. Ibid., 143.

4. Ibid., 144.

5. The British claimed they faced two escorts, *X137* (identified as a torpedo boat) and *Castore* (identified as a destroyer). See also Langtree, *Kellys,* 159.

6. First quote from Carlo D'Este, *World War II in the Mediterranean* (Chapel Hill, N.C.: Algonquin Books, 1990), 39. Final quote from Albert N. Garland and Howard McGaw Smyth, *Sicily and the Surrender of Italy* (Washington, D.C.: U.S. Government Printing Office, 1965), 11.

7. S. W. Roskill, *The War at Sea 1939–1945,* vol. 3, *The Offensive Part I* (London: HMSO, 1960), 121. Quote is from Samuel E. Morison, *The Invasion of France and Germany, 1944–1945* (Boston: Little, Brown), 39.

8. Ibid. 43.

9. Frank, *S-Boats,* 86.

10. Dudley Pope, *Flag 4: The Battle of the Coastal Forces in the Mediterranean 1939–1945* (London: Chatham, 1998), 121.

11. Fioravanzo, *Azioni Navali,* vol. 5, 521–22.

12. *Fuehrer Conferences,* 347.

13. Elio Ando, "Changing Sides: The Italian Fleet and the Armistice: 1943," *Warship* 42 (April 1987): 67.

14. Ibid. Also Theodore R. Tredwell, *Splinter Fleet: The Wooden Subchasers of World War II* (Annapolis, Md.: Naval Institute Press, 2000), 62. *SC 503* was the largest American warship to be engaged by major Italian warships.

15. Bradagin, *Italian Navy,* 260.

16. This section is based on Vincent P. O'Hara and Enrico Cernuschi, *Dark Navy: The Regia Marina and the Armistice of 8 September 1943,*" (Ann Arbor, Mich.: Nimble Books, 2009). See also Elena Agarossi, *A Nation Collapses: The Italian Surrender of September 1943* (Cambridge: Cambridge University Press, 2000); F. W. Deakin, *The Brutal Friendship: Mussolini, Hitler and the Fall of Italian Fascism* (New York: Harper and Row, 1962); and Ando,"Changing Sides."

17. Mario Cardea, "La Brillante Azione della Torpediniera Aliseo," *Mare: L'Italia Marinara* (September 1952), 2.

18. See Giuseppe Fioravanzo, *La Marina Italiana nella Seconda Guerra Mondiale,* vol. 15, *La Marina dall'8 settembre alla fine del conflicto* (Rome: Ufficio Storico Della Marina Militare, 1970).

19. See Alessandro Dondoli, "Piombino, settembre 1943." *Storia Militare* 72 (September 1999): 4–14.

20. Butcher, *My Three Years,* 414.

21. Simpson, *Cunningham Papers,* vol. 2, 129.

22. Samuel E. Morison, *History of United States Naval Operations in World War II,* vol. 9, *Sicily-Salerno-Anzio, January 1943–June 1944* (Boston: Little, Brown, 1990), 244. The *Squadretta* sailed on 19 September for Malta, where it arrived the next day.

23. Bragadin, *Italian Navy,* 340.

24. Frank, *S-Boats,* 87.

25. Bragadin, *Italian Navy,* 346–47.

Chapter 13. Germany's War: 1943–45

1. See Peter Schenk, *Kampf um die Ägäis* (Hamburg: E. S. Mittler and Son, 2000), 32–40; and Zvonimir Freivogel, "*Vasilefs Georgios* and *Vasilissa Olga*: From Sister-Ships to Adversaries," *Warship International* 40(4) (2003).

2. *Fueher Conferences,* 369.

3. See the discussion in Roskill, *The Offensive Part I,* 188ff.

4. "Naval Operations in the Aegean between the 7th September 1943 and 28th November, 1943," *London Gazette,* Supplement, 11 October, 1948, 5372. The Levant Command was formed in February 1943 by detaching from the Mediterranean command the area east of the Tunisian/Libyan border

5. Anthony Rogers, *Churchill's Folly: Leros and the Aegean* (London: Cassell, 2003), 35.

6. The usual number quoted is 4,750. Another 1,264 drowned when mines sank transports filled with Italian prisoners. "It should be noted that when ships carrying German troops were sunk the percentage saved was higher. Apart from there having been insufficient lifesaving equipment on board, there was panic after striking the mines which the crews tried to control with machine gun fire, with hellish results." Schenk, *Kampf um die Ägäis,* 59.

7. Hinsley et al., *British Intelligence,* vol. 3, part 1, 121–22.

8. "Naval Operations in the Aegean," *London Gazette,* 5372; also Rodgers, *Churchill's Folly,* 49

9. Quoted in Hinsley et al., *British Intelligence,* vol. 3, part 1, 122.

10. Rodgers, *Churchill's Folly,* 84.

11. "Improvise and Dare," *Naval Review* 39 (February 1951): 46.

12. Hinsley et al., *British Intelligence,* vol 3, part 1, 128.

13. ADM 234/444, "*Hursley* 17th October 1943."

14. Hinsley et al., *British Intelligence,* vol. 3, part 1, 121–22, 131. For the Children's Crusade, Schenk, *Kampf um die Ägäis,* 81.

15. Rogers, *Churchill's Folly,* 263 fn.

16. *Fuehrer Conferences,* 385.

17. Schenk, *Kampf um die Ägäis,* 112.

18. Charles Koburger, *Wine-Dark, Blood Red Sea: Naval Warfare in the Aegean 1941–1946* (Westport, Conn.: Praeger, 1999), 98. The "KT" ships were mass-produced coastal freighter types—like *KT1,* sunk in the Convoy H action, displacing 800 GRT and capable of 14.5 knots.

19. Schenk, *Kampf um die Ägäis,* 128. This does not include naval losses.

20. Frank, *S-Boats,* 87; and *German Antiguerrilla Operations in the Balkans (1941–1944),* CMH Publication 104-18 (Washington, D.C.: Department of the Army, 1953), chap. 8.

21. See Vladimir Isaic, "Premuda 29 Febbraio 1944," *Storia Militare* 46 (July 1997): 20–26. War Diary quote is from page 25.

22. See Zvonimir Freivogel, "Die Geisterflotte von Pag," *Schiffahrt International Journal* (August/September 2007): 56–65; also Pope, *Flag 4,* 259–60.

23. See Zvonimir Freivogel, "The Attack on *HMS Delhi* at Spalato," *Warship International* 40(2) (2003): 351–64.

24. The RSI's Marina Nazionale Repubblicana operated MAS boats and special attack units. X MAS unit joined the Germans even before the establishment of Mussolini's "republic." See Jack Greene and Alessandro Massignani, *The Black Prince and the Sea Devils* (Cambridge, Mass.: Da Capo, 2004). The RSI navy clashed at least thirty-five times with Allied coastal units and conducted attacks against larger warships, sinking the British *LST305* off Anzio, slightly damaging *Le Fantasque,* and severely damaging *Trombe.*

25. S. W. Roskill, *The War at Sea 1939–1945,* vol. 3, *The Offensive Part II* (Nashville, Tenn.: Battery, 1994), 83.

26. Tomblin, *Utmost Spirit,* 329.

27. Robert J. Bulkley Jr., *At Close Quarters: PT Boats in the United States Navy* (Annapolis, Md.: Naval Institute Press, 2003), 313.

28. See O'Hara, *German Fleet at War,* 236–38.

29. Ibid., 238–41.

30. Samuel E. Morison, *United States Naval Operations in World War II,* vol. 11, *The Invasion of France and Germany* (Boston: Little, Brown, 1975), 311.

31. Vincent P. O'Hara, "Mystery Battle off Imperia, 1 October 1944," *World War II Quarterly* (4)2 (August 2007): 24–33, contains a more detailed account of this action.

32. See O'Hara, *German Fleet at War,* 245–47.

33. Arnold Hague, *The Allied Convoy System 1939–1945* (Annapolis, Md.: Naval Institute Press, 2000), 192.

34. Kenneth Wynn, *U-Boat Operations of the Second World War* (Annapolis, Md.: Naval Institute Press: 1997), 300.

Conclusion

1. These figures are compiled from a number of sources, including Enrico Cernuschi, *Fecero tutti il loro dovere* (Rome: Rivista Maríttima, 2006), 87–97; David Brown, *Warship Losses of World War II* (Annapolis, Md.: Naval Institute Press, 1995); Kemp, *Admiralty Regrets* (Sutton: 1999); Robert Gardiner, ed., *Conway's All the World's Fighting Ships 1922–1946* (New York: Mayflower, 1980); and Erminio Bagnasco and Enrico Cernuschi, *Le Navi da Guerra Italiane 1940–1945* (Parma: Ermanno Albertelli, 2003). They include ships sunk and later salvaged, including *Queen Elizabeth* and *Valiant;* some sources (including Kemp and Cernuschi) consider these ships as only damaged.

2. See chap. 4 and endnote 58.

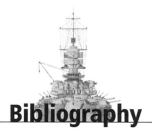

Bibliography

Primary Sources and Official Histories

ADM 199/1048. *Naval Actions in the Mediterranean,* "Action off Calabria." The National Archives.

ADM 199/2068. *Inquiry Operation Headache.* The National Archives.

ADM 199/2378. *Preliminary Narrative of the War at Sea 1940* (1946). Admiralty Historical Section of Tactical, Torpedo and Staff Duties Division, Naval Staff. The National Archives.

ADM 234/317. Battle Summaries. *No. 1, Operations against the French Fleet at Mers-el-Kebir (Oran) 3rd 6th July, 1940.* The National Archives.

ADM 234/323. Battle Summaries. *No. 6, Bombardments of Bardia, June 21st, 1940, August 17th, 1940 and January 3rd, 1941; No. 7, The Bombardment of Genoa February 9th, 1941; No. 8, Mediterranean Operations Operation M.A.5, 7th to 15th July, 1940, Action off Calabria 9th July, 1940.* The National Archives.

ADM 234/325. Battle Summaries. *No. 9, Action off Cape Spartivento, 27th November, 1940; No. 10, Mediterranean Operations 4th to 14th November, 1940 Air Attack on Taranto, 11th November 1940.* The National Archives.

ADM 234/326. *Italian Account of the Action off Cape Spartivento, 27th November 1940.* The National Archives.

ADM 234/335. Battle Summaries. *No. 18, Mediterranean Convoys 1941.* The National Archives.

ADM 234/353. Battle Summaries. *No. 32, Malta Convoys 1942.* The National Archives.

ADM 234/359. *Operation "Torch" Invasion of North Africa November 1942 to February 1943.* The National Archives.

ADM 234/444. *H.M. Ships Damaged or Sunk by Enemy Action 3 Sept. 1939 to 2 Sept. 1945.* The National Archives.

ADM 239/261. *The Fighting Instructions 1939.* The National Archives.

"Action between British and Italian Forces off Cape Spartivento on 27th November, 1940." *London Gazette,* Supplement, 5 May 1948.

Admiralty. *British Merchant Vessels Lost or Damaged by Enemy Action during Second World War: 3rd September 1939 to 2nd September 1945.* London: HMSO, 1947.

———. *Progress in Naval Gunnery.* Gunnery and Anti-Aircraft War Division, Naval Staff, 1942.

———. *Progress in Naval Gunnery.* Gunnery and Anti-Aircraft War Division, Naval Staff, 1943.

———. *Ships of the Royal Navy Statement of Losses during the Second World War: 3rd September 1939 to 2nd September 1945.* London: HMSO, 1947.

Archivio Centrale dello Stato, Rome. Ministero della Marina. Allegato no. 10117 del 14/12/1940; 10521 del 22/12/1940.

———. "Condotta del tiro naval." January 1941.

———. "Direttive e Norme per l'impiego della Squadra nel conflictto attuale." January 1941.

———. *Navi perdute,* cartella R. I. P. *Zara.*

———. "Norme di Máxima per l'impiego in Guerra." January 1941.

———. *Perseo* "Danni inflitti al nemico." 22 April 1943.

———. Relazione sulle operazioni navali dei giorni 6, 7, 8, e 9 luglio 1940 XVIII (Azione di Punta Stilo)" Segreto b) and C) rapporto sulla missione di guerra dei giorni 7–8–9–luglio 1940–XVIII, 24 July 1940.

———. R.C.T. *Oriani.* Considerazioni.

———. Cartella 26, "Messaggi in arrivo comando in capo squadra navale."

Archivio dell'Ufficio Storico della Marina Militare, Rome. Fondo MARICOTRAF, Busta 6, Fascicolo 4, "Corrispondenza tra Maristat—Ispettorato per l'Aviazione della R. Marina e il Comando Superiore M.M. a Tobruch sulla ricognizione aerea contro il traffico inglese tra l'Egitto e Creta."

———. Fondo MARICOSOM, Busta 32, Fascicolo 510, "Studio del S. T. D. M. Rolla per un eventuale piano d'azione contro le forze navali inglesi del Mediterraneo Orientale e successivo sviluppo per lo sbarco di truppe nazionali inn Alessandria d'Egitto." 25 August 1940.

"The Battle of Crete." *London Gazette,* Supplement, 24 May 1948.

"Battle of Matapan." *London Gazette,* Supplement, 31 July 1947.

"The Battle of Sirte of 22nd March, 1942." *London Gazette,* Supplement, 18 September 1947.

Cocchia, Aldo. *La Marina Italiana nella Seconda Guerra Mondiale.* Vol. 8, *La difesa del traffico con 'Africa Settentrionale dal 1 ottobre alla caduta Della Tunisia.* Rome: Ufficio Storico Della Marina Militare, 1964.

"Control of the Sicilian Straits during the Final Stages of the North African Campaign." *London Gazette,* Supplement, 7 October 1948.

Fioravanzo, Giuseppe. *La Marina Italiana nella Seconda Guerra Mondiale.* Vol. 4, *Le Azioni Navali in Mediterraneo Dal 10 Giugno 1940 al 31 Marzo 1941.* Rome: Ufficio Storico Della Marina Militare, 1976.

———. *La Marina Italiana nella Seconda Guerra Mondiale*. Vol. 5, *Le Azioni Navali in Mediterraneo dal 1 Aprile 1941 al'8 Settembre 1943*. Rome: Ufficio Storico Della Marina Militare, 1970.

———. *La Marina Italiana nella Seconda Guerra Mondiale*. Vol. 15, *La Marina dall'8 settembre alla fine del conflicto*. Rome: Ufficio Storico Della Marina Militare, 1970.

"Fleet Air Arm Operations against Taranto on 11th November, 1940." *London Gazette*, Supplement, 24 July 1947.

Franklin D. Roosevelt Presidential Library and Museum. Great Britain Diplomatic Files, box 35 and box 36, War Situation Telegrams.

Fueher Conferences on Naval Affairs, 1939–1945. London: Chatham, 2005.

Garland, Albert N., and Howard McGaw Smyth. *Sicily and the Surrender of Italy*. Washington, D.C.: U.S. Government Printing Office, 1965.

Gill, G. Hermon. *Royal Australian Navy 1939–1942*. Adelaide: Griffin, 1957.

———. *Royal Australian Navy 1942 1945*. Adelaide: Griffin, 1968.

———. *Gli incrociatori italiani 1861–1964*. Ufficio Storico Della Marina Militare, 1964.

Giorgerini, Giorgio, and Augusto Nani. *Le navi di linea italiane*. Rome: Ufficio Storico della Marina Militare, 1962.

Hinsley, F. H., et al. *British Intelligence in the Second World War: Its Influence on Strategy and Operations*. Vol. 1. New York: Cambridge University Press, 1979.

———. *British Intelligence in the Second World War: Its Influence on Strategy and Operations*. Vol. 2. New York: Cambridge University Press, 1981.

———. *British Intelligence in the Second World War: Its Influence on Strategy and Operations*. Vol. 3, Part 1. New York: Cambridge University Press, 1984.

———. *British Intelligence in the Second World War*. Abridged ed. New York: Cambridge University Press, 1993.

Kennedy, Robert M., ed. *German Antiguerrilla Operations in the Balkans (1941–1944)*, CMH Publication 104-18. Washington, D.C.: Department of the Army, 1953.

"The Landings in North Africa." *London Gazette*, Supplement, 23 March 1949.

Lupinacci, Pier Filippo. *La Marina Italiana nella Seconda Guerra Mondiale*. Vol. 9, *La difesa del traffico con l'Albania, la Grecia e l'Egeo*. Rome: Ufficio Storico della Marina Militare, 1965.

———. *La Marina Italiana nella Seconda Guerra Mondiale*. Vol. 10, *Le operazioni in Africa Orientale*. Rome: Ufficio Storico Della Marina Militare, 1976.

"Mediterranean Convoy Operations." *London Gazette*, Supplement, 11 August 1948.

"Naval Operations in the Aegean between the 7th September 1943 and 28th November, 1943." *London Gazette*, Supplement, 11 October, 1948.

Page, Christopher, ed. *The Royal Navy and the Mediterranean*. Vol. 1, *September 1939–October 1940*. Naval Staff Histories. London: Frank Cass, 2002.

———. *The Royal Navy and the Mediterranean*. Vol. 2, *November 1940–December 1941*. Naval Staff Histories. London: Frank Cass, 2002.

Playfair, I. S. O. *The Mediterranean and Middle East*. Vol. 1, *The Early Successes against Italy (to May 1941)*. Uckfield, England: Naval and Military, 2004.

———. *The Mediterranean and Middle East*. Vol. 2, *The Germans Come to the Help of Their Ally (1941)*. Uckfield, England: Naval and Military, 2004.

———. *The Mediterranean and Middle East*. Vol. 3, *British Fortunes Reach Their Lowest Ebb (September 1941 to September 1942)*. Uckfield, England: Naval and Military, 2004.

———. *The Mediterranean and Middle East*. Vol. 4, *The Destruction of the Axis Forces in Africa*. Uckfield, England: Naval and Military, 2004.

"Report of an Action against an Italian Convoy on the Night of the 15th/16th April, 1941." *London Gazette*, Supplement, 12 May 1948.

"Report of an Action with the Italian Fleet off Calabria, 9th July 1940." *London Gazette*, Supplement, 27 April 1948.

Roskill, S. W. *The War at Sea 1939–1945*. Vol. 1, *The Defensive*. London: HMSO, 1954.

———. *The War at Sea 1939–1945*. Vol. 2, *The Period of Balance*. London: HMSO, 1956.

———. *The War at Sea 1939–1945*. Vol. 3, *The Offensive Part I*. London: HMSO, 1960.

———. *The War at Sea 1939–1945*. Vol. 3, *The Offensive Part II*. Nashville, Tenn.: Battery, 1994.

Schreiber, Gerhard, Bernd Stegemann, and Detlef Vogel. *Germany and the Second World War*. Vol. 3, *The Mediterranean, South-East Europe, and North Africa 1939–1941*. Oxford: Clarendon, 1995.

Simpson, Michael, ed. *The Cunningham Papers: Selections from the Private and Official Correspondence of Admiral of the Fleet Viscount Cunningham of Hyndhope, O.M, K.T., G.C.B., D.S.O. and Two Bars*. Vol. 1, *The Mediterranean Fleet, 1939–1942*. Aldershot, England: Ashgate, 1999.

———. *The Cunningham Papers*. Vol. 2, *The Triumph of Allied Sea Power 1942–1946*. Aldershot, England: Ashgate, 2006.

———. *The Somerville Papers: Selections from the Private and Official Correspondence of Admiral of the Fleet Sir James Somervile, G.C.B., G.B.E., D.S.O.* Aldershot, England: Scolar, 1996.

"Transportation of the Army to Greece and Evacuation of the Army from Greece, 1941." *London Gazette*, Supplement, 19 May 1948.

U.S. Navy. World War II Action and Operational Reports, 1941–1947. USS Benson, 2 October 1944. College Park, Md.: Modern Military Records, Textual Archives Service Division, National Archives and Records Administration.

———. USS *Endicott*, 17 August 1944.

———. USS *Gleaves*, 3 October 1944.

———. USS *Somers*, 15 August.

Waters, S. D. *The Royal New Zealand Navy*. Wellington: War History Branch, 1956.

Whelan, J. A. *Malta Airman*. Wellington: Historical Publications Branch, 1950.

Secondary Sources

Agarossi, Elena. *A Nation Collapses: The Italian Surrender of September 1943*. Cambridge: Cambridge University Press, 2000.

Ansel, Walter. *Hitler and the Middle Sea.* Durham, N.C.: Duke University Press, 1972.

Antier, Jean-Jacques. *Les grandes Batailles Navales de la Seconde Guerre mondiale: Le drame de la Marine française*. Paris: Omnibus, 2000.

Arthur, Max. *The Navy 1939 to the Present Day* (London: Coronet Books, 1998).

Atkinson, Rick. *An Army at Dawn: The War in North Africa, 1942–1943*. New York: Henry Holt, 2002.

Auphan, Paul, and Jacques Mordal. *The French Navy in World War II*. Westport, Conn.: Greenwood, 1976.

Badoglio, Pietro. *Italy in the Second World War: Memories and Documents.* Westport, Conn.: Greenwood, 1976.

Bagnasco, Erminio, and Enrico Cernuschi. *Le Navi da Guerra Italiane 1940–1945.* Parma: Ermanno Albertelli, 2003.

Bagnasco, Erminio, and Mark Grossman. *Regia Marina: Italian Battleships of World War Two.* Missoula, Mont.: Pictorial Histories, 1986.

Bagnasco, Erminio, and Maurizio Brescia. *Cacciatorpediniere Classi "Freccia/Folgore" "Maestrale" "Oriani" Parti seconda e terza.* Rome: Ermanno Albertelli, 1997.

Barnett, Correlli. *Engage the Enemy More Closely: The Royal Navy in the Second World War.* New York: W. W. Norton, 1991.

Bartimeus. *East of Malta, West of Suez.* Boston: Little, Brown, 1944.

Bekker, Cajus. *Hitler's Naval War.* New York: Doubleday, 1974.

Bennett, G. H., and R. Bennett. *Hitler's Admirals.* Annapolis, Md.: Naval Institute Press, 2004.

Bennett, Ralph. *Ultra and Mediterranean Strategy: The Never-Before-Told Story of How Ultra First Proved Itself in Battle, Turning Defeat into Victory.* New York: William Morrow, 1989.

Bigi, Luciano. *Una vita in marina.* Milan: Fondazione Italo Zetti, 2003.

Bolla Luigi, *Perchè a Salò.* Milan: Bompiani, 1982.

Borghese, Valerio J. *Sea Devils: Italian Navy Commandos in World War II.* Annapolis, Md.: Naval Institute Press, 1995.

Bragadin, Marc' Antonio. *The Italian Navy in World War II.* Annapolis, Md.: Naval Institute Press, 1957.

Broadberry, Stephen, and Mark Harrison, ed. *The Economics of World War I.* Cambridge: Cambridge University Press, 2005.

Brodie, Bernard. *A Guide to Naval Strategy.* Princeton, N.J.: Princeton University Press, 1944.

Brown, David. *Warship Losses of WWII.* Annapolis, Md.: Naval Institute Press, 1995.

Bulkley, Robert J., Jr. *At Close Quarters: PT Boats in the United States Navy.* Annapolis, Md.: Naval Institute Press, 2003.

Butcher, Harry S. *My Three Years with Eisenhower: The Personal Diary of Captain Harry C. Butcher, USNR, Naval Aide to General Eisenhower, 1942 to 1945.* New York: Simon and Schuster, 1946.

Cameron, Ian. *Red Duster, White Ensign: The Story of Malta and the Malta Convoys.* New York: Bantom Books, 1983.

Campbell, John. *Naval Weapons of World War II.* Annapolis, Md.: Naval Institute Press, 2002.

Cernuschi, Enrico. *Domenico Cavagnari: Storia di un Ammiraglio.* Rome: Revista Marítima, 2001.

———. *Fecero Tutti il Loro Dovere.* Rome: Revista Marítima, 2006.

———. *La Notte del Lupo.* Rome: Revista Marítima, 1997.

Churchill, Winston S. *The Second World War.* Vol. 2, *Their Finest Hour.* Boston: Houghton Mifflin, 1949.

———. *The Second World War.* Vol. 3, *The Grand Alliance.* Boston: Houghton Mifflin, 1950.

———. *The Second World War.* Vol. 4, *The Hinge of Fate.* Boston: Houghton Mifflin, 1950.

Ciano, Galeazzo. *The Ciano Diaries 1939–1943*. Safety Harbor, Fla.: Simon, 2001.

Cocchia, Aldo. *The Hunters and the Hunted*. New York: Arno, 1980.

Cooper, Bryan. *The Battle of the Torpedo Boats*. New York: Stein and Day, 1970.

Cressman, Robert J. *The Official Chronology of the U.S. Navy in World War II*. Annapolis, Md.: Naval Institute Press, 2000.

Cunningham, Andrew Browne. *A Sailor's Odyssey*. London: Hutchinson, 1951.

Dannreuther, Raymond. *Somerville's Force H*. London: Aurum, 2005.

Darrieus, Henri, and Jean Queguiner. *Historique de la Marine française 1922–1942*. St. Malo: l'Ancre de Marine, 1996.

Deakin, F. W. *The Brutal Friendship: Mussolini, Hitler and the Fall of Italian Fascism*. New York: Harper and Row. 1962.

Dear, I. C. B., ed. *The Oxford Companion to World War II*. New York: Oxford University Press, 1995.

De Belot, Raymond. *The Struggle for the Mediterranean 1939–1945*. Princeton, N.J.: Princeton University Press, 1951.

De Gaulle, Charles. *War Memoirs: The Call to Honour, 1940–1942*. New York: Viking, 1955.

D'Este, Carlo. *World War II in the Mediterranean: 1942–1945*. Chapel Hill, N.C.: Algonquin Books, 1990.

Eisenhower, Dwight. *Crusade in Europe*. New York: Doubleday, 1948.

Ellis, John. *World War II: A Statistical Survey*. New York: Facts on File, 1995.

Ellsberg, Edward. *No Banners No Bugles*. New York: Dodd, Mead, 1949.

Felmy, Hellmuth. *The German Air Force in the Mediterranean Theater of War*. U.S. Air Force Historical Study 161. Washington, D.C.: U.S. Air Force, 1955.

Forsyth, Douglas J. *The Crisis of Liberal Italy: Monetary and Financial Policy, 1914–1918*. London: Cambridge University Press, 1993.

Frank, Hans. *German S-Boats in Action in the Second World War*. Annapolis, Md.: Naval Institute Press, 2007.

Friedman, Norman. *Naval Firepower: Battleship Guns and Gunnery in the Dreadnought Era*. Annapolis, Md.: Naval Institute Press, 2008.

Gardiner, Robert, ed. *Conway's All the World's Fighting Ships 1922–1946*. New York: Mayflower, 1980.

———. *Conway's All the World's Fighting Ships 1906–1921*. Annapolis, Md.: Naval Institute Press, 1986.

Gay, Franco, and Valerio Gay. *The Cruiser* Bartolomeo Colleoni. Annapolis, Md.: Naval Institute Press, 1987.

Gooch, John. *Mussolini and His Generals: The Armed Forces and Fascist Foreign Policy 1922–1940*. New York: Cambridge University Press, 2007.

Greene, Jack. *Mare Nostrum: The War in the Mediterranean*. Watsonville, Calif.: Typesetting, Etc., 1990.

Greene, Jack, and Alessandro Massignani. *The Black Prince and the Sea Devils: The Story of Valerio Borghese and the Elite Units of the Decima MAS*. Cambridge, Mass.: Da Capo, 2004.

———. *The Naval War in the Mediterranean 1940–1943*. London: Chatham, 1998.

———. *Rommel's North African Campaign: September 1940–November 1942*. Cambridge, Mass.: Da Capo, 1999.

Gröner, Erich. *German Warships 1815–1945.* Vol. 1. London: Conway Maritime, 1990.
————. *German Warships 1815–1945.* Vol. 2. London: Conway Maritime, 1991.
Grove, Eric. *Sea Battles in Close-Up: World War II.* Vol. 2. Annapolis, Md.: Naval Institute Press, 1993.
Guiot, Pierre. *Combats Sans Espoir: Guerre Navale en Syrie–1941.* Paris: La Couronne Littéraire, no date.
Hague, Arnold. *The Allied Convoy System 1939–1945.* Annapolis, Md.: Naval Institute Press, 2000.
Harker, Jack S. *Well Done* Leander. Auckland: Collins, 1971.
Harrison, Mark, ed. *The Economics of World War II: Six Great Powers in International Competition.* Cambridge: Cambridge University Press, 2000.
Hawkins, Ian, ed. *Destroyer: An Anthology of First-Hand Accounts of the War at Sea 1939–1945.* London: Conway Maritime, 2003.
Heckstall-Smith, Anthony. *The Fleet That Faced Both Ways.* London: Anthony Blond, 1963.
Hocking, Charles. *Dictionary of Disasters at Sea during the Age of Steam: Including Sailing Ships and Ships of War Lost in Action, 1824–1962.* London: Lloyd's Register of Shipping, 1969.
Hone, Thomas C., and Trent Hone. *Battle Line: The United States Navy 1919–1939.* Annapolis, Md.: Naval Institute Press, 2006.
Howard, Michael. *The Mediterranean Strategy in the Second World War.* London: Greenhill, 1993.
Iachino, Angelo. *Tramonto di una grande marina.* Verona: Alberto Mondadori, 1966.
Ireland, Bernard. *The War in the Mediterranean 1940–1943.* London: Arms and Armour, 1993.
Jackson, Robert. *The German Navy in World War II.* London: Brown, 1999.
————. *The Royal Navy in World War II.* Annapolis, Md.: Naval Institute Press, 1997.
Jellison, Charles A. *Besieged: The World War II Ordeal of Malta, 1940–1942.* Hanover, N.H.: University Press of New England, 1984.
Jordan, Roger. *The World's Merchant Fleets 1939.* Annapolis, Md.: Naval Institute Press, 1999.
Karig, Walter, Earl Burton, and Stephen L. Freeland. *Battle Report: The Atlantic War.* New York: Farrar and Rinehard, 1946.
Keegan, John. *The Times Atlas of the Second World War.* New York: Harper and Roe, 1989.
————. *The Admiralty Regrets: British Warship Losses of the 20th Century.* Phoenix Mill, England: Sutton, 1999.
Kemp, Paul. *Friend or Foe, Friendly Fire at Sea 1939–1945.* London: Leo Cooper, 1995.
Kemp, P. K. *H.M. Destroyers.* London: Herbert Jenkins, 1956.
————. *Key to Victory: the Triumph of British Sea Power in WWII.* Boston: Little, Brown, 1957.
Kesselring, Albert. *Kesselring: A Soldier's Record.* New York: William Morrow, 1954.
Knox, MacGregor. *Hitler's Italian Allies.* London: Cambridge University Press, 2000.
————. *Mussolini Unleashed 1939–1941.* London: Cambridge University Press, 1982.
Koburger, Charles, Jr. *The Cyrano Fleet: France and Its Navy, 1940–1942.* Westport, Conn.: Praeger, 1989.
————. *Naval Warfare in the Eastern Mediterranean 1940–1945.* Westport, Conn.: Praeger, 1993.

———. *Wine-Dark, Blood Red Sea: Naval Warfare in the Aegean 1941–1946.* Westport, Conn.: Praeger, 1999.

Langtree, Christopher. *The Kellys: British J, K and N Class Destroyers of World War II.* Annapolis, Md.: Naval Institute Press, 2002.

Levine, Alan J. *The War against Rommel's Supply Lines 1942–1943.* Westport, Conn.: Praeger, 1999.

Liddell Hart, B. H. *The German Generals Talk.* New York: Quill, 1979.

Lind, Lew. *Battle of the Wine Dark Sea: The Aegean Campaign 1941–1945.* Kenthurst, Australia: Kangaroo, 1994.

Lowry, Thomas P., and John W. G. Wellham. *The Attack on Taranto.* Mechanicsburg, Pa.: Stackpole, 2000.

Macintyre, Donald. *The Battle for the Mediterranean.* New York: W. W. Norton, 1965.

———. *The Naval War against Hitler.* New York: Charles Scribner's Sons, 1971.

Mahan, A. T. *The Influence of Sea Power upon History 1660–1783.* Boston: Little, Brown, 1918.

March, Edgar J. *British Destroyers: A History of Development 1892–1953.* Guildford, England: Billing and Sons, 1966.

Marder, Arthur J. *Operation Menace.* Oxford: Oxford University Press, 1976.

Martienssen, Anthony. *Hitler and His Admirals.* New York: E. P. Dutton, 1949.

Mattesini, Francesco. *La battaglia di Punta Stilo.* Rome: Ufficio Storico, 2001.

Maugeri, Franco. *From the Ashes of Disgrace.* New York: Reynal and Hitchcock, 1948.

Messenger, Charles, et al. *The Middle East Commandos.* Wellingborough, England: William Kimber, 1988.

Miller, Nathan. *The War at Sea: A Naval History of WWII.* New York: Charles Scribner's Sons, 1995.

Mockler, Anthony. *Haile Selassie's War: The Italian-Ethiopian Campaign, 1935–1941.* New York: Random House, 1984.

Mollo, Andrew. *The Armed Forces of World War II: Uniforms, Insignia and Organization.* New York: Crown, 1981.

Morgan, Philip. *The Fall of Mussolini.* Oxford: Oxford University Press, 2007.

Morison, Samuel Eliot. *The Two Ocean War.* Boston: Little, Brown, 1963.

———. *History of United States Naval Operations in World War II.* Vol. I, *The Battle of the Atlantic 1939–1943.* Boston: Little, Brown, 1984.

———. *History of United States Naval Operations in World War II.* Vol. 2, *Operations in North African Waters, October 1942–June 1943.* Boston: Little, Brown, 1984.

———. *History of United States Naval Operations in World War II.* Vol. 9, *Sicily-Salerno-Anzio, January 1943–June 1944.* Boston: Little, Brown, 1990.

———. *History of United States Naval Operations in World War II.* Vol. 10, *The Atlantic Battle Won, May 1943–May 1945.* Boston: Little, Brown, 1982.

———. *History of United States Naval Operations in World War II.* Vol. 11, *The Invasion of France and Germany, 1944–1945.* Boston: Little, Brown, 1984.

———. *History of United States Naval Operations in World War II.* Vol. 15, *Supplement and General Index.* Boston: Little, Brown, 1962.

Moses, Sam. *At All Costs.* New York: Random House, 2006.

Mussolini, Benito. *My Rise and Fall.* Cambridge, Mass.: Da Capo, 1998.

O'Hara, Vincent P. *The German Fleet at War 1939–1945.* Annapolis, Md.: Naval Institute Press, 2004.

O'Hara, Vincent P. and Enrico Cernuschi. *Dark Navy: The Italian Navy and the Armistice of September 1943.* Ann Arbor, Mich.: Nimble Books, 2009.

———. *The U.S. Navy against the Axis: Surface Combat 1941–1945.* Annapolis, Md.: Naval Institute Press, 2007.

Oriana, Federico F. *Giuseppe Oriana: Ufficiale e gentiluomo.* Rome: Supplemento alla Rivista Marittima, July 2008.

———. *The Battle of Matapan.* New York: Macmillan, 1961.

Pack, S. W. C. *Night Action off Cape Matapan.* Annapolis, Md.: Naval Institute Press, 1972.

Padfield, Peter. *War beneath the Sea: Submarine Conflict during World War II.* New York: John Wiley and Sons, 1995.

Parrish, Thomas, ed. *The Simon and Schuster Encyclopedia of World War II.* New York: Simon and Schuster, 1978.

Paterson, Lawrence. *U-Boats in the Mediterranean 1941–1945.* Annapolis, Md.: Naval Institute Press, 2007.

Payne, Stanley G. *Franco and Hitler: Spain, Germany, and World War II.* New Haven, Conn.: Yale University Press, 2008.

Plevy, Harry. *Battleship Sailors: The Fighting Career of HMS* Warspite *Recalled by Her Men.* London: Chatham, 2001.

Polmar, Norman. *Aircraft Carriers: A History of Carrier Aviation and Its Influence on World Events.* Vol. 1, *1909–1945.* Washington, D.C.: Potomac Books, 2006.

Poolman, Kenneth. *The Winning Edge: Naval Technology in Action 1939–1945.* Annapolis, Md.: Naval Institute Press, 1997.

Pope, Dudley. *Flag 4: The Battle of the Coastal Forces in the Mediterranean 1939–1945.* London: Chatham, 1998.

Preston, Anthony. *Navies of World War II.* London: Bison, 1976.

Pugsley, A. F. *Destroyer Man.* London: Weidenfeld and Nicolson, 1957.

———. *Grand Admiral.* Cambridge, Mass.: Da Capo, 2001.

Raeder, Erich. *Struggle for the Sea.* London: Kimber, 1959.

Reynolds, Leonard, C. *Dog Boats at War: Royal Navy D Class MTBs and MGBs 1939–1945.* Phoenix Mill, England: Sutton, 2000.

———. *Motor Gunboat 658: The Small Boat War in the Mediterranean.* London: Cassell, 2002.

Ricciardi, Enrico. *Mediterrananeo 1940–1943: Recordi de guerra di un giovane ufficiale di marina.* Rome: Ermanno Albertelli, 2004.

Robertson, Stuart, and Stephen Dent. *Conway's The War at Sea in Photographs 1939–1945.* London: Conway Maritime, 2007.

Rogers, Anthony. *Churchill's Folly: Leros and the Aegean.* London: Cassell, 2003.

———. *Allied Submarine Attacks of World War II.* Annapolis, Md.: Naval Institute Press, 1997.

———. *Axis Submarine Successes of World War II.* Annapolis, Md.: Naval Institute Press, 1999.

Rohwer, Jürgen. *War at Sea 1939–1945.* Annapolis, Md.: Naval Institute Press, 1996.

Rohwer, Jürgen, and Gerhard Hummelchen. *Chronology of the War at Sea 1939–1945.* Annapolis, Md.: Naval Institute Press, 2006.

Rose, Lisle A. *Power at Sea: The Breaking Storm, 1919–1945*. Columbia: University of
     Missouri Press, 2007.
Roskill, S. W. *Churchill and the Admirals*. New York: William Morrow, 1978.
———. Warspite. Annapolis, Md.: Naval Institute Press, 1997.
———. *White Ensign*. Annapolis, Md.: Naval Institute Press, 1960.
Ruge, Friedrich. *Der Seekrieg: The German Navy's Story 1939–1945*. Annapolis, Md.:
     Naval Institute Press, 1957.
Sadkovich, James J. *The Italian Navy in World War II*. Westport, Conn.: Greenwood,
     1994.
———. ed. *Reevaluating Major Naval Combatants of World War II*. New York:
     Greenwood, 1990.
Saibène, Marc. *Les Torpilleurs de 1500 Tonnes du Type Bourrasque*. Rennes: Marines
     Editions, 2001.
Salerno, Reynolds M. *Vital Crossroads: Mediterranean Origins of the Second World War
     1935–1940*. Ithaca, N.Y.: Cornell University Press, 2002.
Santoni, Alberto, and Francesco Mattesini. *La partecipazione aeronavale tedesca alla
     Guerra nel Mediterraneo*. Rome: Ateneo e Bizzarri, 1980.
Schenk, Peter. *Kampf um die Ägäis*. Hamburg: E. S. Mittler and Son, 2000.
Seth, Ronald. *Two Fleets Surprised: The Story of the Battle of Cape Matapan*. London:
     Geoffrey Bles, 1960.
Shores, Christopher, Brian Cull, and Nicola Malizia. *Malta: The Hurricane Years*. London:
     Grub Street, 1987.
Showell, Jak. *The German Navy in WWII*. Annapolis, Md.: Naval Institute Press, 1979.
Smith, Peter C. *Action Imminent*. London: William Kimber, 1980.
———. *Destroyer Leader*. London: New English Library, 1968.
———. *Pedestal: The Convoy That Saved Malta*. Manchester, England: Crecy, 1999.
Smith, Peter C., and John R. Dominy. *Cruisers in Action 1939–1945*. London: William
     Kimber, 1981.
Smith, Peter C., and Edwin Walker. *The Battles of the Malta Striking Forces*. Annapolis,
     Md.: Naval Institute Press, 1974.
Smith, S. E., ed. *The United States Navy in World War II*. New York: Quill, 1966.
Spertini, Marco and Erminio Bagnasco. *I mezzi d'assalto della Xª Flottiglia MAS*. Parma:
     Ermanno Albertelli, 2005.
Stephen, Martin. *The Fighting Admirals: British Admirals of the Second World War*.
     Annapolis, Md.: Naval Institute Press, 1991.
Stephen, Martin, and Eric Grove. *Sea Battles in Close-Up*. Annapolis, Md.: Naval Institute
     Press, 1993.
Stevens, David, ed. *The Royal Australian Navy in World War II*. St. Leonards, Australia:
     Allen and Unwin, 1996.
Stitt, George. *Under Cunningham's Command 1940–1943*. London: George Allen and
     Unwin, 1944.
Tani, Fabio. *Memorie*. Unpublished manuscript; private collection Enrico Cernuschi.
Tarrant, V. E. *The Last Year of the Kriegsmarine*. Annapolis, Md.: Naval Institute Press, 1994.
Thompson, Julian. *The War at Sea: The Royal Navy in the Second World War*. Osceola,
     Wisc.: Motorbooks International, 1996.

Tomblin, Barbara Brooks. *With Utmost Spirit: Allied Naval Operations in the Mediterranean, 1942–1945.* Lexington: University of Kentucky Press, 2004.

Treadwell, Theodore R. *Splinter Fleet: The Wooden Subchasers of World War II.* Annapolis, Md.: Naval Institute Press, 2000.

Tute, Warren. *The Reluctant Enemies: The Story of the Last War between Britain and France 1940–1942.* London: Collins, 1990.

Ugaki, Matome. *Fading Victory.* Pittsburgh, Pa.: University of Pittsburgh Press, 1991.

Uhlig, Frank, Jr. *How Navies Fight: The US Navy and Its Allies.* Annapolis, Md.: Naval Institute Press, 1994.

Vian, Philip. *Action This Day.* London: Frederick Muller, 1960.

Von der Porten, Edward P. *The German Navy in World War II.* New York: Thomas Y. Crowell, 1968.

Von Senger und Etterlin, Frido. *Neither Fear Nor Hope.* New York: E.P. Dutton, 1964.

Wade, Frank. *A Midshipman's War: A Young Man in the Mediterranean Naval War 1941–1943.* Victoria, Canada: Trafford, 2005.

Whitley, M. J. *Battleships of World War Two.* Annapolis, Md.: Naval Institute Press, 1998.

———. *Cruisers of World War Two.* Annapolis, Md.: Naval Institute Press, 1995.

———. *Destroyers of World War Two.* Annapolis, Md.: Naval Institute Press, 1998.

Winton, John, ed. *The War at Sea: The British Navy in World War II.* New York: William Morrow, 1968.

Worth, Richard. *Fleets of World War II.* Cambridge, Mass.: Da Capo, 2001.

Wynn, Kenneth. *U-Boat Operations of the Second World War.* Annapolis, Md.: Naval Institute Press: 1997.

Magazines

Ando, Elio. "Capitani Romani": Part 1, "Design and Construction," and Part 2, "Operational History." *Warship* 2 (1980): 146–57, 246–57.

———. "Changing Sides: The Italian Fleet and the Armistice: 1943." *Warship* 42 (April 1987): 66–73.

———. "The *Gabbiano* Class Corvettes," Parts 1 and 2. *Warship* 9 (1985): 81–89, 198–206.

Aylwin, Ken. "Malta's Years of Siege." *Naval Review* 82 (October 1994): 397–403.

Barker, Edward L. "War without Aircraft Carriers." U.S. Naval Institute *Proceedings* 80 (March 1954): 281–89.

"Battle of Oran Is Challenge of War to Bitter End." *New York Times,* 6 July 1940.

Bernotti, Romeo. "Italian Naval Policy under Fascism." U.S. Naval Institute *Proceedings* 82 (July 1956): 722–31.

Bezard, J. P. "Mers El Kebir–3 July 1940." *Naval Review* 67 (July 1979): 195–97.

Blanchard, W. O. "Seventy Years of Suez." *Scientific Monthly* 50 (April 1940): 299–306.

Bressan, Manlio. "Una corvette sulle rotte per la Tunisia." *Storia Militare* 92 (May 2001): 35–42.

Caravaggio, Angelo N. "The Attack at Taranto: Tactical Success, Operational Failure." *Naval War College Review* 59 (Summer 2006): 103–24.

Cardea, Mario. "La Brillante Azione Della Torpediniera 'Aliseo'." *Mare: L'Italia Marinara* (September 1952): 1–5.

Caruana, Joseph."Decima Flotilla Decimated."*Warship International* 28(2) (1991): 178–86.

————.   "The Demise of Force 'K'." *Warship International* 43(1) (2006): 99–111.

————. "I convogli britannici per Malta."*Storia Militare* 43 (April 1997): 15–24.

Cernuschi, Enrico."Uno scontro rimaste senza nome."*Storia Militare* 67 (April 1999):
      22–30.

Cernuschi, Enrico, and Vincent O'Hara."The Breakout Fleet: The Oceanic Programmes
      of the Regia Marina, 1934–1940."In *Warship 2006*. London: Conway Maritime,
      2006, 86–101.

————. "A Century-Long Dream: Single Purpose Engine Submarines of the Italian
      Navy."In *Warship* 2004. London: Conway Maritime, 2004, 76–91.

————. "Italy and the Pacific War."*World War II Quarterly* 3(1) (2006): 14–19.

————. "In Search of a Flattop: The Italian Navy and the Aircraft Carrier 1907–2007."In
      Warship 2007. London: Conway Maritime, 2007, 61–80.

————. "The Star-Crossed Split: The Troubled Story of an Unlucky Flagship."In *Warship
      2005*. London: Conway Maritime, 2005, 97–110.

————. "The World's Worst Warships: Round Three."In *Warship 2006*. London: Conway
      Maritime, 2006, 158–63.

Channon, R. F."Red Sea Incident."*Naval Review* 82 (October 1994): 404–10.

Clayton, Anthony."A Question of Honour? Scuttling Vichy's Fleet."*History Today*
      (November 1992).

Colliva, Giuliano."Questioni di tiro . . . e alter le artiglierie navali italiane nella Guerra
      nel Mediterraneo."*Bollettino d'archivio dell'Ufficio Storico Della Marina Militare*
      17 (September 2003).

Dickson, David W."Naval Tactics: An Introduction."*Warship International* 3 (1976): 168–76.

Dondoli, Alessandro."Piombino, settembre 1943."*Storia Militare* 72 (September 1999),
      4–14.

Donolo, Luigi, and James J. Tritten."The History of Italian Naval Doctrine."*Naval
      Doctrine Command* (June 1995).

Fioravanzo, Giuseppe."Italian Strategy in the Mediterranean, 1940–43."U.S. Naval
      Institute *Proceedings* 84 (September 1958): 65–72.

————. "The Japanese Military Mission to Italy in 1941."U.S. Naval Institute *Proceedings*
      82 (January 1956): 24–31.

Fraccaroli, Aldo."Il combattimento navale de Gaudo." *Storia Militare* 88 (January 2001):
      4–14.

Freivogel, Zvonimir."The Attack on HMS *Delhi* at Spalato."*Warship International* 40(2)
      (2003): 351–64.

————. "Die Geisterflotte von Pag."*Schiffahrt International Journal* (August/September
      2007): 56–65.

————. "Siluranti ex italiane sotto bandiera tedesca."*Storia Militare* 36 (September
      1996): 18–29; and 37 (October 1996): 22–35.

————. "*Vasilefs Georgios* and *Vasilissa Olga*: From Sister-Ships to Adversaries."*Warship
      International* 40(4) (2003): 351–64.

Hervieux, Pierre."German Auxiliaries at War 1939–45: Minesweepers, Submarine Chasers
      and Patrol Boats."In *Warship 1995*. London: Conway Maritime, 1995, 108–23.

————. "German TA Torpedo Boats at War."In *Warship 1997–1998*. London: Conway
      Maritime, 1998, 133–48.

Hines, Calvin W."The Distorted Danger: Winston Churchill and the French Dreadnoughts." In *Naval History: The Seventh Symposium of the U.S. Naval Academy*, edited by William B. Cogar. Wilmington, Del.: Scholarly Resources, 1988.

"Improvise and Dare." [pseud.]."Naval Operations in the Aegean."*Naval Review* 39 (February 1951): 42–50, (November 1951): 287–95.

Isaic, Vladimir."Premuda 29 Febbraio 1944."*Storia Militare* 46 (July 1997): 20–26.

Jordan, John."2400-Tonnes Series: The Four-Funnelled *Contre-torpilleurs* of the Prewar Marine Nationale."In *Warship 1994*. London: Conway Maritime, 1994, 88–103.

Jori, Gino."I rifornimenti dal mare alle forze italo-tedesche ad El Alamein per la ripresa dell'attacco all'Egitto (2 luglio–2 settembre 1942)."*RID* (February 1986).

Kemp, Paul."Decima MAS."*MHQ* 7 (Autumn 1994): 74–81.

Lasterle, Philippe."Could Admiral Gensoul Have Averted the Tragedy of Mers el-Kebir?" *Journal of Military History* 67 (July 2003): 835–44.

Mancini, Renato."I Porti Della Libia."*Storia Militare* 53 (February 1998): 20–27.

Massimello, Giovanni. "Bombe sul convoglio 'Harpoon'." *Storia Militare* 37 (October 1996): 15–20.

McBride, Keith."'Eight Six-Inch Guns in Pairs': The *Leander* and *Sydney* Class Cruisers." In *Warship 1997–1998*. London: Conway Maritime, 1998, 167–81.

Melka, Robert L."Darlan between Germany and Britain 1940–41."*Journal of Contemporary History* 8 (April 1973): 57–80.

Nailer, Roger."Aircraft to Malta."In *Warship 1990*. Annapolis, Md.: Naval Institute Press, 1990, 151–65.

————. "The Action off Calabria and the Myth of Moral Ascendancy." *Warship 2008*. London: Conway Maritime, 2008, 26–39.

———— "Mystery Battle off Imperia, 1 October 1944."*World War II Quarterly* 4 (August 2007): 24–33.

O'Hara, Vincent P."Attack and Sink."*World War II* (March 2004): 44–48

O'Hara, Vincent P., and Enrico Cernuschi."Battle with No Name."*World War II* (March 2006): 36–41.

Poynder, C. F. T."Midshipman 1942."*Naval Review* 84 (July 1996): 256–61.

Prideaux, A. G."With 'A.B.C.' in the Med."*Naval Review* 65 (April 1977): 133–40; (July 1977): 270–77; (October 1977): 351–60; 66 (January 1978): 46–54.

R. C. [pseud.]."HMS *Decoy* 1940–41."*Naval Review* 68 (April 1980): 131–36.

Ronconi, Guido."L'operazione 'Abstention' in Egeo."*Storia Militare* 92 (May 2001): 4–15; 93 (June 2001): 23–34.

Rotherham, G. A."Naval Operations against Vichy France."*Naval Review* 67 (April 1979): 142–45; (July 1979): 198–206; (October 1979): 304–309.

Roucek Joseph S."The Geopolitics of the Mediterranean."*American Journal of Economics and Sociology* 12 (July 1953): 347–54; 13 (October 1953): 71–86.

Sadkovich, James J. "The Indispensable Navy: Italy as a Great Power, 1911–43."In *Naval Power in the Twentieth Century*, edited by N. A. M. Roger. Annapolis, Md.: Naval Institute Press, 1996.

———. "The Italo-Greek War in Context: Italian Priorities and Axis Diplomacy."*Journal of Contemporary History* 28 (July 1993): 439–64.

———. "Understanding Defeat: Reappraising Italy's Role in World War II."*Journal of Contemporary History* 24 (January 1989): 27–61.

Salerno, Reynolds M. "The French Navy and the Appeasement of Italy, 1937–39." *English Historical Review* 112 (February 1997): 66–104.

Stahl, Frédéric. "La bataille de Punta Stilo." *Navires and Histoire* 45 (December 2007/January 2008): 36–53.

———. "Le Royale à l'assault de Gënes." *Navires et Historie* 44 (October/November 2006): 32–33.

Sullivan, Brian R. "A Fleet in Being: The Rise and Fall of Italian Sea Power, 1861–1943." *International History Review* 10 (February 1980): 106–24.

———. "Prisoner in the Mediterranean: The Evolution and Execution of Italian Naval Strategy, 1919–42." In *Naval History: The Seventh Symposium of the U.S. Naval Academy,* edited by William B. Cogar. Wilmington, Del.: Scholarly Resources, 1988.

Sweetman, Jack. "Great Sea Battles of World War II." *Naval History* 9 (May 1995): 6–57.

Thomas, Martin. "After Mers-el-Kébir: The Armed Neutrality of the Vichy French Navy 1940–1943." *English Historical Review* (June 1997): 643–70.

———. "At the Heart of Things: French Imperial Defense Planning in the Late 1930s." *French Historical Studies* 21 (Spring 1998): 325–61.

T. P. A. [pseud.]. "The Red Sea." *Naval Review* 30 (November 1942): 293–97.

"White Moth" [pseud.]. "The Turn of the Tide." *Naval Review* 53 (July 1966): 256–72.

Internet and Correspondence

Biggs, A. E. P. *Flagship Hood: The Fate of Britain's Mightiest Warship,* http://www.hmshood.com (23 April 2008).

Cernuschi, Enrico, e-mail to author, 30 March 2008, based on diary of Carmelo Zippitelli.

Hyperwar: A Hypertext History of World War II, http://www.ibiblio.org/hyperwar (7 June 2008).

Naval History.net, http://www.naval-history.net (23 May 2008).

Naval Weapons, Naval Technology and Naval Reunions, http://www.navweaps.com (23 April 2008).

People's War, http://www.bbc.co.uk/ww2peopleswar (27 June 2008).

Regia Marina, www.regiamarina.net (7 June 2008).

Royal Australian Navy: The Gun Plot, http://www.gunplot.net (27 June 2008).

Sansonetti, Vito, to Enrico Cernuschi, correspondence dated 31 October 1992.

Index

Page numbers followed by a *t*, *m*, or *c* indicate tables, maps, and charts, respectively.

About the Author

Vincent P. O'Hara is a naval historian and the author of *The German Fleet at War* (2004) and *The U.S. Navy Against the Axis* (2007), both published by the Naval Institute Press. Mr. O'Hara's work has also appeared in periodicals and annuals including *Warship, MHQ, World War II Quarterly, World War II Magazine,* and *Storia Militare.* He holds a history degree from the University of California, Berkeley.